The Struggle for Modern Turkey

The Struggle for Modern Turkey
*Justice, Activism and a
Revolutionary Female Journalist*

Sabiha Sertel
Translated by David Selim Sayers & Evrim Emir-Sayers
Edited by Tia O'Brien & Nur Deriş

I.B. TAURIS
LONDON • NEW YORK • OXFORD • NEW DELHI • SYDNEY

I.B. TAURIS
Bloomsbury Publishing Plc
50 Bedford Square, London, WC1B 3DP, UK
1385 Broadway, New York, NY 10018, USA

BLOOMSBURY, I.B. TAURIS and the Diana logo are trademarks of
Bloomsbury Publishing Plc

First published in Great Britain 2019

Copyright © Tia O'Brien, 2019
English translation copyright © David Selim Sayers and Evrim Emir-Sayers
Published in 2015 by Can Yayinlari

Tia O'Brien and Nur Deriş have asserted their right under the Copyright, Designs and Patents Act, 1988, to be identified as Editors of this work.

Cover design: Adriana Brioso
Cover image © Sertel Family Archives

All rights reserved. No part of this publication may be reproduced or transmitted in any form or by any means, electronic or mechanical, including photocopying, recording, or any information storage or retrieval system, without prior permission in writing from the publishers.

Bloomsbury Publishing Plc does not have any control over, or responsibility for, any third-party websites referred to or in this book. All internet addresses given in this book were correct at the time of going to press. The author and publisher regret any inconvenience caused if addresses have changed or sites have ceased to exist, but can accept no responsibility for any such changes.

A catalogue record for this book is available from the British Library.

A catalog record for this book is available from the Library of Congress.

ISBN:	HB:	978-1-7883-1357-5
	PB:	978-1-8386-0444-8
	eISBN:	978-1-7883-1599-9
	ePDF:	978-1-7883-1600-2

Series: Library of Middle East History

Typeset by RefineCatch Limited, Bungay, Suffolk

To find out more about our authors and books visit www.bloomsbury.com and sign up for our newsletters.

To my grandson, Deniz,

You were only eight years old at the time. We would sit on the balcony of our seaside house in Istanbul's Moda District, and I would tell you rich and colourful tales from the Orient. Leyla and Mecnun, Ferhat and Şirin, Kerem and Aslı ... As you listened with rapt attention, sparks would light up in your blue eyes. As soon as I finished a story, you would jump up and say, 'Come on, Grandma, let's act this out!' You would stage the tale like an expert director, giving me my role and playing your own with excitement and gusto.

Seeing the richness of your imagination and artistic expression, I told your mother, 'This child will either be an actor or a director. Be mindful of his talent, and don't discourage it.'

Many years have passed. These days, I hear, you successfully act in Shakespeare's plays at theatres in the United States. I myself played a small role, not on stage, but in life. I'd like to tell you and my readers about that role. Once again, I will tell it to you as a tale, as a novel.

The time hasn't come to write about my life in exile. When that time comes, if I'm still alive, I will tell you and my readers a tale about that as well.

This is the story of a life of struggle.

Frontispiece New York City, 1919, Sabiha and Zekeriya Sertel with daughter Sevim

Contents

List of figures	x
Preface	xii
Introduction	xvi
Translators' note	xxvii
Biographical and historical timeline	xxix
Acknowledgements	xxxv
Author's note	xxxvii

1	Introduction to life	1
2	In America	19
3	The return home	35
4	Publishing *Resimli Ay*	47
5	Life in politics	105
6	Turkey in the war years	127
7	Turkey at the end of the war	159
8	The *Görüşler* journal	181
9	The *Tan* incidents	191
10	The founding of the Democrat Party and the arrests	205
11	The Human Rights Association	221
12	The provocations continue	229
13	To my countrypeople	241

Glossary	243
Index	245

Figures

Frontispiece New York City, 1919, Sabiha and Zekeriya Sertel with daughter Sevim

0.1 Vienna, 1955, the Sertels' first and only reunion with all three American grandchildren. L to R: Sabiha Sertel, granddaughter Sevim O'Brien, Zekeriya Sertel, granddaughter Tia O'Brien, Sevim Sertel O'Brien. Photograph by grandson Denis O'Brien — xiii

1.1 Istanbul, 1915, Sabiha Nazmi's marriage to Mehmet Zekeriya was hailed as an example of promised secularism in a new Turkish Republic. In Zekeriya's memoirs, he describes Sabiha as the first to publicly marry outside the secretive *Dönme* community — 5

1.2 Salonica (now Thessaloniki, Greece), 1903, Sabiha Nazmi at eight years old. She was heavily influenced by growing up in the cosmopolitan, multicultural, multi-ethnic city, a hub for revolution as the Ottoman Empire collapsed — 9

2.1 New York City, 1919, Turkish scholarship students at Columbia University. They were charged with bringing back pioneering ideas for a new Turkish Republic. Sabiha (second left), Zekeriya and their two-year-old daughter Sevim (bottom right) — 20

2.2 New York, 1919, within days of arriving, Sabiha quickly transformed her look from a Turkish *çarşaf* to Western styles borrowed from a relative — 22

2.3 Central Park in modern dress, Zekeriya, Sevim and Sabiha — 23

4.1 *Resimli Ay* (Illustrated Monthly), the Sertels' groundbreaking magazine, launched in 1924, aimed at a general audience and served as a forum for opposition voices. Sabiha Sertel's advice column 'Cici Anne', published in the magazine, provided a ground-level view of how Turkish families were handling revolutionary social reforms — 47

4.2 An article advocating for child welfare reforms — 48

4.3 Modern young woman exercising in underwear — 49

4.4 Istanbul, 1930s, Zekeriya and Sabiha Sertel. The husband-and-wife publishing team gained influence with the popular success of *Resimli Ay* and later on with their newspaper and publishing house *Tan*, as well as earning them harsh critics loyal to the government — 82

5.1 Magazine profile, 29 April 1935, of Sabiha Sertel at their famed Moda villa, overlooking the Sea of Marmara. It was a salon for intellectuals, writers and artists — 107

6.1 *Tan* publishing house postcard — 140

Figures

6.2 Headline, April 1939, reads: 'Hitler Says Germany Threatens No One'. *Tan* was an early voice warning against the rise of Hitler and fascism. Sertel's articles, critical of the government, landed her in court — 143

8.1 The debut issue of *Görüşler* (Views), 1 December 1945, the Sertels' new political magazine, three days before the destruction of their publishing house. Edited by Sabiha, the magazine was intended to serve as the voice for a new opposition party — 188

9.1 On 4 December 1945, the police watched on as thousands of government-orchestrated rioters, swinging pickaxes and sledge hammers, destroyed the Sertels' publishing house, chanting, 'Damn the communists! Damn *Tan* and *Görüşler*!' — 193

9.2 Rioters ransacking the printing press — 194

9.3 Police make no arrests — 195

9.4 *Cumhuriyet* front page, 5 December 1945. The destruction of *Tan* made headlines in Turkey and worldwide. It effectively silenced the leading progressive voices of the era — 196

9.5 On 5 December 1945, the day after the *Tan* riot, *Cumhuriyet* published this caricature of Sertel, depicting pro-government journalists assaulting her. The sign in the background held by Hüseyin Cahit Yalçın says: 'Rise Up, O Patriots,' the title of Yalçın's editorial that rallied protestors — 197

10.1 Istanbul, March 1946. The only people arrested after the *Tan* riot were the Sertels and *Tan* colleagues. Sabiha defended herself in the headline-making trial — 215

12.1 At the Sertels' villa, 1948, Sabiha reads to their visiting grandchildren Sevim and Denis O'Brien, a respite in the aftermath of *Tan*'s destruction. The Sertels were under a round-the-clock police surveillance and unable to work — 232

13.1 Yalta, 24 April 1966. While exiled in the Soviet Union, two years before her death, Sertel sent this photo to her elder daughter and grandchildren in the USA to show she was well — 242

Preface

The English translation of my Turkish grandmother's autobiography grew out of a personal quest to learn the truth about her revolutionary and elusive life. Her story was wrapped in layers of mystery and I was determined to unravel them.

As the youngest of Sabiha Sertel's three grandchildren growing up in the United States at the height of the Cold War, I couldn't speak or read Turkish. My mother was our window on our past. Her enchanting bedtime tales about her childhood left us begging for more – there was the one about her pet lamb while summering in a Black Sea fishing village. And how she baked gingerbread men at her experimental nursery school at Columbia University in New York City. And the time her mother saved the day while chaperoning a school trip to the islands near Istanbul. When the captain discovered he was speaking to Sabiha Sertel, author of the popular advice column, he waived an onerous fee in return for personal counselling as he ferried the group back to Istanbul.

Many of my mother's adventures hid a complex, historic backstory. Take that idyllic Black Sea fishing village – she'd been sent to visit her father, Zekeriya Sertel, who was under house arrest for stories he'd published while Sabiha stepped in to save their magazine. And her nursery school? Her parents were at Columbia, charged with bringing back cutting-edge Western ideas on the eve of the Turkish Republic's birth.

Questions about our exiled Turkish grandparents often led to simplistic explanations that glazed over the tumultuous politics that had upended their lives. Was it true, we'd ask, that one of our pioneering grandparents' journalistic pursuits had led to their downfall and exile? 'Oh the family is divided over that,' our mother would answer vaguely, artfully preserving an apparent Sertel pact of secrecy. Over time, I realized that even she didn't know all of their secrets.

My journey to learn the truth about my grandmother – my Anneanne – begins in a bathtub.

It's 1955 and I'm three years old. My sister and I are giggling uncontrollably as Anneanne tries to give us a bath in the drafty villa our grandparents have rented for our reunion, set in the mountains near Vienna. Despite the chilly water, we can't stop laughing as the plump woman with a sing-songy foreign accent battles an ancient hot-water heater, running up and down three flights. 'Allah Allah!' we'd hear from the basement, following loud bangs as she gave the faulty heater several powerful kicks.

By the time I met my grandparents in Vienna (Figure 0.1), Zekeriya and Sabiha Sertel were beginning what would become a long, tragic and furtive exile. We knew that they'd fled Turkey in 1950 and had told us they were living in Vienna. Our mother's stories served as a child's primer, filling in the basics about their downfall. On 4 December 1945, a government-orchestrated mob of thousands destroyed the Sertels' publishing house and *Tan* (Dawn) newspaper, the powerful voice of the

Figure 0.1 Vienna, 1955, the Sertels' first and only reunion with all three American grandchildren. L to R: Sabiha Sertel, granddaughter Sevim O'Brien, Zekeriya Sertel, granddaughter Tia O'Brien, Sevim Sertel O'Brien. Photograph by grandson Denis O'Brien.

opposition, fighting for multi-party rule, a democracy with a free press and civil rights for all Turks.

Over the years, I'd scour the few photos of our only reunion, jumbled in with pictures of relatives wearing fezzes and *çarşafs*. Zekeriya – my Dede – remained a vivid memory, a warm and charming stand-in for my father, an Associated Press correspondent, who'd stayed home that summer. But memories of Sabiha quickly faded. I remembered nothing except that bath and a stilted accent.

Letters were rare and they were usually postmarked Vienna until my grandparents moved to Baku. One time, a package arrived with embroidered Chinese silk jackets, souvenirs from the Sertels' trip to what we referred to as Red China. Halloween photos that year showed off our jackets but as Cold War kids, living in the suburbs of the nation's Capitol, these mementos from Communist China flagged up our grandparents as, at a minimum, unusual.

After my mother translated Zekeriya's autobiography, I asked if she'd also translate Sabiha's memoir, *Roman Gibi* (Like A Novel). She shook her head, 'It's very political, not personal. It won't interest you.'

What she didn't explain was that it was a self-censored account, written while living in Baku during the late 1960s, then part of the Soviet Union, where the Sertels were stripped of their passports and trapped. If she'd revealed their full story, it could have jeopardized any hope of returning to their homeland.

In the preface, Sabiha confides to the readers, 'The time hasn't come to write about my life in exile. When that time comes, if I'm still alive, I will tell you and my readers a tale about that, as well. This is the story of a life of struggle.' In 1968, not long after penning those lines, she died from lung cancer and was buried in Baku, never returning to her beloved Turkey.

The irony is I could have posed my questions to Sabiha in person. Just two months before she died, I was on a high school trip to the Soviet Union but Anneanne didn't want her granddaughter to see her so ill and at the time, she didn't know she was dying.

So, the questions that no one else would address remained unanswered for almost forty years until I started on a global trek.

By then, my interest was more than simply a granddaughter's curiosity. As a veteran journalist, instinct told me that my mother's simplistic primer concealed a far more politically loaded, multifaceted account of Anneanne and Dede's pioneering lives. I interviewed scholars, tracked down the Sertels' last remaining friends and colleagues, all octogenarians and nonagenarians. Among the most reticent were my relatives, who politely deferred probing questions, even seemingly harmless queries about where Sabiha was born and her childhood. No amount of time had eased concerns about being associated with their politically volatile relative.

One piece of the puzzle fell into place with the translation of *Annem* (My Mother), a biography authored by my aunt, Yıldız Sertel. She delved into what relatives refused to discuss, describing how Sabiha was raised amid revolution in Salonica (now Thessaloniki), a hub of the movement to abolish the Sultanate. How her fate was influenced by growing up in a non-practicing *Dönme* home, a community of Jewish origin that converted to Islam in the 1600s but secretly preserved many of its traditions. And why she was radicalized as a feminist at the age of eight, pledging to defy tradition and pick her own husband. She kept that pledge. Her marriage was hailed as the first time a *Dönme* wed outside of the community, a symbol of a new secular Turkey.

Still, like other historical works, Sabiha's own narrative and voice were largely missing from this account. I went back to the scholars. Was it worth translating *Roman Gibi*? The unanimous answer was, 'Yes.'

When the first sections finally arrived, page by page, my grandmother's remarkable saga came to life. It was like turning a key in a lock. I could finally meet Sabiha and hear her story in her own words, capturing history in blunt insights, colourful vignettes and humour. My aunt once described her mother as happiest when engaged in fierce battle with her opponents. As I read, Sabiha emerged as a seemingly fearless warrior, who challenged a male-dominated power structure to turn rights promised on paper into true reforms for women and workers. It's filled with intrigue, assassinations, betrayals and a bold idealism that ultimately cost the Sertels their country and freedom.

I was puzzled by my mother's attempt to dissuade me from reading *Roman Gibi*. Deep in the Cold War, had she tried to protect her American children from our grandmother's idealistic embrace of communism, even while fighting for a democracy?

Of all the Sertel mysteries, the most closely held involved Sabiha's ties to the outlawed Turkish Communist Party. In 2009, shortly before Yıldız's death, my aunt revealed a fuller, more complex truth about their lives in her memoir, including the fact that those photos labelled 'Vienna' were taken in Leipzig, East Germany, where they'd actually worked and lived. Yet, like her mother, she held on to some secrets, as though revealing them after a lifetime of persecution would break a family vow. In fact, mother and daughter shared more than a vow. I realized that their allegiance to the Turkish Communist Party was likely the primary reason that had held them back from disclosing a hard-to-tell truth: the role that their political idealism played in the Sertels' downfall.

'Communism is for fools,' Dede once lectured me, stressing that he was a social democrat.

It's 1978, and Dede has recently returned to Turkey after 27 years in exile. We're together in Istanbul, sipping afternoon tea by the Bosporus. I press him. Hadn't his own investigative journalism and tough editorials also put them at risk? Yes, Dede admits, but he insists that if it hadn't been for Sabiha, he wouldn't have been forced to leave the country.

Like everything about my grandparents, I found that the reality was much more complicated. Political scientists and historians I've interviewed conclude that both Sertels' unbending pursuit of democracy, a free press and civil liberties set them on a collision course with the authoritarian regime. The destruction of *Tan* was designed to permanently silence not just the Sertels, but also their platform for the loyal opposition.

Over the years, Aunt Yıldız assured me that, like her parents, she was confident the progress they'd fought for would be achieved despite steps backwards. However, in 2009, as she lay dying, Yıldız was riddled with doubts. A new wave of arrests and crackdowns intensified concerns about the future of a multi-party, secular republic.

I asked my aunt what seemed a rude question for someone who'd devoted her life, along with her parents, to establishing a democratic Turkey.

'*Was it worth it?*'

'This is what's been troubling me,' she confessed. Her eyes were filled with sadness, her expression fallen. 'I wonder. There were such hardships, so much suffering. For what?'

I couldn't pose the same question to my grandparents. But a recently discovered letter from Dede makes it difficult to believe they ever would have abandoned their fight for a Turkish democracy. His words were intended for his 16-year-old granddaughter, but they are just as relevant for new generations of English readers. Writing from exile in Baku, Dede asked if I'd read their memoirs. 'They are sad stories, which show under what conditions we were working and how we have suffered in our time.' He continued, 'But we worked and we fought for our ideal of democracy and for our people. That is our consolation. You must read and learn it.'

Tia O'Brien
San Francisco, 2018

Introduction

Sabiha Sertel (1895–1968) was a woman of firsts. Let me name just three to provide a quick overview of her remarkable life: she was among the first Turkish women – if not the first – to work in professional journalism, to face prosecution and imprisonment for her writings, and to end her life in political exile. And, as though Sertel's own life was not exceptional enough, it was embedded in an era of unprecedented change: Sertel witnessed the demise of the Ottoman Empire, the foundation of the Republic of Turkey, the formative years of the new republic under an oppressive single-party state, the deeply troubled years as Turkey hovered on the edge of the Second World War, and the country's subsequent alignment with the USA and North Atlantic Treaty Organization (NATO).

Throughout these stormy times, Sertel held her finger on the pulse of Turkey's social and political life. In her role as chronicler and commentator, she advocated for the most disadvantaged parts of the population while having the ear of the highest echelons of Turkey's political elite. Her life was truly like a novel, and thus it was only appropriate for her to name her memoirs *Roman Gibi* (Like A Novel). But since the 'novel' was targeted at a domestic audience – this is the first English translation – I will devote this introduction to providing some context that might be useful to the reader not well acquainted with the political history of Turkey or the intellectual history of its elites.

The Ottoman Empire, which traces its origins back to the early fourteenth century, was one of the most powerful and enduring empires in world history. With the conquest of Constantinople in 1453, the Ottomans became major players in world politics, going on to establish their rule over the Balkans as well as most of the Arabian Peninsula and North Africa. At the height of its power, the Ottoman Empire dominated the Mediterranean Sea, controlling Western access to vital trade routes into Asia and forcing the Europeans to explore alternative routes via the Atlantic Ocean.

The empire retained its status as a dominant force in the politics of Europe and the Middle East for centuries. However, the European naval expeditions triggered by the Ottoman threat eventually led to Western colonial expansion across the globe, and European states started overtaking the Ottomans in terms of wealth, knowledge and power. By the nineteenth century, the Ottoman Empire was suffering massive losses at the hands of its main land-based rivals, the Russian and Austro-Hungarian Empires, and its colonial antagonists, the British and French empires. These losses went hand in hand with extreme internal turmoil as many of the empire's ethnic and religious groups vied for independence, inspired by the ascendant ideology of nationalism and supported by the Ottomans' imperial rivals.

It was in these troubled years that Sabiha Sertel was born in the Ottoman port city of Salonica (Selanik in Turkish), today Thessaloniki in Greece. She belonged to a particular ethno-religious group that had made the city its home, namely the *Dönme* (literally, 'those who have turned'), a community of Jewish origin that had converted to Islam in the seventeenth century but retained its own religious profile and sociocultural cohesion through endogamy and self-segregation.

When the Ottoman Empire started embracing major reforms in the nineteenth century, opening itself to the cultural and technological influence of the West, many *Dönme* made their way to the forefront of the empire's modernizing forces. They went on to play an important role in the Committee of Union and Progress (CUP) – also known as the Young Turks – a secret political organization of young Ottoman elites that staged a military coup in 1908, sidelining Sultan Abdülhamid II and assuming de facto rulership of the Ottoman Empire until the end of the First World War. One of Sertel's brothers, Celal, was a member of the Young Turks and participated in the declaration of the new regime on 23 July 1908, at Freedom Square in Salonica. True to the progressive and reform-oriented impetus of her community, Sabiha became one of its first members to publicly marry outside the group, choosing as her husband Mehmet Zekeriya, a staunch secularist and atheist, who descended from a Sunni Muslim family.

As the European and primarily Christian provinces of the Ottoman Empire seceded, one by one – Sabiha and her family had to relocate from Salonica to Constantinople in 1913, after the loss of the city to the Greek army – the empire experienced a massive demographic shift, weakening its multi-religious character and fortifying the predominance of the Sunni Muslim population. The trend was not lost on the ideologues of the Young Turk movement, which struggled for a nationalist ideology of its own to hold the remnants of the Ottoman Empire together. They found it in Turkishness, which they conceived as an ethnic identity with an implied religious, i.e. Sunni Muslim, component. But the ascendancy of Turkish nationalism was by no means a foregone conclusion. Ottoman elites had traditionally used the word 'Turk' as an insult, denoting an uncivilized country bumpkin. More importantly, the empire still contained sizeable populations of non-Turks such as Kurds and Arabs, non-Sunnis such as Alevis, and non-Muslims such as Armenians, Jews and Greeks. But the events and policies of the First World War and its aftermath provided a decisive push for the new national identity. During the war, the empire's Arab provinces seceded, while the Ottoman state exterminated its own Armenian population – as well as certain smaller groups – in a ruthless genocide. And a few years after the war, a 'population exchange' between the states of Turkey and Greece removed the last major community of Orthodox Christians from Anatolian soil. With some exceptions, such as the minorities of Constantinople, soon to be officially renamed Istanbul, the population under Turkish rule was now largely Turkish and overwhelmingly Muslim.

Just as the prevalence of Turkish nationalism was no foregone conclusion, so, too, the establishment of a Turkish nation-state was no foregone conclusion. The Ottoman Empire fought the First World War on the losing side of the Central Powers. After the war, the Allied Powers occupied Constantinople and imposed the Treaty of Sèvres, partitioning the empire's remaining territories among themselves and leaving the Ottomans with an unviable rump state. However, many Anatolian segments of the Ottoman army were still intact and in the process of regrouping under the supreme command of a Young Turk officer by the name of Mustafa Kemal. These troops went on to stage a war of resistance against the implementation of the treaty, a struggle waged against armed forces from Greece, the only country willing to fight for the treaty in the aftermath of the First World War. These times of occupation and resistance are remembered forcefully by Sertel, who devotes vivid chapters to the Greek occupation of the port city Izmir, her participation in Istanbul cells of resistance, and her involvement with the anti-occupation journal *Büyük Mecmua* (Grand Journal), the contents of which she fiercely defended against British censors. Eventually, Turkish troops drove the Greek army from Anatolian territory, forcing a renegotiation of the Sèvres treaty. The result was the 1923 Treaty of Lausanne, which established, with some minor variances, the borders of modern Turkey. The same year, the Turkish republic was proclaimed, with Mustafa Kemal as its president – he would soon assume the family name Atatürk, often translated as 'Father of the Turks'.

Surprisingly, Sertel and her husband spent much of the Turkish–Greek conflict obtaining a university education in the USA. This sojourn was arranged by Halide Edib, a leading female Turkish writer, intellectual and activist, who, at the time, supported the idea of the USA exercising indirect rule over the remaining Ottoman territories through a League of Nations mandate. Edib was instrumental in securing scholarships for the Sertels from Chicago businessman Charles R. Crane. The goal was to educate them as young Turkish elites, who would return home with cutting-edge knowledge in various fields of learning, along with personal connections to the USA. Some of Sertel's most fascinating memories are from this time, detailing her studies at Columbia University in New York City, the fundraising events she staged for the Turkish resistance, and her efforts at organizing and unionizing Turkish and Kurdish factory workers in New York City and Detroit. It was also during her studies in the USA that Sertel first encountered socialist thought in the English translations of authors such as Karl Marx, Friedrich Engels, August Bebel and Karl Kautsky. The ideals of socialism were to guide her for the rest of her political and intellectual life.

The Sertels returned from the USA right around the time the Treaty of Lausanne was ratified in July 1923, and mere months before the Republic of Turkey was proclaimed. They found themselves in the midst of a tremendous sociopolitical paradigm shift, where, in effect, a new country was being created. Everything seemed up for debate, few topics were taboo, and even the wildest dreams seemed to stand a chance of realization. Should the new Turkish state be a republic or some kind of constitutional sultanate? Should its law be secular or religious? Should women be granted equal rights with men? Should the country be self-sufficient or enmeshed in the world economy? Should the land of quasi-feudal lords be redistributed to peasants? Those of us born and raised in established countries with relatively stable political systems will find it hard to imagine taking part in such a momentous process, but Sertel's memoirs do a superb job of reflecting this period in all its excitement and tension, all its hopes and frustrations.

It was in this environment that Sabiha Sertel embarked on her journalistic career. In 1924, her husband Zekeriya established *Resimli Ay* (Illustrated Monthly), a monthly magazine aimed at covering intellectual trends and debates about politics and society and conveying these to the average Turkish population, in an accessible language and engaging manner. The magazine was a first in Turkish publishing both for its editorial approach and for its appearance, which boasted an eye-catching and lavishly illustrated

American-style layout. Encouraged by her husband, Sabiha contributed to the magazine, with feature articles containing social and political analysis as well as the popular advice column 'Cici Anne' (Sweet Mother), in which she answered the queries of readers puzzled by the rapid changes in Turkish social and family life. *Resimli Ay* became a massive success, firmly establishing the Sertels as journalists and publishers of major stature on the emerging Turkish media scene.

Resimli Ay's agenda of conveying progressive ideas to the uneducated masses was buoyed by the direction in which the Turkish state, led by Mustafa Kemal, seemed to be taking the new country. After the proclamation of the republic, Mustafa Kemal and his allies sidelined the broad coalition of political forces that had helped them win the Turkish–Greek War, a coalition that included supporters of the sultanate and defenders of sharia law. Instead of compromising with such groups on matters of government and law, Mustafa Kemal forced the creation of a modern, secular state, following Western models. His goals could hardly have been more ambitious: the Arabic alphabet employed by the Ottomans was replaced with a Latin one. Sharia law was fully abandoned in favour of legal systems adopted from Western countries. The sultanate and caliphate, offices through which the Ottoman dynasty had ruled its empire for many centuries, were abolished and the dynasty itself banned from the country. Religious brotherhoods, a crucial form of social organization in the empire, were outlawed. Women were granted equal rights with men and guaranteed freedom by the state in matters such as education and their choice of clothing. These and many other measures were nothing short of revolutionary and were, indeed, perceived as such: they were called 'revolutions' (*inkilap* in Arabic, *devrim* in Turkish), and to Turkish minds, their combined significance was comparable to that of the October Revolution which had ended the Russian Empire in 1917, a mere five or so years ago.

But while the Kemalist reforms may have had a similar impact to those carried out by the Bolsheviks, they also suffered from some of the same drawbacks: they were decided and carried out in a top-down fashion, and they were implemented by a state that lacked the resources and manpower to spread them across the whole country. As a result, the reforms largely took hold in major urban centres, where the state had a strong presence and where many inhabitants worked as bureaucrats, teachers, doctors, lawyers, or in other white-collar professions dependent on the state. The vast majority of the population, though, continued living in the countryside and working in agriculture as it had done for centuries. These people remained indifferent to the reforms, first because the reforms did not affect their livelihoods, second because there were few schools or other services through which the state could have reached the rural population, and third because the new state, just like the Ottoman one before it, depended on the political support of quasi-feudal local rulers, whose sway over rural communities the state dared not challenge. Sertel experienced the deep divide between city and countryside first-hand when, as she tells us, the first social project she proposed to the state, a survey about children's needs in the countryside, was shot down by none other than Latife Hanım, Atatürk's wife at the time. The plight of peasants became one of Sertel's main preoccupations, and she was repeatedly frustrated by the state's failure to implement a land reform that would have redistributed ownership of arable land from local lords to farmers.

The city–countryside divide was not the only factor complicating the nationalist ideal of a unified Turkish population from the outset. The state continued to harass remaining non-Muslim communities, inducing them to leave the country in successive waves. This was not just a measure to achieve demographic unity, but also a programme of wealth and status redistribution. The trade and economic elite of the Ottoman Empire had largely consisted of non-Muslims, such as Orthodox Christians and Jews, and the emphasis on a Turkish Muslim nationalism gave the founders of the republic the chance to expropriate this elite and redistribute its wealth and power among their own followers. This process continued long after the founding of the republic, with events such as the introduction of the Wealth Tax in 1942, a discriminatory levy that disproportionately affected non-Muslims and was described by Sertel as having 'the stench of fascism'.

The non-Muslim communities were demographically – if not economically – negligible. But the state also had to grapple with large population groups that were either Sunni Muslim but not Turkish, such as the Kurds, or Turkish but not Sunni Muslim, such as the Alevis. Against these groups, each making up about 20 per cent of the population, vehement policies of oppression and assimilation were put into place, including the armed suppression of rebellions, forced migration off ancestral lands and cultural re-education through the banning of native languages and other measures. Rather than a non-negotiable racist exclusion, such policies were – and remain – an attempt at cultural extermination. As long as a person declared themself to be a Turk, with all the cultural and religious characteristics the term implied, they could claim a full stake in the new republic. But in return for this inclusion, the state demanded an abandonment of traditional or alternative national, religious and cultural affiliations. Mustafa Kemal and his followers believed that the Ottoman Empire's multi-ethnic and multi-religious make-up had been a major factor in its disintegration, and assimilationist policies were to prevent the same fate from befalling the new Turkish state.

Sertel takes up minority issues in Turkey at various points in her memoirs. In early chapters, she recounts conflicts between Turkish and Kurdish migrant workers in the USA. Later, she writes about the suppression of the 1925 Sheikh Said rebellion by Turkish armed forces, conceding at the end of her account that the rebellion, for all its flaws from her perspective, should still be appreciated as 'a movement for Kurdish independence'. And she gives a detailed assessment of the Wealth Tax, condemning it as a 'shameful episode' in Turkish history. However, in all these chapters, Sertel cannot help but come across as somewhat apologetic of the actions taken by the Turkish state, while many other atrocities, such as the Ottoman state's genocide against the Armenians, which Turkey officially denies to this day, or the Dersim massacres carried out by the Turkish state against rebellious Alevi groups from 1937 to 1938, find no place in her memoirs at all. Added to this is the fact that Sertel never mentions her own *Dönme* background, except for one instance where her opponents use the term to vilify her, which implies that Sertel herself did not identify with the description. It is evident from her memoirs that Sertel was no racist or cultural chauvinist. But it is equally evident that she was a true believer in the project of Turkish nationalism and the necessity for all parts of the population, including herself, to abandon old identities and contribute to the integrity of the young state.

To Turkey's leaders, this integrity depended not just on domestic factors such as demographic uniformity, but also on a maximum of independence from the influence of foreign states and the global economy. The demise of the Ottoman Empire, they reasoned, was not only due to the disruptive influence of non-Muslim communities within the realm, but also to the interference of the empire's rivals on the stage of world politics. States such as Britain, France and Russia had collaborated with Ottoman non-Muslim communities, fomenting their drive for independence and using them as a wedge to tear the empire apart. But these states had also co-opted the Ottoman economy: by the end of the nineteenth century, the empire was largely running on foreign debt acquired from European creditors. In 1881, these creditors established the Ottoman Public Debt Administration, which was given the right to collect certain Ottoman taxes directly to service the Ottoman debt. At the dawn of the twentieth century, about 30 per cent of the empire's tax income was being funnelled abroad through this system, without ever seeing the vaults of the Ottoman treasury.

To avoid such a trap, the founders of the new Turkey were determined to keep the country as economically self-sufficient and politically independent as possible. They championed 'Westernization' not to bring the country into the orbit of the West, but to help the country catch up with the West. They adopted Western laws, institutions, practices and technologies while dispossessing the most 'Western' parts of Turkey's population, cutting off the country's economy from global currents, and steering a political course that was free of alignment with the West, the Soviet Union or any other global players. This is why intellectuals like Sertel, while keen to learn as much from the West as possible, could at the same time take a highly critical anti-colonialist and anti-imperialist stance, railing against the influence of countries like Britain, France and the United States on the world stage. Sertel devotes many passages to framing the Turkish–Greek War as a national struggle for independence, in line with anti-colonial struggles around the world. And throughout her memoirs, we find her firmly opposing any political or economic concessions to foreign entities that she felt would undermine Turkish sovereignty.

The internal and external threat perception of Turkey's ruling elites helped them justify a very loose attitude – to put it kindly – towards democratic values. Nominally, the republic under Atatürk was holding elections, with women achieving voting rights in local elections as early as 1930. However, the country was, in effect, ruled by a single-party state. The Republican People's Party (Cumhuriyet Halk Partisi or CHP), founded by Atatürk, kept a tight leash on political life and public debate, only allowing a highly circumscribed opposition at certain junctures and on carefully chosen topics. Some of the Sertels' fiercest struggles were against this single-party authoritarianism, which, time and again, resulted in censorship of their writings, banning of their journals or newspapers, as well as trials and imprisonment of newspaper staff, and of the Sertels themselves. Especially after Atatürk's death in 1938, which Sertel recounts in a chapter that is as moving as it is sobering in its critical assessment of the leader's achievements, the authoritarian bent of Turkey's rulers increased. Under Atatürk's successor İsmet İnönü, Sertel witnessed the single-party state move further and further to the right, to the point of establishing various avenues of cooperation with Nazi Germany.

These developments had a major impact on the Sertels and their milieu of leftist thinkers. In 1928, *Resimli Ay* hired the controversial young poet Nazım Hikmet Ran, who had recently returned from studying in Moscow and could not find employment because of his political opinions. In an attempt to ward off criticism that the magazine was harbouring communist writers, the Sertels merely retained the poet as a copy-editor. Nonetheless, Nazım Hikmet quickly emerged as the leading voice of modern Turkish literature, spearheading a literary revolution that turned Turkish poetry away from the formal and thematic preoccupations of Ottoman literature and towards social-realist themes, expressed in free verse. At the same time, his charismatic personality transformed *Resimli Ay* into the gathering place of a whole new generation of leftist Turkish writers and intellectuals, who produced some of their earliest and most seminal works while affiliated with the magazine. Sertel devotes many chapters to the political and literary discussions that were held in this stimulating milieu, the members of which retrospectively read like a who's who of famous Turkish authors, including the eminent novelist Sabahaddin Ali, whose 'discovery' by Nazım Hikmet, Sertel describes in a touching chapter.

The emergence of the *Resimli Ay* milieu gave Sertel the chance to form friendships with some of the most interesting figures in Turkish artistic and intellectual history, and her memoirs clearly show her affection for these friends. It was all the more difficult, then, for Sertel to witness as these figures were silenced, imprisoned or even assassinated at the behest of the Turkish state as anti-left oppression mounted in Turkey. The Sertels themselves had to appear in court numerous times. Sabiha acquired the dubious honour of becoming the first Turkish woman to be prosecuted for her writings. Her husband Zekeriya spent one-and-a-half years imprisoned in exile, with Sabiha running the magazine in his absence. Finally, at the end of 1930, the magazine ceased publishing over a dispute between its investors and the editorial staff: intimidated by the Turkish state's hostile stance towards the magazine, the investors demanded the dismissal of Nazım Hikmet and other leftist writers. The Sertels refused, choosing to discontinue the magazine rather than betray their friends and principles. In 1938, Nazım Hikmet was sentenced to twenty-eight years in prison on trumped-up charges of spreading communist propaganda. He remained incarcerated until 1950, when he was released as part of an amnesty and went into Soviet exile, where he died in 1963 without ever returning to Turkey. Sabahaddin Ali's fate was even more bitter: he was assassinated, by agents of the Turkish state as Sertel suggests, while attempting a clandestine border crossing into Bulgaria in 1948. These tragedies add a deeply emotional side to Sertel's account, which is as much about the struggle for social and political ideals as it is about the personal struggles of the exceptional people who risked life and limb to defend these ideals.

The Sertels' struggle reached its climax with their takeover of the daily newspaper *Tan*, which they were to publish from 1936 to 1945. It was one of the most dangerous and volatile periods in Turkish and world history: in Turkey, the single-party state attained new heights of paranoia and cynicism following Atatürk's death, while internationally, the major world powers were lining up along the ideological fault lines of capitalism, fascism/Nazism and communism, paving the way for the Second World War. In this atmosphere, the Sertels used *Tan* as a platform to call for more democracy and human rights at home and to staunchly oppose far-right, fascist and Nazi thought across the globe. In the process, they transformed *Tan* from a minor and moribund publication into the country's main leftist opposition paper and a journalistic powerhouse. Some of the most riveting sections of Sertel's memoirs cover *Tan*'s struggle against the far right before and during the Second World War, a worthy cause that leaves no doubt as to the couple's political integrity and personal bravery. Shortly before the outbreak of the war, we even find Sabiha travelling across Western Europe, interviewing journalists and state officials who, for the most part, blithely underestimate the threat posed by Nazi Germany or cynically try to play the Nazis and Soviets off against each other. Political frustration turns into existential fear as Sertel is held up by police officers in Fascist Italy, barely avoiding inspection of a trunk full of banned leftist books she is smuggling from France to Turkey.

Much to Sertel's satisfaction, Turkey did not become a party to the Second World War. Nonetheless, the war and its aftermath came at a heavy price for the country, namely the economic and political sovereignty that Atatürk had valued above all else. The country was bankrupted due to maintaining a massive wartime army as well as other factors such as interrupted trade flows. Even during the war, there had been heavy pressure on Turkey to take sides, from the Allies and the Axis powers alike, and the country had wavered greatly in providing support for both sides while trying to keep both at arm's length. As the war ended, though, mounting economic and political pressure forced the Turkish state to align either with the US-led coalition soon to become NATO or with the Soviet Union under Stalin. Turkey's leaders chose the former, mainly because Stalin demanded territorial concessions in north-eastern Anatolia as part of any agreement. And so, Turkey declared war on Nazi Germany during the last days of the Second World War and thus became eligible to join the United Nations as a founding member, and soon went on to receive US aid as part of the Marshall Plan. In 1950, Turkish troops were dispatched to fight in the Korean War to secure Turkey's admission to NATO, in which it remains, to this day, the only Muslim-majority country.

It is one of the great ironies of historiography on Turkey that the post-Second World War line of military integration with NATO, economic opening to global capitalism and political alignment with the European Union have been presented as the continuation and culmination of Atatürk's reformist agenda. In fact, the opposite is true. In rendering the country militarily, economically and politically dependent on the West, Turkey's leaders abandoned the *sine qua non* of Kemalist thought, namely national sovereignty. The Sertels clearly recognized this contradiction and vehemently argued against the undue influence they felt the United States and NATO were beginning to exert over the country. Key passages in Sertel's memoirs describe the anchoring of the US battleship *Missouri* in Istanbul and the participation of Turkish soldiers in the Korean War. 'We sacrificed our sons,' Sertel writes poignantly, 'for the sake of the US monopolies. America sent Turkish soldiers into the line of fire, frittering them away like small chips at the casino. [...] US battleships hadn't conquered the Turkish people's hearts, but their independence. We paid for America's dollars with the blood we shed in Korea, with graves that rose in mounds.'

But at least, one might think, Turkey's alignment with the West must have resulted in more democracy. On the face of it, this did seem to be the case. The first Turkish multi-party elections were held in 1946, and while these were rigged and won by the

CHP, the party lost power to the centrist and populist Democrat Party (DP) in the second elections in 1950. But there were limits to this new freedom. Turkey's Western allies wanted the country to be democratic, but not so democratic as to tolerate a political left that might awaken sympathy for the Soviet Union. 'Free' elections excluded leftist parties, which were usually banned as soon as they emerged. The result was a string of populist, economically liberal and socially conservative governments, all more or less toeing the NATO line. The Turkish military steered the proceedings from behind the scenes when it did not seize power overtly, such as in the military coups of 1960, 1971 and 1980. Leftist thinkers and activists like Sertel, who had been persecuted for opposing Nazism and the far right during the war, were now subjected to a new round of persecution for refusing to endorse the political and economic objectives of NATO and the USA.

The new, post-war persecution resulted in one of the most terrifying events in Turkish media history: on 4 December 1945, the Sertels' newspaper *Tan* was destroyed by a government-instigated mob that demolished the *Tan* printing house and all the technical equipment it contained, along with two other, smaller newspapers. Instead of trying the perpetrators, the prosecutors put the Sertels themselves on trial, accusing them of publishing articles aimed at undermining the Turkish state. Their home was raided, many of their private documents were confiscated and the Sertels were each sentenced to a year in prison. They successfully appealed the verdict, but even though their convictions were overturned and they were released from prison, their lives had changed forever. They found it impossible to return to publishing, were subjected to constant police surveillance and faced the risk of further violent attacks. Many of their closest friends, all of them high-profile writers and intellectuals, were similarly affected by the vehemence with which the Turkish state cracked down on leftist thought in a bid to ingratiate itself with its new strategic partner, the USA. 'One evening,' Sertel recalls, 'we were entertaining some friends on the seaside balcony of our Moda home. They'd all lost their jobs. They weren't just unable to serve the nation; they couldn't even make a living anymore.' In 1950, the Sertels decided, with a heavy heart, to continue their lives in exile.

Sabiha's memoirs come to an end with the Sertels' departure from Turkey. The couple first relocated to Paris, but, with Nazım Hikmet's encouragement, ended up spending the majority of their exile in Eastern Bloc countries, most prominently East Germany and Azerbaijan. It was here, in the city of Baku, that Sabiha decided to write her autobiography. She wanted readers in Turkey to hear her side of the story – what she had seen and done, whom she had known and loved, why she had left the country she fought for, and how she hoped its future could still be redeemed. 'We sacrificed everything for our cause,' she wrote. 'Today, we live in exile, anguished at having to watch from afar as the struggle we began is carried on by capable hands.' But the struggle was destined to outlive her: in 1968, the same year her manuscript was smuggled into Turkey in a suitcase filled with laundry, Sertel died of lung cancer in Baku. Printed the same year by the leftist Turkish publishing house Ant Yayınları, her *apologia* became her farewell.

Since their publication, Sertel's memoirs have only grown in significance. The increased importance of women's studies underlines her value as a rare female voice from Turkey's formative years. Not that Sertel stands on an avowedly feminist platform or makes a consistent point of highlighting women's issues. But her very life story, the goals she set herself, the obstacles she faced and the ways in which she succeeded and failed, vividly illustrate what a 'new woman' of the Turkish Republic – albeit one from a privileged background – could aspire to, accomplish and expect to put up with. Sertel accomplished much: she gained access to the highest ranks of the Turkish intelligentsia; published countless articles, newspapers and books; and was taken seriously enough to face imprisonment and exile. However, her memoirs are also those of a woman who was exploited by business partners when her husband was absent, subjected to sexist slurs by her political opponents, and expected to take full charge of raising her two children in the midst of all her endeavours. Sertel makes light of such issues or only mentions them in passing. Even when she goes into detail regarding her personal life and feelings, she sounds remarkably detached and matter-of-fact. But this literary strategy only exposes another dimension of her gendered experience: clearly, even at her life's end, Sertel was at pains to project the ideal of the enlightened, rational, sexless woman, a twentieth-century ideal encountered across the sphere of influence of 'Western civilization' but perhaps expressed most forcefully in Soviet ideology.

Sertel's seeming indifference to her gender is just one of the 'blind spots' we encounter in her memoirs. Above, I mentioned her tendency to downplay the racist and exclusionary nature of Kemalism in the name of national sovereignty. And the minority issue is not the only one where Sertel seems to toe a 'party line', whether Kemalist, socialist or otherwise. Her take on religion is unreservedly negative. She has nothing but contempt for the moribund Ottoman Empire. Her historical materialist belief in an inevitable sequence of political revolutions is absolute. And often, she seems to regard her opponents as one-dimensionally as they did her: while she is outraged when her detractors paint her as a communist stooge in the pay of the Soviet Union, she is equally liberal in depicting her antagonists as serving the interests of global capitalism and Western imperialism.

Still, despite her political leanings, Sertel is no ideologue. Awed by Atatürk's accomplishments, she, nonetheless, takes him to task for failing to establish a democracy. Supportive of Kemalist reforms, she still laments the wide gap between ideals and implementation. A committed socialist, she does not hesitate to criticize her comrades for internal squabbles and utopian thinking. Throughout her memoirs, she impresses the reader as an independent, critical thinker, offering an honest, personal and thoughtful opinion on matters she experienced first-hand. Her views may not be unbiased, but she always carefully weighs the available ideological and political options against historical realities, and when she speaks and acts, it is not with the fervour of blind faith, but with the conviction of considered thought. Thanks to this attitude, Sertel uses her memoirs to develop an exceptionally nuanced and inquisitive take on Turkish history. Readers only familiar with linear grand narratives depicting the country's supposed progress, Westernization or Islamization, will find in Sertel a refreshing reminder that history is a complex and contradictory affair.

This intellectual honesty and open-mindedness is why Sertel's memoirs are as relevant to contemporary Turkey as to the country's history. Sertel's analytical and largely unromantic gaze allows many issues that plague Turkey today to emerge in their historical continuity. These issues include an authoritarian state with a strong leadership cult; a lack of appreciation for the freedom of opinion and speech; ethnic, religious and regional divides; the wide gap between city and countryside; the disconnect between elites and masses; the exploitation of these masses by the country's power brokers; and the tension between national independence and outside influence. Sertel helps us to see that such issues are not solely to blame on one or the other political group taking power in the country, but must be addressed in a complex analysis that cuts across ideological lines. In many ways, Turkey today is repeating its history, and while the names of the actors may have changed, most of the underlying dynamics remain the same. Thanks to Sertel's account, we gain a closer view of those dynamics than ever before.

David Selim Sayers
Paris, 2018

Translators' note

Sabiha Sertel's autobiography is truly a hybrid text. It is more than a mere memoir, offering a chronicle of upheavals in the outgoing Ottoman Empire and the nascent Turkish Republic. It is also an expert analysis of these events, introducing main players, explaining circumstances, and assessing outcome, success, and failure. In addition, it is an intellectual treatise examining sociopolitical ideas, ideologies, and movements in the first half of the twentieth century, endorsing some of these, and rejecting others. And finally, it is a manifesto, a passionate call to political action informed by Sertel's socialist convictions and deep sense of justice.

To Sertel's credit, she manages to weave these disparate approaches into an intriguing narrative. Still, such a text comes with its unique set of challenges. One of these is the way the text switches back and forth between narration of events and intellectual analysis. For a comparison, readers may imagine a James Bond movie in which 007 takes time out after every action sequence to enlighten the viewer about the geopolitical ramifications of what just happened on screen. While both aspects may be equally fascinating, their combination has the potential to rattle the audience. Sertel does a good job of maintaining a stylistic continuity between the more narrative and scholarly parts of her account, and this translation follows her lead in attempting to render the transitions as smooth as possible.

More challenging for us as translators were certain lapses in Sertel's citations, chronology, and arguments. In her Baku exile, Sertel faced the task of writing without access to crucial primary sources (as she points out herself) or (as we might add) a critical editor. Many of the passages she puts in quotes are either partly inaccurate or not really quotes at all, but rather paraphrases or summaries. We only intervened in a handful of instances when a precise quote from an anglophone source was easy to track and correct. Otherwise, we permitted Sertel to let her characters speak as she saw fit. Further, Sertel can be ambiguous as to the exact chronology of events. We added footnotes to address some of these instances, but others retain their mystery.

Another caveat concerns Sertel's interventions in literary, social, and political debates. In these passages, the author often employs a narrative device much beloved by Turkish writers but harder to decipher for non-Turkish audiences: More is said between the lines than in the actual lines themselves. This may obscure the topic of debates: Precisely what is the argument about? It may also obfuscate the stance of one or more participants: What exactly is X arguing for, why does Y object to this, and which alternative does Z propose? Occasionally, the reason for this opacity is presumed background knowledge. At other times, it feels like Sertel may have benefited from an editor streamlining her thoughts. But in most cases, we assume, Sertel is nebulous on purpose, because crudely spelling things out is something most Turkish political authors simply don't do. In an environment as volatile as the Turkish political scene, it always helps to retain a modicum of deniability, and Sertel in particular was writing in an exile from which she hoped the Turkish state would let her return one day.

Once again, our response as translators has been mixed. In cases where Sertel eventually reaches her point, but does so in a convoluted and repetitive way, we have allowed ourselves to play the role of editor. But in passages signaling a more deliberate ambiguity, we felt that imposing a clear and unretractable argument would have interfered too heavily with the author's style and intent. Therefore, as in the Turkish original, we left it up to the reader to decide exactly what Sertel wants to say, and where on the spectrum of opinion she wishes to come down.

Finally, readers should be aware that Sertel assumes a great deal of prior knowledge on their part. She expects them to be familiar with the main events of Ottoman and Turkish history. She also presupposes intimacy with the urban layouts of Istanbul and Ankara, taking readers through a variety of neighborhoods and locales only introduced by name. Occasionally, she lists the names of people participating in a meeting or other event, tasking the reader with finding out whether the people in question are major figures or mere bit players. And she freely employs the terminology of thought systems like socialism and Kemalism without explaining the meaning of specialist terms.

Introducing brackets or footnotes to address all these issues would have rendered the translation unwieldy. So, in the spirit of Sertel herself, we combined a variety of approaches. We followed Sertel's orthography when it came to names, leaving place names largely uncommented. We inserted the English names of publications in brackets. We added footnotes for historical events and names of persons if they were particularly relevant to Sertel's narrative, leaving inquisitive readers to research the rest for themselves. We explained political and other intellectual terms in footnotes if they were easy to summarize and collected the rest in a brief glossary. And we provided additional footnotes when Sertel's omission of certain events (such as the Armenian Genocide) was significant or when events after the close of the narrative (such as Turkey's military coups) added poignancy to her story. Our goal was to create a text that is neither bewildering to the layperson nor cumbersome to the expert; whether we succeeded is up to the reader to decide.

David Selim Sayers and Evrim Emir-Sayers
Paris, 1 July 2018

Biographical and historical timeline

1876
31 August: Abdülhamid II assumes the Ottoman throne. He is the 34th sultan of the Ottoman Empire, which he will rule until 1909.

1895
Sabiha Nazmi is born in the Ottoman port city of Salonica (now Thessaloniki in Greece) to mother Atiye and father Nazmi. She is the youngest of six children. Her family is part of the *Dönme* community, a small group that converted from Judaism to Islam in the seventeenth century.

1903
Sabiha witnesses her father's domestic abuse of her mother. Subsequently, Nazmi divorces Atiye on the spot, in accordance with Islamic law.

1908
24 July: The Young Turk Revolution. The Committee of Union and Progress (also known as Young Turks) is a secret society, largely consisting of young, Western-educated Ottoman civil servants and military officers. Following the revolution, the Committee of Union and Progress (CUP) gradually assumes political control of the Ottoman Empire, consigning the sultan to a largely symbolic role.

1912
8 October: The First Balkan War breaks out. Over the course of the war, the Ottoman Empire loses nearly all its territory on European soil.
8 November: The city of Salonica surrenders to the Greek army.

1913
30 May: The First Balkan War ends.
Sabiha and her family immigrate from Salonica to Istanbul/Constantinople, capital of the Ottoman Empire.

1914
28 July: First World War breaks out. The Ottoman Empire joins the war on the side of the Central Powers, Germany and Austria-Hungary.

1915

24 April: Ottoman authorities round up hundreds of Armenian intellectuals and community leaders in Istanbul. The event is widely considered the beginning of the Armenian Genocide.

Sabiha marries Mehmet Zekeriya, who hails from a Sunni Muslim family. She is one of the first *Dönme* to publicly marry outside of the community. The wedding is publicized by the Young Turks' central committee as an example of interfaith harmony in the Ottoman Empire.

1917

Sabiha gives birth to her first daughter, Sevim.

1918

30 October: Armistice of Mudros. The Ottoman Empire surrenders to the Allied Powers.

11 November: End of First World War.

13 November: Istanbul is occupied by British, French and Italian forces.

1919

6 March: The first issue of *Büyük Mecmua* (Grand Journal) appears. Zekeriya and Sabiha's first major foray into publishing, the journal focuses on opposing the country's occupation by the Allied Powers. Zekeriya is arrested as a result of the journal's political line. Sabiha takes over the publisher's licence for the duration of his absence.

15 May: Greek forces occupy Izmir/Smyrna, a major Ottoman port city on the Aegean coast of Anatolia, and start proceeding inland. Shortly thereafter, the Turkish National Movement under the leadership of Mustafa Kemal (Atatürk), mainly consisting of remnants of the Ottoman army, launches an armed resistance.

28 November: Sabiha and Zekeriya Sertel move to New York City to study at Columbia University on a scholarship. In the USA, Sabiha becomes familiar with socialist and communist thought. She earns a degree from the New York School of Social Work. She also spends time unionizing Turkish and Kurdish factory workers as well as organizing fundraisers to support the Turkish National Movement.

25 December: The final issue of *Büyük Mecmua* appears. The journal is shut down by British censors for its opposition to the Allied occupation.

1920

10 August: Treaty of Sèvres. The government of the Ottoman sultan agrees to the almost complete dismemberment of the empire by the Allied Powers.

1922

11 October: Armistice of Mudanya. Greek troops are driven out of Anatolia by the Turkish National Movement.

1 November: The Turkish National Movement declares the Ottoman sultanate to be abolished. The same day, Sabiha gives birth to her second daughter, Yıldız, in New York City.

1923

25 May: Sabiha graduates from Columbia University's New York School of Social Work. Shortly thereafter, she and her family return to Turkey.

24 July: Treaty of Lausanne. The Turkish National Movement gains international recognition for a new Turkish state.

13 October: Ankara, the stronghold of the Turkish National Movement, supersedes Istanbul as capital city.

23 September: The last Allied troops depart Istanbul.

29 October: The Turkish Republic is proclaimed.

1924

1 February: The first issue of *Resimli Ay* (Illustrated Monthly), the Sertels' second major publication venture, appears. *Resimli Ay* is an illustrated, American-style magazine aiming to attract an audience among the general public as well as the country's elites. The magazine becomes especially known for its advocacy of Turkey's literary avant-garde and of progressive and socialist political ideas. Among other writings, Sabiha contributes the popular column 'Cici Anne' (Sweet Mother), providing advice to Turkish families struggling with social reforms and upheavals. She also temporarily takes over as editor when Zekeriya is imprisoned once again. It is during her time at *Resimli Ay* that Sabiha is first sued by the Turkish state for the content of her writings.

1928

The Turkish poet Nazım Hikmet returns to Istanbul from his studies at the Communist University of the Toilers of the East in Moscow. He starts working for *Resimli Ay*, where he and his work are introduced to a broad Turkish public for the first time. He will remain a close family friend of the Sertels, as well as a major influence on their artistic and political views, for the rest of their lives.

1930

Sabiha runs unsuccessfully in the Istanbul municipal elections as an independent candidate, calling for greater public funding of homeless shelters and soup kitchens as well as leave from work for new parents.

1931

Resimli Ay is closed due to controversies over the political content of its articles.

1936

Zekeriya becomes co-owner of *Tan* (Dawn), a struggling Turkish daily newspaper and publishing house. Under the Sertels, *Tan* will rise to become Turkey's second-largest newspaper and the couple's final and most prominent publication. In the lead-up to the Second World War and during the war itself, the newspaper becomes known for strongly opposing the ideas and policies of fascist and Nazi movements within Turkey and abroad.

1937

February: The Sertels' older daughter Sevim enrolls at the University of Missouri School of Journalism. She will go on to marry an American journalist and spend the majority of her life in the USA.

1938

10 November: Death of Mustafa Kemal Atatürk, founder and President of the Turkish Republic. Control of the Turkish single-party state passes to his comrade-in-arms and confidant, İsmet İnönü, who had previously served multiple terms as prime minister.

Nazım Hikmet is sentenced to 28 years in prison on fabricated charges of spreading communist propaganda among the Turkish armed forces.

1939

1 September: Nazi Germany invades Poland. Second World War begins. Turkey retains its neutrality, negotiating an opportunistic web of treaties with Britain, Germany and the USA.

1942

11 November: The Turkish National Assembly passes the Wealth Tax Bill, establishing a discriminatory tax on fixed assets that destroys the livelihood of many non-Muslim minority communities in the country.

1945

7 May: The German armed forces surrender.

26 June: The United Nations Charter is signed in San Francisco. Turkey participates as a founding member.

2 September: The Japanese armed forces surrender, bringing the Second World War to a de facto end.

1 December: Sabiha serves as the editor of *Görüşler* (Views), a controversial journal expressing strong opposition to the single-party state.

4 December: The *Tan* publishing house is destroyed by a government-sponsored mob of thousands. The Sertels' publishing career comes to an end. Their request for asylum in the USA is denied.

1946

7 January: The Democrat Party, Turkey's first post-war opposition party, is founded.

7 February: The Sertels are arrested for defaming the Turkish Republic in their writings and held in jail for the duration of their trial.

July: The Sertels are acquitted. However, their home remains under police surveillance and they are effectively blacklisted, no longer able to find work in Turkey.

21 July: Turkey holds its first multi-party elections, which are rigged and won by the Republican People's Party (CHP), the political apparatus controlling Turkey's single-party state.

1948

2 April: Sabahaddin Ali, prominent Turkish novelist and close friend of the Sertels, is assassinated while attempting a clandestine crossing of the Turkish–Bulgarian border.

1950

9 September: The Sertels and their younger daughter Yıldız flee Turkey for Paris. Their forced exile will be spent mostly in Eastern Bloc countries.

14 May: Turkey holds its second general elections. The victory of the Democrat Party puts an end to CHP rule.

19 May: Nazım Hikmet is released from prison as part of a general amnesty, following a lengthy hunger strike and an international campaign on his behalf, in which the Sertels are involved. Shortly thereafter, he goes into exile in the Soviet Union.

25 June: The Korean War breaks out. Turkey dispatches troops to speed up its accession to NATO. While the war will end in 1953, the last Turkish troops will not leave the country until 1971.

1952

18 February: Turkey becomes the first and only Muslim-majority country to join NATO.

1958

The Sertels start a secret collaboration with Nazım Hikmet on *Bizim Radyo* (Our Radio), a Turkish-language communist radio station broadcasting to Turkey from behind the Iron Curtain. Based in Leipzig, East Germany, the Sertels tell family members they are living in Vienna.

1960

27 May: The Democrat Party administration is toppled by a military coup. The following year, former Democrat Party leader and prime minister Adnan Menderes is executed along with two of his cabinet ministers. New multi-party general elections are held on 15 October 1961.

1962

Zekeriya is dismissed from *Bizim Radyo*; Nazım Hikmet arranges for him to relocate to Baku, Azerbaijan. He is followed by his daughter Yıldız.

1963

3 June: Nazım Hikmet dies of a heart attack in Moscow.

Sabiha joins Zekeriya and Yıldız in Baku.

The Sertels' passports are confiscated by Soviet authorities.

1968

2 September: Sabiha Sertel dies from lung cancer in Baku. She has not been able to return to Turkey since her departure in 1950.

1969

Obtaining temporary visas with the help of friends in Paris, Zekeriya and Yıldız defect to France. They settle in Paris, never to return to the Soviet Union.

1971

12 March: Turkey experiences its next military coup. New multi-party general elections are held on 14 October 1973.

1977

March: Zekeriya Sertel is allowed to return to Turkey after 27 years in exile.

1980

11 March: Zekeriya Sertel dies in Paris.

12 September: Turkey experiences its third military coup. New multi-party general elections are held on 6 November 1983.

1991

Yıldız Sertel returns to Turkey after 41 years in exile. On 3 April 1996, she establishes the Sertel Gazetecilik Vakfı (Sertel Journalism Foundation) in memory of her parents. The foundation sponsors an annual award for journalists who advance freedom of the press.

2002

24 June: Sevim Sertel dies in suburban Washington, DC.

2009

17 December: Yıldız Sertel dies in Istanbul. Her foundation is closed shortly thereafter, amidst fears of government retribution.

Acknowledgements

The idea seemed like a straightforward project. Translate my controversial grandmother's autobiography to gain a first-hand understanding of her life and struggles.

It took a decade and a small, dedicated, international team of scholars, journalists, family and friends to accomplish much more than that original goal. *The Struggle for Modern Turkey: Justice, Activism and a Revolutionary Female Journalist* finally allows English-speakers to read Sabiha Sertel's personal account of the Turkish Republic's formative years. It also introduces them to the role that both Zekeriya and Sabiha Sertel played in one of modern Turkey's fieriest clashes – the fight for a free press, which continues unabated.

Through this project, I have gained abundant respect for the art of translating, the ability to capture not just the intent of words but the personality and voice of the characters. It was a stroke of luck that introduced me to our translators, the talented husband-and-wife team David Selim Sayers and Evrim Emir-Sayers. David was my patient and encouraging Turkish-language teacher, who turned out to be much more than a gifted instructor – a Near Eastern Studies scholar with an expertise in Turkish Studies, who understood the historical importance of my grandmother's memoir. There is no way to fully thank David and Evrim for bringing Sabiha to life for English-speakers worldwide. They have generously supported related Sertel projects with their time and enthusiasm, often pitching in at the last minute to overcome hurdles.

Another stroke of luck, an off-hand remark, reunited me with my cousin Nur Deriş, a professional translator. Nur quickly joined forces on the translation, employing her linguistic skills and historical and political knowledge to ensure we remained true to Sabiha's text. She has become more than a cousin and is now a dear and trusted friend and collaborator.

It was the novelist and journalist Ipek Çalışlar who suggested I meet with Nur, one of the many pieces of sage advice that allowed this and other projects to move forward.

A number of Sertel scholars encouraged me to pursue a translation of Sabiha's autobiography and cheered it on through uncertain stretches – thank you Holly Shissler, Kathryn Libal and Christine Philliou. One historian, James Ryan, not only embraced the translation, but also served as an informal tutor, fact-checker, research collaborator and generally did everything possible to make it a success. Boundless thanks, Jim. Our friendship is a gift from this endeavour.

Without Mefra Arkin and Jale Robertson, there would be no book. In Istanbul, our lifelong family friend Mefra helped me navigate the Turkish legal system to prove that my sister and I were heirs to the copyrights for the Sertels' collection of books. Meanwhile, in San Francisco, my neighbour Jale, Turkish tour guide and cultural expert, offered invaluable advice at key junctures. She sorted through stacks of ageing Turkish documents to ensure that nothing politically sensitive jeopardized our legal bid, such as a letter I was about to send, stating that my mother had not written the controversial piece about communism, it was her sister.

Throughout this journey, Rifat Bali, Turkish author and publisher of Libra Books, generously offered his time, providing invaluable advice and guidance to navigate an often unclear course.

Thank you to I.B. Tauris and our skilled editor Sophie Rudland, who believed in this translation, made it better with her insightful notes and buoyed us with her enthusiasm and encouragement.

And thank you to my extraordinary husband David and daughter Kaley Diamond, whose infinite patience, optimism, kindness and generous support endured through passing years. It was good fortune to marry an accomplished author, whose editorial guidance never fails to improve my writing.

And to my sister Sevim, thank you for supporting what seemed like a daunting undertaking when I started out ten years ago. Sabiha dedicated her memoir to our late brother Denis. This book is dedicated to Sabiha's American descendants. They can now read the remarkable story of their grandmother, great-grandmother and great-great-grandmother, who dared to try and make her country a better place for all.

Tia O'Brien
San Francisco, 2018

Author's note

This book chronicles my life, memories and struggles from 1919 to 1950, and is divided into periods and ordered by major events. I am writing in exile, and it has been hard to find the old newspapers, journals and other materials that I need for the book. I could only locate some of these and had to make do with what I found. I humbly ask my readers to excuse any omissions and inaccuracies that resulted from these circumstances.

I would like to thank everyone who helped me assemble my sources: Anna Stepanovna Tveritinova, Head Scientific Researcher of Historical Sources at the Moscow Institute of Asian and African Peoples; Leyla Arkayeva, Head Literary Researcher at the same institute; Ahmet Arunov, a director in the Bulgarian Communist Party's Turkish branch; İbrahim Tatarlı, Professor of Literature; İbrahim Berilov; Saime Hanım at Provada; Mir Mehdi Seyitzade, an Azeri writer; and Kamil Samedov, Professor of Economics at the University of Baku.

Sabiha Sertel

1

Introduction to life

Prelude to the War of Independence

The year is 1919. Turkey has lost the war, along with its allies, the German militarists. Istanbul is under occupation. Foreign officers – such as British Admiral Harrington and American Admiral Bristol – are in charge of governing. The country had been dragged into the First World War by the ringleaders of the Committee of Union and Progress,[1] among them Talat Pasha, Enver Pasha, Cemal Pasha and Doctor Nazım. Now, they have all fled the country. Enemy battleships line the harbour, adorned with a plethora of flags.

Ragged Turkish foot soldiers are carted in by train from Yemen, Galicia[2] and all the empire's battlefields. Haydarpaşa Station is packed with people looking for their sons and brothers. The returning soldiers look so young that they could pass for children. Some still have village *çarıks*[3] on their feet. Trembling in the cold, without so much as an overcoat, they've come home from the deserts of Arabia, or some other theatre of war, with no idea why they fought or for whom. They've left their fallen compatriots behind in foreign lands, with neither a stone to mark their graves nor a piece of paper to record their identities. These are the sons of Anatolia; their lives were wasted in the folly of war.

No one knows how many soldiers were killed, wounded or lost in this catastrophe. No one knows how many civilians died of hunger or disease. No one dares ask what the price of all this has been. People are too busy worrying about the future. What will happen now that the country has collapsed? Will the imperialists carve it up? These are the questions on everyone's lips.

The occupiers, in the meantime, are preparing the Treaty of Sèvres, which will end our national independence.[4] On 30 October 1918, Admiral Galtrop[5] of the Allies and

---

[1] Translation note (TN): The Committee of Union and Progress (CUP) was the political organization that controlled the Ottoman Empire from 1908, when it took power through a military coup, until the end of the First World War.
[2] TN: A province of the former Austrian Empire, located in modern-day Poland and Ukraine.
[3] TN: A rawhide shoe, similar to a moccasin.
[4] TN: The peace treaty signed by the Ottoman Empire and the Allied Powers at the end of the First World War. The treaty, which envisioned an almost complete dismantling of the empire, was superseded in 1923 by the Treaty of Lausanne, which established the borders of the Turkish Republic.
[5] TN: Sertel is referring to Sir Somerset Arthur Gough-Calthorpe (1865–1937), who served as Commander-in-Chief of the Royal Navy's Mediterranean Fleet in the First World War.

Rauf Bey,[6] Turkey's Minister of the Navy, signed an armistice treaty. Thanks to this treaty, the imperialist states have established themselves in key positions throughout the capital.

Colonial soldiers from Senegal, India and Java patrol the streets in their diverse uniforms. Scottish regiments march around as if on an opera stage, playing their bagpipes and drums, their colourful, chequered kilts hanging to their knees. Along the Bosporus, the occupiers' flags wave from the fortresses of Rumeli and Anatolia;[7] the Turkish flag has been banished to the back of the row.

In this time of mourning, only the Greeks still smile. They saunter about, playing the hurdy-gurdy. They sing, drink and carouse day and night, scorning their Turkish compatriots, who have been humbled by war. They tear women's *çarşafs*[8] and attack young girls. No government imposes order, no police reins them in.

The country has descended into the deepest gloom. Gone is the carefree Istanbul of before the war; streets seem narrower, people seem smaller, faces are pale. The collapse of the empire weighs on everyone's shoulders. Civil servants with stern demeanors, *hodjas*[9] with their robes and *sarıks*,[10] workers, guildsmen – all pass over the bridge with their heads hung low. For the first time in their history, the Turkish people are experiencing the pain of losing their independence, and it cuts them to the bone.

The outlying neighbourhoods offer object lessons in destitution. On the one hand, you see barefoot children grinning from behind their rags. On the other, you see war profiteers in their bulgur palaces.[11] People like Topal İsmail Hakkı Pasha, who made millions in wagon trading,[12] use banknotes to light the cigarettes of the Viennese actor Milovich. Those who had to eat bread made of straw during the war come face-to-face with those the war made rich. One side has taken up residence in Şişli and Nişantaşı, the revived districts of Istanbul. The other has retreated to burnt-out ruins in the poor neighbourhoods of Fatih, Aksaray and Cihangir.

The governing cabinet is in constant flux: one day, İzzet Pasha is out and Ferit Pasha is in; the next day, Ferit Pasha is out and Tevfik Pasha is in. The old Ottoman pashas are struggling to salvage the shipwreck that once was the empire, and in their desperation, they turn to the British and American admirals – the imperialist states themselves. Most CUP members who haven't fled the country are locked up in Bekirağa Prison,[13] where they once sent their own enemies, the members of the Freedom and Entente Party.[14] Now, the latter are released as the former are tried by the court martial of Kürt Mustafa Pasha. Some are even executed to appease the court's imperialist masters and to demoralize the people.

---

[6] TN: A title of respect added after the first name, similar to 'Sir' or 'Mr'.
[7] TN: The European and Asian shores of the Bosporus, respectively.
[8] TN: A Turkish Islamic woman's garment, usually consisting of two parts and covering the entire body except the hands and part of the face.
[9] TN: *Hodja* is a teacher or, more specifically, a Muslim preacher.
[10] TN: Turbans.
[11] TN: Mansions built by profiteers who sold staples like bulgur wheat on the black market.
[12] TN: A form of war-profiteering, in which Ottoman troops were sent cheap, substandard supplies, delivered in train wagons.
[13] Part of the Defence Ministry in Beyazıt, this was a penitentiary for political prisoners.
[14] A pro-British party founded in opposition to the CUP.

Foreign officers survey people's homes. If they like a house, they kick out the owners and move in themselves. Foreign censors control the press, and only papers that support the British are published without interference. *İkdam* [Endeavour] and *Sabah* [Morning] – the newspapers of Ali Kemal, a lapdog of British imperialism – embrace the occupiers and shower Unionists[15] with bile.

Capitalists of minority origin cover the display windows in Beyoğlu[16] with ads that read, 'Don't buy Turkish products.' They openly act as agents of foreign capital. The Turkish currency has lost all its value; money changers stand on street corners, eager to exchange it for foreign officers' dollars, pounds and drachmas. The stores of Beyoğlu sport the flags of the occupying states, and Greek-owned stores are guarded by Greek infantrymen in pleated skirts, red fezzes and long, blue tassels.

This is Istanbul under occupation. This is Istanbul, whose people are bereft of identity and hope. It is a city lost amidst the ruins of a shattered empire.

Who is to blame?

Who is to blame for this collapse, people ask each other, and where will it all end? The newly released leaders of the Freedom and Entente Party, backed by the British, blame the CUP for embracing German militarism and taking the country to war. In the CUP itself, the lower echelons blame Enver Pasha.

The Friends of England Society argues that foreign policy should follow Britain's lead, while the Wilson Society pins its hopes on an American mandate. Most intellectuals are gloomy, and some claim that we must give up parts of Turkish territory to maintain our national independence. But the Turkish people sense by intuition that the imperialists will not tolerate an independent Turkey and that independence can only be won by fighting another war.

Meanwhile, the imperialist states of the Triple Entente have already agreed to divide the country. The internal confusion only emboldens them. They've been exploiting Turkey's economy for centuries, and now, they are preparing to carve up the country itself and establish control over the resulting pieces. Never before has Turkey been so close to dismemberment and destruction. Vahdeddin, the Ottoman sultan, is only concerned with preserving his own rule. Politicians and public figures like Damat Ferit and Ali Kemal grovel before Harrington and Bristol, eager to carry out their orders. They despise the CUP and are ready to place the country under the British yoke.

Britain wants to gain control over Turkey, just as it did with Egypt. Its main rival is the USA, which is lobbying among intellectuals, presenting itself as Turkey's guardian and trying to set up a mandate in the country. Some luminaries, such as Halide Edip,[17] Journalist Ahmet Emin Yalman and Rauf Ahmet, prefer an American mandate to British rule. They claim the USA has no imperialist ambitions and will bring democracy

---

[15] TN: Members of the CUP.
[16] TN: A Central Istanbul district, traditionally inhabited by non-Muslims.
[17] TN: Halide Edip Adıvar (1884–1964) is arguably the most prominent and seminal female author in the history of the Turkish Republic.

to Turkey, conveniently ignoring the countries exploited under USA mandates, such as the Philippines and South America. Some Istanbul-based writers, journalists and legal experts who favour the USA founded the Wilson Society in 1918. Faced with the grim prospect of Turkey's dismemberment, they invoke the Wilson Principles,[18] hoping these will help them save the empire from destruction.

In her memoirs,[19] Halide Edip Adıvar describes the political scene of the day as follows:

> Representatives of the press had gathered in the office of the newspaper *Vakit* [Time] and were discussing the memorandum to be sent to President Wilson. It would ask the US to provide Turkey with economic and material aid, send in experts and cadres, and give the country one last chance to establish a stable regime and carry out internal reforms.
>
> On all sides, there was a momentum to unite against the occupiers, and societies were being founded to that end. In June 1919, the National Bloc was established under the leadership of Ahmet Rıza.[20] Prominent countrymen such as former prime ministers and chiefs of staff were joining this organization.
>
> All were looking for a way out. Many new parties were founded, such as the National Liberals or Peace and Welfare, and the National Congress organization convened in the congress building under the presidency of Doctor Esat Pasha. However, the activities of all these groups did not amount to much, and could be summed up in the words 'they convened, they discussed and they disbanded.' Around the same time, the politically significant Karakol society was founded with the Unionist Kara Vasıf Bey at the helm.[21]

With hindsight, this flurry of activity in Istanbul was paving the way for a war of national independence. Even from Anatolia, news was arriving of organizations being founded here and there.

I was very young and not mature enough to grasp the significance of these events. I'd recently gotten married, and my first daughter, Sevim, was two years old. We were a big and busy family. My husband, Zekeriya, was a director in charge of *Aşirets*[22] at the General Directorate for Refugees. His salary was very low; our generation had grown up on straw bread and boiled quinces during the war. We lived in Cağaloğlu, on Molla Fenari Street, the first apartment in a two-storey building owned by Abdullah Cevdet.[23] We followed current events with great concern and sorrow, wishing there was something we could do.

---

[18] TN: Sertel is referring to the 'Fourteen Points' stipulated by US President Woodrow Wilson as the basis for negotiations to end the First World War.
[19] Published in English as *The Turkish Ordeal* (New York: The Century Co., 1928).
[20] A freedom fighter and patriot, who'd fled to Europe during Sultan Abdülhamid's oppressive reign.
[21] *The Turkish Ordeal*, pp. 19–20.
[22] TN: Ethno-religious tribes or clans, many of them displaced by the war, in the eastern regions of Anatolia.
[23] A Turkish intellectual who supported Britain. He took part in the 'Friends of the British' society.

Figure 1.1 Istanbul, 1915, Sabiha Nazmi's marriage to Mehmet Zekeriya was hailed as an example of promised secularism in a new Turkish Republic. In Zekeriya's memoirs, he describes Sabiha as the first to publicly marry outside the secretive *Dönme* community.

The journal *Büyük Mecmua*

Zekeriya and journalist Sedat Simavi decided to publish a satirical magazine called *Diken* [Thorn]. The goal was to publicly expose war profiteers who'd grown rich off wagon trading, while common people couldn't even afford to buy cloth for burial shrouds. The stories and capers of the rich already circulated by mouth like urban legends. Now, they were blown wide open in *Diken*'s humorous exposés and caricatures. The first issue proved very popular.

Our home in Cağaloğlu quickly became a gathering place for the foremost writers, poets and thinkers of the day. They were all desperate about this situation and were struggling to find a solution. Finally, we decided to publish a weekly journal that would awaken people and fire them up. It would be called *Büyük Mecmua* [Grand Journal] and staffed entirely by volunteers. Many leading intellectuals would write for it, including Ömer Seyfeddin,[24] Ali Canip, Falih Rıfkı, the poet Yusuf Ziya, Orhan Seyfi, Faruk Nafiz, Köprülüzade Fuat, Mehmet Emin Yurdakul, Professor İsmail Hakkı, Tekin Alp (Mois Kohen), Reşat Nuri and Professor Mehmet Emin.

The first editorial explained why *Büyük Mecmua* had come into being. It maintained that pessimism was useless and detrimental, and urged the population to struggle

---

[24] TN: Ömer Seyfeddin (1884–1920) is one of the most prominent early nationalist Turkish authors.

bravely: 'We mustn't sink into despair and dishearten those around us, or publicly proclaim there is no hope or future for the country. Instead, we must all work hand in hand to raise the people's cultural level and turn them into a true nation.'

The first issue was published on 6 March 1919, with Zekeriya as the proprietor and contributions by many young writers. Soon, the journal became a beacon of hope for a population that had suffered painful defeat. *Büyük Mecmua* was a forum in the truest sense. It brought together people who had very different perspectives and beliefs, but who were all trying to understand the reasons for the country's collapse and find paths of liberation. There were articles on Turkism,[25] nationalism and New Ottomanism,[26] but also on anti-imperialism and feminism.

Some blamed the empire's collapse on Turkist and nationalist movements, while others blamed Islamist or Pan-Turkist movements. Among the latter was Ahmet Cevat,[27] who wrote for *Yeni Mecmua* [New Journal], another journal published in Istanbul. According to him, 'we should remain true Ottomans and steadfast Muslims. However, we must rapidly distance ourselves from the disastrous ideas of the bloody gang'.[28] Meanwhile, the communists publishing the journal *Kurtuluş* [Liberation] blamed the imperialists and called on the people to wage an anti-imperialist war.

A dispute soon broke out between the nationalists at *Büyük Mecmua* and Ahmet Cevat, but the defenders of nationalism and Turkism also quarrelled among themselves. Some called for a 'return to Turan',[29] emphasizing the deep historical roots of the Turkist movement. Others distanced themselves from Turanist Turkism. To them, Turkism wasn't about liberating Turks in other countries, but protecting the national bourgeoisie[30] in Turkey against the crushing power of minority and foreign capital.

In this crossfire of debate, some retreated into the trenches of New Ottomanism. The empire's minorities, they argued, had been protected by the Ottomans, who'd granted them *reaya*[31] status. But the Unionists, driven by nationalism, had oppressed the minorities, leading them to reject the country. According to these thinkers, the solution was a return to Ottomanism. Even Tekin Alp, who had once joined Ziya Gökalp[32] in defending Turkism and nationalism, now wrote glowingly about 'the first days of the 1908 revolution, when Christian priests and Muslim *hodjas* embraced, brotherhood united different parts of society, and gang unrest abated, especially in

---

[25] TN: An ideology advocating the political union of Turkic-speaking populations spread across Central and Western Asian countries. Sertel uses the term interchangeably with Pan-Turkism and Turanism.

[26] TN: An ideology advocating the reorganization of the Ottoman Empire as a modern nation-state under the continued leadership of the Ottoman sultan. Sertel uses the term interchangeably with Ottomanism.

[27] A teacher who went to the Soviet Union after the Bolshevik Revolution and cooperated with the socialists. He left the party after returning to Turkey.

[28] TN: Ahmet Cevat is referring to the Committee of Union and Progress.

[29] TN: The semi-mythological Central Asian homeland of the first Turkic tribes.

[30] TN: The term, 'national bourgeoisie', refers to a Muslim and ethnically Turkish bourgeoisie. It consciously excludes people who may be bourgeois and citizens of the state, but are non-Turkish and/or non-Muslim.

[31] TN: Tax-paying 'commoners' of the empire, enjoying legal recognition and protection.

[32] TN: Ziya Gökalp (1876–1924) was a founding ideologue of Turkish nationalism.

Rumeli'. Many organizations were founded, he wrote, to reconcile the minorities. But 'soon, regrettable events started occurring', and the minorities became estranged from the country once again. To stop this estrangement, Alp recommended returning to the policy of New Ottomanism.

Ultimately, though, all these intellectuals suffered from the same dearth of ideas. Their analysis of the collapse was superficial: instead of seriously examining the internal and external, economic and political reasons for the debacle, they were casting blame upon this or that intellectual movement that had emerged at the time. Instead of uniting to struggle against imperialism, they were fighting among themselves, suffocating each other and benefitting no one except the imperialists.

The New Turkey

Even with the country under occupation, new movements were rising from the ashes of the empire. Progressive causes gathered momentum, in spite of all hardship and the sheer hopelessness of the situation. There were lively public debates on a number of issues: Should the *sharia* courts be tied to the Ministry of Justice? Should religion and state become separated? Did we need an education reform? Should *madrasas*[33] be attached to the Ministry of Education?

The war had also changed the lives of women. The country's economic collapse had drawn them into public life, despite all resistance by supporters of *sharia* law. Women were beginning to act in ways that went against traditional norms. A small number had even started working – for the state, commercial firms and factories. Women wanted to show that they, too, were strong and smart enough to cope with the struggles of life.

On 27 March 1919, a major debate broke out in newspapers and journals. I will recount it in some detail since it offers a good snapshot of the mindset at the time. The question was whether women should be allowed to study at university, along with men. At that point, women had no access to education beyond high school. The Ministry of Education was willing to let women attend university, but Naim Hoca, the University President, was opposed. The entire press, as well as the people, were in favour of women attending, but reactionary forces had thrived under the occupation. *Hodja*s and *sharia* supporters rose up against the movement. 'Never,' their *fatwa* decreed. 'It is against *sharia* law for women and men to study under the same roof.'

Women could go to university, they argued, only if classes weren't mixed. Professors should teach the same class separately to men and to women, and the two shouldn't work together in laboratories either. In those days, there were curtains in trams that separated men and women. The reactionaries wanted curtains drawn at the university as well. But there was still the danger that girls and boys might encounter each other in hallways and in the conference hall. To prevent this, reactionaries wanted men to be barred from university grounds while women were taking classes and vice versa. The university should be reserved for men until lunch time and for women in the afternoons.

---

[33] TN: Islamic religious colleges.

These arguments, ridiculous and pathetic in equal measure, failed to impress the Council of University Professors. The Council ruled with an absolute majority that, henceforth, male and female students would study together. Only one person voted against the decision, and that was the University President.

Another debate concerned whether the veiling of women could really be justified by religion. But even the most progressive intellectuals were too cowed by the *hodjas* to take a bold stance and argue that the *çarşaf* should be cast off altogether. Still, progress was being made: while people were busy discussing whether women could enroll in departments like medicine, in practice, women were already there.

These developments show that even as the empire collapsed, the Turkish people were determined to break free of old constraints, no matter what the cost. The seeds were being sown for Mustafa Kemal's[34] later reforms.

At the time, I wasn't sophisticated enough to fully participate in these ideological discussions. Instead, I devoted myself solely to women's rights from the day *Büyük Mecmua* first appeared until it ceased publishing. I followed suffragette movements around the world and fought to help liberate women from social pressure, especially oppression by *sharia* law. My commitment to this cause was partly due to personal experiences.

*

I was eight years old, the youngest of six siblings. My father was the chief clerk at the Salonica[35] customs office and supported our family on his meagre income. One day, the customs accountant insulted him, telling him he wasn't fit to be chief clerk. Enraged, my father resigned his post. We were left with only a small pension to live on. Our family became destitute. We lived in a house called the Sunday Tekke,[36] which belonged to my paternal aunt. It was a neat, beautiful house with a garden, but we only had two rooms.

My father was a true patriarch. Every morning, when he went to the outhouse, my mother would wait for him outside the door, holding a pitcher and towel to wash his hands and feet when he emerged. One day, I asked her:

'Are you my father's servant?'
'All women are their husband's servants,' she said.
'I won't be my husband's servant.'
'Yes, you will.'
'Then I won't get married.'
'Yes, you will.'

(I did get married, but I never was my husband's servant.)

This was the first incident that prompted me to defend women's rights. The second was the way in which my parents divorced. It was summer. My maternal aunt was

---

[34] TN: Mustafa Kemal Atatürk (1881–1938) was the founder of modern Turkey.
[35] TN: Now Thessaloniki in Greece.
[36] TN: Dervish Lodge. Sabiha's great-grandfather was a leading figure in the local branch of the Mevlevi Dervish order.

moving to the Salonica resort known as Yalılar.[37] My mother had gone along to help her sister with the move. Eventually, it grew dark, but my mother didn't return. My father paced around the room in a rage, grumbling to himself. When she finally came through the door, he exploded. He kept yelling and yelling, not letting her explain why she was late. I was on the sofa, trembling like a bird. My father grabbed a chair and stormed at my mother. I buried my head in the pillows of the sofa so I wouldn't see what happened next. I was crying.

I heard my father's voice: 'You are hereby divorced! I divorce you!'

I looked up from the sofa. The storm had passed. My mother had shrunk into a corner of the room. Meekly, she emerged and took me by the hand. We went upstairs.

'I have to go now,' she said.

I clung to her hem. 'Take me with you,' I begged. 'Don't leave me here.'

The next day, my maternal uncle came to pick us up. We were given a room in a wooden house left by my grandfather. It had been divided up after his death, so each room was inhabited by a different family. The house was far from the city centre and on the verge of collapse. Our room had a dirt floor. We shared a kitchen at the end of the hallway.

My brothers Mecdi Eren and Hidayet Eren had defended my mother against my father and now took on the responsibility of providing for us. Hidayet, the oldest, was a clerk at a commercial firm. Mecdi, the youngest brother, found a job at the Singer

Figure 1.2 Salonica (now Thessaloniki, Greece), 1903, Sabiha Nazmi at eight years old. She was heavily influenced by growing up in the cosmopolitan, multicultural, multi-ethnic city, a hub for revolution as the Ottoman Empire collapsed.

[37] TN: The district takes its name from *yalı* (pl. *yalılar*), a seaside mansion built out of wood.

machine company. He split his time between school and work. My middle brothers were students: Celal Deriş studied at the Faculty of Law in Istanbul and Neşet Deriş in Paris. My father had always discouraged my brothers from studying and told them to work instead, but thanks to my mother's efforts, we had all gone to school.

My mother herself sewed to shore up the family budget. She was the one who carried the weight of our family of eight on her shoulders. Whenever I think of those days, I am filled with endless love and respect for her. The day she died, at the age of 78, I kissed her cold, lifeless hand with the very same feelings.

My parents' divorce left a deep mark on me as a child. Seeing a mother of six beaten up and thrown out of her home left me with a deep hatred for all forms of coercion and oppression. I found myself rebelling against every injustice I witnessed. I'm sure this is the main reason I embraced women's issues when I first entered public life and started writing for *Büyük Mecmua*.

I also felt miserable for being a burden to my siblings. I wanted to study, make something of myself, earn my own living. When I was younger and couldn't go to university because women weren't allowed, my peers and I founded a reading group called the Society for Advancement. I also furthered my education by taking lessons from three male teachers. My sole desire was to find a vocation. And so, when offered the chance to write for the journal, I chose to devote myself to women's issues.

The journal's war against imperialism

One day, a man came to the editorial office of *Büyük Mecmua*. He was tall and dark, had curly hair and introduced himself as İsmail Hakkı. 'They call me Arab İsmail Hakkı,' he said. 'I'm a friend of Zekeriya's from Paris. I brought an article for the journal. It'll be the first in a series.'

I gave him a seat. He talked about the gravity of the situation in the country and said he'd been closely following *Büyük Mecmua*'s struggle for independence. His articles were anti-imperialist, arguing that Turkey should refuse to pay its war reparations. So far, *Büyük Mecmua* had mostly run pieces on nationalism, Turkism and New Ottomanism. But İsmail Hakkı's articles, published under the pseudonym M. S., advanced a brand new idea. For the first time, we were featuring an open revolt against imperialism.

'Turkey has emerged from the Great War in ruins,' his articles stated. 'The Treasury is completely empty. The Public Debt Administration collects our taxes and uses them to pay our debt to the imperialist states.[38] These war reparations shouldn't be made by the people but by the state. Let the major landlords pay for them, and the capitalists who amassed a fortune during the war. The state should confiscate a share of their profits. Better still, let the state refuse to pay the reparations altogether.'

İsmail Hakkı espoused a form of state capitalism. He wasn't against private enterprise, but argued that its profits should be checked and reined in by the state. 'The

---

[38] TN: The Ottoman Public Debt Administration was established in 1881 and controlled by the European creditors of the heavily indebted Ottoman Empire.

tyranny of the major capitalists must be broken,' he wrote. Hüseyin Ragıp,[39] a diehard supporter of Turkism, also wrote against imperialism and in support of socialism. 'All five continents are racked by hunger,' he wrote, 'and in all of them, socialism is the most highly developed ideal.'[40]

But most intellectuals and statesmen were far from appreciating the gravity of the situation. They continued talking about 'foreign guardianship' and 'taking shelter under Britain's wing', or maintained that the USA should establish a Turkish mandate. Others, like Ali Canip and Köprülüzade Fuat, ignored the occupation and discussed trifles such as whether the epic poem was a contemporary genre. Halide Edip and her ilk fruitlessly beseeched Sultan Vahdettin to somehow save the country. 'My *padişah*,'[41] she wrote, 'the 600-year-old soul of the Turk calls out to you. His most venerable ancestors call out to you.'

While Halide Edip and her circle clamoured for a US mandate, *Büyük Mecmua* was already publishing anti-mandate articles. But soon, supporters of a mandate were silenced by a decisive turn of events: the Greeks landed troops in Izmir.

The occupation of Izmir

It was 1919, during the night between 14 and 15 May. The Greeks, backed by the Allied states, entered Izmir. There was some resistance on the waterfront, but step by step, they took the city.

The news struck Istanbul like a thunderbolt. The Ferit Pasha government[42] tried to reassure the population, claiming that the upcoming peace conference would set things right. But the people were aghast. They saw the writing on the wall: the Greeks wouldn't stop until they'd conquered all of Anatolia. This was a death blow to the nation. Young people and intellectuals rushed from meeting to meeting, trying to find a solution.

The excitement gripped the writers of *Büyük Mecmua* as well. The same evening, many of them gathered in the journal's management office, including Ömer Seyfeddin, Ali Canip, Ruşen Eşref and Falih Rıfkı.

'We have to turn this into a true war journal,' Ömer Seyfeddin said. 'Forget Damat Ferit, Kürt Mustafa's court martial and the British censors – none of them count for spit anymore. It's time we stuck our necks out!'

We decided to hold a larger meeting the next day. But Abdullah Cevdet's house in Cağaloğlu, where we published *Büyük Mecmua*, was under police surveillance. For that reason, a group including Zekeriya, Halide Edip, Hasan Ali Yücel, Köprülüzade Fuat and former Finance Minister Ferit had started meeting at our house. They were planning to establish a secret society.

---

[39] After the War of Independence, he became Atatürk's right-hand man, was made Minister of Education and was appointed ambassador to London and Moscow.
[40] *Büyük Mecmua*, 24 April 1919.
[41] TN: Sultan.
[42] TN: A short-lived administration that governed the Ottoman Empire from March to October 1919. Ferit Pasha, who was married to the daughter of Sultan Abdülmecid (r. 1839–61), was also known as Damat (groom) Ferit.

The day after the occupation of Izmir, Zekeriya was arrested. Abdullah Cevdet, who lived upstairs from us, had informed on him.

Zekeriya had just come home from work. We were both feeling depressed.

'Let's go to Gülhane Park,' he suggested. 'We'll get some fresh air.'
'There's a meeting in the evening,' I said.
'We'll be back by then.'

Our daughter Sevim was just two. We put her in the pram and went out. Soon, a policeman approached us.

'Zekeriya Bey,' he said, 'the Chief of Police wants to see you. You'll be questioned about a certain matter. Then you can leave.'

They started walking away. I followed them.

'Please stay here, *hemşire hanım*,'[43] the policeman said. 'Zekeriya Bey will be back shortly.'

I waited until it was dark. When I realized no one would come, I made my way back home. As people arrived for the meeting, I gave them the news. At ten o'clock, there was still no word from Zekeriya. I had people inquire at the police directorate, but all they were told was, 'She shouldn't worry; he will return.' At midnight, a policeman arrived. He asked for sheets and a blanket to take to Zekeriya. Finally, it dawned on me that Zekeriya's quick visit would last quite a while. The next day, I learned that he'd been sent to Bekirağa Prison.

As soon as the news got out, the writers of *Büyük Mecmua* flocked to our study. They were worried the journal would cease publication. The licence was in Zekeriya's name, and it was illegal for an arrested man to publish a journal. We needed to transfer the licence to someone else.

'I'll take over the licence myself,' I said.

We decided to reconvene once I'd acquired the licence. The next day, I went to Bekirağa Prison for Zekeriya to sign off on the transfer and also to pay him a visit. The prison was in Bayezit, by the Ministry of War. After running around many offices to get permission, I was finally let into the ward.

At first glance, this was just a large hall with beds lined up against the walls. But it was much more than that. It was a forum, a courtroom filled with the guilty and the innocent from all eras of the empire's political history. In one corner, Übeydullah Efendi, a former minister of education, sat cross-legged on his bed, reading the Qur'an. In another, Ziya Gökalp held court, surrounded by an enraptured group, hanging on his every word.

Ağaoğlu Ahmet Bey was also there. 'Don't blame the Turkists and Turanists,' he bellowed. 'It's all the fault of Enver, Talat and their followers. They dragged the people into this folly of a war!'

'No,' someone else retorted, 'the Party of Freedom and Entente is to blame! They sold out the country to our enemies, the British and the French. If not for the CUP, Turkey would've already been torn apart in the Balkan War.'

---

[43] TN: A semi-formal address, combining the words for 'sister' (*hemşire*) and 'lady' (*hanım*).

Zekeriya, Köprülüzade Fuat and Ferit Karakaş[44] were sitting on their beds and talking to each other. As I approached them, I was surrounded by people who knew me.

'What's the news?' they asked. 'We hear the Greeks entered Izmir. What is the National Assembly doing? Is there any word of Mustafa Kemal?'

I could only answer some of their questions.

When I got back home, the writers of *Büyük Mecmua* were already there, among them Ruşen Eşref, Ömer Seyfeddin, Ali Canip, Faruk Nafiz, Falih Rıfkı, Yusuf Ziya and Orhan Seyfi. They were agitated. I told them about Bekirağa Prison. I'd obtained the document from Zekeriya, transferring the licence to me. With that, they considered the matter settled.

What was next for the journal?

'The new issue must be all about grief,' Ömer Seyfeddin said. 'The cover should be absolutely black.'

This sparked a debate. Some said that instead of spreading a feeling of grief, we should call the people to arms. Others countered that appealing to people's feelings was the best way to call them to arms. A third group argued that we should shake off our apathy, go out among the people and lead them in defending our independence. What worried us most was the dissolution of the army. How could we oppose the great Western nations without an army?

Finally, everyone agreed that the next issue's cover should be entirely black. Apart from that, they were free to write what they wanted. Ömer Seyfeddin agreed to manage the printing process.

The journal was under constant scrutiny by the British censors. They would reject some articles and cut others apart. Often, the main point would be lost, leaving only bits and pieces. I was given the task of taking the articles to the censors and re-editing them afterward.

That same day, I went to the notary's office and finalized the transfer of the licence. Later, when I was working in the study, the doorbell rang. It was a short, slender woman dressed in a black *çarşaf*.

'Who would you like to see?' I asked.

'I am Halide Edip,' she answered.

I was stunned – I'd never met her before. She'd been writing for the journal, attending the secret meetings at our house and even presiding over them. I was not allowed to attend those meetings. Still, I'd been an avid reader of Halide Hanım's[45] novels since my childhood and was thrilled to find her in front of me like this. I asked her in. She entered and removed the top part of her *çarşaf*.

'How is Zekeriya?' she asked.

'I went to see him today; he's fine.'

She asked me whom else I'd seen at Bekirağa Prison. I told her.

'What happens to the journal now?' she asked.

'I'll publish it myself. I'm taking over the licence.'

---

[44] He was among the well-known merchants of Istanbul. I don't know why he was in prison.
[45] TN: A title of respect added after the first name, similar to 'Lady,' 'Miss' or 'Mrs'.

Halide Hanım looked me up and down. 'You're just a child,' she said at last.

'I'll grow up eventually.'

That made her smile. She asked what we were doing for the Izmir issue, and I told her about it.

'I can write your editorials if you want,' she said, adding that she'd send me an interview on the Izmir occupation.

On her way out, she said, 'Tomorrow, we'll hold a protest rally in Sultan Ahmet[46] against the occupation of Izmir. Come along.'

The Izmir Rally

Tens of thousands of people are packed into Sultan Ahmet Square. The masses are spilling over into neighbouring areas. It's nearly impossible to enter the square. Balconies, windows, rooftops are all filled with people. They're even hanging from the trees like leaves.

Somehow, I managed to enter the square by the tiny street near Fuat Pasha's tomb. Those were the days of the *çarşaf*, and my face was tightly veiled. The *hodjas* would spit in the face of any woman without a veil, swearing at her: 'It's your fault that all these calamities have befallen us, you with your unveiled faces and exposed calves. It's your fault that people have strayed from the path of religion and faith.'

The murmur of the huge crowd sweeps over me in waves. Halide Hanım is at the pulpit, proud and dignified, even in her black *çarşaf*. A black flag is wrapped around the pulpit; on the flag, below the crescent and star, is the motto, 'Liberty or death.' I notice a poster to one side of the pulpit, listing Wilson's 12 articles.[47] Little black flags adorn the minarets of Sultan Ahmet and Ayasofya[48] mosques, while banners are stretched from one minaret to the other, proclaiming, 'Izmir belongs to us.'

Halide Hanım is speaking now. A wailing rises from the people. The *hodjas* in the minarets keep singing hymns and repeating the confession of faith. Their call is taken up with one voice by the 200,000 people filling the square.

Next, everyone recites the oath read out by Halide Hanım: 'I will fight until the day my people gain independence.' Spoken by 200,000 voices in harmony, the oath becomes a strong and vibrant roar, engulfing us all and echoing through the surrounding neighbourhoods.

This was the ardour of a nation determined to fight for its liberty. All fear and hesitation were dispelled. This was a rehearsal for war.

After the rally, we placed the black cover on the Izmir issue of *Büyük Mecmua*; it was like a manifesto calling the people to war. Gone were the early issues discussing things like epic literature; now, the same writers were demanding national independence.

---

[46] TN: Sultan Ahmet Square is one of the major squares in Istanbul, located between the Hagia Sophia and the Blue Mosque (Sultan Ahmet Mosque).

[47] TN: Again, Sertel is likely referring to Wilson's Fourteen Points.

[48] TN: The Hagia Sophia.

Introduction to life

Once all the articles were completed, I took the journal to Haydar Bey, the Director of Press Affairs for the Damat Ferit Government. When I went back to collect them the next day, Haydar Bey sat me down.

'What are you trying to do?' he asked. 'The country is occupied. Not even Sultan Vahdettin can say what he wants, let alone you. That editorial you handed in – everything in the journal – incites people to revolt. How could I possibly allow this to go to print? Do you really believe you can drive out the occupying armies by holding rallies in Bayezit Square?'[49]

'Aren't you a Turk?' I answered. 'Aren't you bothered that our homeland is under occupation, that we've lost our independence? Don't you feel any need to fight the enemy?'

Haydar Bey laughed.

'Fight against whom?' he asked. 'And with which resources? The army has been smashed to bits. The forces that took Izmir today will take Anatolia tomorrow. There is nothing we can do. We have no choice but to get on with the British, with the powers of the Entente. Otherwise, we might even lose the sultanate.'

Arguing was pointless. Damat Ferit and his entourage had sold out to the enemy. All they could do was feebly bow their heads. I took the articles back. We decided to publish the Izmir edition, leaving the censored passages blank.

I brought the journal to Halide Hanım's house in Gedikpaşa and told her about my argument with Haydar Bey.

'You did well,' she said. 'Keep on leaving blanks in the places they take out.'

By then, Halide Hanım had become a different person. She no longer entreated the sultan, sought refuge with the Entente powers or talked about an American mandate.

There were guests in her living room, and she was telling them: 'Mustafa Kemal Pasha left for Anatolia on 16 May. Three days later, he reached Samsun. War is coming soon. We have an understanding with Ali Fuat Pasha and Rauf Bey, and it looks like Kâzım Karabekir will support Mustafa Kemal as well. They will rendezvous with Refet Pasha in Samsun and proceed together from there.'[50]

'What is the news from the National Assembly?'[51] one of the guests asked.

'Delegates from various groups met at the National Assembly in June,' Halide Hanım said. 'They discussed how to respond to the occupation. Thirty prominent people from around the country are gathered there right now. The nation has finally taken matters into its own hands.'

It was clear from these words that Mustafa Kemal had decided to fight, even before the Izmir occupation. Ignoring the intellectuals' despair, concessions and entreaties,

---

[49] TN: Another historic square within walking distance of Sultan Ahmet Square. Haydar Bey (or Sertel) may be confusing the two.

[50] Ali Fuat Pasha was the Commander of the 20th Army Division in Ankara. Kâzım Karabekir Pasha was the Commander of the 9th Army Division in Erzurum. Refet Pasha was the Commander of the 3rd Army Division in Samsun. Rauf Bey was a former hero of the Hamidiye [TN: an Ottoman cavalry division established in 1891 and notorious for persecuting Armenians] and Minister of the Navy.

[51] TN: Since the Grand National Assembly of Turkey in Ankara was not established until 23 April 1920, it is likely that Halide Edip is referring to the Ottoman National Assembly in Istanbul.

he'd put his trust in the power of the people, their sense of identity, their desire for independence at all costs. Gathering the scattered pieces of the army, he was preparing to face the enemy head-on.

Meanwhile, *Büyük Mecmua* was waging its own small war against Colonel or Major Armstrong, the officer in charge of the British censors.

I kept publishing blanks in place of the passages deleted by the censors. As a result, some issues were so full of blanks as to look ridiculous. This made Armstrong furious; he was, after all, the censor of an occupying force.

One day, I went to collect some articles from Haydar Bey. He was incensed.

'What exactly do you want?' he asked. 'I told you again and again not to leave the censored passages blank. But you just ignore me. Who is the director of press affairs, you or me?'

'You cut out such important parts that we can't rewrite the articles.'

'Then just draw a line as if the article is finished and move on to the next one. Do you seriously want to start a revolt?'

'We want to wake people up.'

This struggle went on for days. Finally, Haydar Bey told me that Armstrong wanted to see me. I went to the Press Directorate, where I was taken to a different room. Inside, a tall, blond officer stood behind a desk. He shook my hand.

'Sit down,' Armstrong said. 'So, you're the rebel who disobeys my orders?'

I didn't answer.

'Why do you leave blanks in place of the censored sentences? Must I remind you that you're under occupation?'

'Is there an international law against publishing blanks?'

'What law are you talking about?' he said. 'Your nation is defeated. You must bow down to your occupiers.'

'Lieutenant Armstrong. Imagine that Britain was occupied by France. The French are plucking words from your journal like feathers from a goose and shaking their fist at you all the while. What would you do?'

'I'd defend my land and liberty, like any Briton would.'

'And we're defending our land and liberty, like any Turk would.'

'Britain is a great, victorious nation under the sovereignty of His Majesty, the King,' he answered. 'Turkey is just the rubble of a ruined empire. Turks must submit to their conquerors' demands. If you keep on publishing articles like this, I'll shut the journal down.'

'You have the power to do that. But until you do, the journal stays as it is.'

Despite Armstrong's threats, the journal came out exactly like that until the day it was closed. It never betrayed the spirit of the war.

The secret cell

Zekeriya had been released from prison. Our work at *Büyük Mecmua* became more passionate than ever: Mustafa Kemal had crossed over to Anatolia, and everyone in Istanbul who supported him and the War of Independence was working as hard as possible. The National Bloc, an organization whose members included Esat Pasha, an ophthalmologist, and Ahmet Rıza Bey, was trying to smuggle men and weapons to Anatolia and strengthen the resistance.

One day, Zekeriya said to me, 'I talked to Halide Hanım today. Mustafa Kemal has begun operations in Anatolia. They want all groups in Istanbul to work together now. An organization was founded specifically to take men and weapons from here to Anatolia. Everyone is working in secret cells. You, me and İnayetullah[52] have been assigned to the same cell; we'll be working together. But you mustn't tell anyone about this.'

'What will we do?'

'I don't know yet. But Halide Hanım wants to meet up with you.'

I met Halide Hanım at the Feyziyye School in Bayezit, where Nakiye Hanım, a close friend of hers, was the principal. She was wearing a long black dress and had covered her head with a black tulle veil resembling the ones used by nuns. She looked formidable as she gave orders to those gathered around her, praising some and scolding others. Once everyone had left, she called me to her side.

'I'm sure Zekeriya already told you,' she said. 'Protesting in *Büyük Mecmua* is no longer enough. Now that the British have landed the Greeks in Izmir, they're preparing to conquer all of Anatolia. Damat Ferit and Sultan Vahdettin are calling on reactionary forces to oppose the national congress held by Mustafa Kemal. But Mustafa Kemal's supporters also are organizing. The National Assembly is hard at work here in Istanbul. Zekeriya and Inayetullah will help smuggle men and weapons to Anatolia. I'll give you a little task as well. You'll visit me every evening, take my letters to Esat Pasha at the National Assembly and bring me his replies.'

'Is that all?' I asked. To be honest, playing such a small part in such an important struggle had wounded my pride.

'What more do you want?' Halide Hanım said. 'You'll also be working on *Büyük Mecmua*.'

And so, every evening, I went to Halide Hanım, picked up her letter, put it in my hair, where it was hidden under my *çarşaf*, and took it to the National Assembly. This had to be done before nightfall since women couldn't go out in the streets after dark; they'd be assaulted by foreign soldiers. Then I delivered the letter to Esat Pasha and took his reply back to Halide Hanım. I'm against the *çarşaf*, but I have to admit it was quite useful for this job.

Büyük Mecmua is closed down

The censorship grew so harsh that *Büyük Mecmua* could no longer write about pressing current affairs. For example, the 25 December 1919 issue was full of irrelevant pieces like 'Winter Illnesses', 'The Matter of Public Language', 'Wedding Customs' and 'The

---

[52] A former member of the nationalist Turkish Hearth organization that was shut down by the occupying forces. Later, he worked in the Ministry of Foreign Affairs and at some embassies.

Plague'. Meanwhile, in Anatolia, the national independence movement was gathering momentum, and its supporters in Istanbul were doing all they could to help the cause.

The British, the Americans and the Sultan all feared the emergence of this movement. Many of its followers were detained and accused of involvement in the CUP or the Armenian massacres.[53] Journalists calling for national liberation were silenced, and many journals were closed down altogether. Eventually, the British censors ordered the Directorate of Print Media to shut down *Büyük Mecmua* as well.

This made it very hard for us to continue our struggle. Around the same time, we received an opportunity to study in the United States. It had always been a dream of mine to obtain higher education. We decided to go.[54]

Fifteen days before we left, the lease on our apartment expired and Abdullah Cevdet refused to let us stay on. We couldn't afford a hotel and didn't know what to do. Ömer Seyfeddin came to the rescue.

'Please don't be upset, my dear,' he said. 'Come to my house in Kalamış. I'll stay at Ali Canib's house.'

Ömer Seyfeddin's house was right by the sea. It was sheltered by trees, like a bird's nest. Once we moved in, the writers of *Büyük Mecmua* and many poets started gathering there, and we discussed the War of Independence and the future of the country. Everyone was full of hope about the war. Some had resolved to join the movement in Ankara. The journal's closure had upset us all.

Soon afterward, Ömer Seyfeddin fell ill and we had to move out again for his sake. He later died of diabetes while we were in the USA; we read about it in the papers. We were doubly bereaved: he was not just a great Turkish author but also a very dear friend.

---

[53] TN: This passage is the most direct reference Sertel makes to the Armenian Genocide.
[54] TN: Halide Edip helped the Sertels secure this scholarship from Charles R. Crane, a Chicago businessman. The goal was to study in the USA and return to Turkey equipped with the most cutting-edge knowledge available in the West.

2

In America

College life

After being tossed to and fro on stormy seas for an entire month, we finally made it to the USA. America was completely uncharted territory to me; the only thing I knew about it – from books – was its prosperity. This wealth, which grew especially after the First World War, was dazzling. The USA had joined the war in its final years and had seen no combat on its soil. It had lent its allies money and sold them weapons, ships and other military equipment. It had obtained cheap goods from colonies and passed them on to the warring states at a handsome profit. In the process, the country had accumulated immense sums of capital.

New York was a city divided in two. The rich lived in the upper part, called uptown, while downtown, the lower part, was mired in poverty. My first encounter was with rich America: Columbia University and Barnard College, where we'd be studying, were uptown. In order to attend Barnard, I first needed to learn English. It wasn't easy getting a college degree in a language I didn't know, with a small child in tow and no help around the house. But nothing could stop me. In the mornings, I left Sevim at Columbia's nursery division, the Horace Mann School. I picked her up again around lunchtime. In the process, I learned a great deal about the new educational methods used at American nursery and primary schools.[1] At night, Zekeriya and I took turns going to the university library: I went one day, he the next.

I wanted to study sociology and started taking courses at Columbia, from Professors Giddings and Ogburn. Giddings was the leading American sociology professor of his day. His courses were taken not just by students, but all kinds of people. Among these were the rich young misses of high society. Most of them came just so they could brag about it afterward. Every morning, their fancy cars lined up at the university gates.

I'd attended Ziya Gökalp's talks on sociology at the Turkish Hearth[2] in Istanbul, so I knew a bit about Durkheim's sociology. But Giddings opened up a whole new world for me. He taught a theory called 'consciousness of kind' and used it to explain not just social and historical events but interpersonal relations as well. He argued that the

---

[1] After I returned to Turkey, I wrote a series of reading primers under the title *Yeni Kıraat* (New Reading). They followed the Thorndike method and were accepted for use by Turkish primary schools.
[2] TN: An early and influential Turkish nationalist society.

Figure 2.1 New York City, 1919, Turkish scholarship students at Columbia University. They were charged with bringing back pioneering ideas for a new Turkish Republic. Sabiha (second left), Zekeriya and their two-year-old daughter Sevim (bottom right).

separation (or antagonism) between races – such as black, white and yellow – was based on kind. Regardless of continent, he said, blacks united in solidarity against whites because they'd achieved consciousness of kind.

According to Giddings, religious hatred was also due to consciousness of kind. The wars of religion that fill history books, the animosity between Christians and Muslims – all of this came about because members of a given religion share a consciousness of kind. Whenever people attained this consciousness, they united and fought against those who didn't belong to the same kind.

Giddings dismissed conflicts of interest between individuals, nations and races, as well as the struggle between capital and labour. He said these were secondary antagonisms that could be addressed by ensuring social justice. They did play a role in rifts and alliances between nations, but, ultimately, it was consciousness of kind that united members of one nation against others. The main human conflict was conflict of kind. This theory took over my thinking, and I found myself interpreting every event according to it.

One day, in Professor Ogburn's sociology class, the subject was women and the family. After we discussed Morgan and Le Play's work on this issue, the professor recommended that we also read Engels' *The Origin of the Family* and August Bebel's *Woman and Socialism*. After reading them, I was dumbfounded. My worldview shifted again. Apparently, in addition to consciousness of kind, there was also something called 'class consciousness'. Engels and Marx used a dialectical method to analyse society. Conflict and convergence between people wasn't due to kind but to class interests, and these were tied to relations of production.

Woman and Socialism became a defining book for me. Fascinated, I started reading more books on socialism by Marx, Engels and Kautsky. At the same time, I devoured the novels of Jack London and Upton Sinclair. They reshaped my views and introduced me to ideas about social relations and a whole new world of thought.

At the School of Social Work

The New York School of Social Work was part of Columbia University.[3] The school conducted research on social issues, using the case method to identify types of unrest in the lives of workers and families. The goal was to develop scientific methods to fix these problems through welfare initiatives. At the school, I studied applied sociology.

The school was located downtown, on Lexington Avenue, in a poor, squalid neighbourhood similar to Harlem or the Bowery. This was where the immigrants lived: Italians, Czechoslovakians, Spaniards, Greeks, Armenians – people from all over the world. One of the school's aims was to adapt these immigrants to the American lifestyle or, in other words, to Americanize them.

Every district had community centres that studied problems experienced by workers, families and children. The centres kept people under constant scrutiny and compiled records on issues that arose. Those who registered with a community centre could benefit from welfare aid. These organizations weren't just funded by the state. Major capitalists donated large sums of money to the centres. The boards of institutions like the School of Social Work always included a few wives of millionaires.

To a certain extent, this system addressed the needs of the workers and the poor. It used science to make social welfare more efficient, providing jobs for workers, treatment for the sick and protection for children. As an added benefit, it yielded plenty of data for sociologists to analyse. But ultimately, its purpose was to restrict the activities of labour and stifle any emerging workers' movements or revolutionary tendencies.

American capitalism had thrived magnificently, especially during the war. While the upper city bathed in wealth and abundance, the masses dwelled in downtown slums, positively eager to be exploited in exchange for a slice of bread. The wealthy did all they could to cripple socialist movements: they bought off union leaders like Gompers[4] and supported moderate wings of leftist parties. During our time in the USA, socialist parties were always weak, some of them fading from the scene altogether.

The most hotly debated issue at Columbia University and at the School of Social Work was the Soviet Revolution. In those days, American intellectuals were still able to discuss such topics without fear. Columbia was a wealthy school, so most of its conferences defended capitalism. But the School of Social Work was deeply involved with the plight of the workers and common people. Its conferences were more objective and featured thinkers from across the political spectrum. Even William Foster, the head of the Communist Party, was able to give public lectures there.

---

[3] TN: Sertel is referring to the Columbia School of Social Work.
[4] TN: Samuel Gompers (1850–1924) was the founder of the American Federation of Labor.

At the Lexington Community Center

Through the School of Social Work, I became familiar with downtown New York and the people who lived there. Most of them were recent immigrants. Each street in the fringe downtown neighbourhoods was a veritable microcosm of an immigrant's home country. One recognized Italians by the strings of pasta hanging in the streets, Muslims by their oriental embroideries and various Balkan populations by whichever national characteristics they still hung on to.

All immigrant groups set up their own vending stalls, chattering away in their native languages. Sometimes, one even heard the heartrending folk songs of fishermen from Capri, their hair gone white in exile, their hearts still yearning for the soil and hot sun of Italy. None of the groups was Americanized yet, and the little English they spoke could hardly be understood. The apartments were jam-packed with people. Black and white children quarrelled in the streets, and the white ones made the black kids cry.

I worked at the Lexington Community Center and had access to the files of the people who were registered there. What a find those files would have been for a novelist! The immigrants' tales filled entire volumes: how they'd come to America, the hardships they'd endured, their struggle with joblessness and exploitation, how they yearned for their homelands and regretted having left.

They'd come from Europe expecting an El Dorado, braving the ocean with their families in the hope of getting rich. But America had turned them into slaves; they worked at factories day and night, barely making enough to buy food. They didn't speak the language and had no technical skills, so they were given the hardest jobs. Their labour was exploited ruthlessly. Women and men, children and elders – they were like mules at a mill, endlessly turning the wheel.

Figure 2.2 New York, 1919, within days of arriving, Sabiha quickly transformed her look from a Turkish *çarşaf* to Western styles borrowed from a relative.

Figure 2.3 Central Park in modern dress, Zekeriya, Sevim and Sabiha.

Some of them borrowed money, defaulted on their debts and moved from town to town. They toiled on the farms of big landlords or in the orchards in the north, and were left with nothing to show for it but their daily bread. They worked in gardens of Eden but never touched the fruit. There was no way out. There was no way back. They'd burnt their bridges, sold their homes and livestock, just to get here. Now, they were resigned to poverty and hunger.

I didn't just read about these people – I visited their homes, listened to their troubles and kept records on them. I saw organizations try to heal this social disease, and I can say without a doubt that in a capitalist society, welfare cannot prevent social misery, no matter what means it employs. As long as the causes of the disease – the terrifying gap between labour and capital, the injustice in their relations – are not addressed, even legions of welfare organizations would only be curing symptoms.

Among the Turkish workers

Scattered across the cities and towns of this vast and endless country, there were a number of Turkish immigrants as well. Almost all of them were workers; the small number of electricians, technicians and engineers, who were more educated, didn't live among the workers, and had nothing to do with them.

In New York, the Turkish workers had no gathering place other than their local coffee house. Zekeriya sometimes went there, but he often told me that I shouldn't go. Even though these Turks lived in America, their mindsets were still Anatolian. Nevertheless, I wanted to mingle with them. As a matter of fact, I needed to.

At college, I was specializing in community organization, and the professors who read my papers chided me again and again: 'Your theoretical work is perfect, but where is the application? How can we trust your ability to apply these theories in real life if you've never organized a community?'

They were right, of course; I couldn't give them a good answer. Was there no Turkish community in the United States, they asked, and I told them that there was, but I couldn't work among them. When I told them why, they said,

> Your task is to work in and for society, regardless of the hurdles you may face. How can you give up without even trying?

Finally, I resolved to take action, no matter what the cost. Perhaps I couldn't organize all the workers in the United States, but I would organize some. I spoke of my ambition with some acquaintances.

'You couldn't even get through the door of that coffee house,' they said. 'You'd be an alien to them. They don't like intellectuals; they're all from Anatolia, from the villages. It's even worse that you're a woman; they'll never tolerate a woman mixing with men. This isn't a regular New York coffee house we're talking about. It might as well be in a Turkish village. And there's so much cigarette smoke in there, you won't even be able to see what's in front of you.'

I knew there was some truth to these words. Why didn't these people like intellectuals? I'd learned the answer while studying other communities. They hated how selfish intellectuals were, how arrogant and how aloof from the rest of the community. Most intellectuals looked down on workers and didn't regard them as equal human beings. It wasn't surprising that workers were offended by them.

Still, I didn't pay heed to these objections. I wanted to work among a Turkish community and employ the new methods I'd learned for its benefit. Zekeriya knew some of these people. He recommended that I meet up with a Turk called Ahmet Osman.

'Talk to him,' he said. 'He's a very smart man. Maybe he can help you make some inroads.'

Ahmet Osman was a tall, dark-skinned man from Eğin.[5] His eyes shimmered with intelligence. Like the others, he'd come to America to find work and had braved many misfortunes. After struggling with hunger and unemployment for years, he'd partnered with a former Turkish civil servant called Refik Bey and opened a workshop that produced electrical batteries. I called him up, and he came to see me, together with Refik Bey. Refik Bey was an Ottoman gentleman of the old school, a bureaucrat who'd served at the Sublime Porte. With his slender figure, his pale, narrow face and his blue eyes, he still had all the bearings of a civil servant. He hadn't become Americanized in the least. I laid out my thoughts to them.

'You can go and talk to them,' they said. 'But organize them? Never.'
'Why?'
'Supposedly, they already have an organization. But they never pay their fees or attend any meetings. And even when they do, all they do is fight.'

---

[5] TN: A town in eastern Anatolia. The name, deriving from the Armenian word for spring, has since been changed to Kemaliye.

Clearly, this wouldn't be a walk in the park.

'Put me in touch with them,' I said, 'and I will try to bring them around. I don't want to just walk into their coffee house unannounced; they would shun me. Talk to them in advance about me and my ideas.'

They accepted.

A letter from Ankara

Meanwhile, in Anatolia, Greeks and Turks were engaged in heavy fighting. The Greeks had advanced all the way to Sakarya. On the eastern front, Turkish forces were clashing with the Dashnak Armenians.[6] Around then, I received a letter from a friend in Ankara. It outlined the situation in the homeland and the calamities of war, and described how Atatürk had abolished unruly armed bands and established a regular army.

From the hunger and misery in Anatolia, the letter went on to describe the plight of orphaned children: droves of children whose parents had been killed on the eastern front were languishing in the streets. 'There are 90,000 Turkish orphans,' it said. 'The orphanages can only hold around 12,000. The Americans just accept Armenian children in their orphanages and turn away the Turkish and Kurdish orphans. If you could convince the Turks in America to help these children somehow, it would be a great service to the homeland.'

This news made it doubly urgent for me to organize the Turks. It was our duty to support the War of Independence, even if modestly and from afar. Ahmet Osman and I agreed to visit the coffee house one night.

On a rainy winter evening, the two of us walked through the dark streets of the Bowery[7] and arrived at a decrepit clapboard building. We climbed a creaky flight of wooden stairs to the second floor and opened the door to the coffee house. Inside, the smoke was so thick that I couldn't see anything. They knew I was coming and had cleaned the stone tables. Ahmet Osman introduced me and talked a little about my interest in them and their lives.

They listened. When he finished, nobody said anything. Finally, I was compelled to break the silence myself. I got up.

'I came here from our homeland,' I said. 'Right now, a war of independence is raging back there. Our Anatolian brothers have put their lives on the line for this cause. We must support them as best we can. It doesn't have to be money; we can help them in many different ways. We can send them our old clothes. We can stage events to support the cause. But above all else, we need to get organized. We need to have a society that will improve our lives in America and aid the homeland in any way possible.'

---

[6] TN: The Dashnaksutyun, or Federation of Armenian Revolutionaries, was a leading force in the struggle to emancipate the Armenian population within, and later from, the Ottoman Empire and the Republic of Turkey.

[7] In those days, the Bowery was the area of downtown New York, where the homeless, the unemployed and the poorest immigrants lived. There, one could have a man killed and have all traces of the murder removed with a five-dollar bribe to the police.

Again, there was no response. Some mumbling could be heard among the tables. Finally, a dark-skinned man, neither short nor tall, got up. Apparently, this was the leader of the workers here, and the owner of the coffee house. He spoke in a faint voice.

'So, a sister of ours has come from the homeland. Well, we welcome her. She says she cares about our living conditions. We sure are grateful for that. Then she talks about getting us organized, about raising our standards of living. With all due respect, I don't see how it can be done. How can our sister help us? Will she find us jobs? Is that possible? Will she help us get a raise? What can she do? We've met many do-gooders like her. They come, fret over us for five or ten days, and then we never see their faces again.'

They wanted concrete answers. I said that in order to help them, I first had to learn about their needs.

'Once we're organized,' I said, 'we can tackle the issue of finding jobs.'

Now, a few men spoke up at the same time.

'We have countless needs,' they said. 'But first, let's see you figure out our graveyard problem. We'll talk about the rest later.'

I had no idea what the graveyard problem was. An old, white-haired man stood up.

'Every community here has its own graveyard,' he said. 'But us, we're scattered like pebbles. They bury our dead in Christian graveyards. We go before Allah as blasphemous infidels. If you want to do something for us, relieve us from this shame.'

I thought about it for a second and decided I could solve this issue with help from my school.

'I will solve your graveyard problem,' I said with a resolute voice.

They looked at me in astonishment.

'It's not about the money, sister. No one will sell us land here.'

'You come up with the money,' I said. 'I'll get you the land.'

They didn't seem convinced, but we parted amicably. They accompanied me to the door and even asked me to come again.

Poor souls, I thought to myself. Stranded in some foreign land, rotting in hunger, poverty and joblessness, and they think their biggest problem is a Christian burial.

The graveyard problem proved easy enough to resolve. I told Walter Pettit, my adviser, about the meeting and the demands. He called the municipality. Apparently, a formal application had to be filed. We prepared it, and I had the community leaders sign it. A month later, a piece of land was surrounded by an iron fence and allotted to the Turks. I don't quite remember where it was. It might have been in Brooklyn.

This feat boosted my credibility with the Turks, and it became much easier to work with them. I'd found their sweet spot – in community organization, finding this spot is the key to success. They eagerly attended the meetings now. Still, holding the meetings in the coffee house was quite unpleasant; we needed a proper gathering place. Once again, I asked my school for help, and we were given a decent-sized room in a community centre. The meetings took on a more formal tone, with the workers airing their complaints, one by one. By then, the Turkish workers living in other US cities had heard of our work and wanted to organize as well. Almost all the Turks living elsewhere were workers. I conducted a survey to determine their numbers and occupations, and received enthusiastic responses from every direction. The results of the survey were quite interesting.

The Turks hadn't immigrated to America as a group. They'd come over one by one, or sometimes in groups of three or four, and settled all over the country. The immigrant wave had started in Anatolian cities like Van, Erzurum and Sivas, spreading from there to other cities, towns and even villages. There were Armenians who'd moved to the States but still went back and forth, and they'd spread the word that everyone in America was rich and jobs were easy to find. They'd enticed many others to join them in the USA. Others had been impelled to move by letters from friends. The number of immigrants had spiked during the Fisrt World War.

Since this immigration had been neither collective nor systematic, there wasn't a common reason behind it either. Some had come to escape Greek oppression in Macedonia; others had come simply to make money. There were Turks, Kurds, Albanians. Those from Anatolia said they'd come to escape landlessness and unemployment. Immigration to the States had spiked again in 1920; most who'd come around then were Cypriot Turks fleeing British subjugation.

Only a few had married and started families in the United States. Differences in religion and language made things hard for them. They said they were unable to get along with American girls or immigrant girls from Europe. Some Turks would receive photographs of girls in Turkey, bring them over and get married.

This crowd of around 9,000 Turks, Kurds, Tatars and Albanians mostly worked in factories, producing soap, furs, gramophones, electricity and cars, as well as in steel foundries. Of those who had a trade, most were shoemakers, hat cleaners, laundry owners, producers of electrical batteries, greengrocers and middlemen in import and export. A Tatar in New York owned a silk factory, while a Turk called Hafız Efendi had a soap factory in Worcester.

The labourers' working conditions were extremely harsh. Not knowing English and having no special skills, they were given the toughest jobs. The lives of the Turks and the Kurds who worked in Ford's automobile factory in Detroit were a special kind of hell. Back then, US technology wasn't as advanced as it is today, and labourers had to work steel furnaces so hot that one couldn't endure the heat for more than a minute. Changing shirts each time they went to the furnace, these labourers were as close as one could get to hell on earth.

Some worked at the factory for ten to fifteen hours a day. Most came in at night and slept during the day. Often, they didn't see daylight for months. Industry-related diseases were common among those working in chemical and tobacco factories. Wages were high compared with those in Europe, but the workers had turned into robots, and higher wages weren't enough to humanize their lives.

The survey showed that Turkish workers were clustered in the cities of New York, Detroit, Worcester, Lawrence, Youngstown, Pittsburgh and Philadelphia.

Thanks to this survey and the ongoing success of our work in New York City, younger and more urbane people joined the society, such as Rahmi Kolçak, who was attending college in New York; Seyfi, an engineer; and İsmail Hakkı, a projectionist. The society's name was changed to Türk Teavün Cemiyeti [Turkish Solidarity Association]. Some members objected, especially the Albanians and Kurds, insisting that it should be

Osmanlı Teavün Cemiyeti [Ottoman Solidarity Association] instead, but the choice of the majority was accepted.

Once the society's work became steady and consistent, we rented a separate building and turned it into a de facto community centre. This saved some of the workers from having to go to the coffee house all the time. Language courses were offered for those who didn't speak English. Conferences were held to inform workers about the situation in their homeland, to review working conditions in the USA and to develop class consciousness.

Unionizing the labourers took a long time and was hard work. At first, they rejected the idea, saying employers were quicker to fire unionized workers. And once an immigrant lost his job, he wouldn't be able to find another. But we used real-life examples to show them the disadvantages of not being unionized and the advantages of joining. Eventually, most of the workers in New York joined, but many Kurds at the Ford factory in Detroit couldn't be persuaded.

After setting up subsidiary institutions, we started using membership fees to publish a weekly bulletin called *Birlik* [Unity]. Prepared by Zekeriya and some students from the New York Teachers College,[8] the bulletin helped establish ties between workers and associations in other US cities.

The first fundraiser

Bad news kept arriving from the homeland. Newspapers reported the progress of the Greek armies and murders committed by Anzavur's[9] bands, *hodjas* loyal to the sultan and other reactionaries. At the society's first meeting, I passed along this news and read aloud the letter I'd received. I talked about how we could help: from the USA, all we could really do was send money and old clothes. We decided to stage an event to raise money, inviting association leaders from other cities and all the workers in New York.

At the fundraiser, we spoke about the atrocities committed by the Greeks and the sacrifices of the Anatolian people, be they men or women, young or old. We pointed out that the imperialist states were intent on dismantling and dividing the country. The assembled Anatolian sons, their hearts ablaze for many years with yearning for the homeland, showed such passion and concern for the cause that it would bring tears to one's eyes. As if bidding at an auction, they engaged in a race of generosity and sacrifice. As far as I can remember, we raised $20,000 at that event.

The event also strengthened the bonds between the association in New York and workers in other cities. Zeki Bey, a delegate from the Detroit Solidarity Association, invited me to come and organize the workers there. Detroit had two societies: the Solidarity Association, founded by the Turks, and the Red Crescent Association, founded by the Kurds. I received invitations from both.

---

[8] TN: Sertel is likely referring to Columbia University's Teachers College.
[9] TN: Ahmet Anzavur (d. 1921) was the commander who was dispatched to Anatolia by Sultan Vahdettin to counter the forces fighting the War of Independence.

When I got off the train in Detroit, I was greeted by a small crowd. After introductions were made, Zeki Bey pulled me aside.

'Sabiha Hanım,' he said, 'we have a big problem. The Turks and the Kurds are quarrelling. The Kurds say, "We will host our sister from the homeland." And the Turks say, "She is our sister as much as yours, so she will be our guest." What should we do?'

'There's an easy way out,' I said. 'I won't stay with you or with them. I'll go to a hotel instead.'

Zeki Bey was a short, pudgy Anatolian. He was smart and knew the mindset of the people well. He balked at my suggestion.

'Unthinkable,' he said. 'They'd regard that as a grave insult. They already fought over the issue at our previous meeting. To calm the commotion, one of our members suggested putting you up at a hotel. The Kurds wouldn't hear of it. "You vile, shameless people," they said. "You would dare let our sister from the homeland sleep at a hotel?" They raised hell!'

I thought about it for a minute. My objective here was to support the independence movement. So, I needed to go wherever I could raise more funds.

'Tell me, then,' I said to Zeki Bey, 'from which side can I expect to raise more money?'

'From the Kurds,' he said without hesitating. 'Because they have the hardest jobs at the Ford factory, they earn and save more money than the Turks.'

'Then I'll stay with the Kurds. Leave it to me to break the news to the Turks.'

Having quarrelled the day before, the Turks and the Kurds welcoming me at the station stood in separate groups. Zeki Bey took me over to the Turks. I plunged in without introduction.

'Brothers,' I said, 'I know what happened yesterday. I appeal to your conscience. Our brethren in Anatolia are being massacred; 90,000 orphans are languishing in the streets. They are hungry and have no roof over their heads. In such a crisis, we can't be discussing with whom I'll be staying. I implore you, don't be offended or hurt; I am your guest no matter whose house I sleep in. Permit me to stay with the Red Crescent Association. It's for the greater good of the homeland.'

The Turks accepted without raising any objections.

Rumi Efendi, the chairman of the Red Crescent Association, was a tall, hulking mountain of a man. His long moustache went all the way up to his ears. He introduced me to the other members, who were overjoyed, and then we got into cars and drove to his house.

Rumi Efendi lived in a modern two-storey house. His furniture, timeworn but clean, seemed oddly Asian in this contemporary setting. For lunch, they placed a gigantic round metal dining tray on the floor and arranged some cushions around it. Then they brought in a big tray of pilaf with meat. Everyone started eating with their hands. They'd brought some cutlery just for me, but I turned it down and joined them in eating out of the tray with my fingers. Clearly, the Americans, who claimed to have brought civilization to the colonies, had not extended this civilization to the immigrants living in their own country.

The meeting was scheduled for Sunday, so the workers took the day off and showed me around the Ford factory. It was a gargantuan building. Every minute, finished cars were lowered from suspended bridges. The labourers worked like robots, not even wasting a moment: the role of speed in production was such that even a second had its monetary value. The exploitation machine was in full steam as well. Foreign workers made half the money Americans made and still had difficulties finding jobs. And since they weren't unionized, they were ruthlessly exploited by employers.

When we arrived at the steel furnace, we had a chance to witness this reality up close. The furnace was in a small room and encircled by glass. Workers ceaselessly fed the furnace with coal, and the molten steel flowed like a crimson flame. It was so hot in there that they said the devil's own hellfire couldn't be hotter. I was told that no workers except the Kurds could make it into this chamber. They would enter the furnace naked like wrestlers and take turns by the minute.

No one working under these harsh conditions belonged to a union. They received no social aid whatsoever. And since they were ill-informed, they saw nothing wrong with this state of affairs. When I tried to explain that they should join the unions, they all objected at once.

'We don't take part in strikes,' they said. 'Whenever there is a strike, the factory is surrounded by Ford's private policemen and soldiers. Ford has a private army that he uses against the workers. We enter the factory and work under their control.'

I saw how the capitalists took advantage of these naive, hard-working people and their lack of knowledge and consciousness. They exploited them and used them as strike-breakers against their fellow labourers. But it was hard to make them understand the evil of this situation. An organization was needed and much work had to be done, I reasoned, for such an awareness to even become possible.

Next, there was a debate about which association would hold the first fundraiser. 'We won't go to the Turks,' the Kurds said. 'We'll host the first meeting, and they can come to us if they want.'

To prevent a row over precedence and location, I made a proposal. 'Neither you nor the Turks should host the meeting,' I said. 'We'll rent out a hall and everyone can go there. That way, we won't need to hold two separate meetings, either.'

The Kurds rejected this offer in one breath. The discussion went on for hours. They insisted that their association should meet first and stonewalled the matter, saying that the meeting would either be held by them or not at all. Finally, I ran out of breath from arguing with them. Clearly, Kurdish obstinacy could not be overcome.

'Fine,' I said. 'Tomorrow night, we'll gather at the Red Crescent Association. If the Turks don't come, we'll hold a separate meeting for them at a later time and I'll speak there as well.'

They accepted. The next morning, I sent for Zeki Bey. I told him about the previous night's discussion and asked him to convey my greetings to the Solidarity Association. It was meaningless to start a quarrel between Turks and Kurds with the homeland in such a predicament, and I hoped they would understand my decision. Zeki Bey accepted my proposal, saying that since the main objective was to help the homeland, everyone else would be on board as well. The Turkish Solidarity Association would hold its own separate meeting.

The next evening, we gathered at the meeting hall of the Red Crescent Association. Most of those in attendance were labourers at the Ford factory, and almost all others were factory workers as well. Not a single one of them was trained in a profession. The hall was wide and long, and they'd set up a table for me at one end. Those who couldn't find seats sat cross-legged on the floor.

Before I could begin talking, a commotion broke out. People started hurling abuse at each other across the hall. One of them jumped up and rushed at a young man sitting by the door.

'Get out,' he said, 'I cannot be in the same room as you!'

'No, you get out!'

They started raining blows on each other. In a flash, they both drew knives from their coat pockets. And before I had a chance to find out what they were fighting about, they were stabbing at each other.

I brought my fist down on the table with all my strength.

'Is this how you show respect for your sister from the homeland?' I asked. 'You didn't want the Turks to host me, so I came to you. You insisted on holding the first meeting, so I met with you. And now you draw your knives to drive me out? Well, goodbye.'

All hell broke loose. They were screaming and yelling. Some tried to separate the brawlers while others clung to my hem, begging me to take the high road and stay.

I turned to the brawlers right away.

'Throw away those knives,' I said.

They let go of the knives as if compelled by a magnet.

'Rumi Efendi, pick them up.'

The knives were gathered up. But the atmosphere was so tense that no good could come from giving a speech. First, we needed to clear the air.

'Countrymen,' I said. 'I came here today to tell you about the wretched state of our homeland. Your brothers in the east were martyred on the fronts of Erzurum and Van,[10] and their children were left on the streets, destitute and hungry. But I see it's impossible for you to consider this matter today. You're angry and resentful of each other. Let's postpone this meeting until tomorrow.'

At once, shouts of 'No!' rang out. A dark-skinned, pockmarked old man shot up from among the assembly.

'Sister,' he said, 'surely, your arrival is a good omen. Don't mind their fighting. They have respect for you. Please, won't you reconcile these two?'

The thought hadn't occurred to me. The old man went on.

'Mehmet is bitter at Derviş over a money affair,' he said. 'They fight like this wherever they go. They both said they wouldn't come if the other was here. But the Red Crescent decided it wouldn't close its doors to anyone, and so they both got in. Please, won't you reconcile them?'

I turned to the brawlers again.

'If what the old man says is true,' I said, 'and you have any respect for me, you'll embrace each other now.'

Mehmet and Derviş had been at each other's throats for seven years, but that day, they kissed and embraced. And that was just the beginning. All those who'd quarrelled were brought to me in pairs, and it fell upon me to reconcile them all.

---

[10] TN: It is notable that in addressing a Kurdish audience, Sertel highlights the conditions in areas heavily populated by Kurds.

Finally, the atmosphere eased, and I was able to address the real issue. They listened to my words in shock and dismay, and they wept openly. It was astounding to see these towering men cry. I could only assume that my words had conjured up visions of their villages, mothers and children, as well as places and loved ones they hadn't seen in years.

After talking about the homeland, I addressed their own situation. I brought up the dreadful conditions in which they lived, scattered across the big cities of this boundless country, and told them this was due to their lack of organization. I stressed that all workers, whether Turkish, Kurdish or Albanian, needed to unite and join the unions. I said that even if the Red Crescent and the Solidarity Association remained separate, they had to join forces to defend workers' rights against their bosses.

I pointed out that strike-breaking was against their own interests. I proposed that the Red Crescent Association form a commission to deal with this matter, and that it cooperate with a similar commission from the Solidarity Association.

Rumi Efendi, the chairman, asked that workers' issues be discussed in a separate meeting. He proposed that today's meeting continue with a fundraiser for the homeland, the children and Mustafa Kemal's soldiers. This met with great enthusiasm, and the ensuing fundraiser became a true race of chivalry and largesse. If one of them gave $50, the other, not to be outdone, donated $75. We ended up collecting over $50,000. And later, we raised nearly as much from the Turks' Solidarity Association as well.

Requesting an ambassador from Ankara

After I returned to New York, we held an administrative council meeting and discussed bringing someone from Ankara over to the United States. A person with first-hand experience of the country's plight could be of great help with our fundraising. We contacted the Association for the Protection of Children in Ankara, and the Ankara Central Committee decided to send over Dr Fuat Bey, the chairman of the Association.

Fuat Bey arrived on the steamer *Gülcemal*.[11] *Gülcemal* was the first Turkish ship to come to America, and its arrival in New York's harbour turned into a major event. All associations sent representatives to welcome the ship. The Turks weren't the only ones in attendance. Greeks, Armenians, Jews and other people from Turkey were present as well, trying to catch a glimpse of the ship's captains.

On the day of Fuat Bey's arrival, we held a meeting in the conference hall of the Astoria Hotel and prepared a programme for the welcoming ceremony. We also made a list of the cities Fuat Bey would be visiting. It was decided that I should serve as his travel companion and interpreter.

The first meeting was held in New York, where we rented out a big hall. Fuat Bey reported on the tragic state of the homeland. I gave an emotional talk. Poems were recited. Throughout the meeting, sobs could be heard from among the audience. After the speeches, we started accepting donations. The table was covered with piles of

---

[11] TN: Literally, 'The Rose-Faced One'.

dollars. A middle-aged man of medium height, his eyebrows thick and black, and his moustache so long that it touched his ears, made his way through the crowd and slowly approached the table. This was the Kurdish Sergeant Yusuf Gülabi. He started out by kissing Fuat Bey's hand.

'You brought me the scent of my soil, my village,' he said. 'Thank you so much for that. Surely, my own children are among those starving back home. I've been working in America for twenty-seven years. I worked as a labourer in the mines. I worked in the automobile factories and the Fruit Company's[12] orchards in the north. I slept in garages and public parks. I saved $10,000 – you can have it all. I've decided to return to the homeland. All I want from you is a ticket on a ship and some help with finding a job back home. Here is my gold watch. Here is my gold belt-buckle. Take them to the homeland with my blessings.'

Everyone was in tears. We raised more than $100,000 that day.

In each city that Fuat Bey and I visited, we encountered men like Sergeant Gülabi. They brought us all the money they'd earned with their blood, sweat and tears in bitter exile, and they poured it out before us like so many pebbles. All they asked in return was for their photos to be hung at the orphanages and hospitals that would be built back in the homeland. It was impossible not to be humbled by their magnanimity.

Thanks to these efforts, more than 1,000,000 Turkish liras were sent back home. The first children's centres, nursing homes, hospitals and kindergartens set up in Ankara by the Society for the Protection of Children were built with this money. But no job was found for Sergeant Yusuf Gülabi. And no workers' pictures adorned the walls next to those children's beds.

Leaving New York

By the end of 1923, I'd completed my last year of college and earned my diploma, so we decided to accompany Fuat Bey back to the homeland. Fuat Bey asked me if I'd like to work for the Society for the Protection of Children, helping its board to address children's issues. I wasn't too fond of the idea. True, I'd dealt with children's issues, along with other social issues, in America. But I wanted to work in my field of specialization, which was community organization. My ambition was to move to an Anatolian village and establish a community centre. Still, I didn't reject Fuat Bey's proposal out of hand. I told him I'd decide after our return.

My experience among the Turkish workers in America had given me first-hand knowledge of the labourers, the villagers, the people of my homeland. Initially, they seemed difficult to work with, but once I found their sweet spots and addressed their specific needs, they weren't difficult at all. It would be a major service to the country to enlighten these people, giving them knowledge to defend their rights and the ability to determine their own fate.

---

[12] TN: Sertel gives the company's name as 'Fruit Company' in English.

The day of our departure came. We were leaving with Fuat Bey, Yusuf Gülabi and some other workers. The labourers with whom I'd worked over the past three years came to see us off, even from other cities. People made their way to the harbour in a crowded throng. They were shaking my hand and kissing it, telling me they wouldn't forget me.

I was in tears. They gave me a gold pen as a parting gift, and I gave them my word that I would use this pen to advocate for workers' rights. I didn't realize at the time how hard a promise that would prove to keep.

Waving from the deck of the ship, I couldn't help but wonder how long the organizations I was leaving behind would survive.

I kept in contact with the New York organization after my return. But weighed down by many years of struggles, the letter exchange broke off. Still, from time to time, Fuat Bey told me that the US organizations remained active and made regular donations.

Twelve years later, in 1937, I visited the US to see my daughter Sevim, who was studying there. The board of the Solidarity Association was full of young people. The connection between the New York organization and others around the country had been lost. Most of my old acquaintances had moved elsewhere, and some had died. The youngsters invited me to their meetings. I learned that the workers belonging to the Association had become unionized, and that some youngsters had joined socialist organizations. They took me to a meeting of the Renters' Association, which had been set up by the workers. The film *Chapaev* was being shown at the association's movie theater, and we watched it together.[13]

They asked me about Nazım Hikmet.[14] They wanted to know everything about him. They recited his poems, telling me they'd received them from their friends back in the homeland.

Some of these young people joined the Lincoln Brigade, which travelled from the United States to Spain during the Spanish Civil War.[15] The youngsters I met in 1937 were no longer the workers of the old days, who were unaware of why they were being exploited and meekly bowed down to their fate. The new workers had acquired the conviction to fight for their rights. They participated in strikes and joined forces with workers from all other nations. I was delighted. These were the fruits of the seeds we had sown.

---

[13] TN: *Chapaev* (dir. Georgi and Sergei Vasiliev, 1934) is a classic of early Soviet cinema.
[14] TN: Nazım Hikmet Ran (1902–63) is widely considered to be the greatest poet of the Turkish Republic. He features prominently in later chapters of Sertel's memoirs.
[15] TN: It is unclear whether these people were part of the Lincoln Brigade before or after Sertel's visit.

3

The return home

In Ankara

We arrived in Istanbul in July 1923. The city hadn't been fully purged of occupying forces yet. The War of Independence was won, but Ankara and many parts of Anatolia were in ruins. Istanbul hadn't suffered any material damage during the war; it hadn't been vandalized or burnt down. Nonetheless, the people were devastated.

The war had dealt a heavy blow to the palace and its supporters – *hodja*s loyal to Anzavur's army of treason, reactionaries, politicians banished from public life and the Ottoman pashas who'd served the interests of British and American imperialism. They were all in mourning. The city smouldered with opposition to the progressive measures taken by Ankara.[1] Some intellectuals and others were trying to incite hostility against Atatürk. Newspapers like *Tasvir-i Efkar* [Depiction of Ideas] were fighting against the ideas he put forward.

But the War of Independence was more than just a victorious military campaign. It had great ideological significance. For the first time, the colonial powers that had exploited Asia, Africa and South America for centuries were defeated through a national liberation struggle. The war also showed that the sultanate and caliphate had become harmful rather than beneficial to the Turkish people. There was no faith left in a sultan and caliph who'd collaborated with the enemy and ordered brothers to kill each other. And the only ones not willing or able to see this were those who still clung to the past.

Atatürk understood why the Ottoman Empire had collapsed. Imperialism from abroad and reactionism at home were the main reasons, and Atatürk had been fighting against both since the war had been won. He'd already mapped out many reforms in his head, and now he wanted to implement them, step by step. And he knew that the surest path to development lay in securing economic independence.

From the very first day he tried to implement his progressive ideas, he came under attack – not just from reactionaries, but even from his own revolutionary comrades. The likes of Kazım Karabekir and Ali Fuat Pasha[2] as well as intellectuals like Halide

---

[1] TN: Ankara, the Anatolian town that served as the headquarters of the Turkish national liberation movement, was proclaimed the capital of the Turkish Republic on 13 October 1923, thereby replacing Istanbul, the capital of the former Ottoman Empire.
[2] TN: Two of the most important generals in the War of Independence.

Edip and Adnan Adıvar[3] were nervous about his political moves. They felt that Atatürk's desire to abolish the sultanate was fuelled by his ambition to become president himself, and they could not grasp the social ramifications and progressive nature of such a step.

This was the atmosphere at home upon our return. My older daughter, Sevim, was six, and my younger daughter, Yıldız, was still a babe in arms. We didn't know what to do with our lives. I wanted to move to a village and found a community organization, but like any dreamy socialist, I had no idea how to do this. Like all youngsters fresh out of college, I was living in a fantasy world. All I knew was that I wanted to be useful to the newly emerging Turkey.

Zekeriya went to Ankara before me. A week or so later, I received a telegraph informing me that he'd been appointed to the Directorate General of the Press.[4] That put an end to my dream of moving to a village and working among the peasants. One month later, when I arrived in Ankara myself, the bitter realities became even clearer. Ankara itself was no more than a village. There were no trees, no dwellings to seek shelter in, and there was no water. Even the Grand National Assembly was just a two-storey building, no bigger than a provincial government office. The so-called Hay Market was a market with neither stores nor goods. The villagers pulled aside their carts in open spaces and slept on the ground next to their oxen. The inner streets were too narrow for even a single car to pass through. The locals lived in a district called Old Ankara, in wooden or tin structures built on top of hills. The only way to reach these houses was to scale the hills like goats. Old Ankara reminded me of the medieval towns that Evliya Çelebi describes in his *Seyahatname* [Book of Travels].[5]

New York and Ankara were truly polar opposites, and I'd just gone from one pole to the other. I already knew of the *çarıks* worn by villagers, but I was struck by their copiously patched cardigans and baggy trousers. Women wrapped in black *çarşafs* and thin cloth towels, only exposing their eyes, wandered the streets like bogeymen. Garbage piled up on street corners, and I doubt if it was ever collected. Children with skinny legs and bulging bellies scuttled down the sidewalks like skeletons, begging for money. The stores were empty and the people tired from shouldering the weight of the war. Terrible poverty was evident at every turn.

It was these villagers, with their patched cardigans, men and women alike, who'd carried ammunition to the fronts and fought in the trenches. All of Anatolia had suffered the same devastation. Now, it was the revolution's task to establish a new country, to carry this society from the Middle Ages to the present.[6]

*

---

[3] Adnan Adıvar (1882–1955), Halide Edip's husband, was a medical doctor and a leading Turkish intellectual.

[4] TN: Through this appointment, Zekeriya Sertel became the founding director of the Turkish Directorate General of the Press.

[5] TN: The *Seyahatname* of Evliya Çelebi (1611–post-1682) is the most extensive travelogue composed in the Ottoman Empire and a major work of Ottoman history and literature.

[6] TN: The Turkish term 'Devrim' (revolution) is somewhat ambiguous. It can refer to actual revolutions, such as the French Revolution, but also – especially in the Kemalist context – to state-led social reforms. For instance, the Turkish term for language reform is *dil devrimi*, or 'language revolution'.

Our house in Ankara was a little outside the centre, near the building of the Turkish Hearth organization. There was a courtyard in the back, but it had no walls around it, and entering it felt like stepping out into the street. Both our kitchen and our toilet were in this courtyard. The first time I took my baby out there in her stroller, I was met with a bizarre sight: intestines were hung up all along the walls of the house. It turned out that the village women were using our walls to dry out tripe. At once, they surrounded me. Talking over each other, they asked me for a patch of cloth. Not even a dress or some shoes. Just a patch. I was stunned by this level of poverty.

They looked at the stroller in awe.

'You come from the palace?' they asked.

'Most assuredly not. I just came out of my house.'

'Only sultans have such carts.'

The state of these people in front of me – the state of the city where I lived – wasn't just due to the War of Independence. Ankara was simply one of the countless Anatolian towns that had been neglected since Ottoman times. My train had passed through many villages and hamlets after leaving Haydarpaşa station in Istanbul, and in all of them, I'd encountered the same sight. Wherever we stopped, children with bare feet and torn trousers approached the train, begging for newspapers, cigarettes, a single cent. Village women tilled the soil in the burning sun, their faces scorched and wrinkled despite their young age. It was in their villages that I'd wanted to work.

But once we arrived in Ankara and I had the chance to listen to those who actually had fought in the war, I realized that I couldn't enter the villages without being affiliated with an organization or getting help from the government. These villages were nothing like the ones I'd seen in America. A single woman with two children couldn't even survive in them, let alone work there. It was time to say farewell to my dreams.

*

In Ankara, the foundations of a new, independent Turkey were being laid. All who'd joined the war at great personal cost were gathered there, around Atatürk. Meanwhile, in Istanbul, the caliph and his entourage of pashas, such as Izzet, Salih and Tevfik were living out their last days in charge of a ruined empire.

My surroundings were abuzz with the rumour that the new Turkey would be a republic. A new draft constitution was in the works. A constitutional commission, consisting of experts such as Ağaoğlu Ahmet and headed by the journalist Yunus Nadi Bey, had been charged with preparing the draft, and its meetings were frequently attended by Atatürk himself. Since Ankara had no proper buildings or halls to house the commission, the meetings were held at the train station, with the Turkish Hearth building reserved for the most important gatherings. The efforts expended here were just as worthy as the sacrifices on the battlefield. With the greatest self-denial, the revolutionaries were toiling to save the homeland.

Even during the war itself, a schism had emerged among the leaders of the struggle. They had tried to keep it a secret, but news had gotten out. Amidst the dangers of the War of Independence, it was said, Atatürk hadn't sought agreement among those fighting for the cause. Instead, he'd made alliances with whoever was opposed to the sultan and the occupiers. And so, this anti-imperialist front had welcomed everyone from conservative pashas and extreme rightists to intellectuals with no idea of the new movement's goals, from high-ranking bureaucrats to local notables and village landlords.

Many former CUP members, such as Kara Vasıf and Çolak Selahaddin, had become involved in these vital state affairs. After Talat, Enver and the other CUP leaders had fled the country, the remaining Unionists had founded a party called Teceddüt [Renewal]. That party had fallen apart before even properly being launched, but the Unionists were still determined to play a role in the country's politics. After riding the coattails of German militarism and driving the homeland to ruin, they were looking for a way to erase their past mistakes.[7]

Some of them had supported Atatürk in the War of Independence, but others now opposed him becoming the head of the state. This second group, headed by some Unionists in the Assembly, was a veritable placeholder for the CUP. It tried to create a united front against Atatürk and his allies, claiming that he was behaving like a dictator. This group included a variety of people, from Rauf Bey, former Minister of the Navy, who was very popular among the common people but wished to retain the sultanate and caliphate, to Kazım Karabekir, who was unable to stomach the revolutionary movements. But what it lacked was cohesion. Atatürk, in the meantime, kept a close eye on these coalitions while devoting most of his time to the new constitution.

The 1924 draft constitution affirmed that '[t]he form of the state is a republic'. This article was hotly debated. Atatürk and his opponents also disagreed on the authority vested in the National Assembly. Atatürk himself wanted all authority to rest with the Assembly. As a result, Article 3 of the Constitution declared, 'The State is governed by the Grand National Assembly, and the government bears the title Government of the Grand National Assembly'. According to this article, even if different parties were founded, the government wouldn't be formed by parties, but by the National Assembly as a whole. This was opposed by those who wanted the Constitution to conform to Western democratic standards. They maintained that the party with the majority of votes should form the government. 'There is no such thing as a parliamentary government anywhere in the world,' they said.

Atatürk's proposal of a parliamentary government was evidence of his desire to establish a truly democratic system. But certain intellectuals wanted to fall in line with the West and base both government and economy on the liberal model. To them, it was enough for the system to be a sheer copy of Western democracies. They desired a multiparty system, in which the Assembly would merely supervise the government.

Atatürk's proposal also entailed that members of the Assembly would be appointed, not elected. Many cried foul, claiming that Atatürk would fill the Assembly with his cronies and that this 'parliamentary government' would be nothing more than an executive office carrying out his orders.

Article 4 of the draft caused much debate as well. This article stated, 'The National Assembly consists of members elected by the residents of the provinces'. But provincial notables, military commanders and some of the landlords were beholden to Atatürk.

---

[7] TN: Sertel omits the fact that Atatürk himself was a high-ranking member of the Committee of Union and Progress.

Critics feared that they would elect whomever he suggested, thus bolstering his dictatorship. For this reason, opponents wanted the right to vote to be granted not just to the provinces, but also to the populations of towns and villages.

This objection was not without merit. With the right to vote curtailed in this way, the new Turkey and its democratic bourgeois revolution[8] could easily slide into a dictatorship. The article ran counter to the Constitution's democratic intent. But the opposition's main aim was not to ensure a democratic regime. Rather, they wanted to undermine Atatürk's personal authority and prevent the reforms he envisioned. Some of them, like Rauf Bey, couldn't accept the abolition of the sultanate and caliphate and the proclamation of the republic. Atatürk's goal in granting himself greater powers was to counter these reactionaries who couldn't tolerate his revolutionary ideas.

After many debates, some changes were made to the draft. Democratic rights were slightly improved. Articles guaranteeing individuals' freedom of thought, opinion and conscience were included. Nevertheless, the 1924 Constitution was not a charter that enabled a democratic bourgeois revolution. There was no mention of land reform. And despite the fact that most Turkish workers had fought in the War of Independence, carried weapons and ammunition from Istanbul to Anatolia and endured great sacrifices on the fronts, workers' rights and the right to strike remained out of the question.

The incoming members of the Assembly fell far short of being true representatives of the people. They were virtual appointees, chosen from among the candidates listed by the People's Party.[9] And without democratic elections, the resulting regime wasn't democratic, either. After Atatürk's death, the People's Party lost its revolutionary élan, relying more and more on slogans like 'One Party' and 'One Chief' to prop up a system of dictatorship.

*

While in Ankara, I closely followed the debates surrounding the Constitution and reforms. We lived right across from Mazhar Müfit Bey, the speaker of the People's Party in the Assembly. He often told us about the parliamentary debates and his replies to the opposition.

One day, I asked him: 'Why doesn't the People's Party trust the popular vote and hold a democratic election? You say the Constitution will be democratic, but if that's true, why are the members of the Assembly appointed and not elected?'

Mazhar Müfit nearly lost his temper at this question. 'What do you think?' he said. 'If we give these people the right to vote, do you know who will end up in the Assembly? Pilgrims, *hodja*s and sheikhs, that's who! The biggest enemies of progress. Mustafa

---

[8] TN: In Marxist thought, a democratic bourgeois revolution aims at abolishing a feudal system and/or wresting national independence from colonial rule while establishing the bourgeoisie as the country's dominant class and capitalism as its economic system. Once these goals are attained, the country may become ready for a proletarian revolution, in which the working class attempts to overthrow the bourgeoisie itself. Throughout the book, Sertel remains convinced that Turkey has not been able to successfully complete its bourgeois revolution.

[9] TN: The first Turkish general election, to which Sertel is referring, was held on 28 June 1923. The *Cumhuriyet Halk Partisi* (Republican People's Party), officially founded on 9 September of the same year, governed the Turkish Republic from its foundation until 1950. During this period, Turkey was officially a one-party state from 1931 to 1945.

Kemal is staging a revolution; he is establishing a whole new order. Until that work is complete, he has no choice but to restrict certain freedoms.'

'But isn't the Assembly already full of such people – provincial bigwigs, landlords, pilgrims and *hodja*s? Will they really support Mustafa Kemal's reforms? No, certainly these reactionaries will continue to oppose his reforms. Mustafa Kemal is relying on such forces instead of the people. The Constitution has no articles on land reform or workers' rights. They say that Turkey is a classless society, but workers and peasants are oppressed. How are they supposed to protect their rights?'

This time, Mazhar Müfit restrained himself. He thought about the question before replying. 'Mustafa Kemal wants to carry out many reforms,' he said. 'He has talked to the landlords about land reform, especially the Kurdish landlords and Assembly members like Feyzi Bey. But the redistribution of land is a tough nut. It's impossible to get the landlords and local notables on board with it. If we force the issue, we'll lose their support. So we've decided to put land reform on the shelf for now.'

And so, the issue was shelved. But it never truly came off the shelf again. Even when it was raised from time to time, it was immediately buried under pressure from the landlords and provincial bigwigs. It took the 27 May movement[10] to bring land reform in the spotlight and finally address it in the Constitution. Until then, the reform proposals brought before the Assembly simply could not be realized. And the same holds true today.

*

One day, at a meeting in the Turkish Hearth building, I talked to Ağaoğlu Ahmet Bey, a member of the Constitutional Commission. I asked him what people meant when they called Turkey a classless society. He replied:

> I don't get that one, either. They say the Turkish nation is one totality without classes. Well, every nation is a totality. But still, there are classes within it. A classless society can only exist under a socialist regime. But we aren't drafting a socialist constitution or fostering a socialist community. The draft we are preparing stresses private property, free competition and free trade. This is a liberal constitution. All articles we have penned so far are built on this foundation.
>
> Now, suddenly, people are talking about a classless society and statism.[11] They want to see the principle of statism in the Constitution. But this goes against all the articles we have ratified so far.
>
> We had a long conversation about this with Mustafa Kemal. Finally, he got angry and said, 'I want state socialism.' I reminded him that this Constitution had been drafted not according to the principles of socialism, but those of liberalism. I said there was no need to enshrine statism in the Constitution. I told him that if he favoured populism, he could achieve it through democracy. And if he wanted the state to control public corporations and regulate profits, he could do that within a capitalist system. But I just can't get through to him.

---

[10] TN: Sertel is referring to the May 27, 1960, military coup in Turkey.
[11] TN: State control over the economy.

This conversation between Ağaoğlu and Atatürk highlights the conditions under which the 1924 Constitution was drafted, and the difficulties Atatürk faced in making it a revolutionary document. To intellectuals like Ağaoğlu, a democratic bourgeois revolution simply meant translating the constitutions of Western nations and copying their institutions. They didn't take local idiosyncrasies and social fabric into account. As a result, it was unclear what kind of revolution they had in mind.

Atatürk was surrounded on all sides by reactionaries, conservatives and liberals. The opposition was strongest in Istanbul. It included supporters of the *sharia*, those whose interests were threatened by the collapse of the sultanate, and conservative intellectuals who were afraid of the reforms. The Istanbul press criticized the new regime and attacked Mustafa Kemal. Those who were scared of his strong personality wanted to strip him of his powers. And even many intellectuals who supported him failed to grasp the significance of his six principles – republicanism, statism, populism, laicism, revolutionism and nationalism. These were the strenuous conditions under which he was working.

All these matters of revolution and affairs of the state were freely discussed at Atatürk's dinner table. At this table, Mustafa Kemal listened to everyone's thoughts and allowed his own sharp mind to draw the necessary conclusions. He made decisions accordingly and implemented them at once. No one was able to withstand his force. But the whole process was very abstract. There was no effort to analyse the objective and subjective conditions existing in the country, or to grasp the country's economic structure through scientific research.

The Ankara of 1923 was tossed to and fro between such diametrically opposed ideas. The Turkish people, in the meantime, were unaware of all these talks and deliberations. The new state would be a republic, but this was only discussed behind closed doors. Then, on 29 October, the republic was sprung on the public – practically overnight – and enshrined in the Constitution. The proclamation hit the nation like a bombshell. In one fell swoop, this change to Turkey's state system destroyed the foundations of the sultanate underlying the Ottoman Empire and laid the groundwork for the new Republic of Turkey.

The social survey project

While Zekeriya was working as the director general of the Press, he was also publishing a journal called *Ayın Tarihi* [History of the Month]. It reported on the political events of the month, compiled political newspaper articles and collected politicians' public statements. I had no job in Ankara. Just around then, Fuat Bey, the chairman of the Society for the Protection of Children, repeated the offer he'd made in New York about working together. Frankly, I wanted to work in community organization, but working on children's issues was better than not doing anything at all.

I told Fuat Bey that I'd work with him, but not as a member of the Society's general assembly or a director on its board. Instead, I told him to employ me as a commissioned expert. I wanted to start by conducting a local survey to understand the scope of children's issues. This social survey would be a first step toward analysing the situation in other parts of the country.

'Let me prepare this social survey project and submit it to you,' I said. 'We'll have it evaluated by a scientific committee and discuss how to carry it out. The Society's general assembly can decide on whether it will be implemented.'

The board of directors approved the project's development. Once it was ready, the project would be discussed by a committee of experts. Children's issues were not just limited to protecting and sheltering the tens of thousands of children who had ended up on the streets in the preceding years of war. They encompassed many topics at the national level, such as children's education and health, the number of available schools, teaching personnel, children of women who were employed, children employed in mines and other hard labour, children born out of wedlock, adopted children and laws for the protection of children. The social survey was intended to lay the whole situation bare so that the state could pursue solutions as necessary.

In order to cure an illness, one must first know what the illness is. To ascertain the realities on the ground as accurately as possible, the project would include many questions and testimonials. I was convinced that real societal change could not be brought about by bureaucrats without knowledge of the country's economic, social and cultural structure, or by simply translating foreign laws into our language. A nation attempting a revolution needed to employ scientific methods in all areas. It needed to assess conditions in the country in order to take measures grounded in science. This social survey would be a trial. It could cause no possible harm, but if successful, it would be of great service to the homeland.

It didn't take me long to prepare the project. We would conduct our first investigation in the villages surrounding Ankara, so I gathered some information about them. Having studied the subject extensively at the School of Social Work, I designed a project that would address the most salient issues according to the country's specific conditions. We talked with Doctor Fuat Bey about the committee to evaluate the project and agreed on some experts: Ziya Gökalp for social issues; Hikmet Bey, an Ankara-based doctor, for health-related issues; Nafi Atuf, a pedagogical expert, for matters related to education; Yusuf Kemal Tengirşenk, the Minister of Justice, for legal matters; Doctor Yusuf for issues related to psychology and psychiatry; and other names I can't recall. The board of directors approved the evaluation of the project by these experts. Everything was in order.

A few days before the meeting of this scientific committee, Fuat Bey said to me:

'Latife Hanım, Mustafa Kemal's wife, is the honorary chairperson of our society.[12] I told her about the project you prepared. She wants to talk to you and hear about the project before the meeting.'

We agreed on a day for her visit. I saw nothing wrong with informing Latife Hanım about the project. After all, she might have had some good ideas to contribute.

Fuat Bey and I met Latife Hanım at the Society's headquarters, in Fuat Bey's office. She was a slender, brunette beauty of medium height, dressed very soberly, her black cloak and headscarf lending her an air of maturity. I shared my ideas with her. She asked for the project to be read out loud. This took some time, but she listened carefully.

---

[12] TN: Latife Uşaklıgil (1898–1975) was married to Mustafa Kemal Atatürk from 1923 to 1925. Neither remarried after their divorce.

Afterward, I asked for her thoughts. She put down the glass ink-well she had been testily twiddling with and spoke up in an assertive manner.

'A well-prepared, comprehensive project,' she said. 'But it cannot be carried out in our country.'

I asked her why.

'These kinds of things can only be done in America,' she replied. 'The conditions here are not suitable for this.' She rose. 'Let the committee of experts review the project. If they approve it, you can implement it. But this is my personal opinion.'

Latife Hanım's words gave me a glimpse of the project's fate. Still, I thought that if the committee approved it, it stood a chance of being realized. The committee needed to convene as soon as possible.

One week after this meeting, the annual convention of the Society for the Protection of Children was held in the Turkish Hearth's conference hall. Atatürk attended together with Fethi Okyar, who was chairman of the Grand National Assembly at the time. Fuat Bey read out the annual statement concerning the society's work. While he was reading, Atatürk whispered something into Fethi Bey's ear. After Fuat Bey concluded, Fethi Bey stepped up to the podium. He said that the society's work didn't even begin to address the existing crises, that the issue wasn't how many children had been provided with milk or shirts and that children's issues needed to be addressed more seriously.

This talk gave me a glimmer of hope. Fethi Bey's words echoed some of the criticism I'd voiced in my project. After hearing this speech, I thought that the project might even have been discussed at Çankaya itself.[13]

A week later, the committee of experts convened in Fuat Bey's office. All those invited had come, with the exception of Yusuf Kemal, the Minister of Justice. After waiting half an hour, we decided to start the meeting without him. I briefly explained the project and read its text out loud. The experts listened with great interest. Afterwards, Ziya Gökalp spoke up.

'In these groundbreaking days,' he said, 'such a social survey might afford us immeasurable benefits. We have no statistics on the economic and social conditions of the people, and even if the results of this investigation should fall short of being fully scientific, they would still give us concrete information on many issues we don't know about and point us in the right direction. The topics to be analysed are well chosen. Still, it would be better to broaden these topics even more and include other issues vital to the homeland as well.'

The other experts concurred. They proposed various questions to be added under the rubrics of education and health. There was no big discussion, just some back and forth on the difficulties the project might face once it had been approved. But in principle, the experts agreed on the usefulness of the project. They also affirmed, in particular, that the project should first have a trial run in Ankara and its surroundings.

As the meeting continued in this enthusiastic manner, the door opened and Yusuf Kemal Bey, the Minister of Justice, came in. By then, the discussions had more or less ended. All that remained was to decide who would take on which task once the General

---

[13] TN: Atatürk's presidential residence. Sertel uses the term not just to refer to a location, but to the President and his office as well.

Assembly had approved the project. Yusuf Kemal apologized for arriving late. Then he turned to Fuat Bey.

'I see that a committee of experts has been assembled here,' he said, 'and some projects are being discussed. Did you get the approval of the General Assembly before inviting such a committee? Do they know about this?'

Fuat Bey turned bright red.

'We discussed and decided on this with the board of directors, sir.'

'The board of directors has no authority on this matter. This meeting is illegal. The General Assembly has to decide whether such a project is necessary or not. You can only invite experts after that.'

Fuat Bey replied that the committee of experts wouldn't make any final decisions about the project anyway. If this scientific committee approved the project, it would come before the Society's General Assembly, which would be the final arbiter. This meeting, he argued, was purely advisory and could, indeed, be convened by the board of directors.

Yusuf Kemal didn't budge. The experts started arguing with him. For more than an hour, they debated whether the meeting was illegal or not, almost all of them maintaining that it was legal. I listened with composure as the discussion went on. The only thing that saddened me was that people should focus on such trifling bureaucratic matters when an issue concerning the homeland was at stake.

It proved impossible to deter Yusuf Kemal from his claim. By now, it was clear to me that Çankaya was behind this turn of events. I hadn't forgotten Latife Hanım's parting words. The discussion went on for another while. Finally, Ziya Gökalp got up in exasperation.

'Let the authorities decide if this meeting is legal or not,' he said. 'Then, they can invite us again. We'll go back to work when they ask us to.' He left, angrily slamming the door behind him. The other experts followed him.

The only ones left in the room were Fuat Bey, Yusuf Kemal, Zekeriya and myself. Another long discussion ensued between Zekeriya and Yusuf Kemal. Finally, the latter said that he was 'under obligation to comply with the law' and left.

I turned to Fuat Bey.

'Fuat Bey, what's the meaning of all this?'

Once again, Fuat Bey turned bright red. He couldn't answer.

'This is Çankaya's doing, isn't it?'

He hung his head. 'Probably,' he said.

'No, not probably. Certainly. You know very well that Latife Hanım was opposed to this project. Yusuf Kemal Bey dissolved this meeting in order to please her ladyship.'

Fuat Bey gave no reply. He was thinking. It was obvious from his face that he was afraid.

'You do understand,' I said, 'that I cannot work here under these conditions? If I'm not even allowed to carry out a simple scientific project, what chance will my other ideas have? Wouldn't I be putting you in a difficult position as well?'

Fuat Bey said nothing.

'Can we expect the General Assembly to vote in favour of convening a committee of experts?'

'I don't think so.' He looked quite miserable.

I took a pen from the table and started writing: 'I don't believe I can be of use at an institution where it is not even possible to perform a scientific investigation.' That was my letter of resignation.

Returning to Istanbul

My younger daughter, Yıldız, was sick, and I needed to take her to Istanbul for treatment. On the train, I thought about the failure of my initiative and tried to find a reason. Perhaps it was really too early for this kind of scientific work. Still, what would have been the harm in getting the opinions of scientific experts on such an issue? The whole thing had been quite an experience for me.

Shortly thereafter, I received a letter from Zekeriya telling me he would be returning to Istanbul as well. He had resigned his post in protest against press censorship. It had started with a news item published in the Istanbul papers, proclaiming that the press would soon be censored. Zekeriya had issued a denial at once. Before long, he had been summoned by Ferit Bey, the Interior Minister. 'How do you know,' Ferit Bey had asked him, 'that the government does not intend to impose censorship?' Zekeriya had responded by handing in his resignation, stating that he 'could not be the press director of a democratic regime while imposing censorship'. After six months of effort, the Ankara experience had ended in failure for both of us.

I had returned from America with such fanciful dreams. I had prepared to work for the good of the people in the heart of Anatolia. But now, the dream was over and reality showed us its true face. Zekeriya told me he would return to journalism, his actual profession, and proposed that I work with him. This meant abandoning my own vocation. But what could I achieve in that field anyway? Teach sociology at a school? I wanted to work in a broader setting, grapple with social issues and disseminate my learning and ideas. Journalism seemed a suitable outlet for this.

4

Publishing *Resimli Ay*

Upon returning from Ankara, Zekeriya founded a company with Suudi Bey, one of the prominent publishers on Istanbul's Ankara Avenue. They conceived a brand new magazine, unique in both form and content. It was called *Resimli Ay* [Illustrated Monthly] and was first published on 1 February 1924. The inaugural issue featured an editorial explaining the goals of the magazine.

Figure 4.1 *Resimli Ay* (Illustrated Monthly), the Sertels' groundbreaking magazine, launched in 1924, aimed at a general audience and served as a forum for opposition voices. Sabiha Sertel's advice column 'Cici Anne',[1] published in the magazine, provided a ground-level view of how Turkish families were handling revolutionary social reforms.

---

[1] TN: "Cici Anne" was a popular advice column that first appeared in two prominent Turkish journals, *Resimli Ay* and *Resimli Hafta*, and subsequently in one of Turkey's preeminent daily newspapers, *Cumhuriyet*, 'Abstract', Ada Holland Shissler, "'If You Ask Me": Sabiha Sertel's Advice Column, Gender Equity, and Social Engineering in the Early Turkish Republic', *Journal of Middle East Women's Studies* 3, 2 (2007), pp. 1–30, see: https://muse.jhu.edu/article/215579.

'So far,' it stated, 'two types of journals have been published in our country. The first type, literary journals, only appeal to a limited audience. The articles in them are written according to the literary tastes of their authors. The other type, second-rate journals, are published by booksellers and amateurs seeking fame and fortune. *Resimli Ay* belongs to neither group. Our goal is to put out a sensible journal that satisfies the reading needs of our country's people. To us, an article's value is not determined by who wrote it, but by how many people read it. The articles, stories and features to be published in *Resimli Ay* will not be geared toward the literary tastes of a rarefied group. They will have a broader appeal and satisfy the people's emotional, intellectual and aesthetic needs. This is a bold new direction in the world of publishing.'

As this editorial suggests, *Resimli Ay* aimed to raise the public's cultural level. The primary goal was to enlighten the 80 per cent of the country who were illiterate, had no decent education and were disregarded by our intellectuals, and to explain to them what democracy actually meant. *Resimli Ay* also hoped to address the social problems of the New Turkey after the War of Independence; to expose the economic, social and cultural deficiencies the republic had inherited from the sultanate; and to search for possible solutions. Its goal was not to analyse the issues from a scholarly and theoretical perspective, but to convey existing theories to common people in a language they could understand. In a way, *Resimli Ay* was a popular magazine. But it was a magazine that would raise the cultural bar for the masses.

The magazine's style of propaganda[2] was also completely new. Instead of dishing up ideas in the form of clichés and dogmas, it wanted to show how these ideas were

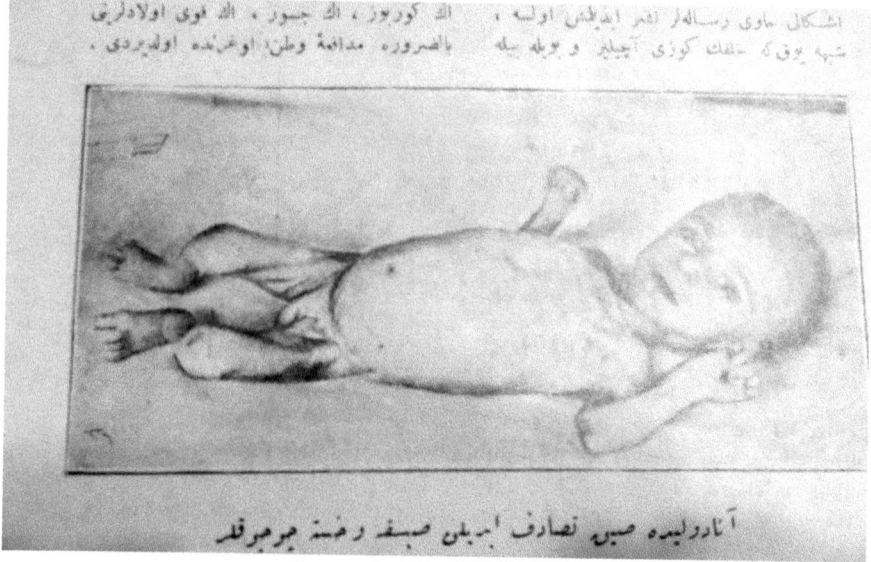

Figure 4.2 An article advocating for child welfare reforms.

---

[2] TN: Sertel uses the word in its value-neutral meaning of 'disseminating ideas and principles'.

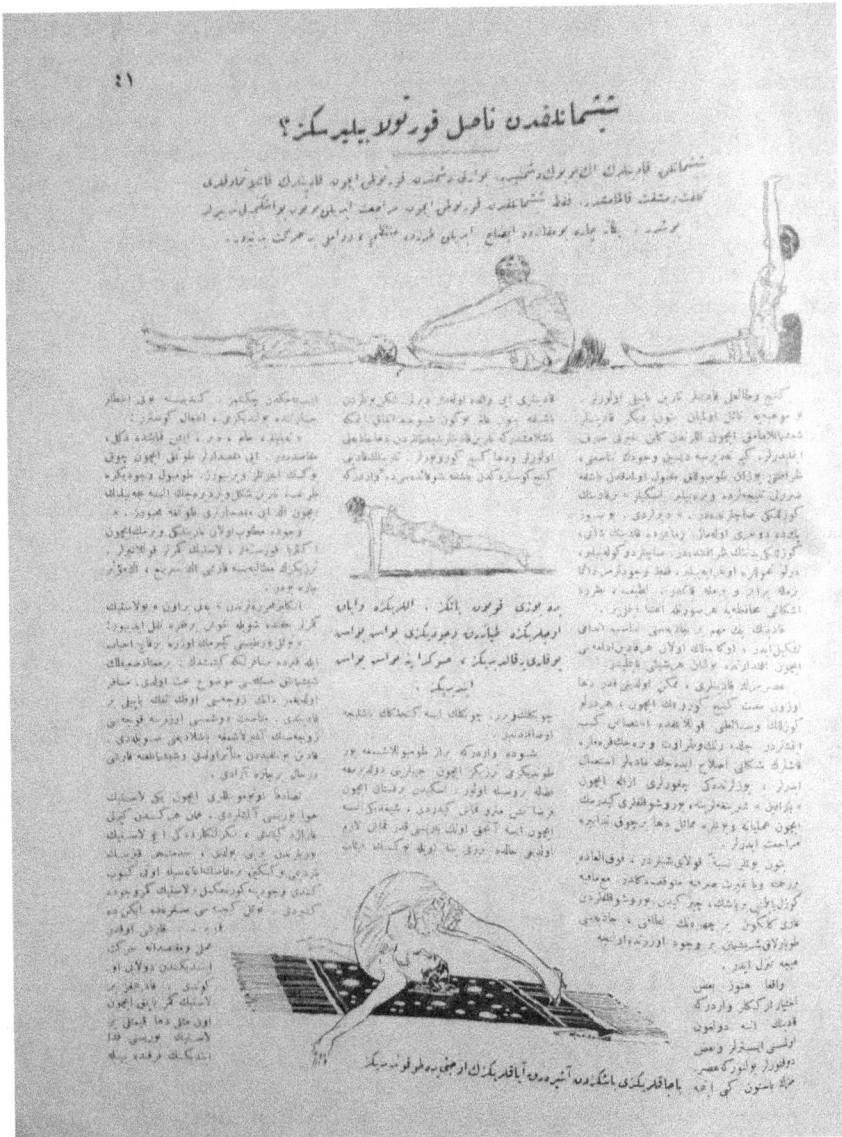

Figure 4.3 Modern young woman exercising in underwear.

relevant to people's daily lives and how they could be implemented. The magazine emphasized real-life topics and articles that would win hearts and minds.

The magazine's novelty in form, content and approach was embraced by the masses and intellectuals alike. The first issue went through three print runs, a very auspicious start. We received letters from different parts of Anatolia showing the interest that the magazine had awakened in people. Other press outlets in Istanbul and the provinces heaped praise on the magazine from the second issue onward. The newspapers *Vakit*, *İkdam*, and *İleri* [Forward], in particular, regarded *Resimli Ay* as the most literary, brilliant and splendid magazine in Turkey.

Resimli Ay's editorial staff was composed of the best-known literati of the age, including Mehmet Rauf, İbnül Refik Ahmet Nuri, Reşat Nuri, Yusuf Ziya, Hakkı Suha, Ercüment Ekrem, Hıfzı Tevfik, Sadri Ertem, Selim Sırrı, Mahmut Yesari and Yakup Kadri.

Resimli Ay was published over seven years, which can be divided into two periods. From 1924 to 1928, the magazine investigated issues related to the recent war and social issues, with an eye to enabling a true democracy. Zekeriya and I were responsible for most of the intellectual content, while the literary pieces were written by the staff mentioned above. In addition, we published articles to enhance people's general knowledge.

The second period lasted from 1928 to 1930 and showcased the birth of a new literature. Progressive and socialist ideas took centre stage in articles and stories. The editorial staff had also changed by then. Writers like Nazım Hikmet, Sabahaddin Ali, Suat Derviş, Vala Nureddin and Sadri Ertem emerged as the champions of a leftist literature. Stories and poems no longer simply reflected the predilections of their authors as in the old days, but exposed social realities. It was impossible to openly voice socialist ideas, and stories and articles had to tread carefully. Still, we can say that those years marked the birth of the country's socialist literature.

In spite of our best efforts, the owners of *Resimli Ay* were taken to court and sentenced again and again on account of these pieces. The remainder of this chapter will recount the various stages of this arduous struggle.

The Age of Reforms

At the time *Resimli Ay* started publishing, the Grand National Assembly was embroiled in crucial debates. The sultanate and caliphate had come to an end, and the republic had been proclaimed. The discussions centred on establishing a regime based on the sovereignty of the people, separating religion and state, and creating an education system that reflected current developments.

Atatürk's progressive ideas caused anxiety among the reactionaries who were eager to preserve the old traditions and whatever else remained from the days of the sultanate. The word in government circles was that a democratic regime would be established. But the specific form of this democracy led to heated debates. Atatürk wanted all authority to be vested in the Grand National Assembly, which would elect the president and also oversee the cabinet.[3] He also argued that the president should have extraordinary powers and participate in cabinet meetings. The Republican People's Party, founded by Atatürk, was to be the leading party.

Conservative circles opposed these ideas and confronted Atatürk. His comrades-in-arms during the War of Independence, his closest friends, such as Refet, Ali Fuat

---

[3] TN: The Council of Ministers.

(Cebesoy), Cevat Pasha, Kazım Karabekir, Doctor Adnan (Adıvar), Halide Edip and Rauf (Orbay), stepped up the opposition they'd started during the war. Members of the Istanbul press, among them Velit Ebuzziya, Hüseyin Cahit, Ahmet Emin Yalman (who had formerly championed a foreign mandate) and Rauf Ahmet, used their papers to denounce his every step and proclaim that the regime was headed toward dictatorship.

The Grand National Assembly, founded in the harsh days of the war, had never been a harmonious gathering. A hodgepodge of *hodja*s, Ottoman intellectuals, high-ranking bureaucrats and military officers, it was unable to carry out decisive change. Its members were committed to opposing tenets of faith and thought, making it impossible for them to unite around a revolutionary programme.

The intellectuals gathered around Atatürk talked about populism[4] and Westernization, claiming that a new Turkey would be established. But they lacked a road map for this revolution. They simply wanted to copy the West, without examining the social and economic structure of the country or determining its objective and subjective conditions. The Justice Minister, Mahmut Esat (Bozkurt), promoted a classless regime based on social justice while his very own party members sought to curtail the most basic rights of workers and peasants. Even İsmet İnönü[5] was afraid of the pace of change and assumed the stance of a mediator between the two sides. The arguments between the Progressive Republican Party,[6] founded by Kazım Karabekir Pasha, and the Republican People's Party turned into a veritable war.

At this moment in time, Atatürk decided to publish a newspaper in Istanbul to disabuse people about the opposition. He assigned the seasoned journalist Yunus Nadi Bey to the task. The resulting paper, *Cumhuriyet* [Republic], joined the fray on 24 May 1924. Zekeriya and Nebizade Hamdi were involved, and I was given my own feature column as well.[7]

Working at *Cumhuriyet*

Until that time, newspaper columns had always adhered to a particular form and content. Even Ahmet Rasim, the most famous columnist of the day, limited himself to recounting the Ramadans, customs and traditions of yore and expounding on the concepts of woman and family in his own distinct style. He didn't touch on daily social matters, and neither did the other columnists.

In my own column, just as in *Resimli Ay*, I examined the grievances of the population and tried to determine the social reasons behind them. This style of column-writing became very successful. Every day, readers' letters piled up on my desk. These letters, in turn, revealed new, unknown problems.

---

[4] TN: As a Kemalist principle, populism proclaims the sovereignty of the people.
[5] TN: İsmet İnönü (1884–1973) was Atatürk's second-in-command, served multiple terms as prime minister under his presidency and succeeded him as the president of Turkey.
[6] TN: Founded upon Atatürk's encouragement on 17 November 1924, this opposition party was banned again on 5 June 1925.
[7] TN: Sertel's column, 'Cici Anne' (Sweet Mother), was a popular advice column aimed at readers grappling with the tensions caused by social reforms, especially women's rights.

One day, I read the following news in the papers:

> A child of three weeks has been found at the Fatih concourse. A tag on his chest states he is Muslim and his name is Mehmet Seyda. The hapless mother asks the finder to take the child to the Darülaceze[8] orphanage.

The next day, the papers reported that the mother had been found and interrogated by the Prosecutor's Office.

'I have four children,' she told the prosecutor. 'My husband used to work for the Reji tobacco factory. He was fired and has been unemployed for six months. My fifth child was about to be born and we had no way of providing for him. So I left him at the concourse three weeks after his birth.'

I covered the issue in a column entitled 'One More Plate Crushed the Table Like a Mountain.'[9] I wrote that no mother would willingly abandon her child, her own flesh and blood, and maintained that the social roots of this issue needed to be addressed:

> If a union had lent its helping hand to the worker who was jobless for months and if society had taken him under its wing, this woman wouldn't have abandoned her child. There are no organizations to protect the hungry, the jobless and the orphans. That's why these social tragedies occur and mothers are forced to abandon their children, who are often born out of wedlock and with no means of subsistence. Society is responsible for this affair, not the unfortunate mother.

A few days later, I received a summons from the Prosecutor's Office. I went over. The prosecutor asked about my intention in writing that column. I smiled.

'I didn't write it for the money,' I said, 'that much is certain. What do you think my intention was? I was criticizing the indifference and lack of institutions, which lead to social tragedies.'

'No. This column was written to denounce the republican regime and to cause enmity between the classes!'

'Cases such as this one,' I answered, 'occurred before the republican regime as well. It was during the sultanate that the poet Tevfik Fikret penned the line, "one more plate crushed the table, like a mountain". I wrote this column to argue that in the republican era, no extra plate should crush a table, like a mountain.'

But I couldn't convince the prosecutor. He indicted me for the crime of denouncing the republican regime and causing hostility between the classes. The authorities in Ankara kept talking about 'social justice', but it was a crime for me to name the causes of a social issue.

Some days later, Yunus Nadi Bey summoned me to his office. *Cumhuriyet* was housed in Cağaloğlu, in an enormous mansion that used to be the headquarters of the

---

[8] TN: An Istanbul-based charitable foundation of the Ottoman and Turkish state, providing aid and shelter to the needy.
[9] TN: The title indicates that the financial weight of one more mouth to feed was too much to bear for the family.

Committee for Union and Progress. Nadi Bey was at work on one of the upper floors, in his immaculately decorated office. When I entered, he stood up, shook my hand and sat me down across from him.

'What happened?' he asked. 'What does that prosecutor want from you?'

I told him what the column was about and gave him my own opinion about it. He listened carefully.

'This court case is not so important, but there is a bit too much criticism in your writings. You criticize the government a lot.'

'No, I'm not criticizing the government. It's not about Fethi Bey replacing Ismet Pasha or someone else replacing Fethi Bey. I'm criticizing the shortcomings of our social institutions.

We're establishing a democratic regime. A democratic regime needs to protect the sovereignty and interests of the people. We can't simply write those words on a sign at the assembly gate; we need to establish the institutions that go along with them. I'm advocating a democratic regime.'

'What does democracy have to do with a woman abandoning her child at a concourse?'

'This case is just a symptom of structural issues in society. As long as these issues are not addressed and remedied by specific institutions, there can be no real democracy. I'm not criticizing the political mechanism but the social mechanism.'

At this, Nadi Bey jumped up.

'That's even worse!' he said. 'That's even worse.'

I said nothing and got up as well. Nadi Bey advised me to be a little more careful in my writings. He shook my hand and we parted.

In court

It was my first time entering a courtroom. In those days, the courthouse was in the Sultan Ahmet District. Above the entrance, there was a depiction of scales. These were supposed to be the scales of justice. They were topped by an inscription that read, 'Justice is the foundation of the state.' I felt calm as I walked into this palace of justice, charged with protecting the foundation of the state. After all, I had committed no crime. I was not the woman who had abandoned the child at the concourse.

The bailiff called out my name, and I went into the courtroom. It was very small and could hold only forty to fifty people. Three judges in black gowns sat behind the slightly raised bench. To one side, the prosecutor had taken his place at his own raised podium. There was a row of chairs surrounded by a circular iron railing. They sat me down in one of them. I didn't have a lawyer. I didn't believe any lawyer could defend this case as well as I could.

After the initial questions, the judge asked about my intentions in writing the column. I repeated the answers I'd given to the prosecutor.

'The column clearly states its own purpose,' I said. 'It describes the hardships that led this mother to commit an offense. It exposes the causes of such events, tries to find ways to prevent or at least reduce them, and suggests precautions. Is that a crime? It's your duty to implement the law, so perhaps you'll condemn the mother for abandoning her child. But I am a writer who investigates social issues, and my duty is to examine the maladies and injustices in society. We need unions to protect workers and community organizations to protect the poor. To me, there is no greater justice than that. Use the scales at the gate of this courthouse to weigh these social issues.'

The prosecutor jumped up at once.

'That is not the subject of this case. This article incites workers against their employers and government. It denounces the regime!'

The judge asked for my response.

'I'm not denouncing the republican regime. I'm asking for social justice within the republican regime. I'm calling for the creation of institutions to protect the unemployed. If that's a crime,' I said, 'I'm guilty as charged.'

The prosecutor rose again. He read out the indictment. Apparently, I had committed all kinds of crimes.

I'd sown discord among workers, employers and unions by pointing out that workers didn't have the right to establish unions and that the existing unions didn't protect them. I'd incited the people against the government and caused enmity between the classes by writing that the government was indifferent to the plight of the people. I'd denounced the republican regime by saying the state hadn't lent a helping hand to a jobless worker. The list went on and on.

The judge asked whether I'd like the case to be adjourned to prepare my defence.

'No,' I said, 'I've already made my defence. It's clear what's going on here. The prosecutor has written this indictment for Machiavellian reasons. He wants to endear himself to Ankara. His statements do not constitute evidence. They are simply inferences based on his own judgement. The words "worker" and "employer" don't even occur in the article. They were supplied by the prosecutor's imagination. He asks for me to be punished because of these imaginary words. It is the judges' duty to administer justice. Let them decide whether this column legally constitutes a crime. I have nothing else to say.'

The judges stood up and retired for their deliberation. I waited in the empty room for half an hour. Finally, they returned. The court clerk read out the verdict. It stated that while the column's language was harsh, it contained no malicious intent. Therefore, I had been acquitted.

I was spared. But no one spared the mothers who were forced to abandon their children because of joblessness and poverty.

Resimli Ay's controversial articles

Resimli Ay continued publishing articles like this. In my pieces, I discussed and praised every progressive development in the homeland as well as Atatürk's reforms. But even the slightest note of criticism was met with disapproval. Some friends from Ankara told us that certain articles in *Resimli Ay* were frowned upon by the upper echelons in Ankara. I asked them which ones. 'For instance,' they said, 'the appeal you made to the country's youth.'

Around that time, the government had published the Declaration of Family Rights. It repealed the remaining portions of sharia law that limited women's rights and introduced certain new rights for women. My article applauded this change. It also argued that the whole world had been witnessing such changes for the better since the October Revolution in the Soviet Union and that it was time for us to catch up with these changes. However, the article criticized the country's youth and intellectuals for not showing enough interest in these issues. In such an age of rapid new developments, it argued, youths should organize to advance the revolution.

'What's wrong with this article?' I asked a friend from Ankara.

'You hold up the Soviets' October Revolution as an example. In other words, you want a socialist regime to be established in Turkey. You say that this country has only accepted a superficial form of democracy and call on the youth to oppose the government.'

'Socialism,' I replied, 'can't be founded just because I say so. For a society to be able to transition to a socialist regime, certain objective and subjective conditions must evolve. Turkey today is nowhere near that point. What I want is a bourgeois democratic revolution. I argue that we must go beyond a superficial democracy and establish a system that grants more equal rights to all classes. I want the youth to have a say in social and cultural matters, and I want them to organize. This is a prerequisite of democracy.'

The prevailing attitude in the National Assembly was to impose limits on freedom of expression, opinion and thought, just as had been the case during the Constitutional Era.[10] They had no tolerance for dissent. This was the main reason that my article was criticized. The governing circles claimed to have carried out a revolution, but some of them hadn't even grasped its nature.

Another example of this was the reaction to an article I wrote for the May 1924 issue of *Resimli Ay*. It was entitled 'When Will We Learn to Respect the Common Soldier?' and can be paraphrased as follows:

> The tram was gliding downhill from the Kroker Hotel toward Bankalar Caddesi.[11] As we descended at dizzying speed, I noticed a soldier through the window of the tram. Patiently, rifle on his shoulder, he was standing outside the gates of the gigantic Ottoman Bank without really knowing what he was doing there. Clearly, he was standing guard, but by whose authority had he been ordered to stand there? Is our common soldier the guardian of foreign capital?[12]
>
> By what privilege is the Ottoman Bank so different from other banks that our common soldier, the symbol of the entire breadth of our country, has to stand guard over it? Is this bank different from the others because the state has granted a

---

[10] TN: Sertel is referring to the Second Constitutional Era of the Ottoman Empire, starting in 1908, during which the Ottoman sultan shared power with Parliament.

[11] TN: 'Avenue of the Banks', a famous business street in Istanbul.

[12] TN: The Ottoman Bank was founded in 1856 as a joint venture between British and French interests and the Ottoman Government. It was heavily involved in the collection of Ottoman debt to foreign creditors and came to be seen as a symbol of Western imperialism.

privilege to foreign capital? Why is the soldier not standing guard at the National Credit Bank instead?

The government's police forces are responsible for maintaining public order in the homeland. The common soldier, on the other hand, represents the people and the army. By what power does he stand here, and what authority does that power wield?

The article led to an investigation. The examining magistrate summoned me and said the piece was hostile to capital. He declared that only communists were enemies of capital, that communism couldn't be defended in our homeland, that the prosecutor had examined the article as well, and that an investigation would be carried out.

I told the magistrate that the article wasn't hostile to all capital, but merely to the privileges enjoyed by foreign capital. Hadn't we, with the Treaty of Lausanne,[13] removed the capitulations[14] granted to foreign nations? Wasn't Atatürk himself an enemy of foreign capital? Didn't he call for the disbanding of foreign companies? And if so, why was the common soldier guarding the Ottoman Bank? Taking this article to court, I said, meant going against the principles of Atatürk himself.

The magistrate was visibly shaken. 'Of course,' he said, 'we will take that into consideration.'

The case never made it to court. Shortly thereafter, the soldier in front of the Ottoman Bank was removed. But this investigation was just one example of how prosecutors and judges failed to understand the nature of the revolution.

Another article that led to censure and showcased the so-called revolutionaries' idea of democracy was my February 1925 piece entitled 'The Democracy of Hüseyin Ağa'. The story went like this:

> Hüseyin Ağa is a peasant. During the last days of the War of Independence, he desires to see Atatürk and is granted an audience. He complains to Atatürk about the swamps on the roads and the destitution of the peasantry.
>
> In 1925, on a trip to Konya, Atatürk visits Hüseyin Ağa's house. He tells Hüseyin Ağa that he 'didn't see any swamps on the way here'.
>
> 'My pasha,' Hüseyin Ağa replies, 'you should see the roads in winter. The municipality started building them but couldn't finish them. Don't funnel all the money to Ankara, son. Leave some of it out here. Let the municipality do its work. They decided to build a school next to our house. They put 300 liras in the bundle (the budget), but it wasn't enough. Show us some charity so the school can get built. At the Agricultural Bank, they give loans to peasants who come in and vouch for each other. But in Konya, they want a merchant to vouch for you. Not everyone can get a merchant to vouch for him. And if you ask me, my pasha, you should appoint the local officials from among the farmers.'

---

[13] TN: The international peace treaty signed in 1923 and establishing Turkish sovereignty within the borders of modern Turkey.

[14] TN: Trading privileges granted by the Ottoman Empire to certain other states and their representatives.

And this was my take on the matter:

> In a mere three or four sentences, Hüseyin Ağa sums up the wishes of the peasants, who form the backbone of Anatolia. In this age when the leaders at the top mingle with the people, Hüseyin Ağa has the right to know how his money is being spent. His vote, interests and grievances are relevant to every affair of the state. In his heartfelt way, Hüseyin Ağa is saying that this new age has not benefitted him all that much. He wants the swamps on the roads to be drained. He wants a school to be built in his village. The peasants can't use the bank. Why not? The democracy that Hüseyin Ağa wants is the one that will uplift his village.

It was clear why Ankara didn't approve of this article. The heady days of the War of Independence were over, and many of those in charge were chasing after their own personal interests. There was no doubt that they saw such criticism as an obstacle to those interests. But the piece that angered Ankara the most was Zekeriya's article entitled 'At the Monument of the Unknown Soldier'. In the September 1924 issue of *Resimli Ay*, Zekeriya wrote in praise of the Victory of Dumlupınar,[15] explained its significance and discussed the importance of the common soldier in the War of Independence:

> Until that point, the common soldier's stake in such victories was seized by haughty pashas and sultans, who took all the credit, lauding themselves by pretending the common soldier's valour and victories were their own.
>
> Today, for the first time, we celebrate the valour and sacrifice of the common soldier himself. In commemorating the War of Independence and the Victory of Dumlupınar, we do not remember some pasha but the common soldier, and we salute the shared ideal, the shared hero of the entire population. The Unknown Soldier is an embodiment of valour, an exemplar of self-sacrifice. The ceremony of Dumlupınar is meaningful to us because it marks this historic day and acquaints the state and the people alike with the Unknown Soldier.

Kılıç Ali Bey, one of Atatürk's comrades in arms, published a reply to this article in the newspaper *Akşam* [Evening]. He maintained that the Anatolian victory was Atatürk's, and Atatürk's alone, that the common soldier was merely following orders and that Atatürk's genius had won the day. He tried to prove his obedience to the pasha by acting as if Zekeriya's piece had been an attack on Atatürk. But all the article did was point out that in the old days, pashas and sultans had denied the importance of the common soldier and that today, for the first time, the common soldier was being acknowledged.

Those who misconstrued *Resimli Ay*'s struggle for democracy, those whose interests were threatened by debate, continued to try and stifle criticism at any price. Further on, I will discuss Zekeriya's trial by the Independence Tribunal.[16] He was ostensibly

---

[15] TN: The decisive victory won by the Turkish national resistance against the Greek army in 1922. The date of the victory, 30 August, is a Turkish national holiday.
[16] TN: The highly controversial Independence Tribunals were special, temporary courts founded between 1920 and 1927 to rapidly condemn perceived enemies of the Turkish independence movement and the early Turkish state.

indicted for a piece he'd published in *Resimli Perşembe* [Illustrated Thursday], but the real reason were the articles, such as the one above, that he'd published in *Resimli Ay*.

Opposition in the National Assembly

Opposition was on the rise, not only in the press but also in the National Assembly. The reactionaries formed a front to counter Atatürk's moves, their heads spinning from all the reforms he made. Following Atatürk's instructions, the press law was changed. But its new articles promising more press freedom also came with provisions curtailing the press. The Constitution was changed. A relatively democratic charter made it through the National Assembly, but neither land reform nor workers' rights were addressed in it. The education and judiciary systems were also changed. Remarkably, all institutions related to organized religion were dissolved within a week. The caliphate was abolished. The caliph and the Ottoman dynasty were banished from the country. The *şeyhülislam*[17] was excluded from the cabinet. The ministries of sharia law and pious foundations were turned into lower-ranking directorates. The homeland was witnessing major transformations in the blink of an eye.

Resimli Ay published articles in praise of all these progressive steps. The magazine was only critical when democracy was not fully put into practice. Were these criticisms appropriate at a time when the revolution was not yet firmly established, when the reactionary opposition was in fact growing stronger? Maybe not. But we genuinely desired the establishment of a democratic regime and wanted to point out the current shortcomings. The reactionary press and the parliamentary opposition, on the other hand, were against these new steps. Even within the People's Party, there was no full agreement on fundamentals, since the party's parliamentary ranks were filled with conservatives, defenders of sharia law, hodjas and revolutionaries alike. The People's Party, founded by Atatürk, had spearheaded the War of Independence. The party's opponents conceded that much. But they claimed that things were back to normal now and that other parties should enjoy equal rights and entitlements. Some went as far as calling for the People's Party to be abolished.

This dissension resulted in the establishment of a splinter party, the Progressive Party, led by people such as Kazım Karabekir Pasha, Rauf Orbay and Ali Fuat Pasha. The party immediately took on the role of opposition in parliament. Where the People's Party wanted elections to be held in two stages, the Progressive Party insisted on one stage. The former party was centralist, the latter against centralization. But most importantly, the People's Party wanted to grant the president extraordinary powers such as the right to veto parliamentary decisions. The Progressive Party objected to this as well. It claimed that giving the president too much power would lead to domination and tyranny down the line. It wanted opposition parties to have the right to investigate the People's Party to keep it in check. Atatürk realized that this group wasn't just targeting him but his reforms as well. They seemed concerned with limiting the

---

[17] TN: The supreme religious official of the Ottoman state.

president's powers, but in reality they wanted to curtail the dizzying steps he was taking. And so, the Assembly turned into a battlefield between these two political parties.

This reactionary opposition movement even included defenders of the caliphate. In order to implement the changes and reforms he had in mind, Atatürk eventually found it necessary to shut down this movement. In the end, the Progressive Party was dissolved.

The Sheikh Said Rebellion

For *Resimli Ay*'s writers, 1925 was a year of mind-boggling work. On the one hand, we kept up the struggle for democracy and our support for reforms. On the other, we continued criticizing the shortcomings in their implementation.

In the meantime, *Resimli Hafta* [Illustrated Week], a popular magazine we published without political objectives, was shut down (I can't remember why). Instead, we started printing a weekly journal called *Resimli Perşembe* and two monthly journals for children, *Resimli Yıl* [Illustrated Year] and *Çocuk Ansiklopedisi* [Children's Encyclopedia]. In just a year, thanks to the interest of the masses, *Resimli Ay* became an institution, accomplishing valuable work. We moved our headquarters to a pasha's mansion in Cağaloğlu, called The House of Koca Bıçak.[18] We used two floors for office space and lived on the upper floor. New writers such as Cevat Şakir (known by his pen name, The Fisherman of Halicarnassus), Ercüment Ekrem and Ömer Bedreddin joined the editorial staff. We worked from eight in the morning until ten at night.

Around that time, a new crisis occurred. The papers reported distressing news from the east: a rebellion had broken out under the command of Sheikh Said.[19] On 21 March 1925, *Cumhuriyet* published the government's official statement: 'On the night of the 18th and 19th, the Koç tribe attacked Çemeşgüzek. Local forces stopped the rebellion.' However, subsequent reports showed that the rebellion was not restricted to such a small area. It had sprung up in many eastern provinces at once and rapidly spread to Elazığ, Diyarbakır and other parts of the east. A short while later, the rebellion was suppressed. An Independence Tribunal was established in Diyarbakır and started carrying out trials at lightning speed. Thousands of rebels were sentenced to death and hanged.

While this rebellion was planned by regressive elements such as sheikhs and feudal landlords, it was also a movement for Kurdish independence. Many documents seized during the trials, as well as articles published in the foreign press, showed that the British had instigated the rebellion. The government, however, merely presented it as a reactionary movement. If the news from Ankara was to be believed, the rebels had read the Istanbul papers, felt that their religion was under threat and taken up arms as a result. The government wanted to use the rebellion as an excuse to silence opposition newspapers and stifle any kind of criticism. Even before the trials ended, the Law on the Maintenance of Order was issued.[20] Journalists in Istanbul and elsewhere were arrested.

---

[18] TN: A nickname meaning 'large knife'.
[19] TN: Sheikh Said (d. 1925) was a Kurdish religious leader.
[20] TN: A law granting the government far-reaching and exceptional powers such as the right to ban opposition groups.

The arrested journalists

Istanbul descended into an atmosphere of terror. As soon as the Law on the Maintenance of Order was passed, the police shut down the papers *Tevhidi Efkar* (which had replaced *Tasviri Efkar*), *Son Telgraf* and *İstiklal*.[21] They also closed the journal *Sebilülreşat*, a reactionary mouthpiece, and the journals *Orak Çekiç* and *Aydınlık*, published by the communists.[22] Many writers and publishers were taken into custody and packed off to the Independence Tribunal in Diyarbakır, among them Velit Ebuzziya, the owner of *Tevhidi Efkar*; Fevzi Lütfü Karaosmanoğlu, owner of the paper *Hareket*; the writer Sadri Ethem (Ertem); Ahmet Emin Yalman from the paper *Vatan*; Şükrü Esmer; Abdülkadir Kemali, owner of Adana's *Tok Söz*; the editors-in-chief of the papers *Sayha*[23] in Adana and *İstiklal* in Trabzon; Eşref Edip from *Sebilülreşat*; and Sadrettin Celal from *Orak Çekiç* and *Aydınlık*. Şefik Hüsnü, the editor-in-chief of the latter journal, couldn't be found and was tried in absentia.

These harsh measures were aimed not just at religious fanatics but also at workers' movements. The emerging bourgeoisie was using the crisis to crush its class enemies. The occasional strikes in big cities like Izmir, Ankara and Istanbul upset the government and employers. These strikes targeted foreign and domestic capital alike. Just as the rebellion broke out, the Assembly was debating changes to the labour law. The secretary general of the Society for the Promotion of Workers had sent private letters to the other workers' societies, inviting them to a meeting on the matter. On 8 May 1925, the newspaper *İkdam* reported that several societies attended the meeting. Among them were the Society of Labourers from the Istanbul Ferryboat Company; the Society for Roads, Transportation and Construction; the Society of Farm Labourers; the Society of Rowboat and Barge Operators; and the tram workers. The same newspaper also reported that Şevki Efendi, a member of the Society for the Promotion of Workers, had been arrested by the political police and sent to the Ankara Independence Tribunal.

Clearly, the Independence Tribunals' goal was to kill three birds with one stone: punish those involved with the Kurdish rebellion, silence the press and stall the workers' movements all at once.

What could the workers possibly have to do with the Sheikh Said rebellion or with religious zealots? They were simply demanding that the Labour Law discussed in the Assembly be changed in their favour. They were holding meetings and publishing pamphlets to inform other workers. In order to nip this movement in the bud, the government lumped the workers in with the reactionaries. That is why police shut down the journals *Orak Çekiç* and *Aydınlık* in Istanbul and why the writers who published them, such as Şefik Hüsnü and Sadreddin Celal, were dragged before the Independence Tribunals.

The Istanbul newspaper *Amele Sedası* [Worker's Voice], published by the Bulgarian immigrant Ethem Ruhi, criticized this attitude on 9 March 1925:

---

[21] TN: 'Unity of Ideas' (*Tevhidi Efkar*), 'The Latest Telegraph' (*Son Telgraf*) and 'Independence' (*İstiklal*).
[22] TN: 'Fountain of Righteousness' (*Sebilülreşat*), 'Sickle and Hammer' (*Orak ve Çekiç*) and 'Illumination' (*Aydınlık*).
[23] TN: 'Movement' (*Hareket*), 'Homeland' (*Vatan*), 'Resounding Word' (*Tok Söz*), 'Call' (*Sayha*).

The cabinet of Ismet Pasha passed a Law on the Maintenance of Order. The first article decrees that societies and newspapers will be shut down not just for evils such as reactionism, but also if they violate the social order and domestic safety. Some daily newspapers have already been closed. A connection was implied between this affair and the newspaper *Orak Çekiç* as well as the journal *Aydınlık*, both of which focus on issues concerning the Turkish worker. We wish the word 'worker' had not been implicated in such a crisis. This event should be a lesson for Turkish workers.

As the trials concluded, Sadreddin Celal from *Orak Çekiç* and *Aydınlık* as well as other journalists were exiled to various locations while Doctor Şefik Hüsnü was sentenced to fifteen years' prison in absentia.

The Ankara Independence Tribunal

The Ankara Independence Tribunal started operating soon thereafter. Following the events in the papers, I realized we were on the brink of a dark age. It didn't occur to me, though, that our own journals might be called into question. After all, *Resimli Ay* was the biggest defender of democracy and the ongoing reforms. But things didn't turn out the way I thought. One evening, two police officers and a soldier with a bayonet showed up at our door. They declared that Zekeriya had been summoned by the Ankara Independence Tribunal and that he needed to pack a change of clothes and go with them. He was taken into custody and transferred to Ankara that night.

What was Zekeriya's crime? I knew that the ruling circles were unhappy with our criticism. But it was hard to fathom what exactly he was accused of.

The next morning, I learned from the papers that Cevat Şakir had been detained because of an article he'd written in *Resimli Perşembe* and that Zekeriya had been detained as the proprietor of the journal. But which article in *Resimli Perşembe*? This was a popular journal exclusively devoted to lighter issues. If none of the important intellectual issues addressed in *Resimli Ay* had led to charges, how could an insignificant article published in *Resimli Perşembe* constitute a crime?

The reason became clear soon enough. Cevat Şakir previously had spent many years in prison for a crime he'd committed. In this new article, he described how during the CUP era, while he was in prison, deserters were hanged without trial in order to serve as a warning to others. The article described a previous era, so I didn't believe it could lead to a sentencing. Still, I was distressed that they had been packed off to Ankara in such an undignified manner.

On the other hand, I now had to think about publishing *Resimli Ay*, *Resimli Perşembe*, *Çocuk Dergisi* [Children's Journal], and *Çocuk Ansiklopedisi* on my own. I didn't know anything about the technical side of publishing. But with two key players like Zekeriya and Cevat gone, I had to shoulder the responsibility myself.

The journals were typeset in Babıali,[24] in a composing room on the upper floor of the Suudi Publishing House. When I went there with the articles that were ready, the

---

[24] TN: Istanbul's publishing district, comparable to London's Fleet Street.

typesetters welcomed me gloomily. Hayri Bey, the chief typesetter, was a master of his art and the chairman of the typesetters' union. He tried to console me and dejectedly told me that some members of the Society for the Promotion of Workers had been sent to the Independence Tribunal as well. But my thoughts were racing, and I didn't have the patience to listen to his comforting words.

'Hayri Bey,' I said, 'enough with the small talk. You need to teach me about the sorts.'[25]

Hayri Bey looked at me in astonishment.

'From now on, I will be binding the journals myself. I need to learn about the sorts.'

Hayri Bey opened a desk drawer and took out the printed booklets showing the letters, sorts and decorative lines used on the pages. The Latin alphabet had not been adopted yet, so everything was in the Ottoman script. Hayri Bey taught me the italics, the headings and the sorts as if he was giving a lesson to a child. I learned which sorts were used to typeset the articles in our journals and how the pages were bound. While the Independence Tribunals went on in Ankara, I was at home memorizing sorts as if studying for a class.

The arrests continued. The papers reported that the writer Hüseyin Cahid, Ata Çelebi from Adana and others had been sent to the Ankara Independence Tribunal. People were executed one after the other. And even though I kept calling my acquaintances in Ankara, I couldn't get any news about Zekeriya.

'It's impossible to see Zekeriya,' they told me. 'Nobody is allowed anywhere near the prison.'

My heart is in knots, I keep binding pages in the composing room. I complete the unfinished articles. Hayri Bey helps me, as does Recep, the typesetter. Recep is a tall, hulking worker, but he wasn't born yesterday. While binding the pages, he says to me: 'They didn't take away Zekeriya Bey for the article in *Resimli Perşembe*. They carried him off for the criticisms you and he made in *Resimli Ay*. Why,' he adds, 'are they mixing up the workers in this whole thing? Are the workers supposed to be reactionaries, too?'

'I know,' I reply, 'but knowing that doesn't change a thing.'

In Istanbul, the air is as heavy as lead.[26] The newspapers keep reporting on the Independence Tribunals in Diyarbakır and Ankara. The rumour mill is working overtime. We hear they are making Velit Ebüzziya Bey, the editor-in-chief of *Tevhidi Efkar*, draw water from a well and carry it to the prison wards. We hear they are making Ahmet Emin Yalman and Şükrü Esmer, the owners of *Vatan*, scrub the wooden floors of the wards.

I decide to delay putting out *Çocuk Ansiklopedisi* and *Çocuk Dergisi* until Zekeriya returns. I don't have enough strength to publish all the journals at once. The writers grow intimidated and stop sending in articles. The only writer who helps in any way he can is Hakkı Suha. I write more and more articles myself, using various male and female pseudonyms. Every day, I work until midnight. Zekeriya ends up spending two weeks in Ankara, but they seem like two years to me.

---

[25] TN: Metal pieces of type representing particular letters or symbols.
[26] TN: Sertel is paraphrasing a verse by Nazım Hikmet.

The papers report on Zekeriya's and Cevat Şakir's defence. No verdict has been reached yet. But even before this news makes it into the papers, I receive a telegraph from Zekeriya.

'Good news,' he writes, 'I've been sentenced to three years of fortress internment in Sinop.[27] I'm returning by train, so meet me at Haydarpaşa at such-and-such hour. From there, I will go right to Sinop.'

Good news? Three years' fortress internment in Sinop is good news? How exhilarating! I can't understand what Zekeriya means by this. But for me, three years of hardship lie ahead.

It was only later that I figured out what he meant by 'good news'. They had thrown Zekeriya in some dark, secluded corner of the prison, along with vicious murderers and people sentenced to death. Even his best friend, the parliamentarian Nebizade Hamdi, who was a member of the Independence Tribunal, hadn't been able to visit him there. From afar, he'd told Zekeriya, 'Don't be afraid. Even if the sentence is death, a way will be found.' After all this, Zekeriya was immensely relieved when he heard of the three years' fortress internment in Sinop. That was his idea of good news.

I turn the telegraph over and over, thinking about how to support a companion in exile and two little children, how to keep on publishing the journals under these harsh conditions. I don't know what fortress internment legally means, so I ask around. Salih Münir, a relative of Zekeriya's, who is a partner in *Resimli Perşembe* and works in the Security Directorate, tells me: 'They will throw him in a dungeon in the fortress and put a chain around his ankles.'

Cradling my face in my hands, I weep silently. I can't sleep until dawn. But when I get up in the morning, I chide myself. 'Sabiha,' I say, 'this is no time to cry. You'll overcome the hardships of life through determination and will.'

Putting my own feelings aside as if nothing has happened, I plan out the articles to be written, the things to be done that day. A chain around his ankles? As if he were a murderer! Lost in such thoughts, I go downstairs. Celal Deriş, my middle brother, is waiting for me there. He looks distraught but tries to hide his sadness and console me.

'What is fortress internment?' I ask him. 'They will put chains around his ankles...'

'That's nonsense. It means he will spend his exile inside the fortress. If the tribunal allows, he won't even be confined to it.'

These words put my mind at ease a little.

'What will you do now?' he asks.

'I'll keep on working.'

'Take your children and go to Sinop. I'll send you money until Zekeriya can return. You can pay me back afterward.'

My thoughts start to race. Three years of doing nothing. Living on borrowed money. Followed by even more years trying to pay back our debt...

'No. I will work. And the journals will come out.'

'You can't do it. These wolves of Babıali will gobble you up.'

'I'll try not to let them catch me.'

---

[27] TN: A town on the Turkish Black Sea Coast, about 643 km (400 miles) from Istanbul.

He does his best to change my mind, but to no avail. I have spent the entire night thinking the matter through, and I have made my decision. Nothing will deter me from it. My younger daughter, Yıldız, is two years old, and my older daughter, Sevim, is seven. She is trying to understand the conversation. She can sense that something is wrong.

'It's nothing,' I tell her. 'Your father is going on a long journey, but he will come back.'

She doesn't really understand.

I wait for Zekeriya at the Haydarpaşa Station, pacing up and down the platform. Finally, the train arrives. He gets off, flanked by two gendarmes carrying bayonets. These two weeks have aged him. He sees me, his arms fall around my neck, he starts crying. I cry as well. They allow us to talk for a couple of minutes. I tell him not to worry, that I will keep on publishing the journals. He is just glad he made it through his ordeal in one piece.

They take him to the police headquarters that night. The next day, they dispatch him to Sinop.

I go to the publisher. Suudi Bey, Zekeriya's partner in *Resimli Ay*, tells me that the journals can't be published under these circumstances.

'A condemned man can't put out a journal,' he adds. 'He can't hold the licence. Also, with the way things stand, the vendors can't make any payments to him. Let's stop now. It's better to lose the saddle than the horse.'

It's clear that he wants to take advantage of Zekeriya's absence to shut down the journals and seize the existing capital.

'We'll find someone to assume the licence, Suudi Bey. And the vendors will keep making their payments.'

After this conversation, I talk to Nebizade Hamdi, and he agrees to take over the licence for *Resimli Ay*.

The journals are about to come out. I send letters to all the vendors, signing them with my own name. I ask them to help me in this difficult situation, to make their payments on time to ensure the journals' survival. I receive very encouraging responses. I also print an appeal to the readers, telling them about the tough position I'm in. I ask for their help.

Days go by and the journals sell well, even better than before. But Suudi Bey tells me that the vendors still haven't made their payments. The money he gives me isn't even enough to pay for the children's expenses. And he doesn't send any money to Zekeriya at all.

I receive many letters from the vendors. Kökçüzade, the owner of the People's Bookstore in Samsun, writes: 'If you need money in order to publish the journals, I'm prepared to send it.'

Encouraged by this, I ask him to send the money for *Resimli Ay* and *Resimli Perşembe* directly to Zekeriya Bey in Sinop. He replies, 'If the income from *Resimli Ay* and *Resimli Perşembe* is not enough to cover Zekeriya Bey's living expenses, I can send him the money he requires.'

I hold the letter with tears in my eyes. The readers' letters I receive are in the same vein. Even today, writing these memoirs, I can't describe my feelings of gratitude to our readers and Kökçüzade for their support in those trying times.

*

I am able to provide for Zekeriya now. But even though the journals sell with great success, the publisher is reluctant to give me any money.

'There's no money coming in from the vendors,' he says, 'and we're running out of revolving funds. We need to top up the capital. Salih Münir Bey is willing to invest in the journals. Let's make him a partner as well.'

They pressure me from two sides. I write to Zekeriya. 'We don't need more capital,' he replies. 'Check Suudi Bey's accounts.'

This answer doesn't satisfy the wolves of Babıali, as my brother calls them. One day, Salih Bey holds a gun to my chest. 'If you don't make me a partner,' he says, 'I'll blow off your head with this gun.'

I keep this threat to myself. I know that if my brother hears about it, he'll close down the journals and send me off to Sinop. But things get so bad that I can't even pay the rent. I can't provide for my children. Zekeriya keeps pressing me to have the accounts checked. Suudi and Salih Bey want to wear me out, fire me from the journal and take over the business themselves. My patience and perseverance seem to be futile. I spend whatever money I get on the house and the children, and eat nothing but bread and cheese during the day. Two days a week, I order a white bean onion salad and a liver salad at the beanery across from the publishing house. These are a feast to me.

There is a young man called Mehmet, who works at the bookstore. He is a tall, skinny village boy. He has only finished primary school; his job is to bundle up the journals and run errands for us. One day, he comes up to me.

'Sabiha Hanım,' he says, 'Suudi Bey is cheating you. He keeps two separate books. One of them is the real book with the income from the vendors, and the other one is the book he shows to you and the government. He keeps these separate books to evade taxes. The money from the vendors is coming in, but he's hiding it from you.'

The situation reaches a breaking point. I appeal to my brothers to have the accounts checked. Mecdi Eren, the youngest of my older brothers, steps up to the task. He is a merchant and not easily fooled. But Suudi Bey doesn't show him the accounts. My older brother, Celal Deriş, decides to press charges.

*

Even amidst these troubles, the journals keep coming out, and I assume I will be able to publish them during the lawsuit as well. But that isn't the case. As soon as the lawsuit is filed, the court appoints a 'committee of deputies', chaired by Sıddık Sami Bey, a university professor.

I am binding pages in the composing room when the committee members arrive. They inform me that until the court case is settled, everything belonging to *Resimli Ay* and *Resimli Perşembe*, including the typesetting equipment, the papers and the accounting books, will be locked and sealed in a room, and that I can continue the journals elsewhere if I want.

I watch them as they rush all the documents and office equipment into the composing room as if saving them from a fire. They take everything they find. The back issues of the journals pile up like a mountain. They shut all the chests in the room itself.

The typesetters have to leave without even taking their aprons. They put a lock on the door and a seal on the lock. I feel like a mother who has lost her children.

My brother is there as well. 'Why are you upset?' he asks. 'You need to get these sleazy people off your back.'

'I'm upset because the journals can't publish under these conditions.'

'Don't worry. I'll give you the capital you need. Go find yourself a room and a printing press.'

The members of the committee shake hands with us and leave. To me, they seem like washers of the dead. They have buried everything, leaving me only the articles for the upcoming issues. I take them out of their drawer and put them into a folder. I'm dragging my feet; I don't want to leave the publishing house.

My brother seizes his chance. 'Didn't I tell you,' he says, 'that these wolves would devour you?'

'Yes, you did. But I couldn't abandon what I'd begun.'

We're leaving the publishing house, my brother in front, me right behind. Hayri Bey, Recep and the other typesetters are with us. Mehmet runs after me.

'If you keep on putting out the journals,' he says, 'I want to work for you.'

We make a deal on the spot.

After all this long and arduous work, I walk down Babıali Hill with a folder in my hand and not a penny to my name.

Sevimli Ay[28]

Mehmet left no stone unturned in Istanbul to find us a new office. But we couldn't go too far from the hub of the publishers and printers. Finally, he found a room for me in the building where the paper *Son Telgraf* was being published. For our typesetting and printing needs, we reached an agreement with the chief printer of the *Tevhidi Efkar* publishing house.

My new office was huge and had floor-to-ceiling windows, but it was absolutely empty. There weren't even curtains on the windows. My brother sent a desk but there was no chair, so I wrote the articles standing up and bent over the desk. I wanted to publish the journals without missing any deadlines. The chief printer had demanded that the *Resimli Ay* articles be delivered in fifteen days. The *Resimli Perşembe* articles were to be submitted three days before the printing date. A week of *Resimli Ay*'s time had already passed.

Fevzi Lütfi Karaosmanoğlu's newspaper *Hareket* was being published in the office next to mine. The door to my room was open, and they saw me writing while standing up. Bless them, they brought me a chair. But our needs didn't end there. There wasn't even a closet or shelves for the printed journals. Most importantly, Suudi Bey notified me that the journal couldn't be published under the name *Resimli Ay*, that this name

---

[28] TN: Roughly translatable as 'The Lovely Month'. The name was probably chosen for both its phonetic resemblance to *Resimli Ay* and the name of Sertel's older daughter (Sevim).

couldn't be used until the end of the trial. Law-abiding citizen that he was, he'd felt the need to let me know. So I had to change the journal's name and get someone to assume a new licence. I wrote to Nebizade Hamdi Bey in Ankara, asking him to send me a statement that he was taking over the licence for *Sevimli Ay* instead of *Resimli Ay*. I asked my brother for money to buy furniture and paper.

All of this went well, but the biggest problem lay ahead. I didn't have the addresses of the vendors to whom I needed to send the printed journals. One day, I was writing articles feverishly, all the while trying to figure out how to distribute the journals. Mehmet was out buying furniture. When he returned, I told him about my worries.

'When I was leaving the bookstore,' he happily told me, 'I saw an old vendors list lying around, so I took it with me. We'll put an announcement in the journal asking for new vendors' addresses as well.'

That resolved the biggest difficulty. I wrote letters to the vendors at once, asking them for help, telling them about what had happened to *Resimli Ay* and asking how many copies of *Sevimli Ay* they would order. The responses were positive. They ordered as many copies as they had of *Resimli Ay* and said they could send funds if needed. All this was thanks to the popularity that *Resimli Ay* and *Resimli Perşembe* had achieved among readers.

Sevimli Ay was ready to go. The covers of the journal were being designed by an artist called Hayri Bey. For the first issue's cover, he brought me a picture of a bride. I took it in my hands and laughed out loud.

'This is just like you, Hayri Bey,' I said. 'Well, it does feel like I'm in the middle of a wedding. This picture of a bride will suit the cover just fine.' He laughed as well.

I went to the *Tasviri Efkar* press to bind the pages. The head typesetter there was Yunus Efendi, a short, fat, stern-looking man who'd been in the trade for fifty years. With his leather apron and white skullcap, he was the very picture of an old-fashioned typesetter. When he saw me bring in the articles, he looked at me in amazement.

'Are you going to bind those pages?' he asked.

'Yes.'

'Now I've really seen it all. How can a woman bind pages?'

I didn't answer and showed him the page design instead. Zekeriya had been using a new style in publishing *Resimli Ay*. The pages were broken up by pictures and the articles' conclusions were left to later pages. I had used the same technique in preparing the page design. When Yunus Efendi saw this design, he threw down his ruler.

'I will not bind pages like this!' he said.

'The typesetter Hayri Bey does.'

'Hayri Bey be damned,' he said, 'what will become of the art of typesetting? Are we to cast aside our century-old traditions? This is a betrayal of the art. I cannot do it.'[29]

I went up to the chief printer's office and told him about the situation. We went back down together. When Yunus Bey saw us, he grimaced.

'These articles,' the chief printer said, 'will be set and bound as the lady wishes. We have a contract with her.'

---

[29] TN: Ironically, the moveable type printing press had only gained widespread acceptance in the Ottoman Empire in the 1860s.

Grudgingly, Yunus Bey got to work, letting out the occasional 'For God's sake' and shooting me angry glances.

At the Prosecutor's Office

Sevimli *Ay* proved to be a great success, but the prosecutors went over each article with a magnifying glass. I was summoned to the Prosecutor's Office over and over again. One day, I came to the office without having had my tea at home. When I saw the court bailiff with his braided gown and ball-shaped face standing outside the building, my heart skipped a beat.

'Not another summons?'

'Yes, the prosecutor would like to see you.'

I tapped him on the shoulder. 'For God's sake,' I said, 'please don't come in until I've had my tea upstairs.'

The bailiff humoured me, but the moment I finished my tea, he entered the room. It turned out the prosecutor was summoning me for an article entitled 'Birth Control'. I had written it myself under a male pseudonym. Before going to the prosecutor, I consulted with friends. They all thought that a woman commenting on this subject would be frowned upon and advised me against revealing that I'd written the article.

Among those present was my aunt's son Ibrahim Refik. 'I'll claim to be the author,' he said.

There was an investigation, and then the trial began. Ibrahim went to court with a lawyer. I learned afterward that the prosecutor claimed the article violated the population policy of the state and that population control was forbidden by law. He asked that the author be punished. The court had adjourned for the defence to prepare its case, but according to Ibrahim's lawyer, there was no hope. My conscience gave me no rest. Someone else was about to be sentenced on my account.

'This can't happen,' I said. 'I will appear in court and confess that I wrote the article.'

All my friends objected. 'If you're convicted,' they said, 'the journals won't come out either. It's crucial that your authorship remain secret.'

The trial concluded. Because Ibrahim was a merchant with no history as a writer, they let him off with a 150 lira fine.

At the time, it was considered shameful for a woman to write an article on gender issues, even if the article was scientific. Today, writing these lines, I'm astonished to see that birth control is openly advocated in the homeland, that female doctors are writing about the issue and that birth control is even part of the government's programme.

By then, I'd moved out of the pasha's mansion in Cağaloğlu and into an apartment near my mother's house in Şişli. My mother and Ayşe Hanım, the daughter of Zekeriya's aunt, looked after my children. I left the house at eight in the morning and didn't return until ten at night. I didn't even see my children's faces except on Sundays, when I stayed at home until noon. The children would come to my bed early in the morning and kiss and cuddle me. They didn't want to leave my side and followed me around, even to the bathroom.

They longed for their father, and it must have seemed to them like their mother was in exile as well. But Ayşe Hanım treated them like her own children. I still think back on my children's second mother with fondness and gratitude. Sadly, she passed away much too young.

Resimli Ay: The second period

Toward the middle of 1925, after one and a half years, Zekeriya returned from his exile. He'd benefitted from the general amnesty granted in honour of the republic's anniversary. *Sevimli Ay* became *Resimli Ay* again. The journal had survived in spite of all the obstacles, and thanks to popular demand it was printing and selling more issues than ever. After Zekeriya's return, the *Resimli Ay* Limited Company was established with my brothers as partners. *Çocuk Ansiklopedisi* started publishing again. We rented a new building on the road to Cağaloğlu and moved the company there. The lower half was turned into a printing press. Besides our own journals, we also printed works by authors such as Reşat Nuri, Vala Nureddin, Aka Gündüz, Ercüment Ekrem, Mahmut Yesari and Peyami Safa. In this way, the company *Resimli Ay* contributed to the development of Turkish literature as well.

The situation in the country remained the same. The other exiled journalists also were set free, but the Independence Tribunals and the Law on the Maintenance of Order had disheartened everyone. Newspapers reported on current affairs and published adventure stories, but no one dared touch on subjects like the development of the country and the advancement of the revolution. Our precious liberty had been gagged and bound. Freedom of ideas, speech and thought hadn't yet made it back from exile. New magazines and literary journals appeared here and there, only to be shut down after a couple of issues. There were no competing intellectual movements. Even the ideology of the revolution could no longer be discussed.

Atatürk's six principles of republicanism, statism, populism, nationalism, revolutionism and secularism were enshrined in the Constitution. But neither the reactionaries in the Assembly nor Atatürk's inner circle really grasped the meaning of these principles. The reforms affected the country's superstructure, but key issues like the development of villages, the education of peasants, industrialization and labour rights remained untouched. Despite Atatürk's sincere efforts, reactionaries prevented his principles from truly taking effect. Even self-proclaimed progressives started claiming that the revolutionary period had run its course. The excitement of the National War of Independence had been snuffed out.

The principle of statism diverged from what Atatürk had in mind. Mustafa Kemal meant for this principle to embody the goal of economic independence, freeing Turkey from the economic pressure of foreign capital. He wanted to develop Turkey by using the country's own resources without becoming indebted to the imperialists. And, indeed, for a long time, no loans were obtained from foreign countries. But reactionaries and opportunists saw statism as a chance to foster the 'rich of the nation', and the policy came to shield and protect both Turkish and minority capitalists.

To aid industrialization, the state was charged with establishing the industries that private enterprise was unable to develop, acting as an investment partner for private capital and granting loans. But private capital only invested in areas that would yield a profit, public enterprises were left to shoulder the losses in other areas, and so the country's industry developed in a lopsided way. Instead of nationalizing sources of wealth for the benefit of the people as intended, the principle of statism came to serve the advancement of capitalists instead.

In the process, the country's commercial bourgeoisie once again fell back on collaborating with foreign capital, allowing the latter to seep back into the country. Since foreign capital was not allowed to enter the country openly, it was masked as Turkish capital via companies founded for this purpose. This practice increased especially after the foundation of İş Bankası[30] and led to the establishment of a whole bourgeoisie of collaborators. As the bourgeoisie's villas and apartment buildings rose, so did the social hardship among workers and peasants, and the gap between labour and capital.

Members of the National Assembly and other fat cats from the People's Party were placed on the boards of the newly established public banks and state enterprises. The labour law was buried in drawers while restrictions on workers' rights to organize and found unions increased by the day. Land reform was shelved as well.

The village remained undiscovered territory. The mechanization of agriculture, the optimization of harvests and the granting of land ownership to peasants were viewed as matters of secondary importance. In the meantime, primitive plows remained the dominant means of agricultural production. Peasants with little or no land burned down whole forests to gain a few square inches, and big landlords engaged in battles to increase their property at each other's expense. These landlords, the relics of a quasi-feudal system, mostly kept exploiting the peasants as before. Villages had few schools and no teachers.

Industrialization followed roughly the same pattern. A few solitary factories were founded here and there. These investments weren't made in a systematic manner, but only occurred in sectors that profited the investor. Labourers in these factories worked like slaves, bereft of any social protections, health regulations and laws to prevent the exploitation of their labour. In the few strikes that occurred, the state's police forces backed the bosses.

Those in charge kept saying, 'There is no class conflict in the homeland,' and used this mantra to prevent workers from defending their rights. The catchphrase of a 'classless society' simply meant that the bourgeois class was bolstered and the working class crushed. Through oppression, this class was prevented from developing and organizing itself. Similarly, low-income civil servants, tradesmen and artisans struggled to make ends meet.

These were the conditions when *Resimli Ay* embarked on its second period.

A summons from the Prosecutor's Office

After the establishment of the *Resimli Ay* Limited Company, a disagreement broke out between several journals, including *Resimli Ay*, and the vendors. In violation of their

---

[30] TN: Founded in 1924, İş Bankası (literally, the 'Work Bank' or the 'Business Bank') remains Turkey's biggest public financial institution to date.

contracts, the vendors were trying to raise their fees for selling the journals. And in order to pressure the journals, they stopped selling them. Some journal owners prepared a letter to the vendors and asked me to join them. So I signed the letter as well.

The vendors used this letter to sue the journals. I became involved in the court case as the representative of *Resimli Ay* and *Çocuk Ansiklopedisi*. In order to defend our rights, we went to the Eminönü notary public and asked for a power of attorney. The notary public demanded that we produce two witnesses. We proposed that two copies of the letter be written and that we act as each other's witnesses.

I was talking to some colleagues when one of our group called out to me.

'Sabiha Hanım, the notary public won't accept your testimony.'

'Why not?'

'He says that women can't act as witnesses.'

I went up to the notary.

'Civil law grants me this right,' I said. 'I can be a witness.'

The notary public kept adjusting his spectacles and addressing me with pompous Ottoman phrases like 'your highness' and 'your excellency'.

'Does your excellency know the laws better than I do?' he asked.

No matter how hard I tried, I couldn't get him to concede my right to act as witness. Finally, I called the office and summoned Mehmet, who was bundling the journals. His testimony was accepted and the certificate was signed. I turned to the notary.

'This boy's only job at the journal is to tie up the bundles and take them to the post office. I, on the other hand, have been writing the articles, binding the pages and running the business for years. He can be a witness but I can't?'

'You can't. That's the law.'

Back at the journal, I wrote an article for *Resimli Ay* entitled 'Am I not Human?' I defended the rights of women as citizens and human beings. In a somewhat harsh tone, I charged that only sharia laws deprived women of the right to act as witnesses, that civil law granted women this right, but that the law was not being implemented.

The news picked up the topic. Gatfranko, a prominent jurist, defended me in *Cumhuriyet* and started publishing articles on the rights that sharia and civil law granted to women. *Cumhuriyet* also asked me to write an article. After its publication, I was summoned to the prosecutor's office.

The prosecutor greeted me kindly. He said that the article was an attack on the laws of the state and that we lived in very sensitive times. The Law on the Maintenance of Public Order, he said, made it punishable to brazenly lash out at the laws as I'd done.

'To criticize the laws,' he said, 'is to erode the authority of the state. Only constructive criticism is allowed.'

'If it isn't constructive criticism to demand my rights and insist that the law be implemented, why don't we just close down the journals on Babıali and sell onions and garlic instead? How can the courts deny a right that is granted by civil law?'

'The existence of such an article in civil law has not been reported to our office,' the prosecutor replied. 'Your aim is to criticize the laws. I called you here with the intention of warning you. I will not press charges. But I will insist that you be cautious in your writings from now on. Even the slightest criticism that might muddle people's minds will not be tolerated.'

This was how prosecutors, notaries and other officials understood the reforms. They were used to pressuring people into silence, so they kept doing just that. I turned to the prosecutor.

'I wrote these articles to report on something that happened to me and to demand the rights granted to women by civil law. This is the aim of my article: As long as individuals don't know how to demand and use a right granted by the law, that right remains on paper. I wrote the article to destroy any lingering hold that the old sharia mentality still has on people's minds. If, in spite of all objections, the notary insists on his point, then he doesn't understand the law. What use is a right granted to me by civil law if notaries and prosecutors aren't aware of it? How can I be attacking the law by pointing out an error and demanding a right that's being ignored?'

The prosecutor listened carefully. He seemed to realize that he was unaware of this article in civil law. He softened.

'I wasn't about to press charges anyway,' he said.

After the newspapers explored the issue in depth, the Ministry of Justice sent out a notice to prosecutors and notaries. And so, my article fulfilled its goal by teaching officials the law.

The reading primers

Zekeriya's return from exile lightened my load considerably. Under my previous, gruelling working conditions, I hadn't even found time to read. Now that I had some free time, I decided to tackle a project I'd been planning for quite a while.

My heart sank whenever I saw the reading primers that my older daughter, Sevim, used in elementary school. Most of these books had no teaching method or awareness of child psychology. During my time in the United States, I'd taken an interest in child education. While Sevim attended kindergarten at the Teachers College, I'd done some research on the school's teaching method and preparation of elementary school primers. So now, I created my own reading primers for the first five grades of elementary school, using an approach called the Thorndike Method.

The Ministry of Education approved the books, and schools started using them. Teachers sent me letters of appreciation. This work helped ease my mind a little. I was finally free of all the bickering and the pacing around courthouse aisles. At the same time, I continued my articles in *Resimli Ay*.

Just around then, a major event occurred – an event that would deeply affect the history of *Resimli Ay*. The great poet Nazım Hikmet joined our ranks.

Nazım Hikmet at *Resimli Ay*

The year was 1928. We were having dinner one evening, when Zekeriya said, 'I want to read you a poem by Nazım Hikmet, one of the new poets.'

I'd never heard of Nazım Hikmet.

Zekeriya read out the poem: 'Trrrrum, Trrrrum, Trak Tiki Tak, I Want to Become a Machine,' it went.

I listened intently until Zekeriya finished.

'So,' he said, 'do you like it?'

'No, I don't like it at all. If he wants to become a machine, he should tie an engine to his back.'

My ear was only accustomed to *aruz* and *hece*, the classic metres of the Ottoman Court and Turkish folklore. This was the first time I heard free verse. It perplexed me.

The next day, I was in the office, writing an article at Zekeriya's desk. The door opened and Vala Nureddin came in, accompanied by a tall man with blond curls and blue eyes. Zekeriya introduced him as Nazım Hikmet.

I shook their hands and sat back down. I already knew Vala. He wrote columns for the *Akşam* newspaper in his elegant, witty style. Apparently, he and Nazım were childhood friends. He'd asked Zekeriya to give Nazım a job at *Resimli Ay*, Zekeriya had agreed, and so he'd brought Nazım to the office. I went back to writing my article. The previous night's poem hadn't made me curious about Nazım.

They settled into the armchairs across the desk and started talking. After a while, Zekeriya asked Nazım to recite a poem. Nazım blushed but didn't hesitate. He started reciting his poem *Bahri Hazer* [The Caspian Sea]. Suddenly, it was as if a river had started flowing down a waterfall. The sounds rose and fell like a symphony, the words breathed fire. I put down the pen, listening to the poem as if it were music.

After returning from Moscow in 1928, Nazım hadn't been able to find work anywhere. Vala Nureddin had told Zekeriya about Nazım's artistic merit and asked him to hire Nazım as a proofreader. That was to be his job at *Resimli Ay*; letting him write articles could have been dangerous.[31]

Nazım was given a desk in the room where I worked. He would come early in the morning, read the articles and sometimes do translations. He was very serious about his work. He didn't say a word while busy and only started talking when he was done, excitedly voicing his thoughts on the events of the day and giving us ideas for the journal.

Once Nazım started working at *Resimli Ay*, he was quickly surrounded by young poets who wrote in his style. The poems that he liked were published in the journal. *Resimli Ay* now became a gathering place for leftist writers like Sadri Ertem, Suat Derviş and Sabahaddin Ali, publishing many of their stories. These new literati gave a strong voice to the social conditions and troubles of workers, peasants and all impoverished people crushed by the wealthy classes.

Nazım was not just laying the foundations for a new form of literature but also trying to convert more people to the socialist cause. At one point, he even became obsessed with the idea of enlisting Peyami Safa. Until that time, Peyami's stories and novels had been mediocre at best. But after connecting with Nazım, he wrote his masterpiece, *Dokuzuncu Hariciye Koğuşu* [Ward Nine, External Diseases]. Reviewing this novel for *Resimli Ay*, Nazım applauded Peyami and proclaimed his own views on art. Praising the novel for its realism, he went on to say:

---

[31] TN: Nazım Hikmet was already an avowed communist at this point.

Documentarism is winning the day in artistic circles around the world. All art, from film to poetry, is turning to documentations of reality to find new phrases, melodies and compositions. On occasion, these reality-based artistic constructions are so awe-inspiringly meaningful that they make novels of intrigue and poems about murmurs of the heart seem pathetic and foolish. Realism must not be the realism of a photograph. It must be a dialectical realism erecting a monument to reality by weaving analysis and synthesis into a composition.[32]

At the time, Peyami was influenced by Nazım to a certain extent. But he disagreed with Nazım on many issues. Nazım spared no effort to win him over to the socialist cause. After all the long discussions between them, Peyami finally said to Nazım, 'You and I are on the same train. We are fellow travellers. But I'm only with you until we reach the station of democracy. After that, it's good-bye.'

But Peyami got off the train before ever reaching that station. During the Second World War, he jumped on Hitler's bandwagon instead. He became the biggest champion of fascism, racism and Hitler himself. Among all the articles targeting Nazım and myself, the nastiest were written by Peyami. Later still, he joined the writers of the old school in attacking Nazım in print. Nazım responded to these crude assaults with a satirical piece entitled 'Yetimi Safa'.[33]

Sometimes, while going over articles at his desk, Nazım would make a face, throw down his pen in anger and lament, 'Isn't it a shame to publish such harebrained ideas in the journal?' During his time at *Resimli Ay*, he prepared his own books of poetry, *835 Satır* [835 Lines], *Portreler* [Portraits] and *Taranta Babu*.

One day, he was at his desk revising *835 Satır*. He read me some poems from the book. After listening to them, I said, 'You can't publish this book.'

This riled him. His face turned beet red.

'Oh, I'll publish it, alright,' he said. 'What's the worst they can do – pull it from the market? And until it gets pulled, it'll sell.'

'What about the courts? What about jail?'

'You reap what you sow.'

Nazım had such determination that no obstacle could deter him from his cause. His works were published. Soon, he shone like a star in the world of literature and art. Every day, the writers' office overflowed with young people who listened to Nazım like disciples, taking lessons from him in the new art. Nazım was the harbinger of a new era in literature. His poems were innovative in both form and content. He wrote in the clearest Turkish imaginable. If a word wasn't used by the common people, he didn't use it in his poems. Only in his prose and articles did he sometimes use Arabic words. Nazım wasn't content with merely abandoning the established poetic meters of *aruz* and *hece*. He also made innovations in the technique and content of poetry. Gathering his themes among the common people, he cast them in the mold of his own personality and system of thought.

---

[32] *Resimli Ay*, 29 February 1930, p. 32.
[33] TN: Roughly translatable as 'The Orphan of Pleasure', this title plays off the sound and meaning of Peyami Safa's name.

Once Nazım's works started appearing in print, many new poets began writing in free verse. Works of this kind became bestsellers in stores. Nazım's poems had an effect not just on young writers, but also on workers, painters and other artists. Nazım himself ventured into the circles of many artists, participated in their discussions, championed the cause of realist art and spread his ideas throughout the art world.

A man of Nazım's stature couldn't remain a mere proofreader at *Resimli Ay* for long. Slowly, he assumed his due position, publishing poems under the pen name 'Man without Signature' and articles under pseudonyms like 'Orhan' and 'Süleyman'.

Nazım Hikmet and Sabahaddin Ali

Sabahaddin Ali was a young man who had recently returned from Germany, where he had been exposed to progressive literature. One day, he brought in a piece to be published in *Resimli Ay*. He and Nazım ended up having a long talk about art and literature. After reading the story, Nazım said: 'There's something special about this kid.'

From then on, Nazım paid great attention to the stories Sabahaddin brought in and engaged him in discussions. He found Sabahaddin's pieces too romantic and advised him to write more realistic stories. Sabahaddin had socialist leanings, but socialism hadn't yet taken a clear shape in his mind. Nazım was trying to nudge him not just toward realist literature, but toward socialism as well. It was Nazım who encouraged Sabahaddin to write novels, and *Kuyucaklı Yusuf* [Yusuf of Kuyucak], Sabahaddin's first novel, was printed by the *Resimli Ay* press. Throughout the printing process, Nazım stood by the machines and watched. The day the first copy was complete, he brought it to the office in delight and showed it off to all of us. The look in his eyes all but proclaimed, 'I created this novelist.'

Another writer in Nazım's circle was Sadri Ertem. Nazım didn't really appreciate Sadri as an artist and story writer, but his knowledge of literature and socialist leanings endeared him to Nazım. Sadri was greatly influenced by Nazım. During the debate on 'Breaking the Idols' that Nazım initiated in *Resimli Ay*,[34] it was Sadri who responded most forcefully to the critics who attacked Nazım.

And so, *Resimli Ay* became the cradle of a new literary movement.

In the 1930s, Nazım's poems 'Bahri Hazer' and 'Salkım Söğüt' [Weeping Willow] were recorded by the Columbia Viva-Tonal Company. It was the first time in Turkey that poetry was recorded. When these recordings started playing in coffee houses and restaurants, the government panicked. The police confiscated the records at once and banned coffee houses from playing them.

One day, Nazım and some friends were sitting at a coffee house in Erenköy. There were only a few people at the tables, mostly construction workers from a site nearby. The manager put on a record of Nazım's poetry. Soon, all the empty tables were full. A fire lit up in Nazım's eyes.

'I could have written twenty manifestos and still not gotten so many workers to read them,' he said.

---

[34] TN: Sertel gives a detailed account of this debate further below.

'How much money did the Columbia Company pay you for these records?' a friend asked.

'It's not about what I was paid. On the contrary, how much money do you think I should pay Columbia? I would give my poems away for free in return for such publicity. If I had the money, I would even pay for it.'

In the wake of this event, Sadri Ertem wrote about these poems in the August 1930 issue of *Resimli Ay*:

> 'Bahri Hazer' represents the pinnacle of modern poetic technique. In this work, we see dialectical materialism[35] become poetry. But before defending the entry of dialectical materialism into poetry, let me point out what a service Nazım has done us by accomplishing this extraordinary feat.
>
> As is widely known, dialectical materialism is a specific kind of worldview. Until now, people who wanted to explain this worldview would draw on passages from *Faust*, the poem by the idealist dialectician Goethe. But now, it is possible for dialectical materialists in Turkey to cite examples from Nazım Hikmet, a poet who is a dialectical materialist himself.
>
> Is the Sufism of Mevlana Celaleddin Rumi anything other than idealism? You all know the poems 'Makber' [The Grave] and 'Ölü' [The Dead] by Abdülhak Hamid; are they not based on idealist philosophy? I assume you have also become familiar with the ardent supporters of symbolism and surrealism. Their philosophy and poetry are inspired by Hegel's and Bergson's philosophy. What, then, could be more natural than to see the philosophical leanings of a dialectical materialist poet reflected in his work? Some say that idealism has a place in poetry, but not dialectical materialism. What nonsense!
>
> The poem 'Salkım Söğüt' accomplishes the same feat. Both 'Bahri Hazer' and 'Salkım Söğüt' describe a procession of people moving at full speed toward a single and definite goal, with all the excitement their hearts can muster, and the state of mind of a random person in that procession when he is shot down by the treacherous bullet of the enemy.
>
> Nazım has outlined the main features of philosophy in his poem 'Berkeley' and provided a peerless illustration of dialectical materialism in 'Bahri Hazer'. What is more, each of his poems shows him to us just as he is, and not as one viewed by those who misunderstand him.

This article by Sadri Ertem was revised by Nazım himself, so it reflects Nazım's own ideas as well.

Nazım didn't just revolutionize the content of poetry but also its form. He demolished the templates of the *aruz* and *hece* meters, the cornerstones of Turkish literature until then, and wrote in free verse instead. In another article, Nazım himself made the case for free verse.

---

[35] TN: Dialectical materialism posits that the world consists solely of matter in motion. This world, or reality, is taken to be in a constant process of change through struggle.

Those days, such literary debates mostly took place at our house. Poems were recited and discussed. As it turned out, my younger daughter, Yıldız, grasped the harmony of free verse by listening to these poems every night. One day, she was sick in bed. She wanted to get up, but her grandmother wouldn't let her. Upset by this, Yıldız wrote a poem.

We told Nazım about this and read the poem to him. Nazım, in turn, wrote the following piece in the October 1930 issue of *Resimli Ay*, to show how well-suited free verse is to life:

> Yıldız is seven years old. She has darting, inquisitive eyes and a broad, pale forehead that looks like it has pondered many things. One day, Yıldız gets sick. Her grandmother wraps her in blankets. She doesn't want her to set one foot outside the room. But the weather is sunny and warm. Yıldız wants to go outside and run in the snow, in the backstreets. She wants to, but her granny won't let her. It's not just her granny, either; it's whoever is in the house. From the housemaid to her own 13-year-old sister, Sevim, everyone is giving Yıldız a hard time.
>
> Yıldız gets upset. She wants to go outside and run until she's out of breath. She gets angry. Her little head is filled with the dream of a bicycle flying at top speed. After giving the matter some thought, Yıldız turns to the poet Nail V., who has come to visit her.
>
> "Pretty please, write down what I tell you."
> "What shall I write, Yıldız?" Nail V. asks.
> "You'll write a poem."
> "Whose poem?"
> "My poem."
> "Gosh, you write poetry?"
> "Yes."
>
> Nail V. laughs. It seems that Yıldız writing a poem is a very funny thing. Yıldız is seven years old.
>
> "Alright, go ahead. I'm writing."
> And Yıldız dictates her poem to Nail V.

> Sickness
>   in bed
>   there is a patient.
>   This patient
>   Wants:
>   get on a bicycle and
> go far away.
> If she gets on a bicycle
>   and goes away:
> the ones who'll shout after her
>   are many.
>   Seven people:

>   – don't run!
>   you are sick,
>   don't go far!
>   you are sick.
>   who cares?
> I
>   am running away:
>   flashes of lightning,
>   just like them.
>   Lightning.

The poem "Seven-Year-Old Yıldız" is finished. Nail V. is dumbfounded. And how could he not be? The poem he just wrote down recognizes all the fine points of the new poetic technique. While dictating the poem, Yıldız even told him when to switch between the beginning, middle and end of the line.

Without a doubt, seven-year-old Yıldız is a very talented, very intelligent girl. Nonetheless, her great triumph also represents a colossal victory for the new poetry. The new poetic technique is so close to life, so closely derived from the living and spoken language that even seven-year-old Yıldız grasped it right away and produced a perfect example of a poem.

What does this show us? Most importantly, it proves that the new technique is not an artificial construct. It fits contemporary language like a skin rather than a dress. Those of us who write with the new poetic technique have Yıldız's generation on their side. This generation will carry the work begun by us to fruition.'

Today, just as Nazım predicted, free verse has been adopted by the young generations. The meters of *aruz* and *hece* have become obsolete. Today, the poets and authors of Turkish literature whose works are most significant in terms of form and content are those inspired by Nazım's art, thoughts and philosophical views.

Nazım breathed a new spirit not just into Turkish literature but into *Resimli Ay* as well. All progressive poets and authors gathered at the journal, and articles started addressing the country's social issues more forcefully.

The war to break the idols

Nazım Hikmet, the proofreader, was at his desk checking articles. *Resimli Ay* had conducted a writers' survey, entitled 'How Do You Write Your Works?' among the literati, and Nazım was going over responses and correcting typesetters' errors. I was working at my own desk.

After reading the replies from Abdülhak Hamid and Halit Ziya, Nazım threw down his pen in exasperation.

'Is any one of these truly a national writer?' he said. 'Asked about the subject they write on, some say "the world abroad" and others list the decadent types in their own bourgeois circles. Are there no people, no workers, no peasants in this country? Such topics don't interest these gentlemen at all. They don't want to see the realities. They are idols that must be torn down.'

Our desks were across from each other. I looked at him in astonishment.

'Is it necessary for a work of art to have a national character?'

'No, but these people claim to be writing national literature. The artist's task is to express the realities of the society he lives in and to use his art for the benefit of that society. But these bourgeois gentlemen only write for their own pleasure.'

Nazım wanted *Resimli Ay* to launch a campaign against these older literati. Zekeriya embraced the idea. And so, Nazım embarked on a series of articles entitled 'We Are Breaking the Idols'. The arrows of his criticism were pointed specifically at Abdülhak Hamid and the poet Mehmet Emin. This campaign hit Babıali Avenue like a bombshell. Hamdullah Suphi published a response full of invective in the *İkdam* newspaper. Senior literati such as Yakup Kadri and Orhan Seyfi unleashed a barrage of criticism, resorting to insults instead of engaging in a literary discussion.

They also denounced the writers at *Resimli Ay* to their politician friends. 'Abdülhak Hamid is a genius,' they said. 'These people aren't trying to tear down some idols. They're trying to tear down our national writers, our geniuses. This is not a literary discussion but communist propaganda.' This was a direct attack on Nazım himself.

Progressive writers responded by saying, 'You cannot resolve a literary debate through abuse and defamation. If you have confidence in your abilities, let us have a discussion.'

The *Akşam* newspaper conducted a survey on the issue. The responses confirmed that the old literati fell short of addressing the public's needs. This verdict, reached by people with no stake in the debate, only fuelled the fire of these old idols, who coasted by on their reputations as masters. They started fabricating lies. One article followed another. The so-called masters had lost their nerve.

Yakup Kadri Bey penned an irate response. 'Today's youth is degenerate,' he wrote. 'During the war years, they were raised on dough mixed with husks.' He depicted the new poets, the new generation, as degenerate on account of starvation.

This claim elicited responses from Vala Nureddin, Peyami Safa (in those days, Peyami appeared to support the Left), Halit Fahri and Sadri Ertem. They all supported the war to break the idols. They asked why the old writers turned a blind eye to the misery of the youth and people who were so poor they had to eat bread made out of husks, and why they didn't lend their voice to this misery in their writing. Sadri Ertem challenged the old literati in the August 1929 issue of *Resimli Ay*:

> If they want to defend Abdülhak Hamid's genius and Mehmet Emin's reputation as a national poet, let them write about it, illustrate their points and offer proof. But it seems like the older generation has grown too feeble to hold a pen. The articles they've published on the issue speak for themselves. What are they after? Why don't they deign to explain these geniuses and national writers to us simpletons? Why do they use their pens to pick their noses instead?

To illustrate the older literati's inability to defend their viewpoint, Sadri Ertem gave an example. 'Throughout all these discussions,' he wrote, 'only Orhan Seyfi Bey actually made an attempt to defend Mehmet Emin Bey. And what a defence it was! Read for yourself:'

> Mehmet Emin Bey spends his every breath on reciting his poetry to the people, whether we call him a national poet or not. His heart is free of all literary ambition. Unlike some upstart poets, he does not demand a high fee for his writings. Unlike the geniuses of the day, he lays no claim to having introduced some incomprehensible artistic innovation, and neither does he brag. To the contrary. In a deeply modest, deeply humble manner, he writes for free, reads for free and publishes for free. He even pays out of his own pocket to publish his works.

Sadri Ertem's response to this laughable argument was as follows:

> This defence merely showcases the true wretchedness of yesterday's generation. Let them explain Hamid and Mehmet Emin to us! What's the use of spinning around like Rufa'i dervishes, baring their chests and bewailing the fact that we don't call Hamid a genius and Mehmet Emin a national poet? They are only raising this ruckus to drown out a legitimate literary issue. Yakup Kadri, for instance, has been lavish in hurling abuse at us, but hasn't answered any of our questions. 'You claim,' we told him, 'that you created the new language. But in the old days, you wrote articles denouncing the new language.'
> Yakup Kadri's only defence was to call us stray dogs.
> But here is what he wrote in an article published in *Rubab*:[36] 'They are selling the new. For how much? And how? I don't know. But they are selling it. Run to Salonica, and you will find *Yeni Fikir* [The New Idea], *Yeni Hayat* [The New Life], *Genç Kalemler* [The Young Pens] and *Yeni Lisan* [The New Language] on sale. Don't laugh, gentlemen. You'll see, people will accept this novelty. For the unknown force called the people is enamoured with idiocy and will rush to its defence, no matter where and when. They say that the emotions and thoughts we've inherited must change. But we are Ottomans and this is the Ottoman language. They would like us to be Chagatais and write in the Chagatai language.[37] No, no, a thousand times no! That would be unnatural! O wretched novelty! O wretched novelty, no more abiding than a fancy holiday dress!'

Back in the day, this had been Yakup Kadri's response to the emergence of literary movements in Salonica that favoured a new language and were aimed at the people. And now, in the literary debate started by Nazım Hikmet and the leftist writers, he was once again opposing innovation. Sadri's article demonstrated how Yakup Kadri's old thoughts were in line with his current conservative view:

> Yakup Kadri Bey doesn't answer our questions. Instead, he finds a thousand ways to make our questions sound like a reactionary attack on the republic and the new

---

[36] TN: This journal takes its name from a stringed instrument of the Middle East.
[37] TN: A Central Asian Turkic language. In their efforts to simplify the Ottoman language, reformers often made reference to Turkic languages such as Chagatai.

regime. While these gentlemen try to drown out the real issue at hand, we can only respond that we were talking about literature. This caused a great commotion and a lot of abuse was thrown around, but we were just expressing a certain idea. Now, perhaps, we can return to the topic of literature.

Once the literati of the old generation realized they'd lost the debate, they tried to find other lines of attack. Hamdullah Suphi stirred up some young people at the Turkish Hearth and had them stage a demonstration outside the *Resimli Ay* offices. After raising a ruckus outside the building, these young people came inside. Their agitation seemed rehearsed. They said that the articles were disrespectful and insulting toward the writers of the old generation. They all talked at once.

Nazım Hikmet, Zekeriya and I were in the writers' office. Nazım became excited. Zekeriya rose from his desk at once and asked the young men to sit down. He said:

You are educated young people. Educated people don't swear and shout at each other. We're happy to see young people join debates on literature and thought. But before you pick a side, you should thoroughly examine the issue at hand and reach a conviction of your own. This is a clash of two movements. It's a fight about literature, but equally, it's a debate between old and new ideas and forms. We want to see young people in the vanguard. It doesn't suit them to be incited by others and parrot their words without understanding.

The young men sat down. The atmosphere became calmer. Nazım told them that this was a literary debate and that with every changing era, literature, too, gained new characteristics. The young men listened to him with great interest, even regret. And they left the printing house peacefully.

After this incident, *Resimli Ay* published an appeal to the youth in its August 1929 issue. In brief, this appeal went as follows:

Resimli Ay merely opened its pages to a literary discussion. Those who make this look like communism are engaged in a nasty form of demagogy. In reality, this is a struggle between the old and the new. What has communism got to do with the statement that Abdülhak Hamid is not a genius and Mehmet Emin not a national writer? By painting our publications as communist and provoking some young people to riot, the perpetrators are just showcasing their own weakness.

Ideas that can be openly discussed need no cover to hide behind. Why do they politicize our claims, dress them up as communism and use this as a shield to defend themselves? If our claims are false, let them prove it. In a democracy, every idea can be defended and discussed. Drowning out ideas with protests and noise is a backward stance unbefitting of twentieth-century youth. In an era of progress, it must be the young who break the idols and advance new ideas and new movements.

Those who feel they will lose the debate are stirring up a panic and taking shelter under the wing of the youth. But they are deceiving both the youth and popular opinion. This is not a matter of communism. It's a struggle between the old and the new.

It didn't take long for these young people to grasp the truth. Once they understood they'd been deceived, they turned on those who'd tried to manipulate them and sent a letter of apology to *Resimli Ay*.

The press and the public were also disgusted by the vicious way that Hamdullah Suphi Bey and Yakup Kadri attacked Nazım and *Resimli Ay*. Hamdullah was roundly reproached and finally had to fall silent. Yakup Kadri was defended by only two journals. One of them was the journal of the American missionaries, and the other was the newspaper of Acem Naci, known in the press world for his sycophancy. It was after these debates that Nazım published his satirical poems 'Karamaça Bey'[38] about Yakup Kadri and 'Sen Zilli Bir Bebeksin'[39] about Hamdullah Suphi.

One evening, after all these discussions and attacks on his status as a senior poet, Abdülhak Hamid invited Nazım over for dinner. We were sitting in the journal's editorial room when the invitation arrived. Nazım thought about it for a moment.

Figure 4.4 Istanbul, 1930s, Zekeriya and Sabiha Sertel. The husband-and-wife publishing team gained influence with the popular success of *Resimli Ay* and later with their newspaper and publishing house *Tan*, as well as earning them harsh critics loyal to the government.

---

[38] TN: Literally meaning 'Mr. Black Spade', this title contains a play on Yakup Kadri's last name, Karaosmanoğlu.

[39] TN: The title of this poem, given by Sertel as 'You Are a Quarrelsome Doll', is actually 'Bir Komik Adem' (A Funny Man).

'I rejected Atatürk's invitation,' he said. 'But I cannot reject the invitation of a poet.' The next day, we asked him for his impressions. He said:

> A bourgeois, but a major poet. He met me at the door with his wife, Lucienne Hanım. He was wearing a frock coat, and, tall as he is, he looked just like an English lord. I was terrified that his monocle would drop at any moment. They took me into a sumptuous drawing room. With all the chandeliers and the Louis XIV furniture, I felt like I was in a palace. And the dining table! What a spread on the dining table! Scotch whiskies imported from London, all kinds of different drinks. Appetizers laid out from one end of the table to the other. Abdülhak Hamid had another visitor as well. The four of us sat down at the table. I felt like a bashful child in this company.
>
> Abdülhak Hamid started a conversation on art. He talked with such eloquence about art history, the various schools of literature and the developments in poetry, literature and theater that I felt ignorant next to him. But I also told him about realist art, things he didn't know. He listened with great interest.
>
> He said, 'You're right to break the idols. When we embarked on a life of letters, we did the same. We tore down *divan* literature and established Tanzimat literature in its place.'[40] We charted new ground in Turkish literature. Just as we demolished them, you will demolish us.'
>
> I couldn't help but admire Abdülhak Hamid's tolerance. And here I'd thought we'd be fighting tooth and nail!

The war against missionaries

The papers reported that Christian missionaries were converting some Turkish girls at the American College for Girls in Istanbul and the American Colleges in Bursa and Izmir. The news caused a wave of public outrage. *Resimli Ay* seized the occasion to launch a campaign against missionaries, publishing a series of articles on the subject.

Missionaries had come to Turkey as early as the reign of Abdülhamid II,[41] under the pretext of bringing culture and civilization to the country. Using money earmarked by American capitalists, they established the Robert College and the College for Girls in Istanbul as well as American Colleges in other cities. They opened hospitals and schools in order to gain the public's favour while spreading their religious propaganda and ideology. In their schools, they tried to Christianize and Americanize the Turks. Maintaining that Americans had a more advanced civilization and that Turkey was a backward nation, they fostered a sense of inferiority in their students. And just as they had done in the Ottoman Empire, they provoked Armenians against Turks and incited religious and ethnic hatred among people.

---

[40] TN: Classical Ottoman court poetry and the first wave of nineteenth-century Ottoman literature to show the influence of Westernization, respectively.
[41] TN: R. 1876–1909.

Their true aim was to pit the minorities in Turkey against the Turkish state and people, weaken the republic and pave the way for foreign capital to enter the country. They'd already infiltrated Africa and Asia, especially China. In the guise of saviours, they'd helped turn these regions into large markets for American capital. These missionaries were sent to every foreign region as the advance guard of capitalism. In Turkey, too, their aim was to incite the minorities against the Turkish people with the promise of independence and to serve as scouts for American capitalists.

In fact, missionary activities in Turkey had a much longer history. Tsarist Russia was once the protector of the Orthodox Patriarchate and population in Turkey. The tsars enshrined this role in their treaties with the Ottoman Empire. Since then, however, the tsarist regime in Russia and the sultanate in Turkey had collapsed and been replaced by the communist and republican regimes. This reduced the influence of the patriarchate and hampered its policy of inflaming the minorities. But the position vacated by Russia after the Soviet Revolution was assumed even more aggressively by the United States, which took over the role of protector of minorities.

At the end of the First World War, during Turkey's occupation by the imperialist states, America revealed its intention of establishing a mandate in Turkey.[42] Those days, as is well known, people like Halide Edip and Ahmet Emin Yalman supported such a mandate. By establishing a zone of influence in Turkey, America wanted to kill three birds with one stone. The first goal was to use Turkey as a springboard against the Soviet Union. The second goal was to use Turkey to make inroads into the Middle East and establish US control over Iraqi oil in Mosul and Iranian oil. And the third goal was to drive the British oil companies out of these regions.

The Bible Society founded in Istanbul translated the Bible into Turkish and distributed it among the youth and general population free of charge. The president of the society was a tall, slender man in a frock coat. He was a Protestant pastor. One day, after our campaign against the missionaries, he came looking for me at *Resimli Ay*. I was alone in the room when he entered with his walking-stick in hand. He introduced himself – I forget his name – and asked me why we'd launched the campaign against missionaries. Before I could answer, he asserted that missionaries hadn't come here to spread Christianity, but to bring culture to this backward country and be of service to the population.

After listening to him, I asked: 'Does one have to use the Bible to bring culture to Turkey? If religious books increase a population's culture, why not use the Qur'an? We are a secular nation. We respect everyone's religious beliefs. But we won't stand for some mystical rhetoric being used to lull people's minds to sleep. Especially if there are political motives involved.'

The president of the Bible Society cut me off: 'You studied in America. You know how Protestant churches strive to increase the people's culture. The Church has shed its old peculiarities and has become a cultural organization, a social organization that addresses public grievances. Our work here serves the same purpose.'

---

[42] TN: Mandates were territories assigned to the control of certain states by the League of Nations after the First World War.

'Yes,' I said, 'the aims of the Church in America are different from its aims in backward countries. In America, the Church follows the policies of the capitalist monopolies and works for their benefit. It assures workers that poverty and wealth are both God's command and advises them to meekly resign themselves to their lot. It tries to turn the blacks into Protestants so that the monopolies can better exploit their black workers. But it never raises its voice against racism. Through various forms of aid, it tries to Americanize the immigrants who come from all around the world, to turn them into slaves who will obey the command of churches and monopolies. Here, on the other hand, the Church serves to drive a wedge between minorities and Turks, and to strengthen the American influence in the country.'

The president of the Bible Society listened to my words with a smile. 'These are just your subjective claims,' he said. 'They don't reflect the truth.'

'They're not my subjective claims. Let me tell you something that happened to me once. I gave birth to my daughter Yıldız at a workers' hospital in America. At the moment of birth, I was alone in the room. I was lying on a high bed, going through my final contractions. A nurse passed through the room. I asked her to hold my hand so I could gather my strength. The lady looked at the chart hanging next to the bed. "You're Turkish," she said, "you're Muslim. I can't give you my hand."'.

'You're the ones who incite this religious and sectarian hatred between people. For my part, I support every nation gaining the right of independence. But I oppose pitting different populations against each other, and I oppose inciting them to hatred for the sake of the imperialists.'

The president listened to me with the patience of a missionary. He answered none of my questions.

'I'll send you the books and pamphlets we've been publishing in Turkey,' he said. 'Then you'll realize your mistake. I'm saddened by your words.' With typical missionary hypocrisy, he shook my hand and left.

After this, the missionaries started attacking *Resimli Ay* in their journal. This marked the second time in the same year that *Resimli Ay* was attacked for one of its campaigns. First it had been the old writers, and now it was the missionaries.

Defending workers' rights

The Labour Law still hadn't made it through Parliament. In spite of all repressive measures, there were strikes in some places. These were brutally suppressed. There were no contracts between workers and employers. The new Labour Law contained some measures to grant social protections, but these couldn't be implemented because the old law was still in effect. And even though that law stipulated an eight-hour work day, many places made labourers work for ten to eleven hours. Women labourers worked even during pregnancy. There was no law protecting children from performing heavy labour. Capitalism wasn't very developed yet, but the existing light industry and small businesses employed workers without any kind of state regulation. The working class couldn't organize, and its living standards declined by the day. Neither the authorities nor the press showed any interest in the issue. Some leftist journals addressed the problem, but they invariably shut down after one or two issues, either because they ran out of funds or because they were outlawed by the government.

Around that time, the workers at printing presses in Ankara and tobacco factories in Samsun and Istanbul decided to go on strike. It looked like a mass movement in the making. We decided to cover this issue in *Resimli Ay* and created a page called 'We See and We Hear'. Nazım came up with the page design. He placed two eyes in the middle of the page and two ears to the sides. In each issue, we used this page to address the strike as well as other worker-related issues. The headlines were in the following vein:

'We see that penniless workers are chased out of hospitals; we hear that workers are beaten in police stations until they spit blood.'

'We see that children with working mothers burn to death in household fires; we hear that unemployment numbers are rising.'

'We see that workers lie in the streets in the heat of noon; we hear that little children are forced to work in mines.'

I wrote many pieces about such real-life events.

'We See and We Hear' proved so successful that every day my desk was covered anew with letters from workers, intellectuals and common people. We responded individually to each letter. Reading and responding to them was Nazım's favourite pastime. Whenever he saw the letters, he put aside his work, read them with fascination and often wrote the responses himself. We also highlighted peasants' issues. Peasant intellectuals showed interest in our articles and sent us their own pieces. *Resimli Ay* became a true people's journal, expressing the grievances and defending the rights of workers, peasants and the general public.

What I saw in my village

One day, Nazım and I were working at our desks when a tall, slender young man came into the office. He put the file in his hand down on my desk.

'I brought you an article,' he said. 'I travelled here from my village. In this article, I talk about what I saw there.'

He was speaking to me but looking over at Nazım in admiration.

Nazım stood up at once.

'Who are you, son?'

'I'm Emin Türk. I'm a peasant boy, who finished the Istanbul Teachers' School. I brought you an article called "What I Saw in My Village".'

Nazım became excited without even reading the piece.

'Dear boy,' he said, 'you should write for us regularly.'

Winning over peasant intellectuals was much more important to him than gaining the approval of the elite intellectuals around him. He asked Emin Türk a lot of questions. He was very satisfied with the answers the boy gave.

'There's something about this boy,' he said.

We published the article in the January 1930 issue.

The same issue also featured a piece I'd translated from an American journal of psychology. The article was entitled 'The Psychology of the Leader'. While Nazım was proofreading it, Vala Nureddin stood next to him. They both came up to me.

'This is a very good article,' Nazım said. 'But let's change the title.'

Vala completed his thought: 'Let's call it "Out of My Way, Here I Come". Just the words to express a leader's psychology.'

'All right,' I said, 'let's do it.' And so, we published the article under that heading.

Shortly thereafter, we received a summons from the investigating judge. The prosecutor had launched a court case against both Emin Türk's article and mine. Behçet Bey, the journal's managing director, was also listed as a defendant in the case. Emin Türk and Behçet Bey were arrested while I wasn't, but we were all taken to the high criminal court. Behçet Bey was an old, seasoned press man, well known around Babıali. When he and Emin Türk were taken to the court in handcuffs, the press took notice. What was our crime? Was it so big that a felony court had to get involved?

All the writers of *Resimli Ay* assembled in the writers' office. We read the articles one by one, again and again. Everyone found Emin Türk's article more perilous, judging mine to be harmless since it was a translation. The trial was to be held very soon, which we were happy about since our colleagues were under arrest.

Unlike us, the lawyers found my article more concerning than Emin Türk's piece. The course of the trial would prove them right.

Resimli Ay on trial

The court case began, as requested by the prosecutor. Since Emin Türk and Behçet Bey were under arrest, gendarmes escorted them to the investigating court. As always, the investigating judge asked us what our intent was in writing these articles. He interrogated me first. I told him that this article was translated from an American journal, that it was a scholarly paper and that scholarly papers did not have ulterior motives. The article, I said, merely outlined how people should act when leading the masses or any group. Emin Türk was questioned next. He said that he was a teacher from a village and he'd seen many people die of disease during a recent trip there. He'd pointed this out in his article, intending to alert authorities to rural problems.

The investigating judge decided to refer our case to the high criminal court. Our first hearing was on 1 February 1930. Once again, Emin Türk and Behçet Bey were brought in by gendarmes. The three of us sat down in the defendants' chairs, surrounded by a railing, with the gendarmes standing guard right next to us. This was the first time in Turkish history that a woman was on trial over an opinion piece, so the press and the public were fascinated by the case. The large courtroom was full of youngsters, journalists and onlookers from all parts of society.

First, the investigating judge's verdict was read out. The names of the defendants were recorded. After the initial questioning was finished, the judge told me to stand up. We had the following exchange:

Chief Judge: Why did you write the article 'Out of My Way, Here I Come'?

Answer: One shouldn't search for ulterior motives in a scholarly paper. This article was translated from an American psychology journal. The writer analyses the psychology of a leader. He gives a definition of leader, saying that leaders are people who head or guide a population, a party, a trade union or any kind of community. The article provides information about leadership to young people and those in positions of power. It explains to them how to assess the group they are heading, how to manage it and which traits a leader should possess. Every issue of *Resimli Ay* features articles translated from this psychology journal. They are meant to energize and motivate young people and help them cultivate self-discipline. When the article 'The Psychology of the Leader' appeared in a recent issue of the psychology journal, I decided to translate it, thinking it would be useful to young people. I changed the title because the expression, 'Out of My Way, Here I Come', better describes the psychology of a leader.

Prosecutor: At the beginning of the article, it says that 'contentment with your lot, settling for little and submissiveness are all traits that impede progress'. There is talk of the submissiveness of the East. Are we included in this definition of the East? I request that the defendant be asked about this.

Answer: The borders of the East are defined by geography. The prosecutor can find these borders on maps and in geography books. There is no doubt that many nations are on the eastern side of the map.

Prosecutor: And does this country have a mass of people that are dissatisfied with their lot?

Answer: All populations on the five continents include groups that are resigned to fate, afraid of innovation and change, tied to tradition and apathetic. We have such a group as well. Then, there are leaders who forge ahead of such apathetic masses and guide them in a new direction through the strength of their will. When this article was written in America, it didn't have a specific population in mind. And its Turkish translation doesn't single out the Turkish people either. Scholarly papers are written objectively. This article is not bound to any specific time, place, race or nationality.

Following this exchange between the prosecutor and myself, the Chief Judge spoke up.

Chief Judge: Did it never occur to you that someone could interpret this article as the prosecutor does?

Answer: No. When I was writing this article, I didn't fancy myself in the Hamidian era. Back then, if I'd just said the word 'star', they would have accused me of referring to Abdülhamid, just because he lived in the Yıldız [Star] Palace. That wasn't the age I thought I lived in. The prosecutor seems to believe that in talking about dictators, this article indirectly refers to the president of the Republic. If so, he should explain what similarities he sees between the president and a dictator.

After my interrogation was finished, the chief judge ordered Emin Türk to rise. He asked why Emin Türk had written about the peasants' plight in such harsh language.

Emin Türk: I am accused of pitting different classes against each other and inciting hatred among them. I am a peasant myself. I spent my childhood and adolescence in the village, before getting my degree from the Teachers' School, one of the best schools in the country. My only desire is to serve my homeland. I wrote about the calamities I witnessed in my village hoping that these issues would be addressed.

Chief Judge: The investigating judge states that the things you wrote about are figments of your imagination. He says that you only wrote this article to incite the peasants. What do you say to that?

Emin Türk: I didn't fabricate the contents of this article. I wrote down what I observed in my village. I'm ready to prove this.

Once the interrogation was over, our lawyer, İrfan Emin Bey, stood up. He maintained that my article was scholarly and should be referred to a board of experts, that this board should consist of scholars and that Emin Türk should be given the right to produce witnesses for his claims. I added that I would be hiring a second lawyer and asked for some time to do so.

The judges withdrew to deliberate. After reviewing the case for about half an hour, they returned to the courtroom. The verdict was read out. The judges didn't object to hearing witnesses who would testify on our behalf. They asked for the names of the witnesses to be recorded and stated that the trial was adjourned until 15 February 1930.

The *Resimli Ay* case caused a sensation among the press and the public. On 15 February, the day the witnesses appeared, the courtroom was packed. All the boxes were full of young people, writers and journalists. Nazım Hikmet and the other *Resimli Ay* writers were in the middle box. Also present was Sami Bey, a former criminal judge, whom I had appointed as my defence attorney. Once again, we sat down in the defendants' chairs. My witnesses were Muslihiddin Adil Bey, president of the bar association and a university professor of law; Şekip Tunç, a professor of philosophy at the University of Istanbul; Hakkı Tarık, a journalist and co-proprietor of the *Vakit* newspaper; and writers Sadri Ertem and Peyami Safa. Emin Türk's witnesses were peasants, including some that he'd brought from his village and others who now lived in Istanbul.

The witnesses were a truly remarkable group. Luminaries and peasants were side by side. The latter had come to defend a teacher from their village, marking the first time that intellectuals and peasants came together to stand up for a social cause.

The session began and the judge asked to hear the witnesses. Muslihiddin Adil Bey, the university law professor, was asked to speak first.

'I know Sabiha Hanım personally as well as through her writings,' he said. 'The article at issue here is a scholarly and objective piece.'

Before Muslihiddin Adil Bey could go on, the prosecutor shot up.

'The topic and contents of the article cannot be discussed. The witnesses are here as experts. They can only comment on the character of the defendants.'

Following this objection, the court didn't ask any more questions about the articles, thereby ignoring the very reason for the trial. The other witnesses only addressed Emin

Türk's and my character. Sadri Ertem said that I was the first influential female journalist of the republican era and that I wrote articles defending democracy. Peyami Safa said that I was the first female Turkish intellectual to deal with sociology and social issues. He said, 'The intellectual world regrets seeing Sabiha Hanım in the defendant's chair rather than at a scholarly institute of higher learning, where she belongs.'[43]

I must say that they praised me quite effusively. But this court case should never have been about my character. It should have been about the article. The court viewed the article as criminal but refused to analyse it, preferring to listen to testimonies about my character instead.

Emin Türk's peasant witnesses were heard next. The witnesses who'd arrived from the village were especially noteworthy. A peasant with *çarıks* on his feet and patches on his cardigan spoke up:

> Emin Türk is from Bey village. He has poured his heart and soul into delivering our village from ignorance and sickness. He even opened our first village school. He is someone who wants the best for the nation, cares about peasants' issues and works for the benefit of all.

The other peasants said similar things. But even though we were flattered by the witnesses' words, they weren't enough to disprove the prosecutor's claims. I looked around at the people gathered in the courtroom, at the intellectual and peasant witnesses. And I couldn't help but feel pity for a system of justice that didn't allow social issues to be discussed, not even in court.

After listening to the witnesses, the judges followed procedure and withdrew again. Finally, they reached the following decision: 'Since the university professors Şekip Tunç and Hakkı Tarık are not in attendance, it has been decided to postpone the session to 27 February 1930, so these witnesses can be summoned one more time.'

The hearing adjourned and we went outside. As soon as we stepped out of the courtroom, we were surrounded by a crowd. Everyone tried to comfort us.

'Even if you're found guilty in this trial,' they said, 'you aren't guilty in our hearts. You only defended the cause of the homeland, and you're still defending it. That's all the honour you need.'

This verdict of the people was our greatest acquittal.

The fourth hearing was held on 27 February. This time, the audience was different. Young female students and university professors filled the boxes. Nazım Hikmet and the writers of *Resimli Ay* were in the same box again. The audience downstairs comprised people from many different classes. The judges and the prosecutor took their places at the bench. My lawyer, Sami Bey, sat down in the lawyers' section.

Nüsret Bey, the chief judge, asked whether the witnesses missing from the prior session were in attendance. Before they were called, Sami Bey requested that all

---

[43] The same Peyami Safa who sang my praises in court that day opposed my struggle against fascism during the Second World War. He tried to tarnish my reputation with his articles in *Cumhuriyet* and the caricatures he commissioned, such as 'The Gypsy with Tongs' and 'The Bolshevik Parrot'.

witnesses also be heard on the subject matter of the article. Hoping this request would be granted, we had brought the earlier witnesses as well. Once again, the peasants and intellectuals sat down next to each other. The judge called on our first witness, the university professor Şekip Tunç Bey.

'I know Sabiha Hanım and Behçet Bey as two esteemed members of the press,' Şekip Tunç said. 'Sabiha Hanım is the first Turkish woman to write on social matters with authority. The article "Out of My Way, Here I Come" is a scholarly, objective piece.'

Before Şekip Tunç could finish, the prosecutor stood up.

'The witness is going off topic. He wasn't asked about the quality of the article. He should only tell us what he knows about the defendants.'

Şekip Bey became angry.

'In that case,' he said, 'why did you summon me here? If you want to know about Sabiha Hanım's character, you shouldn't ask scholars but her friends, who know her better than I do.' He sat down.

And so, the witness hearing concluded. The chief judge called on Cemil Bey, the prosecutor, to read out his indictment. Cemil Bey started reading from the notes in front of him, but he was listless and hesitant. He repeated the factors constituting the crime as enumerated by the investigating judge in his preliminary decision. I will quote some passages from this indictment to show the prosecutor's interpretation of the article.

> By calling dictatorship a microbe that kills the moral quality of a leader and stating that a leader's qualities must include forging ahead of the people, mingling with the people, charging down the path he has created and possessing the immutable quality of being a servant of the masses, the defendant, Sabiha Zekeriya Hanım, has insulted and offended his excellency, the President, claiming that his excellency, the President, has distanced himself from humanity by parting from these principles; that he lacks the eyes to see, the ears to hear and the heart to feel the people's suffering; that he has lost the qualities of leadership; that he has revealed his true intentions by becoming tyrannous; that he has become haughty; and that he does not love the people.
>
> Further, after comparing the Turkish people to sheep that stubbornly and complacently follow the same path, even to the edge of the most dangerous precipice, and stating that they wander around like a blind, aimless and unprincipled dervish who determines his life's path by the whim of his walking stick, she used the abovementioned article to insult Turkishness by claiming that walking down the old path is easy and that the Turkish people are a blind procession, passing like a flock of sheep down a path already worn out by millions of people, and by describing our race as a mass that greets every arising issue with apathy.

The prosecutor continued his indictment with several similarly absurd interpretations of Emin Türk's article. Then, he went on to state:

> In defending his article, Emin Türk Bey states that the typhus epidemic in his village is real and that he will prove it. But even if the existence of this disease in

the village was proven, this would not alter the crime. What we are objecting to is the style in which the article was written.

At the end of his indictment, the prosecutor demanded a prison sentence of up to twenty years for me and up to three years for Emin Türk.

We were visibly shaken by this demand. After the session concluded, all *Resimli Ay* writers left the courthouse together, Nazım Hikmet among us. We arrived at the office. Before even sitting down, Nazım ran over to the staircase. The room we worked in was on the second floor, with a coffee shop downstairs. We were used to drinking coffee in the offices. Nazım called down the stairs:

> 'Mehmet, bring us eight cups of coffee with lots of sugar.'
> 'Why lots of sugar?' our colleagues asked.

All but delighted, Nazım replied:

> 'We won a victory today. We created unity between peasants and intellectuals in the courtroom. Tomorrow, we will create unity between peasants and workers.'

To Nazım, this was the only element of the trial that mattered.

The final session

Soon, the writers' office filled with authors, journalists and friends. They all expressed their sorrow. Some of them told me to flee, saying that one couldn't spend twenty years in prison, while others said the judges might yet reject the sentence demanded by the prosecutor. The trial had adjourned so the defence could prepare its case. Our lawyers were worried. Legally, they said, the charges could be rebutted. But politically, the situation was dangerous.

I was determined to defend myself until the very end.

On the day of the final session, my friends asked me to run my defence by my lawyer Sami Bey. I consulted with him.

'Just say whatever you want,' he told me. 'In the defendant's chair, every defendant can speak freely. There's no need for me to read the defence. I know what I'll say; that's enough.'

He, for one, was very relaxed.

When our group of *Resimli Ay* writers arrived at the courthouse, crowds had already gathered outside the doors. The police barred them from entering and were barely able to clear a path for us to go inside. When we entered the courtroom, it was absolutely packed. Once again, gendarmes had escorted Emin Türk and Behçet Bey from prison in handcuffs. We took our seats in the defendants' chairs.

The court clerk briefly recounted what had been said at the previous session and went over the legal principles underlying the prosecutor's claims. Then Nüsret Bey, the chief judge, motioned for me to begin.

In the course of our defences, Emin Türk and I drew on our answers from the preceding hearings. At length, we dissected the illogic and fanciful interpretations of the prosecutor's indictment. Once we were finished, the judge called on our lawyers. İrfan Emin Bey spoke first. After a long defence of his own, he asked for our acquittal. Then it was Sami Bey's turn to speak. In a bare three sentences, he went beyond what we'd been able to say in three hours. In brief, his defence was as follows:

> There is nothing to be added to Sabiha Hanım's defence. I will restrict myself to pointing out some legal issues. The prosecutor states that the article uses innuendo and insinuation to target his Excellency, the President. But the punishment he demands is not legally applicable. The crimes of insult that result from innuendo and insinuation are noted in Chapter Seven, Article 484 of the Penal Code. Punishment for these crimes ranges from three to twenty years. The prosecutor, however, bases his indictment not on Article 484, but on Article 185 of the Penal Code. A punishment detailed in the seventh chapter cannot be applied to a crime from the first chapter. That would mean making the two crimes analogous, and no justice system will stand for that. The prosecution has committed a brazen error in executing the law. The defendant's article is scholarly, social and general. It does not target a specific person. I ask that any verdict be based on Article 185.

By proving that the case had referenced the wrong article of the penal code, Sami Bey put the prosecutor in a very tight spot. After the defence concluded, the council of judges withdrew. Their deliberation took five hours. I will summarize the verdict that was read out:

> We sentence Sabiha Hanım and Behçet Bey to two months in prison and a fine of 30 liras each. The actions of Emin Türk Bey, the author of the article 'What I Saw in My Village', fall under Article 16 of the Penal Code. However, he has only recently joined the world of publishing and is not intimately familiar with journalism. This counts as an extenuating circumstance. Therefore, in accordance with Article 16, we sentence him to one month in prison and a fine of 25 liras.

We left the courthouse pleased. To be sure, being convicted wasn't a cause for celebration, but compared to twenty years, two months seemed like two days to us. For me, the biggest victory was the concession that my article contained no insult against the Turkish people or president. Nonetheless, the article had been deemed an 'untruthful publication', and I'd been sentenced to two months in prison for writing it. This seemed odd. How could legal scholars judge whether the thoughts and writings of a psychology scholar were untruthful? Still, we accepted the sentence as a compromise partly intended to appease the prosecutor. The verdict was based on the penal code article suggested by Sami Bey. Without his strong defence, Emin Türk and I could have been sent to jail for three and twenty years, respectively. My gratitude goes out to him if he is still alive. If he has passed away, may he rest in peace.

I'm recounting this trial at such length to demonstrate the mentality of the times. The trial's aim was to use the law to silence *Resimli Ay*. The journal defended the public interest. Those upset by this tried to have us sentenced, based on fantasies and conjectures incompatible with law or reason. But rather than harming *Resimli Ay*, the trial ended up helping it, bolstering its reputation among the people.

One day, shortly after the trial, I was working in the writers' office with Nazım and the others. The door opened and a peasant came in, wearing *çarıks* on his feet, a backward cap on his head and his black *şalvar*.[44]

'I come from Malkara,' he said. 'I bring you the greetings and gratitude of my compatriots. We followed your trial with bated breath. This cause was our cause, too. We'd like to buy ten subscriptions for *Resimli Ay*. You should know that these subscriptions are for peasants who can't even afford corn bread, which only costs three *kuruş*[45] per *okka*.[46] Now, I will present you with a defect[47] sent by my friends.'

He took a piece of paper from his pocket. The text written on it thanked us for voicing peasants' troubles in *Resimli Ay* and *Resimli Perşembe*.

Yes, we'd been convicted. But our cause wasn't defeated. These words were the strongest proof of our victory and its greatest reward. As long as peasants go hungry in their villages, as long as workers are deprived of the right to live with dignity, it is our right and duty to raise our voices as loudly as possible to protest the forces of exploitation that keep peasants, workers and the impoverished masses in their place. It is our duty to demand their rights, and if we are convicted for doing so, this is not a defeat but a victory.

We appealed the court's decision. The court of appeals ruled that the charge of personal insult had not been proven and that the articles contained nothing that might inflame public opinion. Therefore, it overturned the verdict. In a session held on 4 September, the previous court accepted this decision and lifted our sentences. And this was how the 'Out of My Way, Here I Come' case ended.

The literary debates at *Resimli Ay*

In the evenings, after finishing our work at the office, we usually gathered at our house on Şair Nefi Street in Kadıköy to debate literature and socialism. Writers like Nazım, Sabahaddin Ali, Naci Saadullah, Vala Nureddin, Peyami Safa and Kemal Tahir attended these gatherings, and the debates were always exciting.

Nazım was a new voice in literature. With his revolutionary ideas and his knowledge of contemporary art, he had a great influence on the young writers of his generation. Claiming that the poetic era of *aruz* and *hece* was over, he heralded the birth of a new literature. He elaborated on these views in a piece he wrote for *Resimli Ay*:

> The writings of bourgeois literati can only be understood by a bunch of bourgeois intellectuals, not by the public. And mediocre intellectuals have a misconception of art.

---

[44] TN: Traditional baggy trousers worn by the rural population.
[45] TN: A Turkish currency unit: 100 *kuruş* are equal to 1 Turkish lira.
[46] TN: A unit of measurement equalling 1,283 grammes.
[47] TN: The word used here is *arıza*. It is likely that the peasant meant to say *maruzat*, meaning 'submission' or 'petition', but mistakenly chose the similar-sounding *arıza*, meaning 'defect'.

Those who offer us ornate, gilded glassware filled with the saccharine, syrupy stories of Yakup Kadri, such as 'Erenlerin Bağı', 'Nur Baba' and 'Damla',[48] have long since become history along with their works. I have no reverence at all for this bygone literary generation.

Nazım's sweeping rejection of the past sparked many debates. One of these concerned the idea that literature should reach down to the masses, an idea vehemently defended by Nazım. Of course, the idea of literature reaching out to the people wasn't new. It first emerged with the *Edebiyatı Cedide* movement,[49] where it was championed by literati like Tevfik Fikret and Hüseyin Siret. But their language was incomprehensible to their own generation and their themes only reflected the upper classes.

One mustn't forget, however, that these authors lived in a different age with different conditions. The eras of Abdülaziz[50] or Abdülhamid couldn't have produced a Nazım Hikmet. All literati and poets are the products of their own age and society. Changes in the social structure lead to changes in literature. *Divan* literature, *Tanzimat* literature and *Edebiyatı Cedide* are all links in an evolutionary chain.

Rejecting these movements as a whole means rejecting the idea of evolution in the course of history. And tossing them aside as bourgeois can only be a product of narrow-mindedness. Most objections to Nazım were based on this argument, and I was among those who opposed him on this point. Nazım's statement that he felt no reverence whatsoever toward these movements struck me as somewhat nihilistic.

Language was another matter of debate. Nazım favoured the simplification of literary language and was against employing words that weren't used by common people. Peyami Safa, in contrast, argued that refined Istanbul Turkish represented the zenith of the language. To him, depleting the language by reducing it to common parlance was a mistake.

Many of us agreed with Nazım on language, but we still believed that Turkish was enriched by Arabic and Persian words. It was hard to find Turkish equivalents for these words, and we were against replacing them with words that were newly made up or adopted from Chagatai dictionaries. Nazım agreed with us on this latter point. But he insisted that the Turkish language didn't need these Arabic and Persian words. He backed up his claim with the evidence of his own poems.

It's undeniable that Nazım introduced the same simplicity to the Turkish language that he introduced in poetic technique. Everyone, even the simplest person, could easily understand his poems. Nazım didn't use recently created words, either. One could say that the language he used was Turkish in its most accomplished form.

Realism in literature was also a topic of debate. Some writers who adhered to the old traditions insisted that artists shouldn't be bound by rules of realism and that it was their duty to reflect mystical philosophy as much as the material world. This argument made Nazım furious.

---

[48] TN: The titles can be translated as 'The Vineyard of Mystics', 'Father Radiance' and 'Drop'.
[49] TN: *Edebiyatı Cedide* or 'New Literature' was an Ottoman literary movement most influential in the last decade of the nineteenth century.
[50] TN: R. 1861–76.

'The mystical world,' he said, 'is where the writer entrenches himself to obscure his lack of talent. Hiding reality from the people and encouraging them to live in a dream world merely pacifies them. The artist mustn't write for himself but for his readers, the people. Art doesn't exist for art's sake. It's a tool in the artist's hands, to be used for a purpose. The artist must use this tool for the benefit of the masses.'

The debates about whether art should be for art's sake or serve a specific purpose often raged on until midnight.

Nazım's own poems were the most beautiful examples of realist literature. His verses proclaimed his realist point of view, and his poems expressed reality in all its clarity. These poems united emotion, reason, upheaval and harmony, to reflect reality through a new language and technique. With his materialist outlook, Nazım broke the mold of metaphysics and focused on the material world. He searched for truth not in the realm of emotions but in the midst of society. One can say that the soul of Nazım's poems is his love for the oppressed, exploited human being and his hatred for the oppressors.

It is this ideology and philosophy that makes Nazım a revolutionary. In his hands, poetry becomes a tool that reflects his emotions, excitement, ideas and ideology, all at the same time. Nazım put his art at the service of the revolution, and as a revolutionary poet, he attacked the 'egoistic' works of the old literati and poets, works that tranquillized the masses.

Nazım can be said to have written his most revolutionary poems during his time at *Resimli Ay*. Among these, the poems 'Yürüyen Adam' (1929), 'Gayemin Yolcularına' (1928), 'Güneşin Sofrasında Söylenen Türkü' and 'Kerem Gibi'[51] made a great impression on the new generation, infusing the young, intellectuals and workers with the will to struggle. Every line of the poem 'Yürüyen Adam' is a call to arms.

> He walks
>   whistling
>   an angry march of death.
>   He walks,
>   his body rising like a ship,
>   falling,
>   He walks, step by step
>   He walks, little by little,
>   he walks
>   naked
>   like two blades
>   in his strained face
>   are his eyes.
>   He walks toward the enemy.
>   He walks, step by step,
>   he walks, little by little,
>   he walks.

---

[51] TN: The titles can be translated as 'The Man Who Walks', 'To the Travelling Companions of My Purpose', 'The Song Performed at the Sun's Dining Table' and 'Just Like Kerem', respectively.

These verses convey a revolutionary fervour, as do the verses from his poem 'Kerem Gibi':

> The air is heavy as lead,
>   shout
>   shout
>   I shout.
>   Run,
>   I call you
>   to melt
>   the lead.
>   Let me be ash
>   just like
>   kerem
>   burning
>   burning.
> If I don't burn
>   if you don't burn
>   if we don't burn
> how will
>   the dark
>   ness
>   come to
>   light.[52]

These and his other revolutionary poems inspire his own generation – and all generations to come – with the will to defend their cause until the end, fearlessly, unwaveringly and without losing heart.

Yet another topic of discussion was that of national literature and class literature. According to Nazım, there was no national literature, only class literature. Just as bourgeois writers had produced the literature of their own class, proletarian poets and artists had to create the literature of the class they championed. A proletarian writer had to go beyond simply writing about the working class and actually make his literature accessible to that class. For this reason, he had to avoid words that workers and common people didn't know. According to Nazım, the proletarian artist had to do more than just convey the life of workers. He had to imbue the workers with a fighting spirit, to defend their rights against their exploiters.

Nazım embedded his thoughts and philosophical views in his poems with such power that even those who were hostile to his ideology couldn't help but enjoy reading them.

The writer most opposed to the concept of class literature was Peyami Safa. He believed in national literature. Every work written by a Turkish poet or author, next to

---

[52] TN: These poems were translated following Sertel's renditions rather than Nazım Hikmet's originals, meaning that many lines were omitted and Sertel's orthographic quirks were respected.

expressing his own feelings and excitement, was a work of national character. The writer didn't have to consider which class he was addressing. To Peyami Safa, there could be no separate category such as common people's literature. Nazım responded that just as bourgeois writers dealt with the issues of their own class, proletarian writers were obliged to address the issues of the oppressed working and peasant classes and to expose social inequities.

When faced with the objection that a proletarian artist addressing only his class was no longer a national artist, Nazım retorted that any literature expressing the suffering of the masses was much more national than literature aimed only at a handful of bourgeois readers.

Nazım gave a perfect example of this nationalist perspective in his epic about the War of Independence, *Kurtuluş Savaşı Destanı*.[53] This epic, which he composed while imprisoned in Bursa, is a masterpiece expressing his patriotism. None of the writers and poets of the time were able to describe the War of Independence with as much patriotic fervour as he did.

These gatherings weren't the only place where Nazım expressed his thoughts and views. In spite of all the pressure, he also tried to disseminate them through his books. At our debates, his forceful personality and literary talent prevailed over all those around him, and any minor objections melted away before his genius and self-confidence.

Debates on socialism

At our gatherings, we also discussed the matter of socialism. About ten years had passed since the end of the War of Independence. Some very progressive steps had been taken, reforms carried out and new principles put forward to advance the underdeveloped nation. Among the principles defended by Atatürk, statism was the most important. The Treaty of Lausanne had done away with the capitulations and erected barriers against the entry of foreign capital into the country. Statism aimed to create a national bourgeoisie and encourage private enterprise. It did so through state subsidies and state-owned credit institutions such as İş Bankası, Kredi Bankası, Sümerbank, and Etibank. The state itself was only supposed to manage the industries that private enterprise couldn't handle.

In our debates, there were those who believed that Turkey couldn't advance toward socialism by promoting private enterprise, but who nonetheless accepted statism as an appropriate response to the country's conditions, a necessary phase to pass through.

On the other side, there were those who thought it was possible to skip statism and transition directly to socialism. At present, they argued, the country lacked the accumulated capital to establish the industries it needed. It was surrendering to capitalism to build these vital industries, but private enterprise couldn't be trusted to do the job. Capitalists would only invest in areas that increased their profit, exploiting

---

[53] TN: *Epic of the War of Liberation*. The words used by Sertel (*istiklal*, independence) and Nazım Hikmet (*kurtuluş*, liberation) are often employed interchangeably to describe the same war in Turkish literature and historiography.

the country's resources for their own benefit. To properly manage these resources, the state needed to nationalize them. Otherwise, the argument went, private enterprise would simply use state capital for its own purposes.

There was some truth to this. But given the conditions at the time, was a direct transition to socialism really possible? Here, opinions diverged. Some argued that social development couldn't always follow the straight line found in theory books, passing through private enterprise and democracy before reaching socialism. Certain leaps, they said, were necessary from time to time. It was wrong for the state to assist private enterprise. Instead, the state itself had to manage the country's resources and distribute national income in an equitable way. When asked which social class would accomplish this leap, they pointed to the proletariat.

But back then, the Turkish working class was extremely underdeveloped, both in numbers and in class consciousness. The peasant class was scattered and divided. Agricultural workers had no organizations of their own, and the ones that did exist at the village level were dominated by local landlords. Though legally abolished, the feudal system's remnants survived and thrived in many places. The sharecropping system continued. Neither objective nor subjective conditions were ripe for a socialist revolution in Turkey.

These circumstances prompted some of us to support the struggle for democracy. Even if the socialist revolution remained out of reach, they argued, a democratic bourgeois revolution was at least a step in the right direction. But such a revolution could also lead to a dictatorship of the bourgeoisie, making it impossible for the working class to develop and organize. Already, the ruling class was trying to prevent the working class and progressive forces from engaging in class struggle. The most crucial issue of the day was to enlighten workers and peasants about their own cause and to unite them against exploitation by the nascent bourgeoisie and the landlords.

For those who wanted Turkey to transition to socialism without first going through a bourgeois democratic revolution, the only hope was to educate the people through publications and organize them. But the bourgeois revolution had already started, and the bourgeoisie was targeting leftist movements, inducing the state to outlaw communist and socialist parties, and waging a relentless war against the left. In this climate, it was very hard to spread socialist ideas and organize the working class. We were all searching for new ways to accomplish this.

The only issue we agreed on was the necessity of fighting against imperialism and liberating the underdeveloped nation from foreign capital's yoke.

A fatal flaw of these discussions was their sectarian and dogmatic nature. At this stage, I must admit, we were all caught up in sectarianism to some extent. Some of us believed that world revolution was just around the corner, proclaimed that Turkey would transition to socialism soon, and dismissed the objective and subjective conditions in the country. Some among us predicted that the imperialists would quickly start a second world war. According to them, just as the First World War had led to the October Revolution and the rise of socialism in the Soviet Union, this new war would destroy the foundations of imperialism and lead to the establishment of socialist states in many parts of Europe, if not everywhere. Without such a war, they said, socialism couldn't be established in Turkey, either.

For this group, the rise of socialism in the country depended on outside factors rather than on the development of internal forces and conditions. They were far from conceding the masses an active role in the revolution.

The hardline sectarians insisted on a rigorous fight against reactionary religious figures and entrepreneurs who collaborated with foreign capital. But they also opposed cooperating with the national bourgeoisie, even on matters of common interest. To them, even the slightest rapprochement with progressive bourgeois intellectuals was a sign of opportunism. They repeated the trite cliché that peasants were our allies but ignored the reality that there was no connection at all between Turkish peasants and workers yet. These hardliners were dead set against any alliance with the middle class. The latter could have united with the workers against reactionaries and imperialists, but the hardliners dismissed them out of hand as petty bourgeois.[54]

There was no full agreement on the matter of democracy, either. The hardline faction claimed that any real democracy had to be preceded by a socialist revolution. To them, bourgeois democracy as found in the West was democracy in name only. Rejecting it utterly, they dreamed of a more advanced democracy established by a proletarian state. They disregarded the fact that socialism was only made possible by the democratic bourgeois revolutions of Europe, and that Turkey had yet to complete such a revolution. By insisting on an immediate socialist revolution, they actually blocked the way of any progressive movement.

There were even people who attacked *Resimli Ay* for its support of democracy and were offended by my pieces in *Cumhuriyet*. They rejected bourgeois scholarship as if it was taboo and considered it a crime to benefit from the findings of this scholarship. To them, no good could come from studying bourgeois culture.

The hardliners didn't trust bourgeois intellectuals and refused to cooperate with them in any way. These intellectuals were deemed suspect since they didn't belong to the working class. But this argument ignored the fact that during the October Revolution, many bourgeois intellectuals had switched classes and made important contributions to the movement. Just like the starry-eyed socialist Fourier Owen, our hardliners reduced socialism to equality in poverty. They rejected anything that could be labeled 'bourgeois', even a decent standard of living like the wearing of nice clothes. They felt virtuous running around in collarless shirts, workers' caps and ragged clothes, forgetting that the goal of socialism was to raise all workers' living standards. In their opinion, one wasn't a proper socialist if one hadn't been in prison. To them, there was no 'people' as a whole, only the working class. They had no idea how their attitudes estranged the revolutionary movement from the masses.

Our political debates were dominated by fruitless matters like this. At the time, I'm sorry to say, socialist thought in Turkey was little more than romanticism.

---

[54] TN: In Marxist thought, petty bourgeoisie denotes a class above the proletariat, but below and beholden to the capitalist high bourgeoisie. Often, the petty bourgeoisie is a clerical and managerial class employed by the high bourgeoisie.

Some words on Nazım Hikmet

Nazım was a realist poet. His poems showcased this realism with the artistry of a genius. He took a stand against mystical and romantic literature. The skill with which he crafted a new perspective on history out of dialectical materialist philosophy set him apart from earlier Turkish literati and most of his contemporaries. Nazım defended not just his own countrymen but oppressed people all over the world. His love for humans and humanity, his ideas and commitment to the liberation of the oppressed made him an international poet. Unity, solidarity and internationalism among the workers of the world were the foundations of his ideology. At the same time, he was a national poet in his affection for the exploited workers, peasants and common people of his own country. But he wasn't merely a poet who expressed these thoughts and feelings in his work; he was also a revolutionary who defended his cause as a militant.

His verses and words were like sparks, not just in their simplicity, but also in how they conveyed his fervour, emotions and thoughts to his audience. His strong personality and literary genius had a major impact on the youth in his day. The most influential new literati, poets and novelists of today are those who build on the foundations laid by him. Thanks to Nazım, an entirely new literature emerged. Those in the vanguard of this new literature, people like Yaşar Kemal, Kemal Tahir, Orhan Kemal, Orhan Veli, Oktay Rıfat, Melih Cevdet, Mahmut Makal and Fakir Baykurt, are the most significant names in contemporary Turkish literature, and they all follow in his footsteps.

The ruling elite didn't understand – or rather, wilfully refused to recognize – his genius and artistic merit. They left him to rot in prison for the most mundane reasons. But even though his homeland failed to grasp his importance, Nazım Hikmet took his place in the annals of world literature. His works were translated into sixty or seventy languages. His masterpieces are part of the world's cultural heritage.

Nazım is a proletarian poet, but also a patriotic poet. His epic of national liberation and the poems of longing he penned in exile are examples of his patriotism. The poems he wrote in Varna for his son, Mehmed, and his wife, Münevver, express his yearning for the homeland. As delighted as Nazım was to see his poems translated into many languages and read by common people around the world, he was endlessly tortured by the fact that they were banned in his own country and that his own people couldn't read them. Like Alfred Dreyfus, he spent years in prison although he was innocent. Attempts on his life eventually forced him into exile. He was never able to return. The greatest agony of his final years was his longing for the homeland and the ban on his poems there.

Letting such a poet, one of the country's rare talents, rot away in prison was a crime that neither history nor generations to come will ever forgive.

*

When I met him again in Vienna in 1960, he was thrilled to see me. We reminisced about old times.

'I spent the most passionate days of my youth at *Resimli Ay*,' he said. 'What joyful days they were!'

We talked about our discussions at *Resimli Ay*. Life and experience had taught us a great deal by then. We recalled the mistakes we'd made. Nâzım smiled.

'We were such sectarians back then,' he said. 'For example, what was the point of the whole "Breaking the Idols" campaign? All that big talk about Abdülhak Hamit not being a national poet, not caring about the country's problems, not being a proletarian poet ... How could we expect him to be a proletarian poet in the age of the sultanate? The proletariat itself had hardly been born! He managed to exceed his own horizons and deal with global matters. That makes him a major poet.

'Abdülhak Hamit was a product of his own time and conditions. Mehmet Emin wasn't even really a poet. Mehmet Akif's mystical ideology was one we should have refuted through our realist works and not through polemics. Namık Kemal was a patriotic poet who fought against the dictatorship of Abdülhamit and suffered for it in exile. But we lashed out at people like him. We summarily dismissed them as bourgeois literati.

'What was that poem of mine, "Berkeley", all about? What was I thinking, using a poem to teach people about dialectical materialism? We insisted that a proletarian poet couldn't write love poetry. In our dogmatism, we forgot about nature and humanity.'

Nâzım had finally accepted that literature and art couldn't be judged independently of their historical context, that their form and content depended on external conditions, that it wasn't fair to dismiss earlier writers and poets as bourgeois, and that rejecting them out of hand amounted to a rigid factionalism. 'Instead,' he now said, 'we should have simply rendered them obsolete through our own literature.'

Nâzım died without seeing the workers' movement advance in his homeland, without seeing the day his poems went back into print in Turkey.

It was, and will always be, an honour for the writers of *Resimli Ay* to have welcomed Nâzım and worked by his side.

The closure of *Resimli Ay*

Resimli Ay continued its progressive writings even after the trial over 'Out of My Way, Here I Come'. Apart from addressing workers' and peasants' issues, the journal also ran articles against imperialism and reported on the progress made by the republics in the Soviet Union, such as Azerbaijan and Uzbekistan.[55] The most popular pieces in this second phase were short stories by Sabahaddin Ali, Sadri Ertem and Suat Derviş; articles written by Nâzım Hikmet under the pseudonyms 'Orhan' and 'Süleyman'; and poems he wrote as the 'Man without Signature'.

The gathering of progressive writers at *Resimli Ay* didn't fail to attract police attention. From the building across the street, they kept tabs on who came and went. They also tried to plant undercover agents among us. These agents arrived under the pretext of pitching new articles. But each of their pieces was designed as provocation.[56]

---

[55] TN: Sertel seems to be referring to Turkic-speaking Soviet republics, in particular.
[56] TN: I.e. the articles were so provocative that had they been published, they would have given the police an excuse to shut down the magazine.

The situation frightened our business partners. They'd invested in the *Resimli Ay* Limited Company to make a profit and had no political or social goals. To us, however, *Resimli Ay* was not a means to make money. It was a vehicle for defending democracy, progressive ideas and the interests of the workers, peasants and impoverished population.

Our business partners demanded that Nazım Hikmet and other leftist writers be dismissed from the journal. Zekeriya and I refused. The rift resulted in the dissolution of the partnership. In the final months of 1930, a curious newspaper announcement was posted by the *Resimli Ay* Limited Company:

> Recently, the *Resimli Ay* magazine has been publishing pointless articles on outdated topics that satisfy none of the needs of the country or readership. In light of this, our corporation has decided to terminate the contracts of the editors-in-chief and shut down the magazine.

The announcement also proclaimed that the publishing licence belonged to the company and that our former partners would publish the magazine without us. But we, the founders of *Resimli Ay*, were determined to continue putting out the journal ourselves. We left the company and rented a small office on Babıali Slope. In our first issue, published on 1 January 1931, we recounted the story of *Resimli Ay* as follows:

> We started *Resimli Ay* seven years ago. In these seven years, the journal encountered many difficulties. But it kept publishing in spite of these hardships, prison sentences and ceaseless court cases because *Resimli Ay* was a journal of ideals. It kept publishing to make a small contribution to the literary and intellectual life of this country, to express the grievances of the anguished masses and to ensure the establishment of a democratic order. The difficulties it encountered did not shake its will and resolve even as we scrambled from one court case to the next. This latest obstacle will not stop *Resimli Ay* from appearing. Our business partners want to take over the magazine's name. But *Resimli Ay* is ours. And it will continue publishing.

Shortly thereafter, in early 1931, the last issue of *Resimli Ay* appeared. Our business partners took us to court, claiming that the publishing licence was the company's property. They managed to block publication of the journal. And this was how *Resimli Ay* ended its life in print.

We'd set out with the goal of serving a useful purpose, and we believe we achieved that goal. On this note, I can't pass up the opportunity to cite something Nazım Hikmet wrote about *Resimli Ay* in his foreword to Sabahaddin Ali's novel, *İçimizdeki Şeytan* [The Devil within Us], printed in Czechoslovakia:

> At one point, I was the technical secretary and copy editor of the magazine *Resimli Ay*, published by Sabiha and Zekeriya Sertel. *Resimli Ay* fought against imperialism and defended democracy.
>
> Back then, just as now, enemies of democracy, pan-Turkists, and agents of imperialism formed a united front. *Resimli Ay* challenged this front with its publications.

The magazine's columns featured literary debates under the heading of 'Falling Idols'. In reality, these debates were a means of defending the political rights of the common people. At the same time, the magazine published poems urging people to support the striking Istanbul tramway labourers. It exposed the hidden agendas of the Young Christians' Organization, the Bible Society, the American colleges in Istanbul and other organizations that acted as imperialist agents. In retaliation, the Young Christians' Organization and the pan-Turkists of the Turkish Hearth banded together with the Istanbul police and attacked the magazine's printing house.

I do not mention *Resimli Ay* on a whim. This magazine played an important role in the literary and political life of Sabahaddin Ali and many other progressive writers.

Nazım Hikmet's words about *Resimli Ay* are a source of pride for us to this day.

5

Life in politics

The translation of socialist works

Before *Resimli Ay* was shut down, Zekeriya had entered into a partnership with journalist Selim Ragıp as well as Ekrem Uşaklıgil and Halil Lütfi Dördüncü to publish a daily newspaper called *Son Posta* [The Latest Edition]. But his partners had imposed the condition that I shouldn't write for the paper. As a result, I was left without a job. This period in time, however, was quite suitable for working a little more independently.

The effects of the 1928–9 global economic crisis were also being felt in Turkey. A poor harvest caused further economic hardship. People had difficulty making ends meet. In line with its policy of statism, the administration established monopolies on many commodities. This increased the trade bourgeoisie's[1] opposition to the government. The worsening economic situation led to cuts in workers' wages, which also deepened the antagonism between the bourgeoisie and workers.

The single-party rule of the People's Party prevented democratic rights from being implemented. The imperialist press portrayed Atatürk as a dictator. And pressure from European monopolies on the Turkish economy forced him to change his economic policy. He and his inner circle decided to adopt a more liberal line, founding a second party to allow some outside scrutiny of the state and government. They also found it necessary to grant certain allowances to foreign capital in order to break the economic deadlock.

On 12 August 1930, the Liberal Republican Party was founded at the behest of Mustafa Kemal. Initially developed in secret, it was presented to the public as an opposition party. Its aim was to appease the people's grievances and search for ways to overcome the economic crisis. Fethi Okyar, one of Atatürk's most trusted friends, and Ağaoğlu Ahmet Bey, a longtime supporter of liberal economic policy, were appointed as its leaders.

Along with the founding of the Liberal Party, the 1930s also witnessed the establishment of certain press freedoms. Prosecutors no longer interrogated writers about every article. Taking advantage of this opportunity, I decided to translate some works about socialism. Since these books couldn't enter the country, the only ones I could use were those sent to me by a friend in London. First, I translated Kautsky's *Class Struggle*.

---

[1] TN: A bourgeoisie that comes into being as a result of commerce rather than capitalist production. Sertel uses the term interchangeably with 'trade capitalists'.

I reached an agreement with a publisher on Babıali. 'I'll finance the book myself,' I told him. 'You can keep the profit. Once you've sold enough copies, you can pay me back my capital.' The bookseller accepted this condition. I wasn't interested in profit but in disseminating these ideas.

The book was on sale for six months, until the police decided to confiscate all copies. By that point, most of the copies had been sold, but the bookseller used the confiscation as an excuse to pocket my investment. Nonetheless, I'd achieved my wish. The book had been on sale for half a year.

In the years that followed, from 1930 to 1936, I translated Adoratsky's *Dialectical Materialism* and *The 1936 Soviet Constitution*, Lenin's *War and Socialism* and August's *Woman and Socialism* into Turkish. I published these books with the money I made from articles I wrote for *Tan* [Dawn].[2] But I didn't have enough money to publish *Woman and Socialism*. The book ended up sitting at home, fully translated.

Around that time, Haydar Rifat Bey, the president of the Bar Association and one of Turkey's prominent lawyers, and Hakkı Tarık, a co-owner of *Vakit* newspaper, founded a company that translated Marxist works into Turkish. They'd launched the company after seeing that such books and Nazım's poems sold like hot cakes and were hoping to make a profit. Somehow, Haydar Rifat heard that I'd translated *Woman and Socialism* but was unable to print it. He offered to publish the book.

'Let's make a deal,' he said. 'We'll split the profit in two.'

I didn't care about the profit. My goal was to get the book printed. So we made an agreement, the book was published, and it remained on sale for years. On this note, I'd like to recount one of my later memories.

One day, during the Second World War, I came to the publishing house.[3] As soon as I entered the printing room, I was told that the police were looking for me and that they wanted to confiscate *Woman and Socialism* and Kautsky's *Class Struggle*. By then, *Class Struggle* had sold out, and I didn't have the inventory for *Woman and Socialism*. I'd only put aside fifteen copies of each book. The rest were with Haydar Rifat Bey.

I went upstairs and the telephone rang before I could sit down at my desk. Police Chief Muzaffer Bey was on the line.

'Madam,' he said, 'the police has decided to confiscate the books *Woman and Socialism* and *Class Struggle*. Please surrender those books to the officers I'm sending over.'

'I don't have the books, sir,' I replied. 'Please contact Haydar Rifat Bey. He published the books and has the remaining copies.'

'Haydar Rifat Bey says that you have them.'

'He's mistaken.'

Muzaffer Bey hung up. Not much later, the phone rang again.

'This is Haydar Rifat speaking. Sabiha Hanım, my dear girl, I like you very much, and we did print that book of yours, but we can't for the life of us sell any copies of it. You have a printing house and a network of vendors. You could sell it easily. Let me

---

[2] TN: This daily newspaper, which came to define the life and work of Sabiha and Zekeriya Sertel, will be described in much detail below.

[3] TN: At this point, Sertel and her husband, Zekeriya, were publishing the daily newspaper *Tan*.

Figure 5.1 Magazine profile, 29 April 1935, of Sabiha Sertel at their famed Moda villa, overlooking the Sea of Marmara. It was a salon for intellectuals, writers and artists.

turn the book over to you at cost. You can keep the profit. These books have a bright future. Let me come over there, and we'll sign an agreement. I'll give you the books at whatever price we agree on. If you want, you can pay it off in installments.'

'Sir, the *Tan* publishing house won't sell those books. And I don't want any profit, either. To this day, I've never asked you for an accounting.'

'I know, my dear girl, but I have nowhere to put the books. You can store them at the publishing house and sell them.'

'Are you looking for a storehouse? Muzaffer Bey, the chief of police, has one at the police directorate. You can send the books over there.'

Haydar Rifat Bey hung up.

Even though the police confiscated the books, the prosecutor's office took no action. This was due to the relative freedom granted us in that period, and I was glad to make use of the opportunity. But when I returned home that evening, I met with an unexpected scene. Books were burning in the back yard. These were the few copies of each book that I'd kept for myself. Nakiye Hanım, who worked with us, knew that I had some copies. She'd come home without telling me, found the books in the library, and now she and my mother were burning them in the garden. I gazed at the scene in sorrow.

'Hitler burns Marxist books,' I said. 'But now they burn in our own garden?'

'Better them than you,' my mother snapped.

And so, I didn't have a single copy left for myself. Much later, in Paris in 1950 and Vienna in 1955, the young people I met told me, 'We received our first Marxist education from the books you translated into Turkish.' I was filled with joy. My efforts hadn't been in vain.

At the *Hayat Ansiklopedisi*

Atatürk disbanded the Liberal Party shortly after its foundation. There were two main reasons, the first of which was political. Founded upon the principle of liberalism, the party had galvanized the entire trade bourgeoisie to create a front against the government policy of statism. Also, the revolution hadn't fulfilled the common people's hopes of advancement. They were turning their backs on the People's Party and supporting this new party in hope of attaining prosperity. The People's Party had lost its credibility with the public. In order to save it from collapse, Atatürk found it necessary to abolish the Liberal Party.

The second reason was economic. Atatürk's system of statism aimed to liberate the national economy from foreign capital domination and to develop the local bourgeoisie with the state's help. The purpose of İş Bankası, founded in 1924, was to provide credit to domestic industries. In 1925, Sümerbank was founded, also with the goal of aiding Turkish industrial development. And the aim of the Central Bank, founded in 1931, was to provide financial backing for these newly established banks.

In spite of all these measures, the economy grew very slowly. Private enterprise developed with state support, but state-owned corporations became unprofitable. In the 1930s, when the Liberal Party was founded, the government tended to grant private enterprise more freedom from state control. The accumulation of capital gained momentum. Around this time, a private sugar factory, called Alpullu,[4] was established in Thrace. The owners of this factory, Hayri İpar and Şakir Kesebir, who was also Minister of Trade, created a virtual sugar monopoly. They were profiteering by buying up sugar at 36 *kuruş* and selling it at 70.

---

[4] TN: The name of the town in which the factory was located.

The *Son Posta* newspaper started a campaign against sugar profiteering. It exposed and published evidence of the graft committed by Hayri İpar. İpar sued Zekeriya as the writer of the article and Selim Ragıp as the paper's managing director, for damaging his reputation as a businessman and his personal honor and dignity.

According to the laws back then, even if a man's thievery and profiteering were proven with evidence, it was illegal to publish his name and the specifics of his wrongdoing in the papers. The public interest couldn't be defended against profiteers. Based on these laws, the court sentenced both Zekeriya and Selim Ragıp to three years of prison.

At the time, Zekeriya was publishing *Hayat Ansiklopedisi* [Life Encyclopedia] together with Yunus Nadi Bey. When he was imprisoned, the job fell to me. The content already was completed. I just had to handle technical matters. I worked on the encyclopedia during the day and continued translating Marxist works at night. But I'd lost touch with the common people. I was removed from their daily grievances and social issues. I yearned for the life of struggle at *Resimli Ay*.

A year and a half later, Zekeriya was released from prison during another general amnesty. Around 1934, he started publishing the *Tan* newspaper with Halil Lütfi.[5] And so, I gained the opportunity to write about politics.

At the *Tan* newspaper

Zekeriya left *Son Posta* because of a disagreement with his partners. He and Halil Lütfi decided to buy the newspaper *Tan*, published by Mahmut Bey, the representative for Siirt in the National Assembly. The government had established this paper while the Liberal Party still existed; its aim was to champion liberalism and protect the interests of the emerging bourgeoisie. The newspaper had the financial backing of İş Bankası, headed by Celal Bayar. Bayar was moderately opposed to the government policy of statism. He accepted it in principle but wanted the policy to support the trade bourgeoisie rather than interfere with its business or development. The *Tan* newspaper was founded as a platform for such ideas.

Atatürk had repeatedly explained what he meant by a statist regime. In his parliamentary speeches and his statements to foreign journalists, he asserted that statism was not opposed to private enterprise. The state would merely establish the corporations that private enterprise couldn't create. And with the founding of the Liberal Party, he even allowed the espousal of economic liberalism. Eventually, the issue of statism caused a split within the People's Party. While İnönü envisaged the state intervening in private enterprise, Bayar resisted such intervention. *Tan* covered this conflict within the party. But the paper was unsuccessful, never really catching on with the public. Its printing house, its equipment and even its name were put up for sale.

Zekeriya and Halil Lütfi bought the printing house and the paper. For some reason, they decided to keep the name. Shortly thereafter, they took on Ahmet Emin Yalman as a partner. Yalman was an agent of American imperialism, who'd previously defended

---

[5] TN: The exact year was 1936.

an American mandate in Turkey. He wrote the paper's editorials while Zekeriya dealt with technical matters. This put Yalman in charge of the paper's political direction. In his editorials, he denied that America was imperialist and defended private enterprise against statism. In each of his pieces, he contrasted the forces of 'good' and 'evil'. To him, the forces of good were private entrepreneurs, while leftists were the forces of evil.

Yalman also filled the paper with reactionaries like Ulunay and caliphate supporters like Refik Halit. During the War of Independence, Ulunay and Refik Halit had served the government of Damat Ferit Pasha. As a result, they were among the 150 people Atatürk had banished from the country for supporting the caliphate. Despite his backward ideas, Refik Halit was a forceful writer.

With this team, *Tan* resembled the famous Tower of Babel and its hanging gardens. Reactionaries were on one floor, fantasists like Burhan Felek on the next, hardcore Islamists like Ömer Rıza on another floor, and progressives on yet another. I started writing for *Tan* under these circumstances. The ban on my writing at *Son Posta* was lifted, and I attained a certain amount of freedom.

I wanted to use every opportunity to disseminate my views. My articles didn't pass through government censorship, but they still required approval by the editor-in-chief. I couldn't discuss American imperialism. I couldn't defend the workers against the bosses. In those days, simply speaking out on behalf of workers was already considered communism.

One day, a large group of workers came to my office. A disagreement had broken out between them and their employer. Apparently, he wasn't paying them their promised wages. Instead, he lowered them, claiming he was suffering a loss. At the time, there were no collective bargaining laws. Workers weren't allowed to strike to defend their rights. Bosses could reduce wages as they wanted. The workers who came to me had written a petition to the government. They wanted us to print it in the newspaper. The editor-in-chief had refused, and so they'd come to me.

They didn't know I was just a refugee in a corner of the Tower of Babel.

'Write me a letter,' I said. 'Point out your grievances. I can write a response that conveys your plight to the readership.'

Sometime after my article was published, they dropped by again. They thanked me and said they'd reached an agreement with their employer. Their wages wouldn't be cut.

Ultimately, Yalman fell out with Zekeriya and left the paper. Zekeriya started writing the editorials himself. I gained a little more freedom and started dealing with social issues in my columns and articles. Until 1945, when *Tan* was shut down, I used these columns to fight against fascists and reactionaries.

The *Pocket Books*

During my time at *Tan*, I published a series called *Pocket Books*. These were books initially published in the United States, under the title *One Hundred Books a Year* and covering a variety of topics. They included accounts of revolutions from all historical periods, literary works from various countries, and writings on economic and social issues. I picked the most progressive among these books for translation. I also had experts write new ones about issues concerning the homeland. The books were in high demand with the public.

I did some of the translations myself and gave others to Cevat Şakir and Ömer Rıza. Cevat Şakir had studied at Oxford and knew the language of Shakespeare better than an Englishman. Ömer Rıza's English was quite good as well.

One day, something strange happened. I'd asked Ömer Rıza to translate Anatole France's *The Majesty of Justice*. But when I read the proofs, I was dumbfounded. Apparently, Anatole France was deeply religious, opposed socialism and defended religious philosophy! I was sure these weren't the opinions expressed by Anatole France. I had the original brought to me and compared it with the translation. The two were completely different. I called Ömer Rıza and showed him some passages.

'What's this supposed to mean?' I asked.

Ömer Rıza turned red. 'My dear lady,' he said, 'I'm a religious man, but Anatole France writes against religion. I'm an opponent of socialism, but he defends social justice. I changed the text so people wouldn't learn about these ideas.'

'What gives you the right to do that?' I asked. I had to terminate his employment.

Halikarnas Balıkçısı[6] had other idiosyncrasies. He wasn't a reactionary, but if he didn't approve of an idea in the original text, he added a parenthesis in the translation, insulted the original author and wrote his own ideas, saying, 'the truth of the matter is not like that but like this'. It was easy to fix. I just crossed out the parentheses while reading the proofs.

I also tried my hand at a novel, writing a book entitled *Çitra Royla Babası* [Chitra Roy and Her Father]. The subject was British imperialism and how Indian socialists were arrested and tortured in the course of British oppression. In those days, the British newspapers were writing about a trial in India called the 'Meerut Case'. The socialist girl who stood trial had been reported to the police by her own father. I used the story as the basis of my novel. It went on sale without encountering any obstacles.

I fought my biggest battle at *Tan* during the years of the Second World War. As a matter of fact, that story is the main reason I'm writing this memoir. In the following chapters, I will recount that period, step by step.

A journey to America

We'd sent our older daughter, Sevim, to study in America. We wanted her to attend Columbia University in New York, but Ragıp Nureddin, the Turkish Attaché for Education in New York, sent her to a university in Missouri. We decided I should go to America to sort out this issue.

It was 1937, and Germany was preparing for war. Its goal was to regain lost territory from the First World War and to claim a share of the colonies and raw material markets

---

[6] TN: 'The Fisherman of Halicarnassus' was Cevat Şakir's pen name.

controlled by the imperialist powers. That same year, Japanese imperialists had invaded the central regions of China, starting a war to subdue and colonize the country.

In Spain, there was a civil war between the democratic forces[7] and those of fascism led by Franco. Fascist Italy and Germany supported Franco, while volunteer brigades from all over the world went to Spain and fought side by side with the people's army. The war had turned into a bloody struggle to the death.

The Turkish reactionary press distorted the news from Spain, branding the Spanish democrats as communists and hailing Franco instead. French reactionaries also aligned themselves against the democratic Spanish government, supplying Franco's troops with weapons from across the French border.

Before I embarked on my journey, *Tan* asked me to write some articles from France and America. Suat Derviş, who also wrote for *Tan*, was going on a trip to the Soviet Union around the same time. The articles I sent back were supposed to appear in *Tan*, but, in fact, only some of them were published.

While in Paris, I requested a meeting with the foreign minister.[8] With French courtesy, he received me at the ministry. He was surprised that a Turkish woman was interested in politics. I asked him why the French government tolerated fascists and pursued a soft policy toward the German government, when the latter had always been the enemy of France. The minister thought about this for a while.

'We don't tolerate fascists in France,' he finally said. 'But this is a democratic country. Everyone is free to voice his opinion and to found any organization he wants. We don't see fascism as a danger to France.'

'Germany, Italy and Japan have formed an axis,' I replied. 'These countries are preparing for war in order to redistribute the existing colonies. Germany wants to expand into world markets. It demands land from Czechoslovakia and Poland. Isn't this the beginning of a new world war and a danger to France and the entire world?'

The Minister answered at once: 'Germany won't attack us. Its goal is to expand toward the Soviet borders. It has declared a holy war on communism. But even if a real war breaks out between those two countries, we'll stay out of it. If we start aiding the Spanish government, it will provoke Germany. The Spanish War won't result in a world war. We believe that the monarchy in Spain will collapse and democratic forces will prevail. We've also taken precautions against the smuggling of weapons across the French border into Spain.'

The French Foreign Minister was serene. He believed that war could be avoided if concessions were made to Germany. And so, as Germany and Italy supported Franco in the Spanish Civil War, France watched on. For a long time, it allowed weapons to be smuggled across its borders. In the end, the democratic Spanish government collapsed and Franco took over. When the German armies finally attacked France, I couldn't stop thinking about that minister. Like an ostrich, he'd dug his head in the sand but left his feet outside. Then one day, the fascist armies pulled that ostrich out by its legs and plucked its feathers.

---

[7] TN: Sertel is referring to the forces supporting the democratically elected Spanish Republic against Franco's rebellion.
[8] TN: The French Minister of Foreign Affairs in 1937 was Yvon Delbos.

A meeting with Geneviève Tabouis

Geneviève Tabouis was a French writer who played a major role in French political life those days. She claimed to be a socialist and was in touch with important statesmen around the world. She was the first to break many stories when nobody else had even heard of them.

Tabouis was a frail, gaunt middle-aged woman who couldn't sit still. She received me in the sumptuously furnished study of her luxurious apartment. I asked her why French socialists supported the imperialist government of France and didn't join forces with communists against fascism.

Tabouis laughed.

'Don't you know that the French socialists always ride the coattails of imperialism? The Socialist Party in France is just like the Labour Party in Britain: its first priority is the protection of national capital. It regards the dominance of French capital in the global markets as a national cause. As for the communists, they're tied to the Third International[9] and the Soviet Union. But the Soviets have retreated into their shell to protect their own regime. The only voices you hear out of Moscow today are those calling for peace. And that with mankind on the brink of a second world war! The Soviets left the revolution half-finished. They're content with establishing socialism in a single country. But capitalism in Europe can only be overthrown by violent means, through perpetual war. What we need is a fourth international.'

I understood that Geneviève Tabouis was not a socialist but a Trotskyist.

'Don't you think socialism is a process that each country needs to develop according to its own circumstances and by its own efforts? Wouldn't it be a kind of imperialism to spread socialism or communism by force of arms, to force nations to accept regimes they don't want?'

Tabouis frowned.

'Do you think imperialism will just collapse by itself? Today's socialist and communist parties in Europe can't be expected to overthrow capitalism and imperialism. Only the Soviet Union could have done this, by military force and under the banner of the perpetual revolution. But the Soviets missed that chance.'

'What you want isn't socialism,' I said. 'What you want is for the Soviet Union to succumb to the imperialist forces.' I changed the topic, asking no further questions on this issue.

'Do you think a second world war is near?'

This roused Tabouis from her seat. She started pacing up and down the room, talking all the while.

'It's near,' she said, 'very near. Hitler's war machine is in high gear. Everyone – the Tories and Labour in Britain, our own government and Socialist Party – everyone thinks war can be avoided by appeasing Hitler. I've met with statesmen from many countries. They all believe Hitler will only attack the Soviets and expand along their

---

[9] TN: The Third International (1919–43), also known as the Communist International or Comintern, was a Soviet-led international organization advocating world communism.

borders. They even aid the Germans in this goal. But you'll see, the Germans will attack us even before they attack the Soviets.'

On this matter, I agreed with Geneviève Tabouis. I thanked her and left.

At the *Voix Européenne* journal

A while before embarking on this journey, I'd received a letter from a Michel Loren[10] at the French journal *Voix Européenne*. Someone had recommended me to him, and he'd asked me for three articles – one on the economic situation in Turkey, one on the land reform bill that Turkey was preparing at that time and one on the state of the Turkish woman. I'd sent him the three articles, and the journal had published them.

I took some time in France to visit the journal's offices. They received me with great interest, and we talked at length about world politics. When I told them about the interviews I'd conducted with Geneviève Tabouis and the Foreign Minister, they were delighted.

'You must publish those interviews,' they said. 'Your statesmen and people should find out about the apathy that reigns in France.'

From France, I went on to America. But it wasn't possible to rectify my daughter's school placement. In any case, she'd already settled in at the University of Missouri. The two of us spent the summer holidays together at a resort, where I wrote up my articles about America and mailed them home.

My journey back was somewhat troublesome. After returning to Europe, I was supposed to travel from Paris to Milan, spend the night there and then take the train to Venice. I'd already reserved my ticket for the steamer from Venice to Istanbul.

While in America and France, I'd bought a great many leftist books. Before leaving for Italy, I put them in a wooden trunk, covered them with two layers of novels and disposable books, and had the trunk nailed shut. At the station, I checked in my luggage and bought a copy of the paper *L'Humanité* to read on the train. The coach was empty when I boarded. Sometime later, a married Italian couple sat down in my compartment. I kept reading my paper. The Italian woman looked me up and down with a frown.

'You can't take that newspaper to Italy,' she said at last.

'I'll throw it away at the border,' I said.

After that, we didn't speak at all. At one o'clock, the train arrived at the border. The inspector came into the compartment to check our belongings.

'I'm on a transit journey,' I said. 'But please, go ahead and check.'

I had a little bag with me. He looked through it casually and then left. But the Italian couple immediately went after him. They must have told him that I was reading *L'Humanité*, for the inspector returned.

'Do you have Italian money on you?' he asked.

---

[10] TN: Sertel uses the Turkish spelling of this French journalist's name. It has not been possible to ascertain the accurate French spelling.

Before leaving Paris, I'd converted a hundred francs into liras at the travel agency. I'd been told this was an acceptable amount to carry.

'I have liras in the value of a hundred francs,' I said.

The inspector took out a pen and paper and wrote something down.

'Come with me,' he said, 'we're going to the police station.'

'You can't be serious,' I said. 'If it's illegal to bring in the liras, just take them.'

'That won't do,' he said. 'You have to pay a fine.'

'Then let me pay it here.'

He insisted on taking me with him. It was a rainy night. We got off the train and went to the police station, which was a short walk away. The inspector told his chief something in Italian.

I started getting impatient. 'The train is about to leave,' I said. 'Please, just tell me what the fine is and I'll pay it.'

'No, just wait. If the train leaves, you'll stay here tonight.'

Spending the night at a police station in fascist Italy wasn't a pleasant thought.

Eventually, the inspector left. I went up to the chief. I told him in French that I was a foreigner and that I didn't know the Italian laws. I slipped him two dollars. 'Please count that toward my fine,' I said.

When the chief saw the dollars, his face lit up. He pocketed them without writing up a receipt. 'You're free to leave now,' he said.

Back on the train, I was gripped by anxiety. What if these Italians caused me some trouble in Milan? Finally, we arrived in the city. I took my luggage to the checkroom at the station and went to the hotel. My train was leaving at one o'clock the next day.

An hour before departure time, I went to the checkroom to pick up my luggage. At once, I was approached by a militiaman in black.

'We're going to inspect these things,' he said.

'I'm a transit passenger,' I said. 'You have no right to go through my belongings.'

'We have our orders. We will search them.'

I opened the suitcases. They went through everything one by one. My train was already sounding its horn. When they got to the wooden trunk, my heart sank. If a copy of *L'Humanité* was enough to get me into such trouble, who knew what the Italians would do when they saw the leftist books?

I stepped up to the inspecting officer.

'My train is leaving,' I said. 'I'm a foreigner. I don't have enough money on me to stay here.'

'What's in this trunk?' he asked.

'Novels.'

The train was sounding its horn more urgently now. Finally, the militiaman relented. And when I gave him two dollars, he even escorted me to my coach, carrying my bags himself.

The train was about to leave. I barely managed to jump on and couldn't find any place to sit. But the hardest part was over.

I was still worried about how to get the books through customs in Turkey. But the Turkish customs officers were only looking for contraband and I was a journalist. And so, I made it to Istanbul without any further difficulties.

An invitation by the Interior Minister

I went on publishing my reports and articles in *Tan*. One day, I received an invitation from Interior Minister Şükrü Kaya. His aide, who made the phone call, told me that Kaya wanted to talk to me and would be waiting for me at the Pera Palas Hotel at two o'clock the next day.

When I went to the Pera Palas at the appointed hour, I saw Suat Derviş and her husband, Nizameddin Nazif, sitting in the hotel lobby.[11]

'Did Şükrü Kaya summon you as well?' I asked.

'Yes,' they said.

Since they'd come before me, Kaya invited them in first. I waited quite a while. When they came out, Suat was frowning.

'What happened?' I asked. 'What does he want?'

'Go in. You'll see,' Suat said. 'He came down quite hard on me. Who knows what he'll do to you?'

Shortly thereafter, a young official called me inside. I entered the reception hall of the Pera Palas. Şükrü Kaya had turned the hall into a huge office, with desks set up everywhere. At some, people were writing on typewriters and at others they were reading through files. Kaya himself was sitting at a lavish writing desk in one corner of the hall. When I approached him, he stood up.

'Have a seat, please,' he said. On his desk were some issues of *Voix Européenne*. When I saw the journals, I understood what was going on.

'Why did you call me here?' I asked.

He pointed at the journals on his desk.

'What are these?' he asked.

'It says on them what they are.'

'You wrote articles for this journal.'

Şükrü Kaya was taking a familiar tone with me, as if we were old friends.

'Yes, I did. A while ago, I received a letter from this journal. It's based in Paris. They wanted some articles from me. I saw nothing wrong with writing them.'

'Don't you know this is a communist journal?'

'No, I don't. And I would have written for them even if I'd known. If I've committed a crime in writing these articles, the prosecutor's office can call me to account for it. You're the Interior Minister, not an investigating judge.'

'I'm the one who'll call you to account. You criticize the land reform law. And as if that wasn't enough, you do it in a foreign country, in a communist journal!'

The Land Reform Bill had been drafted by Şükrü Kaya himself and was currently being debated in the Assembly. In my article, I'd pointed out the good sides of this bill as well as its insufficiencies. Apparently, Kaya wasn't pleased.

'There is no law that says one cannot write articles for foreign newspapers or journals,' I said. 'And besides, just last night, I was invited to the garden party of Muammer Eriş, the manager of İş Bankası, along with other journalists. Celal Bayar[12]

---

[11] At that point, Suat was still married to Nizameddin Nazif. They would separate later.
[12] TN: By then, the prime minister of Turkey.

came up to me and introduced himself. He told me he enjoyed the articles I'd written for *Voix Européenne*. If even our prime minister likes them, what are you accusing me of?'

Şükrü Kaya was a man who spoke in a rakish manner.

'Now look here,' he said, 'Celal Bayar doesn't know what kind of journal this is. You should ditch these ideas of yours. Your file at the police directorate is so thick that it's reached the ceiling. You're a valuable writer for this country. We could get you into parliament. We could make better use of your ideas.'

I got up at once.

'You're offering me an Assembly seat in exchange for my beliefs? Thank you and good-bye.'

He grabbed me by the arm and sat me down.

'Don't get mad,' he said. 'I want to set you straight because I like you. What about that *Projektör* [Projector] journal you people put out? I had that one confiscated just because of your article.'

I'd published the journal *Projektör* with some friends, as a single issue. I wrote an article for it entitled 'Ladies in Parliament, Why are You Silent?' At the time, the Assembly was debating a law to extend the road tax to female workers as well. My piece argued that it was unjust for female labourers who worked in front of machines all day to pay the road tax while bourgeois women who sat at home like parasites and did nothing at all for the country were exempt from it. I called on the female Assembly members to defend women labourers' rights.

'Why did you confiscate the journal because of that article? Is what I say untrue, wrong or unjust?'

'It's nothing but communist propaganda! That journal is full of worthless articles like this. Look, nobody cares about articles on things like the "Michurin Method" in the Soviet Union. And neither do I. I'm not afraid of such articles. I'm afraid of articles like yours. Not only do you provoke female workers, you also accuse the female deputies of not doing their duty. This is the kind of article people notice. That's why I had it confiscated.'

'And by doing that, you put democracy on ice.'

'Think hard about what I've told you. One day you'll say, "Şükrü Kaya told me so." I turned socialist too while I was studying in France. But when I came back home, I saw that it wouldn't take off over here. So I served the country in more useful ways.'

What Kaya called 'more useful ways' were his posts as a deputy and a cabinet member. Now, he was advising me to be just as opportunistic.

'You may have given up on your beliefs,' I said, 'but I want a real democracy to emerge. The conditions in the country aren't ripe for socialism. The danger is not to the left; it's to the right. But you strike the left and turn a blind eye to the right. Why can't you see that people are using nationalism as an excuse to spread racist and Nazi propaganda? They're trying to sway Turkish public opinion into supporting Germany and a second world war. Why can't you see that?'

'That's just a handful of people. Their cause will never catch on in this country. I'm not afraid of them, but of you. If there is a second world war, Atatürk won't enter it. He won't yield to fascism; he'll remain neutral. What we really need to watch is the danger from the east.'

Şükrü Kaya was unconcerned. Eventually, the Second World War did break out. At first, Turkey remained neutral, but when the German armies reached the gates of Stalingrad, commanders like Emin Erkilet Pasha were deployed at the eastern border, ready to invade the Caucasus and help the Germans. If the Soviet troops hadn't stopped the Germans at Stalingrad, Turkey would have entered the war. But Şükrü Kaya wasn't afraid of the racist, fascist movements in the country.

Turkey on the eve of the Second World War

Hitler came to power in 1933 and soon started preparing for a second world war. The terrible fog of impending war engulfed the skies of Europe. Turkey started looking for allies, and the Balkan Pact between Romania, Turkey and Greece was established with much fanfare.

In July 1938, my younger daughter, Yıldız, and I paid a therapeutic visit to the Herculane hot springs in Romania. *Tan* asked me to conduct an interview with Bratianu, Romania's Foreign Minister. He received me at his ministry office in Bucharest.

The Minister was a heavy, rather short man with a round face. I explained the purpose of my interview and asked whether he thought a second world war was near. He answered without hesitation.

'In all probability,' he said, 'such a war will be prevented. Germany was treated very unjustly after the Great War. The British and French statesmen realize this was a mistake and are trying to rectify it.'

'And at whose expense will they rectify it?'

'The region of the Sudetes, for instance, is German territory. Hitler also wants land from Poland, which is a justified request. If we follow a policy of appeasement toward the Germans, both the Balkans and Europe will be saved.'

'Are you sure that Hitler won't attack France and England?'

'He can't. The experience of the Great War will have taught him that he cannot oppose those nations. He knows that if he attempts such a war, America will join in as well. But he is sure that if he fights the Soviets instead, France and England will support him. Hitler's ideological war on communism is the first step of the war that he is planning against the Soviet Union.'

'Germany doesn't just want the region of the Sudetes, but Alsace-Lorraine as well.'

'He cannot cross the Maginot Line.'

'Hitler is spreading fascist propaganda in the Balkans. Many Balkan statesmen support his wishes. Will the Balkan Pact prevent Hitler from invading the region?'

'The Balkan Pact creates a buffer between Germany and the Soviet Union. This pact will prevent the Germans as well as the Soviets from invading the Balkans or Turkey. For that reason, Turkey's participation in the pact is very beneficial for Turkey and the Balkan countries.'

'Hitler claims that the regime he founded will last a thousand years and become a world state. That means Hitler's plans of invasion include the Balkans as well.'

'These are just pipe dreams. They cannot be realized. The Balkan Pact has the support of England, France and the United States. The dangers you envision are unlikely to materialize.'

Just like the French statesmen, Bratianu was in a blissful state of sleep. I forgot my glasses on his desk when I left. If only putting them on could have helped him view world affairs differently. But we were unlikely to ever see eye to eye. I gave him a call after arriving at Herculane, and he had my glasses sent over within 24 hours.

Exactly ten years later, in the summer of 1948, we were visiting Italy. Bratianu was there as well. He had fled Romania when the Soviets invaded the country. He was being accused of aiding the fascists after they'd come to power in Romania. Now, he was looking for a chance to move to the United States. I remembered our interview and his assurance that Hitler couldn't invade the Balkans.

Atatürk's death

After a long illness, Atatürk died in November 1938, at Dolmabahçe Palace in Istanbul. The whole country went into mourning. For three days and three nights, statesmen, youths, unionists and representatives of other organizations stood at attention before his catafalque in the palace. Six torches symbolizing Atatürk's six principles were positioned around the catafalque and burned day and night.

As the vigil drew to a close, the reporters and writers of *Tan* took up positions along the planned route of the funeral procession. My assignment was to climb up a minaret of the Dolmabahçe mosque and view the procession's departure from the palace. A curfew had been imposed, starting at seven in the morning, but the police were granting special permissions to journalists.

I left the house at half past six, just as dawn was breaking, and went down from Nişantaşı to Dolmabahçe by way of Beşiktaş. On the way, I kept having to show my press card to policemen in order to proceed. When I reached the entrance to the mosque, I was welcomed by the imam, who'd been informed about my arrival. I climbed the narrow, winding stairs of the minaret, reaching the first balcony, from where I would watch the procession. There was neither sound nor movement anywhere. Black flags hung from the windows of all houses.

The Bosporus, the Sea of Marmara, Beylerbeyi Palace and the Asiatic shore spread out before my eyes. The sea was perfectly still. Even the white passenger ferries of the Bosporus silently skimmed across the water as if they, too, were wary of spoiling the air of mourning.

I pace about on the minaret, unable to stand still. As the sun rises, balconies and windows start filling with people. Groups of them even gather on crumbling walls. People hang like pears from tree branches. I look down into the garden of Dolmabahçe Palace, where the catafalque is positioned. Celal Bayar, Şükrü Saraçoğlu, Recep Peker, all the statesmen, generals and high officials are walking back, one by one, after standing at attention. As the coffin is loaded onto a gun carriage, the marching band strikes up a mournful tune. The procession advances slowly, step by step. These calm and dignified steps are a mark of respect for the great, departed man.

Among the scenes I witnessed from the minaret that day, the one inspiring the most awe and pride was the sight of sobbing people, standing on their balconies, peering out of their windows, perched on top of the walls. These sobs never let up throughout the processional route. An entire nation wept. The Turkish people expressed their gratitude to their saviour through these tears. No statesman, sultan or hero in the history of Turkey had ever been shown such love and respect.

Atatürk built the new Turkey out of the rubble of an empire that had utterly collapsed after the First World War. Despite severe hardships, he fought a national war of independence against imperialist states. He laid the foundations of an independent Turkey. He abolished the sultanate and the caliphate. He replaced sharia law with civil law. He carried out a number of reforms. This was a revolution encompassing the entirety of Turkey. With the six principles he put forth (republicanism, secularism, populism, nationalism, statism and revolutionism), he instituted momentous changes in society and culture. He liberated Turkey, tied down by religious law and obsolete Islamic doctrines, from the tyranny of the sharia.

He separated religion and state, and he broke the reactionary stranglehold that religion had on education. He enshrined republicanism in the Constitution as the unalterable system of governance. His desire was to create a state based on the sovereignty of the people. He tried to apply democracy, as practised in contemporary European societies, to Turkish society. But he also needed to protect the regime against reactionary and fanatical factions that were the enemies of anything new. And so, circumstances forced him to shift to an oppressive system. Since he had depended on feudal landlords and a newly developing bourgeoisie to fight the War of Independence, he was not able to implement the principle of populism in an effective way. Under the pretext of a classless society, the nascent working class was denied any chance to come into its own. Progressives who wanted true democracy were countered with oppressive measures from the very outset.

Atatürk was a nationalist. But unlike the nationalists who emerged from the 1908 revolution, his nationalism was not based on the principle of race. He was opposed to Pan-Turkism. He had no interest in liberating those Turks who were dispersed in various areas outside of Turkey. Nonetheless, he desired to strengthen the Turkish bourgeoisie against foreign capital as well as the minority capital that controlled the country's economy. This nationalist perspective also informed his principle of statism. Rather than nationalizing the resources of the country and managing them in favour of the people, statism would only allow the state to make those investments that were beyond the means of private capital. In effect, the state became the handmaiden of private capital.

The other aim of statism was to protect the Turkish bourgeoisie against foreign capital and to break the economic and political influence of the imperialists. To achieve this aim, many foreign firms were disbanded and limitations were imposed on foreign capital. However, mounting pressure from the emerging bourgeoisie, underdeveloped conditions, the lack of executives to implement this principle for the benefit of the people, and the persistence of landlords and propertied classes in the Assembly, all made sure that the regime of statism did not yield the desired benefits. With the foundation of İş Bankası and the pressure that foreign banks were exerting on the

Turkish economy, state-run enterprises became enterprises that ran the state into the ground, particularly after Atatürk's death. All of this resulted in the establishment of a trade bourgeoisie that collaborated with foreign capital and amassed huge fortunes at the expense of the population. The attempt at industrialization failed.

Atatürk was a revolutionary. He was influenced by the French Revolution and, to some extent, by the October Revolution that created the Soviet Union. But in terms of the changes he envisioned in Turkey, he put social reforms on the back burner. A land reform, which would have cleared away the remnants of feudalism, was not attempted, and the proletariat of the newly industrializing country was held back from developing class consciousness and defending its rights. In the end, the changes resulted in nothing more than a few super-structural reforms. And progressives, leftists and workers found themselves subjected to unrelenting oppression.

İnönü becomes President

After Atatürk's death, İsmet İnönü became president. İnönü had been sidelined in Atatürk's final years because of differences in opinion between the two. But Celal Bayar, who was prime minister when Atatürk died, appointed İnönü president upon the request of the People's Party.

Atatürk hadn't been able to establish a democratic regime, veering toward a dictatorship instead. But this dictatorship had never turned into a reign of terror. From time to time, it had granted freedom to the press. A lot of progressive journals were published and Nazım's poems and the Marxist works I translated were printed and sold, and even though they were confiscated by the police, they didn't lead to trials.

İnönü, however, was the most hardline proponent of the 'One Party, One Chief' system.[13] He showed zero tolerance for progressive ideas or even their discussion. Even when Atatürk was alive, it was mostly İnönü who had resorted to violent measures of repression. After he came to power, the bureaucrats within the People's Party gained influence. Immediately, a Law of Associations was passed that abolished the freedom to found organizations and brought already existing organizations under state control. The press came under tremendous scrutiny. As more laws changed, even the limited freedoms granted by the 1924 Constitution were abolished. The pressure against leftists increased as well. Progressive journals on the left were shut down. Increasingly violent repressive measures were taken against communists, who were forced to start operating in secret.

In 1938, Nazım Hikmet was arrested and referred to a military tribunal on charges of spreading communist propaganda among the army to incite an uprising. There was no evidence to support the charges, and the pretext for his arrest was so flimsy that no law could have condemned him. Some students at the War Academy had asked him for signed copies of his books and he had obliged, that was all. The books he'd given them

---

[13] TN: Sertel is referring to the Turkish political system consisting of a single-party state led by a party chief with dictatorial powers.

were freely sold at bookstores. But Nazım was locked up in a cell on the battleship *Yavuz* [Grim] and tortured. Then, he was sentenced to twenty-eight years in prison.

The whole thing was a political conspiracy planned in high circles and carried out by the security forces in order to intimidate progressives and leftists. Nazım ended up spending fourteen years in prison. Another Dreyfus, he suffered the cruel fate of spending the most productive years of his youth and life behind bars. From then on, progressive movements in the country were hindered at every turn. Reactionaries, racists and fascists won the day.

The rise of the Pan-Turkists

It is spring 1939. Hitler has increased his demands and is preparing to attack Poland. In all this, he is aided by the imperialist states of Britain and France, who want to stay out of a war with Germany at any cost. They keep making concessions to Germany and Italy, thereby emboldening these fascist states in their expansionist aims.

My articles for *Tan* criticize the precarious peace achieved by the Munich Agreement,[14] declaring that peace cannot be saved by compromising with the fascists. To the contrary, I argue that the concessions just encourage Hitler's warmongering goals. I also write against the racism and 'New Order' propaganda[15] that is spreading in Turkey day by day. My writings are attacked in the fascist press.

The smell of gunpowder is in the air. The opinions of statesmen and the press are becoming polarized. Some believe that the Germans will defeat Britain and France in a second world war and oppose any pact against Germany. Others say that Germany, in spite of all its power, will be vanquished by an alliance of the imperialists and the Soviet Union. Believing that sooner or later, the Soviets will reach an agreement with Britain and France, they demand that Turkey join the Western bloc.

Hitler's Germany is making efforts to gain Turkey's support in these days of turmoil. Secret operations are staged in political circles as well as among the racists and Pan-Turkists. The Germans and their sympathizers are trying to win over some Turkish generals who were comrades-in-arms with the German army in the First World War. They are also secretly organizing the Pan-Turkists, whose policies are opposed to the communists and the Soviet Union.

The Turkist movement is not new in Turkey. It began in the First World War, when people like Resulzade Emin, Ayaz İshaki, Sadri Maksudi, Yusuf Akçora and Ahmet Ağaoğlu escaped from Tsarist Russia to Turkey and put forward the ideal of Turan.[16] Their dream was to liberate all people of Turkish origin living in Tsarist Russia. And since they couldn't achieve this by themselves, they wanted to use Turkey as a vehicle.

---

[14] TN: Signed on 30 September 1938, this agreement between Germany, France, the United Kingdom and Italy endorsed Nazi Germany in annexing parts of Czechoslovakia.
[15] TN: The 'New Order' (German: *Neuordnung*) refers to the political order, envisioned by Nazi thinkers, for the territories to be conquered by the Third Reich.
[16] TN: The semi-mythical ancestral homeland of Turks in Central Asia. The central idea of Pan-Turkism is to unite all Turkish-speaking peoples from Turkey to northern China in one political entity.

It is one thing to propose that people with the same ancestral roots should feel affinity and sympathy for each other. It is an entirely other thing to try and rally the various Turkish populations of the world around the Turkish flag. This was not only a pipe dream but also an imperialist movement. Dragging Turkey into such a misadventure just as it was being founded would have led the country into the same ruin as followed the First World War.

It was no coincidence that this movement, suppressed during Atatürk's time, reared its ugly head again on the eve of the Second World War. Hitler's Germany, preparing for a second world war, wanted to use this movement to gain Turkey's support. The Turan Society was founded with Goebbels' help[17] and began its political efforts to strengthen the Turkist movement. New journals, big and small, started spreading Turkist ideas. Their ranks included *Bozkurt, Çınaraltı, Börü, Millet, Orhun, Dönüm* and *Türk Yurdu*.[18] Some writers in daily newspapers like *Cumhuriyet* and *Tasviri Efkar* started defending Turkist ideas as well. Under the guise of nationalism, these journals argued that Turkey should enter the war on Hitler's side while Germany was winning.

The Turanists published pamphlets, in particular *Dalkavuklar Gecesi* [Night of the Lackeys] by Nihal Adsız,[19] in which they attacked Atatürk's nationalism and tried to spread anti-Soviet sentiment among the people. Adsız, leader of the Turanists, cut his bangs like Hitler, wore white pants and shirts like Gandhi, and walked around his garden delivering sermons to his devotees.

At *Tan*, we started a campaign against this reactionary movement. We pointed out that Atatürk's foreign policy was anti-imperialist, that Turkey didn't covet anyone else's land and that the country's sole desire was to protect its independence within its own borders. We tried to explain that entering the war at Germany's side was the biggest danger of all. I went to court many times over my disputes with the racists. I suffered many insults. I'll recount these instances in detail in the pages that follow.

The Anglo-Turkish Agreement

When the Western nations signed the Munich Agreement, they believed they had deflected the war toward the Soviet Union. This, they hoped, would resolve the conflict of interest between themselves and the fascist nations. In March 1939, Hitler's forces occupied what remained of Czechoslovakia beyond the Sudetes. After eliminating Czechoslovakia, Hitler immediately started preparing for the occupation of Poland.

In April 1939, Italy unexpectedly landed soldiers in Albania. Seeing Germany emboldened by the impotence of Britain and France, Italy now embarked on the invasion of the Balkans. The country had coveted the southern shores of Turkey for a

---

[17] TN: Joseph Goebbels (1897–1945), German Minister of Propaganda under Adolf Hitler.
[18] TN: 'Grey Wolf', 'Under the Plane Tree', 'Wolf', 'People', 'Orkhon' (a river and valley in Mongolia), 'Turning Point' and 'Turkish Hearth'.
[19] Hüseyin Nihal Atsız (1905–75; Sertel employs a variant spelling of his family name) was a pivotal ideologue in the history of Turkism and Turkish racism.

long time. Its invasion of Albania worried Turkish statesmen. They were beginning to understand that the Balkan Pact would not protect Turkey or the Balkans. Amid their unease, an event occurred that shocked not only the Turkish people but all of Europe.

After becoming president, İnönü had sidelined Celal Bayar, whom he considered an opponent, and installed Dr Refik Saydam as prime minister. On 12 May 1939, a declaration was read by Refik Saydam at the National Assembly in Ankara and, simultaneously, by the British Prime Minister Chamberlain at the House of Commons in London. The declaration stated that 'after close consultation, the United Kingdom and Turkey have decided to conclude a long-term reciprocal agreement in the interest of their national security'.

This meant that Turkey was abandoning neutrality and siding with the Western nations. The declaration was well received by the people and the press. Only the Turanists and fascists who wanted an alliance with Germany criticized the pact, all the while continuing to attack the Soviets.

In the meantime, the people of Britain and France demanded that their governments cooperate with the Soviets. Under popular pressure, the British and French governments started talks with the Soviet Union. But their commitment to a common resistance against the fascist aggressors was not sincere. They still hadn't given up working with Hitler against the Soviet Union, and while they were talking with the Soviets, they were also trying to reach an agreement with him. They wanted to pressure Hitler, hoping that he would soften once he saw the formidable alliance being forged against him.

For the Soviet Union, it was imperative to reach an agreement with Britain and France in order to prevent war. But the talks showed that the British and the French had no real intention of cooperating with the Soviet Union. Stafford Cripps, dispatched to Moscow by Britain to reach an agreement with the Soviets, returned empty-handed. Britain and France's real aim was to redirect the war to the east. They were just using the talks to win time.

The two nations approached the Soviets with a proposal the latter couldn't accept. If Britain and France were dragged into a war with Germany, the Soviet Union would support them. But if war broke out between Germany and the Soviet Union, Britain and France would remain neutral. The imperialist nations refused to take any responsibility, leaving the Soviets to shoulder it all on their own.

The Soviets rejected this inequitable proposal. They demanded a treaty of mutual assistance among all three nations. The three states would pledge to assist each other in case of an attack in Europe and also assist Poland, the Baltic States, Belgium and Turkey if these countries were attacked. Such an alliance would have built a mighty front against Germany and perhaps even prevented the war. But the British and French governments shied away from the reciprocal obligations that came with such a treaty. As a result, talks broke off.

The outlook appeared bleak for the Soviet Union. The country was completely isolated. It had given up hope on reaching an agreement with Britain and France. It was faced with the threat of war. The Soviets wanted to avoid this danger at any cost. Around that time, the German government approached the Soviet Union and proposed a non-aggression pact. The Germans dispatched Foreign Minister von Ribbentrop to engage in talks with Moscow.

Hitler hadn't abandoned the idea of fighting a war against the Soviets. But he'd decided to defeat the imperialists first and attack the Soviets afterward. In order not to fight on two fronts, he wanted to keep the Soviets at bay for the time being. The Soviet Union needed time to prepare for Hitler's eventual attack. And so, the Soviets signed the pact.

The war begins

On 1 September 1939, Germany attacked Poland. The Polish people put up a fierce resistance against the invading fascist armies. The workers and the common people defended their country heroically. But Poland was in no shape to withstand Hitler's relentless attacks. His fascist armies put the Polish people to the sword. They set up concentration camps, where they burned hundreds of thousands of Poles in furnaces and tortured them to death in various ways. The Poles lived to regret turning down the Soviets' help. Their fascist government betrayed them, and Britain and France reneged on their promises.

On 3 September 1939, Britain and France declared war on Germany. And thus began the Second World War, which would end in the death of millions and the collapse of entire nations.

6

Turkey in the war years

Press reactions to the Soviet–German Pact

After the Soviet–German Pact, Britain and France realized the war had changed direction and was headed toward them. They convened a Supreme War Council in Paris. Britain dispatched Chamberlain; Lord Halifax; Churchill; Sir Kingsley Wood, the Secretary of State for Air; and Oliver Stanley, the Secretary of State for War. France sent Édouard Daladier, General Gamelin and Admiral Darlan. Many military officers and the British and French ambassadors were present as well. After the meeting, the two countries issued a declaration announcing closer cooperation.

In February 1940, a treaty between Britain, France and Turkey was signed by Numan Menemencioğlu, Turkish ambassador in Paris, as well as by British and French representatives. According to this treaty, drafted by Dr Refik Saydam, Turkey was no longer neutral but aligned with the Western Allies. Around the same time, on his way to the Council of the Balkan Entente in Belgrade, Foreign Minister Şükrü Saraçoğlu made the following statement to a reporter from *Ulus* [Nation] newspaper: 'Turkey is not neutral. It is merely not at war. But being either neutral or not at war means that Turkey is taking all necessary precautions to prevent the war from spilling over into the country.'

The treaty between Britain, France and Turkey was welcomed by the press. The Soviet–German Pact, however, led to differing opinions.

Asım Us, editor-in-chief of the *Vakit* newspaper, wrote on 15 February 1940 that '[t]he treaty of mutual assistance between Turkey, Britain and France guarantees Turkish neutrality in the case of a war between Britain, France and the Soviet Union. Surely, then, the Soviets can't be taking such important military steps solely for defence'.

On the same date, Hüseyin Cahit Yalçın at *Yeni Sabah* [New Morning] wrote the following about a speech by Chamberlain: 'As always, Chamberlain's words were clear and encouraging. But by now, his language has become even softer, taking on a virtually luminous sweetness. Chamberlain doesn't want land from Germany. He says he won't ask for reparations. Neither does he want a regime change. All he asks for is good will.'

Germany showed its good will by attacking Poland after occupying Austria and Czechoslovakia. Even after that, Yalçın didn't change his line that the Western imperialists and fascist Germany should reach an agreement. He kept insisting the war should be redirected toward the Soviets and criticizing the Soviet–German Pact. Yalçın had made hundreds of thousands of liras in wagon trading with Germany during the First World War. That was why he didn't want the fascist regime to change. He went on praising Chamberlain for his soft approach toward Germany and hoping for a British–German agreement.

The public was unsettled by such articles supporting Nazi Germany and antagonizing the Soviet Union. They hadn't forgotten the catastrophic results of being dragged into the First World War as Germany's ally. The people were fearful of an alliance with Germany and the possibility of another war. Their feelings of friendship toward the Soviets, instilled by Atatürk, were still unshaken. And so, they wanted Turkey to sign a treaty with the Soviets, just as it had with Britain and France.

Tan was the only newspaper fighting tooth and nail against the propaganda of the reactionary press and articles defending Nazism. The paper kept up its struggle, arguing that Turkey shouldn't take part in a war against the Soviets. The Turkish fascists, infuriated by our articles, declared war on all progressive forces, on *Tan*, and especially on me.

As a new way of disseminating their propaganda, the fascists started attacking progressive writers from the past. They leafed through the pages of history, lashed out at progressive writers from all periods, and tried to discredit the Tanzimat movement[1] as well as Atatürk's reforms. Their aim was to prime people for the New Order they had in mind. And because I opposed them in my writings, I landed in court once again.

The Tevfik Fikret Trial

In 1940, when fascist propaganda was in high gear, the *Yeni Sabah* newspaper published an article by Kâmuran Demir, entitled 'We Must Burn the Works of Poet Tevfik Fikret'.[2] The article attacked Fikret's revolutionary ideas, humanism and atheism, as well as his person. It accused Fikret of not being nationalistic or religious. As proof, the article stated that Fikret had taught at Robert College, an institution founded by the Americans.

Shortly thereafter, the same newspaper conducted a poll about Fikret. Some participants came out in his favour. These were people who didn't know why the campaign had been started in the first place. But a majority – purposefully chosen from among Fikret's opponents – showered the poet with nasty attacks.

Following this campaign, *Sebilülreşat*, a journal run by religious fanatics, joined the fray, with Eşref Edip, the proprietor, taking centre stage. The journal started rehashing the debates between Tevfik Fikret and the poet Mehmet Akif after the 1908 Revolution. This was a calculated operation. These articles didn't just retrace the argument between two poets but also declared war on humanist, progressive and revolutionary ideas.

Times of war offer the best opportunity for reactionary ideologies to attack progressive ones. In such times, reactionaries often resort to slandering their opponents. Their greatest ideological ally in this task is religion. If necessary, the dead are exhumed,

---

[1] TN: The Tanzimat period ('reorganization', 1839–76) witnessed the most important Westernizing measures taken in Ottoman history, reforming many aspects of the state, from the legal system to education.
[2] TN: Tevfik Fikret (1867–1915) was one of the most influential Ottoman poets of the late-nineteenth and early-twentieth centuries.

their ideas reexamined and their graves used as trenches from which to snipe at progressive thought.

This was why the reactionaries hauled Fikret back on stage twenty-four years after his death, aiming their guns at his decomposing bones. They attacked him as a way of defending the ideology of Nazism and refuting the principles of Atatürk.

Turkey's youth split into two camps: the Fikretists and the Akifists. They started arguing and fighting with each other. Those who defended reactionism under the guise of nationalism and Turkism sided with Akif, while those who supported free thought, humanism and revolutionism championed Fikret. Racists and religious fanatics lost no time in joining forces in these premeditated attacks. They claimed that Tefvik Fikret was a communist and that his statue had been erected in the Soviet Union. The real aim of these attacks was to spread anti-communist and anti-Soviet propaganda by using Fikret as a straw man.

The fascists championed Turkism for the same anti-communist reason and spread Nazi propaganda disguised as nationalism. They stepped up their efforts to commit Turkey to war at Germany's side, just as in 1914. Thanks to the support they received from within and outside the country, they founded a plethora of organizations. They published journals, daily newspapers and pamphlets to promote their reactionary cause. They warned young people that humanism was a communist ideology at odds with nationalism and that communism itself was a form of barbarism.

Pursuing a policy of race in Turkey meant rekindling old flames of racial and religious animosity among Turkish citizens. And pursuing a policy of Turanism against the Soviet Union meant turning a friendship that took twenty years to build into hostility. With their ubiquitous organizations and publications, the racists and fascists largely achieved these goals. The public reassessment of Fikret in the 1940s was a result of these systematic operations.

I countered the *Yeni Sabah* and *Sebilülreşat* attacks on Fikret with some articles in *Tan*, entitled 'The Arsonist', 'Are They Trying to Make Fikret a Target for Reactionism?' and 'Youth and Fikret'. In response, *Yeni Sabah* and Eşref Edip, the owner of *Sebilülreşat*, took me to court.

Fikret was a poet who held an important place in the history of Turkish literature and was loved by the common people. His mention in a court case led to debates in the newspapers. I had the task of defending Fikret in court. For me, it was an honour to have this responsibility placed on my humble shoulders. But for the country, the very existence of such a court case was a disgrace.

On the first day of the trial, I went to the courtroom without a lawyer. I was certain that no lawyer could defend this case better than myself. Eşref Edip Hoca, the owner of *Sebilülreşat*, didn't deign to attend in person and sent his lawyer instead, depriving me of the pleasure of meeting him. The managing director of *Yeni Sabah* came with his lawyer.

The courtroom was full of young people. The racist, fascist youth had gathered on one side and the progressive, democrat, socialist youth on the other. In order to prevent an argument or brawl between the two sides, the court had stationed policemen throughout the hall.

After the initial questioning, the judge ordered me to rise.

'You are accused,' he said, 'of insulting the *Yeni Sabah* newspaper and Eşref Edip Hoca, the owner of the *Sebilülreşat* journal, in your articles about the poet Tevfik Fikret. Have you anything to say regarding these accusations?'

'I do,' I replied. 'I insulted no one in those articles. I merely defended the poet Tevfik Fikret against insults.'

'You called them fascist and reactionary. They consider this to be an insult.'

'According to Turkish law, it isn't an insult to call someone a reactionary, a conservative or a fascist.'

'Is it true that a statue of Tevfik Fikret was erected in Moscow?'

'No, it is not. And besides, it would be an honour for the Turkish people if it were.'

After this, the plaintiffs' lawyers rose to speak. They tried to prove that I had indeed insulted their clients. They said I was a communist and that was why I defended Fikret. After listening to their claims, the prosecutor stood up.

'I demand that the defendant, Sabiha Hanım, be asked whether she is a communist or not.'

This was how they tried to ensnare me. But the judge didn't let me speak. Instead, he turned to the prosecutor.

'Our laws do not require our court to inquire into individuals' moral and philosophical convictions,' he said. 'They only require us to determine whether these articles contain an insult.'

The prosecutor sat down, his tail between his legs. But it was clear that his indictment would be unfavourable to me. And so it was. In summary, it maintained that 'even though it is no crime to call someone a reactionary or a fascist, an air of insult pervades the entire article. It is insulting to accuse a person of spreading propaganda on behalf of a foreign nation'.

The bill of indictment was quite long. The prosecutor scrutinized Tevfik Fikret's ideology, claiming it had incited debate again and again, that an atheist poet was bound to offend the sensibilities of religious people and that their opposition to such a poet was not a crime. Afterward, the plaintiffs' lawyers made their final speeches. At that point, it was already quite late, and the judge postponed my defence to another day.

It was during this second hearing that I spoke in my own defence. I don't have a copy of the speech any longer, so I can't remember the exact wording. But I pointed out that Fikret had been able to freely express his beliefs even in his day, without having to defend them in court. It was a scandal for our country, I maintained, that his beliefs were insulted in the Republican era, twenty-four years after his death. I stated that Fikret's beliefs were a long-standing point of contention between progressive, humanist poets and reactionaries and religious fanatics, and that the issue was being rehashed today for political reasons. The attack on Fikret's humanist ideology was just a pretext, I claimed, to defend racist and Nazi ideas. And I tried to prove that my claims didn't constitute an insult.

There were a few more hearings. Finally, the panel of judges reached its verdict. In summary, it proclaimed that 'the articles published in *Tan*, *Yeni Sabah* and *Sebilülreşat* constitute an intellectual debate; the articles written by Sabiha Sertel in *Tan* contain no insult; and she is acquitted of all charges'.

As I left the courtroom, I was surrounded by progressive-minded young people. They thanked me for defending Tevfik Fikret and progressive and humanist thought in general. I told them I would research the background of the whole Fikret affair and write a book about it. I'd already made the same promise in my defence speech. In 1946, the book was published in Istanbul, with the title *Fikret's Ideology and Philosophy*. And it wasn't confiscated by the police.[3]

The German victories

The war escalated. France was entirely occupied by the fascists. In Turkey, pro-government newspapers and the free press alike were astounded. Most of the military officials who wrote columns now joined the racists and fascists in proclaiming that the Western democracies were collapsing and doomed to be crushed by Germany's military might. In this New Order, they claimed, smaller nations had no right to an independent existence, and it was a historical necessity for them to be swallowed up by larger ones.

Peyami Safa, along with his coterie of journalists, started a campaign in support of Nazism and Pan-Turkism at *Cumhuriyet*. Rather than sullying his own name, Peyami orchestrated the campaign from behind the scenes. Zeyyad Ebüzziya at *Tasviri Efkar* held up German imperialism as a nationalistic ideal. In an article from 30 December 1941, he claimed that 'in this age, the German nation has fully achieved its historical purpose' and that 'this cohesion will give rise to great events'.

'What,' he went on to ask, 'has changed about Turkish nationalism? What is its new programme? I know this new cause is so weighty that even the most competent hands will tremble in taking it up. Yes, it is weighty indeed. But I also know the day is near when the enemies of the Turkist cause will be the ones to tremble. We stand united with two and a half nations raised in this belief, with all our Turkish brethren who populate not just one, but two whole continents.'

Behind its façade of nationalism, *Tasviri Efkar* was advocating a Turanist, fascist cause. When they called for 'a programme of Turkism that has more authentic and tangible racial, geographical, social and political orientations', they really meant an invasion of the Soviet Union with the help of German troops. And so, they threw in their lot with German militarism and imperialism.

This movement was supported by the trade bourgeoisie with economic ties to Germany, by some landlords and reactionaries in the political parties, and by some petty bourgeois intellectuals. Worse, it even had supporters in the Assembly and cabinet. With their slogans of Turkism, religion, morality and a 'Greater Turkey', these people tried to delude the youth and segments of the population. *Tan*'s struggle against these reactionary forces met with great sympathy from many intellectuals and progressives.

---

[3] The second edition of this book was printed in Sofia, Bulgaria, in 1957, and the third edition, again in Sofia, in 1965, with the revised title *Tevfik Fikret's Role in the Struggle between Progressives and Reactionaries*.

Von Papen in Turkey

The defeat of France caused anxiety not just in the press but also in government circles. Around this time, in May 1939, von Papen[4] brought a message from Hitler to İsmet İnönü. His message was followed by an amicable exchange of telegraphs between the two leaders. Von Papen had been appointed German ambassador to Turkey. The appointment of this man, who had brought about the *Anschluss*[5] in Austria, destroying Austrian independence, was not a good sign. Hitler was trying to exploit his victories to split Turkey off from its pact with England and France, and use the isolated country for his own purposes.

After the German victories of 1941, Turkey's foreign policy underwent an important change. German planes landed soldiers in Crete, sending waves of euphoria through Hitler's supporters in Turkey. The idea of an agreement with Germany spread beyond the fascist press to other newspapers.

At *Tan*, we kept publishing articles that cautioned against this propaganda by the reactionary press. In my own column, 'Görüşler' [Views], I tried to alert the Turkish public to the realities of the situation, stressing the dangers of Turkey fighting a war at Germany's side. In June 1941, I wrote a piece about how the Germans oppressed the populations of occupied countries and burned Jews in furnaces.

At the instigation of Peyami Safa, *Cumhuriyet* launched a campaign against my writings. They started attacking me *ad hominem*, publishing column after column about me every day. They also published caricatures of me with insulting titles such as 'The Bolshevik Wench' and 'The Gypsy with a Pair of Tongs'.[6]

I avoided personal attacks in my articles, focusing instead on the theory of Nazism and the barbarism of the fascists. My friends said that remaining silent in the face of such insults would be construed as weakness. Still, I did not stoop to personal polemics. Instead, I took *Cumhuriyet* to court.

All my life, I'd been forced to sit in the defendant's chair. Now, for the first time, I was the plaintiff. I brought a lawsuit against Yunus Nadi Bey as the proprietor of the newspaper. But since he enjoyed immunity as an Assembly member, the court barred me from suing him. Instead, Agah Bey, the managing director of the paper, showed up in court with his lawyer. Since the articles had been published anonymously, he was legally responsible. This was how Peyami managed to remain behind the scenes.

Agah Bey produced a document stating he was hospitalized when the articles appeared. He maintained that the articles had slipped by due to the inexperience of colleagues filling in for him, and he regretted their publication. The court accepted his pretext of illness as an extenuating circumstance. It didn't inquire who had written the anonymous pieces and didn't find it necessary to punish the authors. All it did was sentence *Cumhuriyet* to pay me a 150 lira fine. Apparently, that was the price of a defamed person's honour and dignity. If I'd been the one hurling these insults, I would have certainly ended up in Sultan Ahmet Prison.

---

[4] TN: Franz von Papen (1879–1969) was former Chancellor of Germany and served as German Ambassador to Turkey from 1939 to 1944.
[5] TN: Germany's annexation of Austria in 1938.
[6] TN: A denigrating idiom in Turkish, comparable in meaning to 'shrew' or 'virago'.

The Turkish–German Pact

In April 1941, the fascist armies invaded Yugoslavia, rudely awakening those who claimed Hitler's Germany wouldn't touch the Balkans. Next, the Germans parachuted soldiers onto the coasts of North Africa. These developments caused tumult in Turkish government circles and among the pro-German bourgeoisie.

On 18 June 1941, at the Foreign Ministry in Ankara, Turkey and Germany entered into a pact. The pact was signed by von Papen, the German ambassador to Ankara, as well as İsmet İnönü and Turkish Foreign Minister Şükrü Saraçoğlu. It stipulated that the two countries would respect each other's territorial integrity and refrain from taking any direct or indirect action against each other. As two friends, they would seek each other's approval on all matters of mutual interest. The pact was to last eighteen years. Once ratified by the National Assembly, the agreement would be sent to Berlin for approval.

Turkey's treaty with Britain continued, but this new pact meant that the country was no longer neutral and 'out of war'. Once it was signed, Turkish journalists flocked to Germany at Hitler's invitation. Proclamations of Turkish–German friendship echoed through the country.

The pact came before the National Assembly on 20 June 1941. Saraçoğlu demanded that it be discussed and approved quickly. 'I regard it as a duty,' he said, 'to thank, before you all, the German statesmen who gave us a chance to build the foundations of German–Turkish friendship. As a precondition for keeping the promises we made to our friends, we must now ratify this pact.' The Assembly unanimously approved the pact.

The Turkish–German pact wasn't well received by the British. In a statement before the House of Commons on 24 June 1941, British Foreign Minister Devin stated,

> Turkey had declared its neutrality in this new war. Since the treaty of mutual assistance we signed in October 1939, our relations with Turkey have been exceptionally strong. Turkey is our friend and ally. I am probably divulging no secret in stating that we would have preferred the Turkish government not to sign any treaties with its German counterpart.

After this statement, Winterstone, a member of Parliament, spoke up. 'The days are over when a country like Turkey could remain neutral,' he said. 'Sooner or later, Turkey will have to declare which side it is on.'

The Turkish racists and fascists benefitted most from the German pact. In their journals and in the newspapers *Yeni Sabah* and *Tasviri Efkar*, they extolled German military power and claimed that Britain, France and the Soviet Union were doomed to perish by the end of the war. They also called for the treaty with Britain to be annulled.

On 22 June 1941, the Germans attacked the Soviets. The same day, the editorial in the German *Frankfurter Zeitung* read as follows:

> This pact is a success for Turkish–German diplomacy. Turkey must embrace a destiny that is clearly outlined and independent from foreign allies. Turkish diplomats understand this now.

The recent crisis in relations between Ankara and Berlin was nothing but a veil concealing an old and strong friendship. Undeterred by outward appearances, the German diplomats persevered and patiently bided their time, finally crafting this new agreement.

Without a doubt, this pact was von Papen's achievement.

Letters from my readers

My desk was covered in letters from my readers. I remember them like yesterday – reading them left me speechless. One reader wrote, 'We entered the First World War chasing the fantasy of invading the Caucasus and expanding the borders of the empire. We sent our sons from one front to the next, from Galicia[7] all the way to Yemen, under German command. But all we left behind in those lands were some abandoned graves. And now they want to drag us into another calamity with Germany?'

Another letter stated, 'Our government's foreign policy resembles a fickle woman's attitude. We got engaged to the Soviet Union. We got married to England. And now we're flirting with Germany.' Most letters opposed the Turkish–German Pact. I was astounded by the common sense of ordinary people.

The domestic ramifications of the pact were tragic. On 21 June 1941, the government extended the martial law, which was already in effect. The press came under even stricter surveillance. The Directorate General of the Press issued instructions about how newspapers should write about each new development. Papers that disobeyed were shut down. Parts of fascist Italy's penal law were translated and incorporated, and so was the German police law. The police cracked down even more forcefully on leftists and communists, arresting them under the most trifling pretexts. In anti-democratic laws and suspensions of the Constitution, this period surpassed all previous ones. İnönü brutally enforced the 'One Party, One Chief' system. We'd complained about lack of freedom under Atatürk, but now we yearned for those days.

Writing for *Tan* became more difficult. I couldn't touch on social issues. I couldn't discuss foreign policy. I kept analysing the nature of fascism in my articles, and the racist journals kept attacking my writings. Thankfully, the public didn't respond well to racist propaganda. The idea that 'a Turk should have seven generations of Turkish blood' didn't just disturb progressives and leftists but anyone with common sense. Instead, the masses agreed with the articles in *Tan*. I was encouraged by the letters that arrived from my readers each day.

But the fascists doggedly reported me to the police, and their efforts were rewarded. Policemen started tailing me, around the clock. A street vendor appeared across from our house. Every morning, he spread out some handkerchiefs on a board opposite our door, pretending to sell them. Even though he never had customers, he sat there all day long. One day, the neighbourhood grocer called me over. He told me that two plainclothes officers came to his store every evening around five and watched our

---

[7] TN: A border region in modern-day Poland and Ukraine.

house from there. Wherever I went, whether by ferry, taxi or foot, I always had someone on my heels.

The political branch of the security forces kept *Tan* under constant surveillance, sending in undercover agents as writers and proofreaders, or under other pretexts. They even managed to plant someone in our home. We were looking for domestic help, and a supposed friend of ours recommended an Armenian woman. I asked her what kind of work she could do. 'Anything,' she said. 'I used to work in embassies. I cook very well and bake great pies.'

What a lucky break, I thought at first. But soon, I started finding my desk drawers in disarray. This happened every day. Finally, I asked her about it.

'They get messy while I'm dusting,' she said.

'Leave the dusting to me,' I told her, 'and don't go through my drawers.'

One day, I was looking for an English journal.

'Are you looking for *Harper's Magazine*?' she asked, and brought it over.

'Do you speak English?'

'Yes, I studied at the American High School for Girls.'

'Then why do you work as domestic help?'

'What can I do? I couldn't find anything else. My mother is blind, and I have to work to support her.'

I thought about it. A college education, experience at embassies, my papers in disarray... I was becoming suspicious.

One evening, we had guests over for dinner. After they left, we were removing the extension panels from the table. The woman was about to pinch her finger.

'Watch out,' I said, 'you'll hurt your finger.'

She pulled it away.

'One of my thumbs is missing anyway,' she said. 'I'd better not lose the other one as well.'

'How did you lose your thumb?'

'The police chief placed me in a factory once. It got caught in a machine.'

There was no more room for doubt. Shortly thereafter, she cleared out.

At the Military Investigative Court

One day, I received a phone call from Suat Derviş. She said she was involved with a new journal called *Yeni Edebiyat* [New Literature] and asked me to contribute a piece. I accepted and sent her the article. A short while later, I received a summons from the military court. I never guessed that it could be about the piece in *Yeni Edebiyat*.

On the day the interrogation was scheduled, I went to the garrison courthouse in Fındıklı. It was a sizeable building surrounded by a yard. Two soldiers with bayonets stood guard at a large door with iron bars. I showed them the summons. They read it. 'Come this way,' one of them said. 'Follow me!'

I entered the building with the soldier at my side. He took me to a small room in the basement. Six other people were already waiting there – Reşat Fuat, Hasan Dinamo, Suat Derviş and three others I didn't know. It was clear now why I'd been summoned.

The bailiff took the suspects upstairs, one by one, calling the next in line once each interrogation ended. Those who had been interrogated weren't allowed back to where we were waiting. Finally, it was my turn. I went upstairs with the soldier. We entered a large hall with rooms on all sides. The soldier escorted me into one of these small rooms. Inside, a young officer was seated at a desk. When he saw me, he told me to sit down in the armchair across from him. After confirming my name and identity, he asked:

'What was your purpose in submitting this article to the *Edebiyat* journal?'
'Suat Derviş called me and said they'd be publishing a literary journal. She asked me for an article, so I accepted and wrote this piece.'
'Do you know Suat Derviş?'
'I've known her for a very long time. We used to publish her short stories in *Resimli Ay*, and she also wrote for *Tan*. I saw nothing wrong with accepting her offer.'
'Have you read all the articles in the journal?'
'I have.'
'What's your impression of it?'
'It's a progressive art journal. It covers the latest views and topics about literature. Abidin Dino's piece on realism and surrealism, for instance, offers a brand new perspective on literature. The article about the poet Tevfik Fikret analyses Fikret's qualities as a humanist. The other poems and articles are in the same revolutionary vein.'
'Aren't these articles communist propaganda?'
'Scholarly articles can never be propaganda.'
'In your article entitled "The New and the Old", what do you mean by "the Old"?'
'The article as a whole conveys what I mean. I am referring to the conservatives who oppose the principles of Atatürk, such as revolutionism, secularism and populism, and who resist all forms of change.'
'And what do you mean by "the New"?'
'Society is engaged in a constant process of change. As times and conditions change, the foundations of society change, and so do ideas and views. Progressive forces break the old patterns and voice new opinions that challenge established ideas and systems of thought. Progressives fight to advance the public to a new stage. This is how I assessed the division between reactionaries and progressives.'
'When you say "the New" and "progressives", don't you really mean the communists?'
'Communists, socialists or even capitalists can defend progressive ideas. Was Atatürk a communist? No, but he defended progressives. As I just explained, the *Edebiyat* journal hasn't spread communist propaganda. It's a scholarly journal expressing its views on art. The ideas I defend in "The Old and the New" are of a scholarly character as well.'

The interrogation was over. The officer stood up and told me I could leave. He was very polite and even walked me to the door.

Ultimately, I wasn't sued, but the other writers were. However, at the end of the trial, they were all acquitted.

Sabahaddin Ali's trial

Just like *Tan* in Istanbul, the journals *Yurt ve Dünya* [The Homeland and the World] and *Adımlar* [Steps] were fighting racists and fascists in Ankara. The owners of these two journals were viciously attacked by *Çığır* [Epoch], a journal with Anatolianist leanings,[8] published by Hıfzı Oğuz Bekata and Samet Ağaoğlu. They accused *Yurt ve Dünya* and *Adımlar* of being Americanist.[9] Faced with this Anatolianist and Pan-Turkist onslaught, *Yurt ve Dünya* and *Adımlar* were forced to close down.

Pertev N. Boratav, one of the journals' founders, told me what happened:

> Hasan Ali Yücel, minister of education at the time, summoned me, as the owner of *Yurt ve Dünya*, and Behice Boran, the owner of *Adımlar*. He demanded that we discontinue the journals. As he put it, this was to avoid possible provocations and to prevent the obstruction of important work underway on education policy. He said this was merely his advice. We complied. And so, both journals shut down voluntarily.
>
> The two journals were under attack by the Turanist and Anatolianist press, namely *Çınaraltı*, published by the poet Orhan Seyfi; *Çığır*, published by the Anatolianists; and *Ergenekon*,[10] published by the well-known Turkist Reha Oğuz Türkkan.
>
> We also heard rumours from parliamentary circles that both journals would soon come under surveillance. The Anatolianist wing of the People's Party was planning a move against us. It was led by Reşat Şemseddin Sirer and Şevket Raşit Hatipoğlu, the former minister of agriculture. One of our most vociferous detractors was Fahri Ecevit [father of Bülent Ecevit, who, at the time of writing, is the leader of the 'Left of the Middle' movement in the People's Party].[11]

As these debates between the racists, Anatolianists and progressives raged on, Nihal Adsız, the leader of the racists, published an open letter to Şükrü Saraçoğlu. Sabahaddin Ali, who was verbally abused in the letter, took Adsız to court.

At that time, Sabahaddin Ali worked as assistant director of the State Conservatory in Ankara. Quite a while after the trial, he visited Istanbul and described the proceedings:

> On the day of the trial, the courthouse was surrounded by mounted police. They were afraid of an incident since the racists viewed this trial as an opportunity to make a move. Suddenly, the rightists and fascists who'd managed to get in the courtroom raised a ruckus. The judge tried to postpone the hearing, but the racists started singing the national anthem, and of course, the judge couldn't say anything. The noise both in and outside the building was deafening. I realized I was in great danger. Fortunately, the trial was being held on the first floor. I jumped out of the window. I barely saved my hide.

---

[8] TN: A movement that regarded Anatolia as the origin of Turkish culture.
[9] TN: In this context, supporting US interests at the expense of Turkey.
[10] TN: The name of a Mongolian creation myth popular in Turkist ideology.
[11] TN: One of the most prominent Turkish politicians of his generation, Bülent Ecevit passed away in 2006.

While recounting his story, Sabahaddin kept jumping up and down like a firecracker and laughing out loud. 'The fascists' scheming isn't over,' he said. 'Saraçoğlu is their biggest supporter. We all have to be very careful.'

The attacks on Sabahaddin Ali continued after the trial. They even tried to assassinate him. I was told about this attempt by Hayrünnisa, Pertev Boratav's wife.

'On some nights,' she said,

> the students at the State Conservatory staged plays in the theatre hall of the *halkevi* building.[12] The plays were directed by Ebert, who had been brought in from Germany. As Ebert's assistant, Sabahaddin had to attend all the performances. Since I taught at the school, I attended the plays as well. On the day of the trial, Pertev and I were worried about Sabahaddin, so we dropped by his house in the evening on our way to the theatre. He lived in Kızılay. We picked him up and headed for the *halkevi* building together. Sabahaddin was very excited. He told us about the trial, railed against the rightists and even broke into laughter a couple of times. He seemed to enjoy casting himself as the hero of the day. He was in high spirits.
>
> We arrived in front of the Faculty of Language, History and Geography. From there, we took a shortcut, a dark road that led to the *halkevi*. Suddenly, a huge stone fell in front of us. Then, another one came flying from behind, scraping Sabahaddin's shoulder. He whirled around. Before we knew what was happening, a third stone hurled by. I don't know how, but Sabahaddin, small as he was, started running at full speed toward where the stones had come from. A person emerged from a boxwood in the faculty yard and ran away. Sabahaddin raced after him as fast as he could. Of course, Pertev and I also started running after them. We were afraid something might happen to Sabahaddin.
>
> When we crossed Atatürk Boulevard, we saw that Sabahaddin had caught someone and was pounding him with his hands and feet, with all his might. Pertev tried to restrain Sabahaddin to avoid a public incident. This continued for a while. There was a police booth ten steps away. The police ran over to us. It turned out that the attacker was a young man called Osman Yüksel.[13]
>
> Feeling safe near the policemen, Yüksel threw a punch at Sabahaddin and broke his glasses.
>
> The policemen took Yüksel into custody for the night. The next day, all four of us were in court for having been at the scene, even poor Pertev, who'd only tried to separate the two. The judge ordered both to pay a small fine. But since one of them had thrown stones and the other was guilty of battery, the fines cancelled each other out.

This incident shows that the racists and fascists wanted to neutralize Sabahaddin even back then – and even if it meant killing him. These events were a prelude to Sabahaddin's assassination in 1948.[14]

---

[12] TN: The *halkevi* (People's House) project was an initiative by the Turkish state to convey the fundamentals of a modern education and worldview to adults in cities and the countryside.
[13] Osman Yüksel is a well-known racist. In 1964, he was elected to Parliament on the Adalet Partisi (Justice Party) ticket, but later expelled from the party.
[14] I will write more about this event further in the book.

After 1944, progressives were granted a modicum of freedom. This was largely because the Turkish government had signed the Treaty of San Francisco and the Atlantic Charter.[15] A number of progressive journals started publishing, and people discussed national issues a little more openly. But the attacks on the progressives only intensified. The government employed the fascists as squads to crack down on progressive movements and used many roundabout ways to stifle them.

I am banned from writing

In early 1941, *Tan* was shut down by the government. The reasons were unclear. Ahmet Emin Yalman went to Ankara to try and convince the politicians to reopen the paper. One day, after midnight, we woke up to the ringing of the phone. It was Ahmet Emin, calling from Ankara. He and Zekeriya talked for a long time. Ahmet Emin had managed to salvage *Tan*, but there was one condition: Sabiha Hanım was not allowed to write for the paper anymore. Out of concern for the future of the paper, Zekeriya agreed at once.

I already knew what Interior Minister Şükrü Kaya thought about me. But what were his specific reasons for banning me from writing?

Ahmet Emin returned from Ankara. I was working in my office when he came in.

'I spent a long time defending you to Şükrü Kaya,' he said. 'But he thinks the tone of our foreign policy articles is too harsh. He doesn't like us railing against fascism and Germany. "We've signed an agreement with the Germans," he says. "Attacking them wouldn't be right at this point. Britain is our ally as well, and Sabiha Hanım harshly criticizes British imperialist policies. On top of all this, she defends Soviet imperialism. It's best if she doesn't write for a while." So we sacrificed you to save *Tan*.'

'You did the right thing,' I said. '*Tan* needs to keep publishing; that's the most important issue.'

I wrote Şükrü Kaya a letter. I asked him what law entitled him to take away my constitutionally guaranteed right to write.

> If the government doesn't think these matters should be discussed right now, it can only offer me suggestions. Britain might be our ally, but doesn't the British press itself criticize the country's imperialist policy? We may have a pact with Germany, but how is it against Turkish interests to write about the calamities that fascism has in store for the world?

---

[15] TN: The Atlantic Charter, issued on 14 August 1941, was a policy statement that defined the Allied goals for after the Second World War. The Treaty of San Francisco referred to by Sertel is somewhat more ambiguous. Sertel might mean the Treaty of Peace with Japan, which was signed by forty-eight nations on 8 September 1951, and served to officially end the Second World War. In this case, though, her dating would be off by almost ten years. It is more likely that she is referring to the United Nations Conference on International Organization, or the San Francisco Conference, held from 25 April to 26 June 1945, and resulting in the creation of the United Nations Charter.

Figure 6.1 *Tan* publishing house postcard.

And finally, I do not believe the Soviets are imperialists. They gave us financial and moral support during the War of Independence. They tore up the capitulations signed between the Ottoman Empire and Tsarist Russia. Atatürk made Soviet friendship the foundation of his foreign policy. If the Soviets attack us one day, as you claim they will, of course I will oppose them. But it's the British Tories, Hitler and Mussolini, who dragged mankind into a second world war by spreading this anti-communism, this animosity against the Soviets.

Not just Turkey but the whole world must be freed from the calamity of war and the savagery of fascism. This is why I write. But since you don't want me to, I will stop. I can only hope that one day, you too will see I was right. I look forward to having my freedom to write reinstated as soon as possible.

Şükrü Kaya didn't respond.

I felt in limbo. Just when it was most important to fight against war and fascism, I'd lost my freedom to do so. I decided to write a book so my time wouldn't be wasted. The book was about the conditions that had ushered in fascism, the ways in which British and French imperialism had given rise to Hitler's increasing military power, and the schemes concocted by Britain and France to deflect the war toward the Soviet Union. Of course, it couldn't be published under these circumstances. I also continued translating Marxist works into Turkish. I translated Lenin's *Imperialism is the Highest Stage of Capitalism* and Stalin's *Problems of Leninism*. These translations couldn't be published, either. When leaving the country in 1950, I gave the manuscripts to my brother Neşet Deriş. He died in 1956. I don't know who has them now.

A long time went by. One night, I was at the Marine Club, a gathering place for the rich, intellectuals and statesmen. While I was sitting with some friends on the terrace overlooking the sea, Şükrü Kaya came in with Kılıç Ali, a member of Atatürk's inner circle. Passing by our table, he greeted us and shook our hands. We offered him a seat. He sat down without hesitating. We started talking about the weakness of the British and French. He said he didn't believe the Germans would win the war.

'America will join the war,' he said. 'Once that happens, Germany's chances of victory are slim. Fascism won't be able to take root in Europe.'

'Then why did you ban me from writing?' I said.

'When you wrote those articles, we were trying to reach an agreement with Germany. They came at the wrong time.'

'When is the right time? When do I regain my freedom to write?'

'Go ahead and write,' he said, 'but don't touch on foreign affairs.'

The ice was broken. I could write for *Tan* again. I returned to my column, 'Görüşler'.

Those were days when a person's freedom could be removed and restored at the whim of an interior minister.

Germany attacks the Soviet Union

On 22 June 1941, Germany attacked the Soviet Union in violation of international law, without any formal declaration of war, and in spite of the non-aggression pact between the two countries. Its aim was to destroy the Soviet system and expand to the east. The German armies amassed at the western borders of the Soviet Union and launched an all-out attack from the north to the shores of the Black Sea. The war's centre of gravity shifted from the west to the east.

I was at the hot springs in Bursa when the Soviet–German war broke out. As soon as I heard the news on the radio, I called up Nazım Hikmet, who was in Bursa Prison, and told him what had happened.

Nazım was surprised. 'If it's a dog's time to die,' he said, 'he'll go and piss on the wall of a mosque.'[16]

The next day, I went to the prison to visit him. We met in the warden's office. 'The Germans are finished now,' he said, pacing up and down. 'Even if they advance all the way to Moscow, they'll lose in the end.'

Nazım believed in the power of the Soviet people, in their determination to face all hardships. History proved him right.

The German–Soviet war deeply affected Turkish foreign policy. The day the war broke out, *Anadolu Ajansı*[17] issued the Turkish government's official statement: 'The Government of the Turkish Republic has decided to declare Turkey's neutrality in the war between Germany and the Soviet Union.' We were no longer simply 'out of war,' as Saraçoğlu had stated. We were 'neutral' now, and one step closer to aligning with Germany.

---

[16] TN: This Turkish proverb is used to describe a suicidal act that will provoke certain doom. Hikmet is maintaining that Hitler's attack on the Soviet Union was foolish and self-destructive.

[17] TN: The official news agency of the Turkish state.

This turn of events unsettled the British government. On 30 June *Anadolu Ajansı* cited the following news from the French press agency:

> The British Foreign Minister Eden, the Turkish Ambassador Tevfik Rüştü Aras and the Soviet Ambassador Maisky have held an important meeting. Von Papen is thought to be planning a new manoeuvre: Germany may offer Turkey the lands inhabited by Muslims in Georgia and the Caucasus in return for Turkey allowing German troops to pass through its territory into the Caucasus. Mr Eden explained to Tevfik Rüştü Aras that Turkey's renouncing its neutrality and aiding the Germans in any way would breach the spirit of friendship between Turkey and Britain.

Hitler's victories in Europe and his subsequent attack on the Soviets forced the British government to change its policy. If the Germans were victorious in the east as well, the Western imperialists would be hard pressed to face the might of the German armies. For this reason, the British government announced in June 1941 that it was ready to aid the Soviets against Germany. On 24 June the US Government followed suit. And so, the two mightiest capitalist nations of the world joined forces with the Soviets in the war against German fascism.

The war sharpened the divisions between Germany on the one hand and Britain, France and the USA on the other. Germany now occupied nearly all of Western Europe and threatened the British Isles. The countries conquered by the Germans were unable to drive out the fascist hordes on their own. The Soviets were the only force strong enough to stop Hitler's army and prevent Germany from taking over the entire world. In Britain and the US, people staged rallies in favour of aiding the Soviets, putting pressure on their governments. And so, the Western allies finally recognized that it was in their interest to reach an agreement with the Soviet Union against their common enemy.

This agreement didn't mean that Britain and the US had given up their hostility toward the Soviets. The day after Germany attacked the Soviet Union, US Vice President Truman[18] stated, 'If we see that Germany is winning we ought to help Russia, and if Russia is winning we ought to help Germany, and that way let them kill as many as possible.'

At the end of 1941, the imperialist nations of Britain and the USA entered an alliance against Hitler. This alliance won the sympathy of anti-fascist and democratic forces everywhere. But Turkey was headed in the opposite direction. Still beguiled by the German–Turkish Pact and Germany's victories, Turkish newspapers paid lip service to the agreement with Britain while filling their inside pages with exaggerated accounts of German victories and triumphant reports on the Soviets' retreat. Some newspapers published serialized accounts of Napoleon's life and his Russian campaign while vilifying contemporary France as well as the French and Soviet Revolutions. Marshal Petain and Pierre Laval, traitors to the French nation, were held up as heroes.[19]

---

[18] TN: In fact, Harry Truman was a senator from Missouri at the time. He became Vice President in 1945.

[19] TN: Respectively, Prime Minister and Minister of State of the French Vichy regime, which collaborated with Nazi Germany.

Figure 6.2 Headline, April 1939, reads: 'Hitler Says Germany Threatens No One'. *Tan* was an early voice warning against the rise of Hitler and fascism. Sertel's articles, critical of the government, landed her in court.

To counter this propaganda effort, we stepped up our anti-fascist campaign at *Tan*. We expanded the paper's editorial staff. Many leftist writers like Sadrettin Celal, Sabahaddin Ali, Sadri Ertem, Naci Saadullah and Burhan Arpad were writing for us now. Defying Şükrü Kaya, I also wrote anti-fascist articles in my column as well as anonymous ones in the paper's inside pages.

Britain and the USA were growing alarmed by the fascist movements in Turkey and started pressuring the Turkish government to take action against them. Intimidated by this pressure, Ankara stopped interfering with anti-fascist articles, and our campaign was able to continue without being silenced.

The German armies reach Moscow

The war rages on in all its ferocity. Leningrad is under siege. Belorussia, Moldavia, Lithuania, Latvia, Estonia and the Crimea have fallen to German forces. The Nazis establish a reign of terror wherever they go. They destroy and burn down villages and cities, evacuate factories and farm collectives, and confiscate the people's grain and animals. They torture and kill their prisoners of war and deport the civilian population to Germany. The whole Soviet Union is convulsed by famine. The people are suffering untold misery.

The Second Front still hasn't opened up. The Soviet Union faces the German armies alone. The Japanese are in Manchuria and Korea, preparing to attack the Soviets. The Germans are approaching Moscow. Soviet partisans are giving their all to support the Red Army. The entire Soviet population stands united in defence of the nation.

These are days of joy for the Turkish fascist press, pro-German statesmen and the bourgeoisie engaged in trade with Germany. Even Turkish government circles regard a German victory as inevitable. The spectre of entering the war at Germany's side grows more menacing by the day. If Hitler wins, Turkey will come under fascist Germany's control, and those who realize this are horrified.

The racists' New Order propaganda is in high gear. Falih Rıfkı Atay, editor-in-chief of the *Ulus* newspaper, proclaims that the establishment of new Western societies after the war won't be easy and will require time. In his editorial of 3 January 1942, he writes, 'Now we must start envisioning a nation without class conflict, and an order of nations under its hegemony. We must establish a planned and strictly supervised economy of statism and advance class interests through New Order organizations. And we must bring the same spirit of justice, equality and discipline to bear upon international relations.'

A nation without class conflict, and an order of nations under its hegemony! This is nothing but red-hot fascism. I take up my pen and, without mentioning Falih by name, explain just what such an order of nations would mean. Fearfully, I await the backlash. But the article causes no incident.

A meeting with Celal Bayar and Tevfik Rüştü Aras

By the end of 1942, the Red Army had launched a massive counteroffensive against the Germans. The fascist German armies were stuck outside Moscow. For the first time since the beginning of the Second World War, they were facing a major defeat.

My daughter Sevim was in Ankara, and I paid her a visit. One day, while I was walking across Kızılay Square, I ran into Tevfik Rüştü Aras. I'd known him for a long time. At my wedding, he'd even been my witness. We started talking as we walked. He mentioned that he read *Tan* and enjoyed my work. 'You're fighting bravely,' he said. He invited me to his house that evening.

When I arrived, the former prime minister, Celal Bayar, was there as well. We discussed the course of the war, the state of the nation and foreign policy. Bayar approved of Turkey's agreements with Germany and advised caution against our ally, Britain. In matters of foreign policy, he and İsmet İnönü saw eye to eye. Their quarrel was over economic policy, especially the issue of statism. Bayar explained his own economic view.

'Statism has fulfilled its role,' he said. 'For a while, it was useful in helping individuals accumulate capital. But now the situation has changed. The state must readjust the economy and grant more freedom to private capital. I'm not saying that statism should be discontinued, at least not for the time being. But it must be recalibrated. The state must only invest in fields that aren't profitable for private capital. Its involvement in the economy should be limited. The state's job is to unite and coordinate the different actors in the economy.'

Bayar had distanced himself from Atatürk's policy of statism and was defending liberalism. İnönü, however, wanted no changes whatsoever to the policy of statism. This was a major point of discord between them.

As for Tevfik Rüştü Aras, he opposed the government's foreign policy. He was critical of the harmful role played by von Papen, dissatisfied with Saraçoğlu's support of Germany and fearful that the country would ride the coattails of Germany into another war. In particular, he sharply criticized the government's policy toward the Soviet Union.

'Our latest agreements with Germany violate our treaty with our allies,' he said. 'We also risk incurring the wrath of the Soviets. As Atatürk said, we must never pursue a hostile policy toward the Soviet Union. The Soviets were the only ones to support us during the War of Independence. Further, they were the only ones to support our demands in the League of Nations. Whenever I ran into trouble as an ambassador, I could count on their help.'

Celal Bayar listened carefully, raising no objections to Tevfik Rüştü's views on foreign policy. Then, changing the subject, he started talking about İnönü's oppressive policies. 'We can't speak up in the Assembly,' he said. 'He keeps me under surveillance at all times. I hear about it from policemen I know.'

Bayar had been prime minister when Şükrü Kaya banned me from writing. Now he was the one complaining about restrictions on himself and the press. I thought about bringing this up but decided against it.

'You are a member of Parliament,' I said. 'You have the freedom to speak as you wish in the National Assembly. Why don't you raise these issues? As ordinary citizens, we can't prevent the state from silencing us or spying on us. But why don't you, of all people, speak up?'

He sat up in his chair. 'An opposition against İnönü's despotic leadership is starting to form in parliament. But there is a time for everything. It wouldn't be right to disrupt our national unity with the country at risk of war.'

I met Celal Bayar and Tevfik Rüştü Aras a couple more times after that. As Bayar said, a parliamentary opposition against İnönü and his faction was emerging within the Republican People's Party. Eventually, Bayar and his supporters made their move and founded the Democrat Party, with Bayar as chairman.

*

In Ankara, I also regularly met with longtime friends, including Niyazi Berkes, Pertev Boratav, Behice Boran, Muvaffak Şeref and Sabahaddin Ali. They had all been young people with socialist leanings, who'd been educated in the USA or Europe. Many of them were teaching at the Faculty of Language, History and Geography. Pertev Boratav was a professor of folklore, and Niyazi Berkes and Behice Boran were associate professors of sociology. If I remember correctly, Muvaffak Şeref and Adnan Cemgil were high school teachers; one taught economics and the other literature.

All of them were involved with the journals *Yurt ve Dünya* and *Adımlar*. *Yurt ve Dünya*, founded by Berkes, Cemgil, Boran, Boratav and Muzaffer Şerif, had started publishing in January 1941. The editorial staff also included Mediha Berkes, Sabahaddin Ali, Orhan Kemal, Necmi Sarıoğlu, Cevdet Kudret, Muvaffak Şeref and Halil Aytekin. Later, Muzaffer Şerif and Behice Boran left *Yurt ve Dünya* and started the journal *Adımlar*. That journal didn't cover current affairs but featured anti-fascist articles on ideology, literature and art. We had many discussions on the state of the nation, the war and the oppressive policies of the government.

*

While I was in Ankara, the Press and Broadcasting Association held its annual convention. The Association consisted of media bosses, workers and government representatives. The event was chaired by Selim Sarper, chair of the State Directorate for Press and Broadcasting. I was invited as well.

The convention had hardly begun when I was surrounded by media workers of all kinds. They complained that the Association prevented them from defending any of their rights. They wanted to split off and found their own organization.

The convention began with a report on the past year. Afterward, various matters were brought up. Those who had proposals submitted motions to the steering committee. I submitted one, too, expressing the wishes of the media workers and demanding they be allowed to found their own independent organization. The same motion was put forward by others as well. When my turn came, I stood up and defended my proposal.

The motions were put to the vote, but none of the proposals favouring the workers was approved. For some reason, the bosses' proposals always won out.

I was leaving the convention when Selim Sarper approached me.

'You're the wife of a boss yourself,' he said. 'How come you're defending an idea against your own interests?'

'I may be a boss's wife, but I'm a media worker first,' I replied. 'We're all in the same boat. I'm just as unhappy as my colleagues about the pay at *Tan* and the censorship I have to endure. And even if I wasn't, this is a just cause. I don't care about my own interests. I care about who is right.'

Sarper laughed. 'Everything you said in there was recorded on tape,' he said.

'This wasn't a secret meeting. I spoke in front of everyone. So what if I was recorded?'
'It wasn't just you,' Sarper went on. 'All media workers' statements were recorded.'
'Then I suppose you must be pretty pleased with yourself.'
The whole thing was just another example of the government's efforts to browbeat the progressives.

The Wealth Tax is imposed

Even though Turkey stayed out of the Second World War, its economy was hit as if at war. More and more trade capitalists emerged. Traders with Germany, brokers and black marketeers started amassing great fortunes. The low-income population became destitute because of war shortages while the wealthy classes used their ill-gotten gains to lead lives of luxury. The country's budget deficit increased by the year. Finally, the government decided to issue a new tax in order to erase the deficit and quell unrest among the masses.

On 11 November 1942, the Saraçoğlu cabinet submitted the Wealth Tax Bill, prepared by government bureaucrats and selected businessmen, to the National Assembly. For a long time, the bill wasn't brought up for debate. But in 1943, the Ministry of Finance approached the Assembly with a package of new laws. The package contained the following statement:

> Since the Wealth Tax is not just an income tax but encompasses fixed assets as well, it would be inappropriate to deduct it from the income tax. For this reason, the finance minister has decided not to declare the Wealth Tax as already collected in his annual budget.[20]

Merchants, brokers, black marketeers and big landowners were making huge profits by exploiting wartime hardships. Taxing them would help the government with its financial troubles as well as somewhat reduce growing social injustices along class lines.

Before discussing the bill in the Assembly, Prime Minister Şükrü Saraçoğlu held a press conference in Ankara. He invited all editors-in-chief. Zekeriya wasn't in Istanbul at the time and I was writing *Tan*'s editorials, so I went to Ankara to represent the paper.

On the train, I discussed the Wealth Tax with Necmeddin Sadak, the editor-in-chief of *Akşam*, and Hakkı Tarık Us, one of the owners and writers of *Vakit*. Necmeddin Sadak said: 'It's only right to tax the major estates. But we're only just beginning to create a national bourgeoisie. Won't this tax stop the emergence of such a class in its tracks?'

Hakkı Tarık smiled. 'Old sport,' he said, 'this tax will mainly hit the non-Muslim minority capitalists. Turkish capitalists will be spared.[21] I have it on good authority.'

---

[20] TN: In other words, the Wealth Tax would need to be collected separately.
[21] TN: Sertel omits the fact that the non-Muslim minorities in question were Turkish citizens as well. The discrimination was not aimed at foreigners, but at non-Muslim citizens of the Turkish Republic.

'Impossible,' Sadak replied. 'The law applies to everyone equally.'

I agreed with the idea of taxing major estates. But if Hakkı Tarık was right about the implementation of the tax, it would be an unpleasant affair.

Emin Karakuş, *Tan*'s Ankara correspondent, picked me up at the Ankara train station. The only lodging I could find was at a grungy hotel called *Cihan* [World]. I asked Emin some questions about the bill. He didn't know any more than I did. In fact, he knew even less.

The press conference took place the next day. My colleagues there confirmed what Hakkı Tarık had said. I don't remember the hall in which the conference was held, but it was spacious, with a long, narrow table at its centre. Saraçoğlu sat down at the head of the table and read his statement. It can be summarized as follows:

> We are living in historic times. The war has thrown the entire world economy off balance. Our imports and exports have ground to a halt. We cannot take our goods out of the country or acquire the raw materials we need. Our remaining trade with Britain is not enough to keep our markets afloat.
>
> So far, the war hasn't reached our borders. But we must be prepared for all eventualities. Our military expenditures are large, and we are running a budget deficit. We cannot erase this deficit with the current level of state income and taxes.
>
> Some capitalists, brokers and black marketeers in Turkey have found questionable ways to conduct business with foreign countries. They have made great fortunes while most of the population suffers from poverty and the deprivations of war.
>
> The government has decided to collect a Wealth Tax to overcome the budgetary crisis and alleviate the suffering of those with low incomes. I would like journalists to explain this law to the people and tell them that the tax is in the interest of the citizens and the country.

The statement was followed by questions, but all of them were trivial. No one asked a question that would reveal the true nature of the law. Finally, Necmeddin Sadak spoke up.

'I believe this law is in the country's interest,' he said. 'But I would like the Prime Minister to explain something to me. We have long been trying to foster a national bourgeoisie in this country. Won't such an extraordinary tax weaken our nascent bourgeoisie?'

Saraçoğlu answered without hesitating: 'They will suffer a temporary setback. But the state economy as a whole will grow stronger, and this will make it easier for them to create new areas of profit. We are about to sign new trade agreements with Germany. Once those agreements are in place, the bourgeoisie will be able to conduct its trade legally and increase its profits. This tax will mainly affect those who exploit the hardships of war by raising prices at the expense of the common people.'

But if the tax was equally applied to everyone, how would the state distinguish war profiteers from those who were conducting legitimate business? I spoke up.

'The bill compels all people with income and estates to submit declarations of wealth. Have these declarations already been collected? How can one ascertain that they contain no tax fraud, that no one has concealed his true wealth? And when will the tax take effect?'

'The law will take effect as soon as the Assembly ratifies it,' Saraçoğlu answered. 'The bill was prepared on 11 November 1942, and treasury commissions have examined the wealth declarations.'

He left it at that. He didn't touch on the possibility of concealing wealth in the declarations.

Hakkı Tarık hadn't been able to find a place to sit and was standing in front of the bookshelves across from the table. He raised his voice.

'The largest fortunes in our country belong to minority capitalists. Turkish capitalists are only just emerging. Wouldn't it harm our national economy to tax all of them equally?'

'We cannot discriminate among our citizens under the law,' Saraçoğlu replied. 'Whoever owns the biggest estates will pay the highest taxes. The tax must be paid within fifteen days. The properties of those who don't pay the full amount will be confiscated.'

It was clear from Saraçoğlu's words that after fifteen days, the government would collect the tax by force.

In principle, this was a justified law. But once it went into effect, the Wealth Tax was primarily collected from non-Muslim minority capitalists while Turkish capitalists were protected. This was unjust. Whether their name was Yorgi, Avram or Mehmet, those who made fortunes by robbing the Turkish people were all the same, and their punishment should have been the same as well. The Wealth Tax carried the stench of fascism.[22]

I returned to Istanbul. We weren't allowed to criticize the law, so I didn't write a single word about the Wealth Tax in *Tan*. Shortly thereafter, the tax law was passed by the Assembly and went into effect. Those who needed to pay their tax debt in fifteen days were panicked. They claimed they didn't have the necessary cash. All their capital was invested in assets, and it was impossible to sell them in such a short time. Some sold their wives' jewelry, others went into debt. Some sold or pawned their homes and belongings to speculators at trifling prices. Others simply gave up, saying, 'I don't have the money. If they want, let them take my life instead.'

The government had decided to deport those who couldn't pay to Aşkale in Eastern Anatolia. I went to the Haydarpaşa train station to witness the deportation. It was a scene of pandemonium. The women who came to see off their husbands, sons and brothers were crying. The men were wringing their hands and running up and down the platform. Their friends were promising to save them, to find money and send it to them.

The deportation of the tax debtors to Aşkale caused a frenzy among the grand bourgeoisie. Those deported wrote letters describing how they lived in tents and sheds in the middle of the steppe, how they couldn't find anything to eat, how they had to break stones from dawn till dusk every day. The law was enforced with Nazi methods.

---

[22] TN: Sertel does not mention that the Wealth Tax systematically discriminated against non-Muslims. Each major ethno-religious group had to pay a different percentage of tax on their fixed assets. Armenians paid 232 per cent; Jews paid 179 per cent; Greeks paid 156 per cent; Muslims only paid 4.94 per cent. Sertel's own *Dönme* community was taxed at non-Muslim rates even though the community was officially Muslim.

Şükrü Saraçoğlu had learned well from his masters, von Papen and Hitler. Even though all tax debtors were supposed to be deported, there were only a few Turks among those sent to Aşkale. These methods of tax collection caused outrage in the country and abroad. The articles published in the world press were a disgrace to Turkish society.

In spite of all the clamour and coercion that surrounded the Wealth Tax, it didn't yield the anticipated income. In fact, the economic situation grew even worse. Only the biggest companies survived, while others went bankrupt. Businessmen kept raising prices on all kinds of merchandise to compensate for their losses. The common people grew even poorer.

Faced with internal and external pressure, the government eased the tax collection. The tax had such a devastating effect on businessmen and ethnic minorities that the government finally had to amend the Wealth Tax Law. This amendment, submitted to the Assembly on 18 September 1943, stated that 'the Finance Minister is authorized to erase the tax debts of employees who prove they cannot pay their taxes and of citizens who pay tax on their gross daily income.'

The Wealth Tax was finally abolished on 15 March 1944. But by then, history had already recorded this shameful episode.

The *İğneli Fıçı* brochure and yet another trial

Heavy fighting rages around Stalingrad. With temperatures near 30 degrees Celsius below zero, the Germans aren't able to leave their trenches. The fascist armies are stuck in the steppes and can't come to the aid of their troops encircled in Stalingrad. The Soviet soldiers fight heroically in the inferno created by the fascists' tanks.

The Turkish press, especially military columnists, were so sure of a German victory that they wrote Stalingrad off as a temporary impediment. They maintained that German reinforcements would ultimately take the city and urged the Turkish government to support Germany in these difficult days.

The racists in Turkey launched a nationalist campaign. Using nationalism as a pretext, they defended the ideology of Nazism, praised the Wealth Tax and promoted hatred of minorities. On ferries and trams, they handed out flyers with slogans like 'Citizen, speak Turkish!' to those who spoke Greek, Armenian, Jewish and other foreign languages. They spewed insults at minorities. They tore down storefront signs written in languages like Greek and French. They demanded that minorities should not be employed as civil servants and that minority capital should be heavily taxed. They spread xenophobia wherever they went.

Around this time, these racists published a brochure called *İğneli Fıçı* [The Needle-Studded Barrel], promoting hatred of Jews.[23] They claimed that our country needed to launch a policy of state terror against the Jews and wipe them out as a race. They

---

[23] TN: The title of the brochure references the 'blood libel', which claimed that Jews were sacrificing gentile babies in religious rituals. One such claim held that babies were rolled in needle-studded barrels to collect their blood for sacrifice. Ironically, the 'blood libel' was outlawed in the Ottoman Empire under Suleyman I (r. 1520–66), while persecution of Jews was widespread in Europe.

advised the Turkish population not to shop at Jewish stores and to insult Jews wherever they saw them. They demanded that Jews be barred from participating in the country's economy.

I wrote in *Tan* that anti-Jewish sentiment, anti-Semitism and racial hatred in general had never existed in Turkey. While Tsarist Russia carried out programmes and the USA discriminated against blacks, there was no hatred of either Jews or blacks in Turkey.[24] I pointed out that such inflammatory attitudes violated our laws as well as our Constitution. Clearly, *İğneli Fıçı* was intended to incite racial hatred and animosity among Turkish citizens. I wrote that such incitement could be considered treason.

The racists lost no time in attacking me through their journals. They showered me with insults, claimed that I was the one betraying the fatherland and filed a lawsuit against me.

The trial was held in a civil court. After the judge conducted a preliminary interrogation, the prosecutor read his indictment. He requested that both sides be punished, stating that 'even though Sabiha Sertel accused the plaintiffs of treason first, the insults she endured in return were harsher'. The judge pressed the publishers of *İğneli Fıçı*, asking them why they thought hatred of Jews was in the nation's interest. The racists' lawyer argued that this question exposed the judge's own prejudice. He vowed to file a motion to recuse the judge.

The trial was adjourned. Many more sessions were held. I spent days languishing in court hallways. The plaintiffs' motion to recuse the judge was denied. Finally, the court ruled that both parties had committed the same offense in accusing each other of treason, and therefore the case was dropped.

I am banned from writing for the second time

The German defeat before Stalingrad plunged Turkish bourgeois writers into deep thought. They feared that a Soviet victory would expose the entire world to the 'peril of communism'. After the trial over *İğneli Fıçı*, I wrote a series of articles in *Tan* opposing these fascist sentiments of the bourgeoisie.

I avoided personal polemics, writing instead on the theoretical foundations and imperialist aims of fascism. I pointed out that the Constitution of the Republic counted everyone as a citizen as long as he was a Turkish national, paid his taxes and fulfilled his citizenship duties, no matter what his race, religion or language. I explained that minorities could no longer be treated as *reaya*.[25] Turkish nationalism, I maintained, was an anti-imperialist nationalism concerned with protecting the national wealth against foreign capital bent on colonizing the country. I reiterated Atatürk's comments on the issue of Pan-Turkism. In his historic speech, the *Nutuk*, Atatürk rebuked those who wanted to unite the Turkish and Islamic worlds:

---

[24] TN: Sertel omits mention of numerous atrocities against ethnic and religious groups in Turkey and the Ottoman Empire, most prominently the Armenian Genocide (1915–16).
[25] TN: Literally 'flock', *reaya* was a term used by the Ottomans to describe the populations under their rule, especially, but not exclusively, non-Muslims.

> Let us suppose for a moment that we take on the aforesaid responsibility [of uniting all people of Turkish origin] and succeed in merging and ruling the entire Islamic world. What if the nations you wish to bring under our control say to us, 'We are thankful for your great service and assistance. But we wish to remain independent. We deem it inappropriate for anyone to interfere with our autonomy and self-rule. We are capable of ruling ourselves.' Will these words of gratitude be sufficient to reward the Turkish people's toil and sacrifice?

Atatürk shunned this imperialist Turkism, rejecting its champions such as Ziya Gökalp. As his own words confirm, he had no imperialist goals like uniting the Turkish races and bringing them under his control.

At present, Turkish nationalism can only aspire to defend the nation's interests against capitalists exploiting workers' labour and foreign capital exploiting the nation's sources of wealth. If, for instance, a sugar profiteer exposes children to bone tuberculosis and various other illnesses, he undermines national interest regardless of his race.

Today's nationalism is about protecting the rights of the masses against local and foreign exploiters, and maintaining the nation's economic and political independence. Turkism, in contrast, uses nationalism as a pretext to defend local and foreign capital and to foment hatred among different races. In so doing, it also opposes the republic's principle of populism.

My articles were vehemently criticized and attacked by the reactionary press. For some reason, the debate was taken up in the Grand National Assembly. Some deputies asked the Prime Minister to take a position on the issue.

Here is what Saraçoğlu had to say on the matter: 'Turkish nationalism is not a passive nationalism. We have cordial ties with the Turkish races that live in other countries. It is every Turk's obligation to desire the well-being of these races. We are Turkists, and Turkists we shall remain.'

These words didn't just have ideological ramifications but political ones as well. They were uttered during the Battle of Stalingrad, when Emin Erkilet and other Turkish generals were dispatched to Turkey's Caucasian borders, ready, it was rumoured, to aid the Germans. This policy of Turkism was diametrically opposed to Atatürk's nationalism and anti-imperialist policy.

It is natural for Turks to feel affinity and affection for Turks living in other countries. But establishing ties with those other Turks in the pursuit of imperialist political goals was another thing. The Turkists who followed this policy were aiding the cause of fascist Germany.

The fascist press was ecstatic. To them, *Tan* and Sabiha Sertel, in particular, had lost their case. After all, Saraçoğlu himself was on the Turanists' side. He himself defended Turkism. I didn't respond to these claims. I hadn't lost my case. I understood the magnitude of the danger facing the country, and I understood that siding with Germany was taking us down the wrong path once again. And time would prove me right.

After these discussions, *Tan* received a phone call from the Press Directorate in Ankara. I was told to stop provoking such debates in these delicate times and to refrain from writing for two months. And so, my freedom to write was taken away for the second time. The first time around, I had been muzzled for criticizing Turkey's cooperation with fascist Germany. Now, I was being muzzled for fighting against racism and Turkism. But time would show just how right I was on both of these counts.

The pamphlet *En Büyük Tehlike*

In June 1943, a citizen by the name of Faris Erkman published a pamphlet called *En Büyük Tehlike* [The Greatest Peril]. In his words, the greatest peril to the country was fascism. Erkman's pamphlet was confiscated, while the fascists' pamphlets and journals kept circulating with impunity.

On 6 July 1943, the Assembly took up the matter. Cevdet Kerim İncedayı, deputy for Sinop and secretary general of the People's Party, started the discussion by speaking of the need to approach all ideologies and propaganda with the utmost caution. He said he'd read *En Büyük Tehlike* and added:

> This pamphlet describes a movement created in Turkey to serve foreign interests. It claims that Turkist groups are being fostered under the pretext of Turkish citizenship and patriotism. It further claims that Turkey is being pushed toward imperialist policies, such as liberating the Turks who live in other countries. I am unaware of any such movement or interpretation of nationalism in our country. What are the intentions of this pamphlet's publisher? What are his political and social credentials? I demand an explanation from the relevant authorities.

Foreign Minister Numan Menemencioğlu replied that he too had read the pamphlet and that it had even been mentioned in a foreign journal. He went on to say:

> One needs to dig a bit deeper to get at the heart of the matter here. This book creates the impression that there are certain movements in this country, and that exposing these movements as dangerous is a valuable service to the nation. What are we to make of this?
>
> The political programme of the People's Party describes the Turkish population as 'a social and political entity made up of citizens united by language, culture and ideals'. This is Turkey's motto.
>
> We say that we are Turks and Turkists. But you know better than I do what we mean by this. For centuries, the Turk has been burdened with all responsibilities and deprived of all blessings in this country, and that despite officially being the 'sovereign *millet*'.[26] Our goal is to carry this Turk to the loftiest heights of economy, culture and values. There is no nationalism in this country that exceeds these goals, and there is no evidence that such a movement exists.

---

[26] TN: The Ottoman Empire was structured along religious lines, with the Muslim religious community enjoying primacy over all others. Menemencioğlu here conflates Turks with Muslims. The term *millet* to describe the Ottoman religious communities first came into wide usage in the nineteenth century.

I knew that Menemencioğlu was deaf, but I didn't know he was blind as well. How could he fail to notice the mounting piles of journals published by the fascists since before the war? How could he ignore all the propaganda about a 'Greater Turkey' that would extend all the way to the Ural Mountains? Had he never read the disputes between *Tan* and reactionary papers like *Cumhuriyet* and *Tasviri Efkar*?

By declaring there were no fascist or Pan-Turkist movements in the country, Menemencioğlu was actually covering for them and ingratiating himself with his true overlord, von Papen. His feigned indignation with *En Büyük Tehlike* was meant to protect the interests of his own class. The ruling class had staunchly backed the Turanist movement and viciously attacked the progressives ever since Atatürk's death. Now, anti-fascist sentiment was rising among the common people and the country's intellectuals, and Menemencioğlu needed to stifle it.

The Assembly dismissed *En Büyük Tehlike* to reassure Hitler that Turkey wouldn't tolerate Germany's enemies. By then, the Saraçoğlu government had largely come under von Papen's and Hitler's tutelage. It would go on to prove its servitude to Germany by devising many ways to increase the Germans' military power.

Faris Erkman was arrested and brutally tortured by the police. Already suffering from tuberculosis, he rotted in prison for years and developed stomach cancer, spitting up blood and finally dying at a young age.

I lose my right to write for the third time

When I was a child, my mother told me a story: A little girl was walking down the street when she found five *kuruş*. She wanted to buy something with the money but her stepmother was a tyrant, and the girl was afraid of making her angry. If I buy walnuts, she thought, the shells will dirty the house. If I buy a pear, the leftover stem will dirty the house. And if I buy a pomegranate, the seeds will dirty the house. And so, she ended up buying nothing at all.

I felt like that little girl. If I wrote against fascism, I'd stir up a hornet's nest. If I criticized the government's foreign policy, *Tan* would get shut down. If I defended the rights of workers and peasants, I would be branded a communist. Finally, I resolved to write a series of articles against imperialism.

I wrote about the difference between justified wars and imperialist wars. I described the colonized peoples' struggle against oppression. I recounted how the imperialists had conquered the lucrative markets of Asia and Africa in the nineteenth century, and how they had colonized these regions. The First World War had been waged over possession of colonies, I pointed out. And now, the Second World War was being waged for the same reason, with British, French and American capitalists on one side and German and Japanese capitalists on the other. I argued that Britain and the USA refrained from opening up a second front against Germany because they hoped to weaken Germany and Japan, their commercial enemies, and the Soviet Union, their ideological enemy, by playing them off against each other.

Shortly after the articles were published, we received another letter from the Press Directorate. I was banned from writing for a year.

I felt like a train that was derailed at full speed. I had so much to say. I had so many social, economic and political causes to defend. But I couldn't write about any of them anymore. I bought a large notebook. On the first page, I wrote the following line from Nazım Hikmet's poem 'Jokond ile Si-Ya-U' [La Joconde and Si-Ya-U]:

I have decided, from now on, to keep a diary.

On the same page, I also wrote, 'I have declared my independence. I am no longer afraid of any oppression. I will follow current affairs and write my thoughts down in this notebook.'

And so I did. Every day, I analysed the tortuous statements of politicians in the newspapers and wrote down my own thoughts on the issues, just as I'd done in my 'Görüşler' column in *Tan*. I filled up three notebooks this way. In 1945, after the *Tan* publishing house was destroyed by fascist mobs, the police conducted a search of our house. Along with many other documents, they took away my notebooks. And they never gave them back.

Supplying Germany with chrome

As the Second World War enters its fifth year, the Soviet armies are fighting to recapture the cities under Nazi occupation. The German defence is buckling under the force of the Soviet attacks. The Second Front, made up of Britain and the USA, is fostering national resistance movements in Nazi-occupied countries.

Tan applauded Turkish statesmen's efforts to keep the country out of war but criticized the excessive friendship they showed toward Germany. This policy of support for fascist Germany continued even as the war turned completely against the Germans. In January 1944, the Soviet armies broke the siege around Leningrad. They entered Estonia and Moldavia. They smashed the enemy's resistance in the Crimea. They chased Hitler's armies all the way back to Romania.

Those who'd believed that fascist Germany would win the war were deeply disappointed. When the Soviet armies started freeing Romania from fascist occupation, Falih Rıfkı Atay urged the Germans not to withdraw. In an article for *Ulus*, published on April 1, 1944, he surmised that the Führer wouldn't let political concerns override military strategy anymore and would cut his losses when it came to territory. He wrote:

> What remains to be seen is how Germany will deploy the forces still at its disposal. Abandoning Romania wouldn't just mean surrendering the country's oil reserves, but surrendering the Balkans altogether. If the Germans leave, the remaining Axis forces will not engage the Red Army in battle, and it is said that Romania will reach an agreement with the Soviets. If that happens, Russia can wreak havoc in the Balkans even without deploying significant forces.

Necmeddin Sadak, the editor-in-chief of *Akşam*, was similarly angered by the sight of Soviets chasing Germans. On 4 April 1944, he published an article entitled 'As Soviet

Troops Enter Romanian Territory'. In it, he maintained that 'it is of utmost military and political importance that Russia stay within its existing borders after liberating its own territory'.

The Turkish government did all it could to support fascist Germany, ignoring the Soviet victories and the Allied armies' advances in Europe. For instance, Turkey supplied Germany with raw materials, especially chrome, used to produce armaments. This caused outrage in Britain, the USA and the Soviet Union. In mid-April 1944, these three countries put Turkey on notice and demanded an end to the chrome exports.

In his editorial dated 18 April 1944, Necmeddin Sadak responded to this demand:

> If a neutral country helps Germany, the Allies might consider this collaboration with the enemy. But one mustn't forget the neutral country's economic needs. It is natural for a country at war to try and squeeze its opponent in all possible ways. But it is equally natural for neutral countries to put their own needs above those of the countries at war in order to avoid internal collapse.

Sadak's protestations notwithstanding, the Turkish government bowed to Allied pressure. On 21 April 1944, Numan Menemencioğlu responded to the Allies' notice: 'From this evening onward, the supply of chrome to Germany and the Axis nations will be halted. Our treaty with Britain forms the foundation of our foreign policy, and therefore, we cannot be impartial in this matter.'

Allowing German ships to pass through the Bosporus

The Saraçoğlu administration's support of fascist Germany wasn't just limited to supplying the country with chrome and other raw materials for arms. In 1944, when the tide of the war had already turned against the Germans, the Turkish Foreign Ministry allowed German ships to pass through the Bosporus. Britain and the Soviet Union protested this move, stating that it breached the Montreux Convention.[27]

The Turkish government came under fire in the British House of Commons. Britain's foreign secretary, Anthony Eden, claimed that Turkish authorities had examined the German ships hastily and insufficiently, declaring them to be trade vessels when in reality they were warships or part of the war effort. Eden maintained that the Montreux Convention was clear beyond a doubt on this matter. He quoted Article 19: 'In time of war, Turkey not being belligerent, [...] vessels of war belonging to belligerent Powers shall not [...] pass through the Straits.'

Newspapers around the world condemned Turkey's decision, and the Turkish public wasn't pleased, either. Bowing to domestic and foreign pressure, Foreign Minister Numan Menemencioğlu resigned on 16 June 1944. On the same day, Şükrü Saraçoğlu

---

[27] TN: The Montreux Convention Regarding the Regime of the Straits, signed in 1936, is an international convention regulating access to the Bosporus Straits and the Dardanelles. Also known as the Turkish Straits, these waterways offer the only maritime connection between the Black Sea and the Aegean and Mediterranean Seas.

made a statement to the foreign press: 'The powers and rights that Turkey enjoys must not and can never be used against our ally Britain and our friends, Soviet Russia and the United States of America.'

The Times correspondent asked why the ships had been allowed to pass. The acting foreign minister replied, 'Since you bring up the subject, I have three more pieces of important news for you:

1. The passage of the German ship *Kessel*, still being examined in the Bosporus, has been blocked;
2. From now on, all vessels of the Mannheim and Ems classes will be blocked from heading through the Straits;
3. All German vessels that reach the Straits will be examined to determine whether they are commercial or not.'

This statement confirmed that until then, the Turkish Foreign Ministry had been allowing vessels to pass without oversight. Saraçoğlu, who now maintained that Turkey's powers and rights couldn't be used against its allies, had allowed German ships to go unchecked.

The Saraçoğlu administration's foreign policy kept flip-flopping as the war progressed. In the beginning, Turkey was neutral. Then, it was no longer neutral, but merely 'out of the war'. Later, the country allied with Britain and became Germany's opponent. When the Nazis started winning, Turkey signed a treaty with Germany and endeavored to aid the country's war effort. And once the Nazis were defeated, Turkey declared war on Germany.

The Saraçoğlu administration doggedly defended the Turkish fascists who spread New Order propaganda in the country. It prevented progressives from fighting this reactionary movement. It violated its treaty with Britain by supplying Germany with chrome and allowing German ships to pass through the straits. It disregarded its agreements with the Soviet Union as well. As a result, relations with both these nations cooled.

Throughout the war, *Tan* was constantly penalized for fighting against fascism, imperialism and the movements that wanted Turkey to fight alongside Germany. But history proved that the paper fought for a just cause.

We may concede that the Saraçoğlu administration's goal was to keep Turkey out of war, and we may even be thankful on that count. But the ways in which the government supported Germany's war effort and Turkey's racist movements cannot be excused.

7

Turkey at the end of the war

In the end, the tide of war turned fully against Germany. Soviet troops inflicted heavy defeats on the enemy everywhere from the Baltic Sea to the Carpathian Mountains. German defences collapsed. Hitler was forced to divert more troops to the Soviet–German front, and British and American units used the opportunity to start an offensive in the west.

In spring 1945, the Red Army occupied Silesia and Eastern Prussia, the cradle of German militarism. It entered Austrian territory and started marching on Berlin. Poland, Hungary, eastern Czechoslovakia and a large part of Austria were liberated from German occupation.

Turkish politicians were anxious. They felt isolated. They had angered Britain and the USA by aiding the German war effort. They had alienated the Soviet Union through their hostile policy. Saraçoğlu was under great domestic and international pressure.

The Allies openly condemned the fascist movements in Turkey. The British and American press harshly criticized Turkey's stance during the war. In the Turkish Assembly as well as among the public, opposition against the oppressive regime grew stronger.

It was clear now that Germany had lost the war. Fear of the Soviets forced Turkish politicians to try and reconcile with Britain and the USA. The moneyed classes that had flourished during the war and accumulated great wealth also urged the government to reach an agreement with the Western imperialists. Turkey wanted to join the United Nations, sign the UN Charter and align itself with Western nations. Under these circumstances, the single-party system became hard to defend. İnönü knew he couldn't placate the West as long as he didn't establish a democratic regime and make some concessions to the Western imperialists.

The Turkish press changed its tone along with the politicians. The papers stopped defending fascist Germany and jumped on the Allied bandwagon. They championed Turkey's entry into the Western bloc. To prove that his domestic policy was changing, İnönü started openly persecuting the Turanists and fascists, who were taken to court.

With this change in atmosphere, I also regained my freedom to write.

The trial of the Turanists

At the end of January 1945, some Turanists were arrested and taken to court. On 3 February, newspapers published the prosecutor's indictment. It was hundreds of pages long. *Akşam* published a summary; I'll quote some sections from it here:

The Turanists are accused of forming a secret society to overthrow the government. Zeki Velidi Togan has confessed in court that he exploited the political crisis caused by the war to engage in illegal activities aimed at the political unification of Turkestan.[1] Togan stated: 'The secret society National Unity of Turkestan, founded to liberate Turkestan and with headquarters in Tashkent, authorized me to represent it abroad. I turned over the European branch of this society to Mustafa Çokay in Berlin. At the urging of Dr Rıza Nur, I travelled from Berlin to Turkey and commenced activities here, recruiting members for the society in Istanbul.' As part of these clandestine political activities, the suspect did not hesitate to enlist Nihal Adsız, Reha Oğuz Türkkan and their comrades for his cause.

The suspect further stated: 'I confess that after the outbreak of the Soviet–German war, I wanted to go to Germany and resume my activities there.' He also wrote the following in his diary: 'The interior and foreign ministers will not allow me to go to Germany, even to conduct scientific research. The German Ambassador Von Papen demanded that I be officially authorized to travel, but the Foreign Ministry refused. This refusal violates our government's policy of neutrality.'

The suspect criticized our government in conversations with Ahmet Karadağlı and Neriman Karadağlı, who were still in Germany at the end of 1941. According to him, the Turkish Government was missing a historic opportunity by not immediately uniting with the Germans and attacking Russia, thereby promoting the independence of Turkestan and the establishment of a 'Great Turkish Union'.

When Germany appeared victorious, these suspects decided to found a secret society aimed at creating a disturbance in order to overthrow the Turkish government. Zeki Velidi Togan, Ahmet Karadağlı, Neriman Karadağlı, Reha Oğuz Türkkan, Cihat Savaşfer, Heybetullah İdil and Nurullah Bariman assembled at Neriman Karadağlı's apartment in Taksim and swore to lay down their lives for this cause if necessary. They decided to organize their followers in Germany through a society known as 'Aid for the Turkestanis in Istanbul,' and commenced activities to this end. Four of the suspects have confirmed these endeavours in their statements.

To promote his political activities, Zeki Velidi Togan also founded other societies, including the 'Union of Captive Turkish Lands' and the 'Turkestan National Union', as well as publishing the journal *Türk Yurdu*.

The suspect Cihat Savaşfer made the following confession: 'At the end of 1941, Nurullah Bariman told me that Zeki Velidi and his circle were part of a secret and powerful organization. Nurullah and Oğuz had already joined this society, and he promised to enlist me as well. The three of us went to Neriman Karadağlı's apartment. There, Zeki Velidi Togan made Heybetullah and myself take an oath on a Qur'an, a gun and the flags of Turkey and Turkestan.'

---

[1] TN: The settlement area of Turkic peoples in Central Asia, today encompassing the states of Turkmenistan, Kazakhstan, Uzbekistan, Kyrgyzstan and Turkic-speaking regions of Russia and China.

The suspect outlined the society's aims as follows:

1. Liberate Turkestan and establish a Great Turkish Union;
2. Overthrow the Turkish Government as soon as German victory became certain;
3. Operate secretly in order to recruit members for the organization;
4. Enable Zeki Velidi Togan to contact the societies in Germany and travel there to organize our followers.

The prosecutor also outlined the confessions of Nihal Adsız, the leader of the Turanists:

He confessed his crime by stating: 'I consider it an honour to be charged with fascism and Turanism.' Further, he stated: 'Turanism is the *sine qua non* of Turkism. Only those who have been Turkish for three generations can be considered Turks. The state must be led by members of the Turkish race. Today, our government includes many people from mixed races. The Albanians, Circassians, Bosnians, Kurds, Laz and others are non-Turks who live in Turkey as Turkish nationals. They must be deported to their countries of origin.'

The indictment had the following to say about Alpaslan Türkeş:[2]

This suspect confessed his guilt during the investigation and repeated his confession in court, stating: 'Only members of the Turkish race should live in Turkey. But if the other races leave the country, the population will decline. Therefore, it is necessary to form a Great Turkish Union.'

These statements are confirmed by the suspect's letters to Nihal Adsız. In his letter dated 28 February 1943, he states: 'Unfortunately, we are proceeding in a very disorganized and leaderless fashion. For Turkism to prevail, we need unity and leadership. When will we attain these two? I fervently implore you to redouble your lofty efforts in this matter.' The suspect, who acted as Nihal Adsız's agent in the army, all but incites Adsız to rebellion in this letter.

Türkeş' guilt is also confirmed by other letters to Adsız, such as the following one dated April 4, 1944: 'I hope the Turkish nation will overcome the perils that threaten it. In all probability, Adsız's pen, sharper than a sword, will carry our cause to victory. But if the pen does not suffice, we will let our weapons speak. Our soul, our heart and our swords are with you.'

The prosecutor moved on to Dr Fethi Tevetoğlu, one of the leaders of the present-day Adalet Partisi:[3]

---

[2] TN: Türkeş was one of the military officers involved in the 1960 Turkish coup d'état and went on to found the extreme right Nationalist Movement Party (MHP) and its notorious youth organization, the Grey Wolves. He dominated these organizations until his death in 1997.
[3] TN: The Justice Party (1961–80) was a major Turkish centre-right political party. In 1968, as Sertel was writing her memoirs, it was the party in government.

During the investigation, he confessed that he is a fascist and Turanist. Nihal Adsız provided the following information on him: 'I have known Fethi Tevetoğlu for a long time. I told him my views regarding the republic, the government and the Grand National Assembly, and he shares my convictions. Being a military officer, he promoted our cause among the young officers in his circle and the cadets at the military academy. He is a Turkist and therefore a Turanist.' Apart from the letters read out in court, Tevetoğlu's guilt is also confirmed by the letter he wrote to Nihal Adsız on February 22, 1939.

The next person mentioned in the indictment was Reha Oğuz Türkkan:[4]

> He is a member of the abovementioned secret society aimed at overthrowing the government. He and his friends Ceyhun Tansu, Cihat Savaşfer, Hikmet Tanyu and Bülent[5] founded another society called *Gürem*[6] to overthrow the current government, to form a new one consisting of members of the Turkish race, and to bring about the Great Turkish Union. The suspects published the journal *Ergenekon* as a front for their activities and contacted Nihal Adsız and Hüseyin Namık Orkun to expand their organization. After the government shut down *Ergenekon*, they started the journal *Bozkurt*.
>
> It appears that Türkkan founded the *Gürem* society at a meeting he convened at his Ankara residence. The meeting was attended by Hikmet Tanyu, Nurullah Bariman, Hamza Saadi Özbek and Tahsin Ergun. Türkkan proclaimed: 'It is time to put our cards on the table. I belong to a secret organization that counts some generals among its members. Our society is a network of cells with five people to a cell. I will be the leader of our cell.' All except Tahsin Ergun accepted his proposal.
>
> The suspects commenced activities, using the offices of *Bozkurt*, founded in 1941, as their headquarters. From there, they planned and organized the actions of various secret societies.
>
> The Turanists' aims were as follows:
>
> 1. Create a nation of pure Turkish race by uniting the Turks in Asia and Turkey;
> 2. Overthrow the current Turkish government, which opposes this aim, through a sudden and rapid coup from within. Install a new government with a policy of racism and Turanism;
> 3. Spread propaganda to recruit members of the Turkish race for the secret society, and have them take ceremonial oaths.

The prosecutor also mentioned the events surrounding Sabahaddin Ali's trial:

---

[4] TN: A respected academic, Türkkan went on to teach at Columbia University and the City College of New York (CCNY) from 1947 to 1972. He died in 2010.
[5] TN: No last name provided.
[6] TN: An archaic Turkish word roughly translatable as 'collective'.

Another suspect, Orhan Şaik Gökyay,[7] facilitated the acquisition of publishing rights for the journal *Orhun* and became the journal's copy editor. He invited Nihal Adsız and Cemal Oğuz to his house, where he told them that Sabahaddin Ali had provoked the trial against the racists and that newspaper stories about Ali being temporarily removed from his government post were untrue. In so doing, Gökyay incited Adsız and Oğuz to take wrongful actions against Ali.

The suspect, Gökyay, was the director of the public institution that employed Ali. If Ali was engaged in questionable activities, why did the suspect not report this to the relevant authorities? Did the suspect not engage in questionable activities himself by inciting his close friends Adsız and Oğuz and causing regrettable events in the nation's capital – and that at a delicate time of political crisis? The suspect is clearly affiliated with Nihal Adsız and insisted on hosting the latter at his home after the demonstrations surrounding the Sabahaddin Ali trial. He has acted as Adsız's agent in Ankara. His letter dated 5 March 1944, also confirms his guilt.

Another suspect, Fazıl Hisarcıklı, confessed in court to being a close collaborator in Nihal Adsız's propaganda activities. He attended secret meetings in Ankara and became an important member of the society. From his letter to Nihal Adsız, dated 17 May 1944, it emerges that he engaged in the same activities in Kayseri: 'We know what kind of people our cause requires; which tactics need to be employed; and how much patience, resolve and energy we need to reach our goals. We have already determined those who would stand in our way. Now, we must disseminate works about racism and Turanism among the people we were able to contact in Konya, Adana and Kayseri.' Nihal Adsız himself maintains in his statement: 'I know Fazıl Hisarcıklı well. Our ideas and activities regarding racism and Turanism are in tandem.'

Cemal Oğuz Öçal and Zeki Özgür made similar confessions during the investigation.

The prosecutor demanded that the accused be sentenced as follows:

> At the instigation of Zeki Velidi Togan, he and Reha Oğuz Türkkan, Cihat Savaşfer and Nurullah Bariman conspired to form a secret society. The members of this society swore, during a special ceremony, to overthrow our government, which refused to enter the war as Germany's ally. They continued their activities until they were arrested. The motives and evidence for these crimes have been established above. I demand that the accused be sentenced according to Article 171, Clause 2 of the Turkish Penal Code.
>
> Reha Oğuz Türkkan, Cihat Savaşfer, Muzaffer Eriş, Zeki Özgür, Hikmet Tanyu and İsmet Tümtürk conspired for the same reasons, swearing to overthrow the government through a sudden coup from within, and continued their activities until they were arrested. I demand that they too be sentenced according to Article 171, Clause 2 of the Turkish Penal Code.

---

[7] TN: Gökyay was an important Turkish literary historian. He died in 1994.

The racists' trial concluded on 30 March 1945. They were sentenced to police surveillance and a maximum of six years in prison.

It is painful to read about this trial and its outcome. The Turkish justice system sentenced the poet Nazım Hikmet to twenty-eight years in prison without evidence of any crime. How compassionately the same system dealt with those who had tried to overthrow the government by force of arms!

As evident from the prosecutor's indictment, the racists founded secret societies to drag Turkey into war alongside fascist Germany. They established contact with the Turkestanis who were headquartered in Germany. They were active, secretly and openly, since 1941 or even 1939. As the confessions in court showed, even some generals were involved in these societies. The roots of the organization were based abroad. How could the Turkish police and government not have noticed these activities until 1945?

This trial demonstrates how right we were in our fight against the Turanists and all those who wanted Turkey to ally itself with Germany in the Second World War. In our years of struggle against them, I was repeatedly muzzled and dragged into court by the Turkish Government. Why did the same government tolerate the racists and fascists who openly trumpeted their cause in their publications?

Was it not Foreign Minister Numan Menemencioğlu who stated that 'there are no racist and Turanist movements in our country' when the brochure *En Büyük Tehlike* was debated in the Assembly?

Was it not Prime Minister Şükrü Saraçoğlu who proclaimed from his pulpit in the Assembly that 'we are Turkists, and Turkists we shall remain'?

The Opposition in the Assembly reveals itself

The Saraçoğlu Government, its supporters and the state-run press seemed to have given up hope of a German victory. İnönü kept promising that the country would become more democratic and revise undemocratic laws.

Celal Bayar and his circle had been secretly forming an opposition faction within the People's Party. Now, emboldened by changes at home and abroad, they stepped out of the shadows. At the party caucus meeting on 23 April 1945, İzmir Representative Celal Bayar, İçel Representative Refik Koraltan, Kars Representative Fuat Köprülü and Aydın Representative Adnan Menderes submitted a motion demanding changes to the People's Party's charter and some laws.

Many representatives spoke up after reading the motion. Their views were summed up by Şükrü Saraçoğlu. Any motion to modify laws, he said, had to follow due process. Further, the party's charter could only be changed in the general assembly. Therefore, he went on, there was no need to discuss these matters at the caucus meeting or to form a commission to deal with them. The motion was rejected unanimously except by those who had proposed it.

Bayar had already foreseen this unanimous rejection. But he was encouraged in his efforts by the common people who had suffered for years under the yoke of 'One Party, One Chief' and by his own constituency, the trade bourgeoisie. The public wanted freedom and democracy. And the interest groups who opposed the policy of statism hoped for greater profits under a Bayar administration. Bayar wanted to position himself as a champion of democracy and freedom, but he was afraid of the pro-İnönü bureaucratic circles in the Assembly, the petty bourgeois intellectuals who supported the one-party state, and, above all else, the political machinations of İnönü himself.

Tan had launched a campaign advocating for more democracy. Heartened by this, Bayar got in touch with us. He started inviting us to join him when he came to see his friends in Moda, and sometimes visited us as well. In one of our conversations, he openly expressed his fears:

> We need to assume power in order to change the laws and establish a more democratic regime. But if an election were held today, İnönü would win all the votes regardless of how disenchanted the common people are. I know how elections work in our country. The government sends its list of candidates to loyal governors and high officials in the provinces. These people go about collecting votes according to these lists, sometimes by force, sometimes by pandering to local interests. At the moment, our opposition group is too small. We need to toe the party line.

Back then, Bayar wasn't thinking of forming an opposition party. Or at least, he wasn't talking about it. His goal was to win over more supporters. He knew that a widely popular newspaper like *Tan* could strengthen his cause, and so he continued meeting with us.

Around that time, the newspaper *La Turquie*, which appeared in French, started a campaign against the İnönü dictatorship. Editor-in-chief Cami Baykut, the first Turkish interior minister during the War of Independence, wrote that the changes in world politics had plunged the regime into crisis. He claimed that serious steps were needed to establish true democracy in Turkey's socio-economic system. The political views of *Tan* and *La Turquie* were in agreement. Cami Bey was troubled because the population at large couldn't read his French editorials, and so he started writing for *Tan* as well.

Tan expanded its editorial staff to include progressive, leftist writers like Esat Adil Müstecablıoğlu, the founder of the Socialist Party; Behice Boran, associate professor at the Ankara Faculty of Language, History, and Geography and among the future leaders of the Workers' Party; Adnan Cemgil, a teacher; Muvaffak Şeref, a university professor; the novelist Sabahaddin Ali; Dr. Hulusi Dosdoğru; and Aziz Nesin.

The paper's struggle against fascism and dictatorship gained momentum. Former Foreign Minister Tevfik Rüştü Aras, part of the Bayar faction, was sending us articles as well. The opposition gradually gathered strength, and *Tan* raised its profile as an anti-fascist, anti-imperialist newspaper fully devoted to progressive ideas.

Toward the end of the war

On 16 April 1945, the Red Army begins a massive assault on Berlin. The city surrenders. Soviet flags wave in the streets. British and Soviet forces meet up on the Elbe. Neither strategic obstacles nor the resistance of Hitler's forces are able to halt the Soviet advance. Soviet forces enter Berlin from three sides. The foundations of fascism are crumbling.

On May 1, 1945, Himmler submits his final conditions for surrender. On 2 May, the Berlin garrison lays down its arms. On May 8, the treaty of unconditional surrender is signed at the headquarters of the Allied Commander Eisenhower. Peace celebrations break out in Western countries and the Soviet Union. Goebbels commits suicide with his wife and children, in his bunker at Unter den Linden. Adolf Hitler disappears in his Berlin bunker. Admiral Dönitz is declared Germany's new Führer. The Germans withdraw from Denmark. In Italy, the common people track down Mussolini in his island hideout and hang him from a tree. On May 3, the one million German soldiers in Italy surrender unconditionally. The German navy hoists the white flag.

Prime Minister Şükrü Saraçoğlu's statement after this victory was a history lesson in duplicity. Saraçoğlu spoke before the Grand National Assembly on 12 May. He eulogized Britain's sacrifices, the USA'S contribution to the fight for humanity and the Soviet Union's heroism. He went on to state:

> The leading nations of the world have assembled in San Francisco to put war to rest and let peace, civilization, freedom and humanity prosper and rejoice.[8] The Turkish nation is confident of its own prosperity and power. As a nation and a state, we were wary of those who led the German nation, and we predicted the calamities they would bring upon the world. We had no trouble recognizing those who had right, justice and victory on their side.
>
> In light of this understanding and good judgement, we gradually took the appropriate measures, steering our foreign policy in a clear and consistent direction. We realized we might not get through the war without fighting, and so, four months before the war broke out, we made pacts with Britain and France to preserve peace in the Mediterranean. We went on to sign alliance treaties with both these countries. At every stage of the war, we provided our friends and allies with all the aid we could muster.

As I write these words, I am reminded of a verse written by the poet Süleyman Nazif about Dr Abdullah Cevdet: 'With its nails, the hand of creation tears the decency off his face.'

News of the German surrender hit the Turkish press like a bomb. The fascist and government-run papers were filled with doom and gloom. 'Are we on the brink of a Third World War?' they asked. The Allied victory, ending the slaughter of millions, filled them with concern rather than joy. They were especially vocal in their anguish about the Soviet victories.

At this point, I can't help but interject another memory from the war years. It was during the German attack on Stalingrad. Zekeriya and I were out on a walk. We arrived at Falih Rıfkı Atay's seaside mansion in Caddebostan. He was leaning on an armchair

---

[8] TN: Saraçoğlu is referring to the United Nations Conference on International Organization, or the San Francisco Conference, held from 25 April to 26 June, 1945, and resulting in the creation of the United Nations Charter.

in the large garden surrounding the house. He saw us and invited us in. We started talking about the war.

'The Soviet Union cannot recover at this point,' he said firmly. 'Communism will become history and fascism will rule the world.'

The idea of a world ruled by fascism made me shudder. Still, I didn't answer.

In those years, the British and American embassies and the Press Attaché's office in Istanbul used to screen films about the war. Soon, the Soviet Consulate followed suit. One evening, they were showing a film about the battle of Stalingrad. All the journalists were invited, and we went as well. We watched the film with bated breath. It was impossible not to admire the heroic resistance and counterattacks of the Soviet troops in Stalingrad.

After the film, guests were served dinner at a long, narrow table in a hall lit by large chandeliers. Most of those at the table were journalists. Necmeddin Sadak and Falih Rıfkı Atay sat down across from me. Sadak looked at me and raised his glass.

'The Soviets are winning the war,' he said.

I remembered what Falih had said in his garden, with the fascist armies at the gates of Stalingrad and Moscow, and I smiled. I answered Sadak, but kept my eyes on Falih:

'The Germans will recover one day. But fascism cannot recover at this point. It was pretty short-lived for a regime meant to last a thousand years.'

Falih turned away and started talking to the person next to him.

The end of the Second World War

After unleashing hell on earth for almost six years, the Second World War finally reaches its end. The murderous fascist armies have drenched the European soil in blood from one end of the continent to the other. Whole generations have been extinguished. The ground has filled up with bones, the sea with corpses. Monuments built in times of peace have been ground into the dust. The furnaces lit by the fascists are still coughing up the smoke of their incinerated victims. Mankind yearns for peace and for the punishment of the fascist barbarians.

In August 1945, Roosevelt, Stalin and Churchill come together in Potsdam to discuss Germany's future and what policy the Allies should pursue toward the nation. Their aim is to eradicate fascism and democratize Germany. The leaders of the three great nations promise to take precautions that will stop Germany from ever threatening peace again. In order to render future militarist and fascist activity impossible, they resolve to disarm Germany, destroy the German military industry, and disband the Nazi Party and its auxiliary organizations. Upon the Soviets' request, they also promise to hold a trial for the main war criminals.

Germany's surrender didn't mean the war was over. In the Far East, Japan was still fighting China and the United States. Japanese armies were stationed in Korea, ready to attack the Soviet Union. The Japanese presence had tied up many Soviet troops on this front of the war. Now, the three Allies decided to end the war in the Far East.

At the Yalta Conference, the Soviet Union had promised to join the Allied war against Japan once the German war was over. To hasten the end of the Second World

War, the Soviet government annuls the Soviet–Japanese Neutrality Pact on 5 April and declares war on Japan on 8 August.

While the USA war against Japan rages on, something happens that leaves the entire world aghast. On 6 and 9 August 1945, US planes drop nuclear missiles on two major Japanese cities, Hiroshima and Nagasaki.

Hiroshima and Nagasaki. A mere two bombs in three days. But Emperor Nero's burning of Rome is just a bonfire compared to this massacre. People turned to ash in an instant. Human bones tossed up in an inferno of flames. Incinerated corpses spewing from rooftops like lava from a volcano. Survivors reduced to poisoned, crippled, diseased shadows of human beings for generations to come.

Dropping nuclear bombs on an innocent population, condemning whole generations to a slow death over time – even if they were meant to end a war, these are not actions that mankind can forgive.

On 2 September 1945, Japanese forces surrender unconditionally. With this bloody calamity, after six years of death and tears, the Second World War comes to an end.

Domestic changes in Turkey

On 3 May 1945, the San Francisco Conference of the United Nations convenes[9] to formulate new principles aimed to protect mankind against a third world war. Turkey is represented by Interior Minister Hasan Saka. Upon his return, Saka informs journalists that Turkey will abide by the resolutions of this conference and that the country's policy will be based on the principles of peace, security, rights and justice.

Turkish progressives and intellectuals embrace US President Roosevelt's Four Freedoms: four principles meant to rescue mankind from four terrors (hunger, unemployment and impediments to free speech and opinion). İnönü constantly makes statements reassuring the public and the Western Allies that Turkey will transition to a full democracy.

Encouraged by these developments, the group around Celal Bayar submitted its 'Declaration of Four' to the People's Party caucus on 4 June 1945. Once again, the declaration was signed by Bayar, Menderes, Köprülü and Koraltan. They demanded an end to oppression and permission to found a second party in the Assembly to monitor the government. The People's Party rejected this proposal at its meeting on 12 June, stating that such requests could only be discussed in the Assembly. Some deputies even demanded that the signatories of the declaration be expelled from the People's Party.

The Bayar group's declaration resonated with the common people, who were fed up with the oppressive 'One Party, One Chief' system created by İnönü. The Republican People's Party had been founded to carry out a democratic bourgeois revolution. But it had strayed from its purpose, suspending freedom of speech, freedom of opinion and the right to form associations. Workers and intellectuals alike longed for these freedoms.

At *Tan*, we supported the founding of a second party as a step toward completing the democratic bourgeois revolution. But the idea caused a backlash among party

---

[9] TN: The starting date of the conference was 25 April.

loyalists, the high-ranking bureaucracy and the reactionary press. On August 20, *Ulus*, the official newspaper of the government, published an article by Falih Rıfkı Atay. In it, he rebuked the call of progressive papers for Turkey to adapt to the changing world:

> They say that because we went to San Francisco, signed the UN Charter and ratified it in the Grand National Assembly, we should immediately reform our regime to reflect this charter and the principles of human rights and freedoms. Otherwise, they say, we can't be part of the new world order of democracies. Both the Left and the Right make this claim. But both sides have ulterior motives.
>
> The laws of this country are meant to protect us from being drawn back into currents of religious fundamentalism or fragmentation and anarchy. Let no one dare accuse Turkish democracy of being hostile to freedom because of such laws! Across the democratic countries that won the war, we can clearly see different fronts, made up of single-party states, two-party states and multiparty states. Our take on Turkish democracy should only reflect our own interests. If genuine differences in opinion necessitate a splintering of parties, we should not shy away from it. But if the political struggle is just about personal jealousy and ambition, we mustn't allow it to turn the country into a patchwork of battles and alliances.

On the same date, Asım Us, the editor-in-chief of *Vakit*, wrote:

> It is clear that we are entering a new period of change. More and more people are babbling about democratic government and how multiparty competition is beneficial, necessary or even inevitable. In our opinion, those who urge Turks to take up party struggles in the name of democracy must have lost their minds. If not, they are enemies of the Turkish nation's unity, or at the service of such enemies.

This was how the reactionary bloc countered efforts to found a second party. As progressives who defended freedom and democracy, we were obliged to oppose this stance. It was clear why such people rejected the articles published in *Tan*. The ruling class and its government had held a grip on power for years. Now, they feared that the exploited classes would rise up and advance toward a free, democratic and socially equitable system.

To prevent the birth of a second party, deputies in the Assembly started drowning out Bayar's and Menderes' speeches by slamming the lids of their desks. Finally, in July, Bayar, Köprülü and Koraltan submitted a motion to the party council. They proposed convening a party congress to expel those deputies for transgressions against party principles, and forming a commission to change the laws that violated the Constitution. The party council rejected these proposals as well. Then, the party moved to expel Köprülü and Menderes for breaching party discipline by writing newspaper articles that criticized the government. A short while later, Bayar resigned his seat in the Assembly. By the middle of 1945, the signatories of the Declaration of Four had severed all ties with the People's Party.

On 1 November, İnönü reconvened the Assembly with a speech that encouraged the opposition. He stated that the country was moving toward freedom and democracy, and that the Assembly needed an opposition party. He was probably confident that the People's Party would win any upcoming elections. He wanted a pliant opposition like the Liberal Republican Party founded and then disbanded by Atatürk.

The attempt to publish a journal with the Bayar Group

After resigning from his seat in the Assembly and severing his ties with the People's Party, Celal Bayar started working on founding a new party. He contacted Zekeriya to obtain *Tan*'s support, and visited us at our house in Moda with Tevfik Rüştü Aras, who wasn't a deputy at the time but worked with Bayar's group. They told me they intended to launch a journal and asked me to publish it for them. They were willing to provide the funds.

I asked Bayar about the aim of this journal, and whether he intended to found a new party.

'Yes, we are working on that,' he answered. 'Our aim is to complete the unfinished democratic revolution in this country. We will fight to rescind unconstitutional laws, grant autonomy to universities, change the Police Law stifling liberties, and give opposition parties the right to monitor the Assembly. The journal will defend these principles.'

'Will your party programme include land reform?'

'Our programme isn't ready yet. But land reform is a long-term endeavour. As long as we lack a land survey based on extensive research, it's impossible. But we will work to give peasants ownership of land and to develop the agriculture sector. First, though, we must secure citizens' freedom of speech, freedom of thought and right to form associations, and we must ensure human rights.'

'Will you give workers the right to organize, form unions and strike?'

'Those are rights that any democratic regime has to grant. If we take office one day, we will definitely defend those rights.'

(After assuming power, Bayar reneged on all these promises. He established an even more draconian dictatorship than İnönü. He acted as the mouthpiece of big landowners and the trade bourgeoisie. And that was the cause of his downfall.)

I was highly sceptical about Bayar's promises. The Assembly had shelved the Labour Law while he was prime minister, and in more recent discussions about the new Land Law, he and his circle had opposed land reform. Still, the country needed to move toward a democracy. The oppressive system, fascist in all but name, had to go.

'The People's Party has lost its revolutionary spirit,' I said. 'The mission of any new party must be to complete the democratic bourgeois revolution. This can only be accomplished by creating a broad opposition front. The objections of a few party members in the Assembly won't create a mass movement. The new party must draw on support from the working class, peasants, progressive intellectuals, the army and the general population. The press already has an opposition front. *Tan*, *La Turquie* and even *Vatan* defend the establishment of a democratic regime, albeit for different reasons. Just as in the press, all pro-democratic forces must create a united front against the "One Party, One Chief" system.'

Bayar and Aras affirmed the need for a united front. I told them my thoughts for the journal: 'We've been thinking for a long time about publishing a journal that defends democracy, but for a variety of reasons, we haven't been able to do it. I don't need capital to launch it. But I need it to be a platform for the entire democratic front. Not just you, but all intellectuals and leftists must be allowed to write for it. If you can guarantee that, I'll publish the journal.'

Aras said he regretted not having the money to become a partner in the journal. But that suited me fine; I didn't want to lose my editorial independence by accepting outside funds. Bayar said he wouldn't write articles himself but would provide interviews.

Approaching the United States

As Bayar's Democrat Party prepared its launch, the People's Party made a new move. Under pressure at home and abroad, the party hoped to strengthen its hold on power by salvaging the crumbling economy. To this end, it tried to obtain credit from foreign countries. Turkey's foreign policy had already turned to the West, and now the People's Party wanted to team up with the American imperialists. Talks were held with the USA. Pro-American propaganda started appearing in the government press.

All progressives stood up against this rapprochement with the United States. The Saraçoğlu administration, assailed on various fronts, decided to rein in the opposition. The promises of more democracy were forgotten. Journals were shut down, one after the other. The supply of paper to newspapers was cut off, and licences allowing them to acquire paper from abroad were restricted. Saraçoğlu ordered the pro-government press to launch a vicious assault on the progressives, especially *Tan*.

A pitched battle in the press

Our battle with the pro-government press began on 6 May 1945, when I published a 'Görüşler' column entitled 'He Couldn't Cut off My Tongue After All'. Here is what I wrote:

> The year was 1937. Germany was building fifth columns around the world. The fascist movements in Turkey were particularly conspicuous. To stop the spread of this virus in our country, I tried to unmask the fascists and wrote articles against these movements.
>
> Around that time, a female German journalist visited me at our publishing house in Istanbul. After extolling the virtues of fascism to me, she said: 'Your articles are getting a very poor reception in Germany. Goebbels sends his regards. He says, "If I lay my hands on her one day, I will cut off her tongue."'
>
> I told her to give her master my regards and to inform him that I would continue my struggle against fascism until he cut off my tongue. Goebbels didn't manage to keep his promise. But he ordered his dogs on Ankara Avenue[10] to attack

---

[10] TN: The extension of Babıali Avenue, where most of the Istanbul press was headquartered in Sertel's days.

me. Time and again, he had me dragged into court. Time and again, he inspired people to gag me. Time and again, I suffered the anguish of not being able to warn the Turkish public about the disinformation it was fed. But I never missed a chance to use this tongue of mine to speak out against Goebbels and fascism. Eventually, Goebbels himself was muzzled by the turn of events. And he failed to cut off my tongue.

Hakkı Tarık Us, one of the owners of *Vakit*, published an open letter to me, asking whom I meant by the 'dogs on Babıali'. My response appeared in *Tan* on May 26:

> From 1933 onward, the press on Ankara Avenue unleashed a torrent of fascist propaganda in newspapers, journals, pamphlets and books. They used all kinds of fascist tactics to win over the Turkish public and induce Turkey to join the war as Germany's ally. They published a book called *İğneli Fıçı*,[11] which spread anti-Jewish propaganda and tried to sow discord among Turkish citizens. I countered this propaganda and was taken to court for that. But you remained silent.
>
> The same press encouraged religious fundamentalism in this country. They praised fascism for promoting religion and opposed the Kemalist revolution. They branded the poet Tevfik Fikret a communist. Fikret is a beacon of Turkish literature, for his ideas if not his poems. In defending him, I defended revolutionary and progressive ideas. Once again, I was taken to court. I was called a *Dönme*,[12] a 'Bolshevik wench', a traitor to the fatherland and many other insulting names. In courtrooms and newspaper columns, I spoke out against the fascists who attacked me, like dogs. But you, my dear sir, remained silent.
>
> Today, you speak up to protect the dignity of the journalists I call dogs. But I am a journalist too, and you were chairman of the Press Association back then. Why didn't you speak up to protect my dignity? Where were you then?

Hakkı Tarık didn't respond to this article. But the pro-government press launched a massive polemic against *Tan* and myself. For years, *Tan* had defended the completion of the unfinished bourgeois democratic revolution, freedom of speech, freedom of thought and the right to form associations. *Tan*'s fight was against racism and fascism. It was a fight to protect Turkey's independence against imperialism. Now that the President had promised full democracy, we should have been able to debate these issues openly. But the opposite happened. The attacks on *Tan* increased. Each and every one of our articles was scrutinized in an attempt to discredit our struggle.

Here are some examples of the ensuing debates. Around that time, an election was scheduled to replace six deputies who had died or resigned. The party announced it would select candidates for these posts. I responded with an article, 'Let's Not Play Democracy', maintaining it was high time that candidates were chosen by the people rather than the party:

---

[11] TN: 'The Needle-Studded Barrel'; see Chapter 6.
[12] TN: The community of Jewish converts to Islam from which Sertel descended.

Asım Us claims that we, too, are a leftist and socialist state. And indeed, the Constitution is democratic, and the party programme endorses the principle of statism. But our recent and not-so-recent past have shown that written laws are of no use as long as they aren't put into practice. Statism, democracy and socialism are not some clichéd formulas, but actual programmes that require implementation.

Socialists and communists aren't the only statists. Fascism and Nazism are statist, too. But the two approaches to statism are completely opposed. Fascist statism exploits the workers and masses for the sake of a monopolist bourgeois class. Socialist or communist statism curbs or abolishes that plundering gang for the benefit of the masses.

How can you speak of socialism in Turkey? While the Nazis were in power, it was in vogue to say that our regime was in essence fascist. And now, the same people claim our regime is leftist! This regime antagonized the leftists. It treated democrats, socialists and leftists of all persuasions like felons. What kind of socialist regime considers leftist thinking a felony?

When fascism collapsed, these new 'leftists' had a hard time accepting the Allied victory. Then, when that victory became certain, they suddenly proclaimed that we, too, were a democratic country. They warned against the left, though, saying it was no different from religious fundamentalism. They defended the liberal democracy of the British Conservative Party. Then, when the socialists came to power in Britain, they suddenly claimed that they, too, were leftists and socialists.

Is the Turkish regime a system that changes its character depending on the whims of a particular group? Is it a variety show?

The first act of the variety show set the stage for Nazism, and the second act for democracy, with the same players switching from Hitler to Abraham Lincoln. The third act portrayed socialism, with the actors playing Fourier or Saint-Simon. What kind of sham is this? Which other regime in history has ever displayed such an erratic nature?

Yesterday, they attacked us for being leftists. Now, the same people make us look like rightists by proclaiming how leftist they are. Really, the whole thing is funny enough to entertain a variety show audience.

This article prompted an assault by Necmeddin Sadak, who demanded to know what I meant by 'show'. I answered him on 13 June 1945:

Presumably, Necmeddin Sadak has read the speech the President gave on 19 May, promising a transition to a broader democracy. A broader democracy means political freedoms (speech, opinion, assembly, organizing) and economic freedoms (freedom from unemployment and a secure livelihood). These are the freedoms we expect, but we see no effort to change the laws that curtail them, no effort to liberate the people from destitution and the high cost of living. As things stand, the party's election of six new deputies seems less like a serious democratic step than a show.

Sadak was determined to continue the polemic. 'Who wants liberation?' he replied. 'Liberation is a word used by communists. It implies liberation from the current regime. Is this the liberation Mrs. Sertel awaits?'

This was a clear attempt to sidetrack the debate. On 24 June, I wrote an article called 'Let's Stick to the Topic':

> Necmeddin Sadak wants to turn this into a debate about communism. But our topic is not communism; it is the transition to more freedom and democracy. It is the rejection of fascism. By branding all this as communism and ignoring the actual topic, this editor-in-chief acts against the nation's interest and the rules of civilized debate. Debates should stay focused on the topic at hand. Introducing unrelated topics smacks of ill intent. Communism is not the topic of this debate, and introducing it is nothing but demagogy.

The pro-government papers showed no consistency in their attacks on *Tan* and myself. Some maintained that we already had a model democracy, while others claimed that granting more freedom would plunge the country into anarchy.

Amidst all this, at the beginning of August, Asım Us wrote an article stating that our regime was socialist indeed. This being the case, he asked what kind of socialism I desired. On 8 August, I replied with my article 'Conviction Crisis, Opportunism':

> The rise of a socialist government in Britain has led to a number of articles on socialism in the Turkish press. But even if we ignore the fact that these descriptions of socialism are completely unscholarly, some of the fallacies expressed on the topic are truly astounding.
>
> Some writers, who seem to think they have a monopoly on Turkish nationalism, used the ascent of German Nazism to claim that the Turkish regime was Nazist as well. They even stated that Hitler learned a lot from this regime. These people were the first in Turkey to defend a type of fascist nationalism.
>
> As soon as Nazism collapsed, these fascist nationalists suddenly announced that they were democrats. But to them, defending democracy meant defending the conservative Churchill and the imperialist, capitalist Tories. Churchill's statement that he was a nationalist made them so happy that they wanted to kiss him.
>
> Then, Churchill and his party lost the election to the socialists. And those in Turkey who'd defended liberal democracy yesterday and fascism the day before immediately converted to socialism.
>
> Now they are trying to contend that the Turkish regime is socialist. One writer opines that 'not every socialist is a nationalist, but every nationalist is a socialist'. To disprove this claim, it is enough to consider Churchill himself. Churchill called himself a nationalist, but he would never label himself a socialist. This is because nationalism, by which Churchill means economic nationalism, defends the interests of the British bourgeoisie. Socialism, on the other hand, doesn't defend the interests of this class, but those of the common people.
>
> A regime that tries to fool the workers and common people by combining nationalism and socialism is national socialist, or, in other words, fascist. So, in

claiming that 'not every socialist is a nationalist, but every nationalist is a socialist', the abovementioned writer is really defending national socialism. But the complete opposite of this claim is true.

All socialists are nationalists, but they are also internationalists. They are nationalists because they defend the interests of their own people, and internationalists because they defend international peace and the solidarity of nations against imperialism and colonization. But not all nationalists are socialists, because nationalists uphold the interests of the ruling bourgeois class over the interests of the common people.

A person should have a specific set of convictions and defend them. If he is a fascist initially, then tries to dress himself up as a democrat, and finally adds socialism to the mix by claiming that every nationalist is a socialist, he is nothing but an opportunist. This kind of fallacious nonsense can only fool those with no understanding of the issues. The public mustn't be fooled by those who embody this crisis of conviction and reinvent themselves with each passing day.

Tan's line was that the government saw the need for progressive change, but that its hardened mindset prevented it from implementing such change. On 27 August, the paper published three articles by Zekeriya Sertel, under the heading 'This Assembly, Government and Party Cannot Carry Out the Necessary Change'. He wrote that the Assembly wasn't democratically elected, the government wasn't a democratic government and the party wasn't a democratic party. Therefore, he argued, they couldn't create a democratic regime. A true democracy could only be created by a newly elected Assembly and a new, democratic administration.

These articles drew the ire of the government and the press. On 27 August, Hüseyin Cahit Yalçın attacked me in *Tanin*, with the article 'Conspicuous Truths':

> According to Sabiha Sertel, the government and even the head of state should change, and the People's Party should share its authority with other parties. But this is also what Moscow wants. Today, Sabiha Sertel demands democracy. Tomorrow, she will demand other things.

Hüseyin Cahit harshly claimed that my call for democracy wasn't sincere. He was trying to get me to state that I desired a communist regime. Then, I could have been sued for defending communism, which was illegal under Articles 141 and 142 of the Penal Code. I responded that a large part of the population wanted freedom and democracy, that even the press was split into supporters of this cause (*Tan, La Turquie, Vatan*) and its opponents (the government press), and that he was among those who feared democracy. I asked him the following questions:

> What is the purpose of these repetitive and systematic attacks on *Tan* and *Vatan*? To destroy the movement for freedom and democracy? Don't our opponents want freedom and democracy as well? They claim that they do. So why are they attacking us? Because their claims are not sincere.

To discredit *Tan*'s struggle for freedom and democracy, the reactionary press tries to paint the paper as Moscow's agent. Is Moscow alone in demanding that the nations of the world become truly democratic? Didn't Roosevelt want the same, proclaiming his Four Freedoms until the day he died? Don't the common people in Turkey want this as well? Why are these truths not conspicuous enough for the author of 'Conspicuous Truths?'

Nations keep evolving; there is no permanent and unchangeable form of government. If the Turkish nation advances to a higher stage in the future, if the objective and subjective conditions become ripe for socialism, maybe I will call for more. Finally, I never mentioned changing the head of state. That is nothing but a fabrication.

Hüseyin Cahit didn't want to end the argument. In another article, he asked me: 'Are you a Marxist or a socialist? What are you?' I read the article and laughed. I responded with a piece called 'Is Mrs Sertel Sunni or Shia?' I wrote:

This question reminds me of the fanaticism during the age of religious wars, when the bigots were at each other's throats, asking, 'Are you Sunni or Shia?' and beheading those who didn't belong to their own sect. We are discussing democracy in Turkey, but Hüseyin Cahit Yalçın asks, 'Tell me, is there democracy in Soviet Russia?' I don't care if there is democracy in the Soviet Union, Mr Yalçın. Just tell me if there is democracy in Turkey.

Necmeddin Sadak kept asking me the same question as Yalçın. I responded with a question of my own:

Mr Necmeddin Sadak, why don't you first tell me what you are? Some of your friends defend a dictatorship, some of you are Kemalists and some of you claim to be Bevinist socialists.

Everybody should calm down – I am neither Sunni nor Shia, and *Tan* is not communist. I don't believe that socialism or similar systems can work in a country that hasn't even experienced a bourgeois democratic revolution, a country in which the conditions for a socialist revolution aren't yet ripe. I only want democracy.

The reactionaries who oppose democracy also oppose *Tan* and its struggle. Their attitude is proof that Turkey cannot become a democracy under its current leaders. One only needs to look at the debates in the press to see how undemocratic Turkey is today. But no one seems to care about the urgent affairs of the nation. The only thing that matters is whether Mrs Sertel is Sunni or Shia.

Celal Bayar and his faction had openly declared their opposition in the Assembly. The People's Party and the Saraçoğlu administration felt threatened by the democratic movements among the people and in the press. They were afraid that granting more democratic rights would jeopardize their power. It was this fear that motivated their systematic attacks against pro-democracy newspapers. But at the same time, they were trying to show Britain, America and the world at large that Turkey was a democratic state.

Our struggle for freedom and democracy was inseparable from our struggle against fascism. But those who had wholeheartedly endorsed the current regime during the war years now felt the need to justify themselves. When the government attacked the progressive press, they jumped on the bandwagon. *Tasviri Efkar* dissected my series of articles, 'What is Nationalism?' and rehashed old accusations against me. Peyami Safa published an article entitled 'Mrs Sertel Is Insulting the Kemalist Revolution'. He denied my claims that the government was protecting the fascists. The government, he insisted, was protecting the leftists, not the Turanists. I answered him as well:

> Even though Turkish fascists used all the methods of international fascism to promote their cause during the war years, they were let off the hook except for a handful of scapegoats. But the newspapers supporting democracy and anti-fascist journals, such as *Yurt ve Dünya*, *Ses*, *Yeni Ses* and *Adımlar*[13] were all muzzled.
>
> Peyami asks: 'How can Sabiha Sertel claim that leftist beliefs are considered a felony in our country? Engels' book *Woman and Socialism*, which she translated and published through the *Vakit* press, is sold in stores!' Well, let me answer his question. First, *Woman and Socialism*, which I translated from English, is not by Engels but by August Bebel. Further, the book was published by the *Dün ve Yarın* [Yesterday and Tomorrow] press, where Hakkı Tarık was a partner. Finally, the book was confiscated by the police, along with the other books I translated. These are academic and scholarly books. Which democratic or leftist country would have outlawed and confiscated them?
>
> Our laws and all the leftists they deprived of freedom prove that leftist beliefs are a felony in our country. I myself am an example of this. In your fascist mindset, you keep using your newspapers to accuse me of treason when all I do is struggle for freedom, democracy and human rights. Over and over again, I was taken to court, our newspapers and journals were shut down, and my freedom to write was taken away. Not because I committed some theft or fraud, but because I fought for democracy.
>
> When all of Europe was under the yoke of German fascism, I was banned from writing for a year because I defended national liberation movements across Europe. How can a revolutionary Turkey, a Turkey with its own struggle for national liberation, consider it a crime to defend resistance movements in occupied countries?
>
> There is no difference between banning an intellectual from writing and putting him in jail. The article 'Mrs Sertel is Insulting the Kemalist Revolution' is fascist Peyami's way of denouncing me to the prosecutor. It proves how strong the fascist mindset still is in our country.

---

[13] TN: 'Homeland and World', 'Voice', 'New Voice' and 'Steps'.

Tan's debate with the press supporting the government and the People's Party raged on. On 21 October 1945, Hüseyin Cahit Yalçın published a long editorial in *Tanin*:

> For quite some time now, the Turkish press has conducted a debate about fascism and communism. Those who dredge up this matter most frequently are *Tan* and Mrs Sabiha. The good intentions and sincerity of this esteemed lady are beyond question. But we are saddened by one point. Mrs Sabiha Sertel's views, thoughts and writings on this matter are not just similar, but virtually identical in style, form and spirit to the anti-Turkish publications coming out of Moscow.
>
> We need to unmask this point of view, which, to us, is the biggest obstacle to true freedom and a European-style democratic regime in our country. There is no difference between it and the fascist point of view.

Moscow wasn't the only hotbed of anti-fascist publishing at the time. Scores of articles were published in Britain, the USA and France as well. The form and content of the argument were virtually identical everywhere. All countries were trying to stamp out the fascists; hence the trials in Nuremberg. But Hüseyin Cahit implied that only Moscow took this position. And in trying to link me to Moscow, he revealed his malicious intent.

The aim of all these attacks was to defend the Saraçoğlu administration, which had helped Germany during the war by supplying it with chrome and opening the Straits to its ships. The Turkish racists were now being exonerated as nationalists, and their collaboration with the German fascists was swept under the rug.

Pro-government papers also targeted anti-imperialist articles. Some time ago, I'd published a series, 'Imperialism and the Colonies', in *Tan*. In response, *Ulus*, *Vatan* and *Akşam* published columns contending that Britain and France didn't oppress their colonies. Apparently, these countries invested heavily in the colonies to improve them and had even partially succeeded. Other writers, led by Ahmet Emin Yalman, wrote commentaries arguing that the United States wasn't imperialist. The public applauded *Tan*'s refutation of these articles, and *Tan* became one of the most popular papers in the country.

This success infuriated government and party circles. In a press conference on 6 October 1945, Prime Minister Saraçoğlu touched on the emerging opposition in the country, the Assembly and the press. He specifically singled out *Tan* and *Vatan* for admonition. After outlining the government's stance, he ordered the papers to toe the line as if it was their own. His statement was published as follows:

> In the past weeks, parts of the Istanbul press have embarked on a passionate campaign. They lecture the government and people on foreign policy, even though they only grasp one side of this multifaceted affair. They accuse the People's Party and its governments of an endless list of sins in domestic policy. The two newspapers (*Tan* and *Vatan*) say they want freedom and democracy. But let us all ask ourselves: Are we not already free? Are we not already democratic?
>
> When the flames of the last world war threatened to engulf everything in sight, the world's nations started shifting toward one of two ideologies: democracy and fascism. And when the war ended, nearly all nations except the vanquished

declared themselves democratic. The only dissonant voice came from Turkey. A representative (Adnan Menderes) declared from the pulpit of the Grand National Assembly that 'our Constitution is democratic, but our governance is not'. The two Istanbul newspapers applauded these words.

Soon, they started enumerating undemocratic aspects of our laws. They referred to Article 50 of the Press Law[14] and to various articles of the Penal Code and Law of Associations. They raised issues like single-stage elections, autonomy for universities and a second political party. They even demanded the resignation of our current deputies and the People's Party's Chairman.

In another press conference, Saraçoğlu said, 'I am considering working on easing the provisions of Article 50 when the time is right. But I fear that journalists themselves may be the biggest obstacle to doing so.'

The fact that Saraçoğlu considered a revision of the Press Law and other restrictive laws proved that the pro-democracy papers were right. Why, then, couldn't the government accept their criticism?

The Prime Minister's real concern was that opposition in the Assembly and the press would give rise to a new party. Celal Bayar had already resigned from his Assembly seat. The signatories of the 'Declaration of Four' and their supporters openly opposed the People's Party dictatorship. Now, the government was trying to scare all these people into submission. It wanted to brand all criticism of the People's Party and its mistakes as treason. On 11 October, I addressed these issues in *Tan*:

> Everyone who criticizes the government and party is accused of treason. As if opposition was a crime! This is the hallmark of fascist regimes. They put people's heads in a totalitarian vice, try to turn them into machines, imprison their critics, and eventually incinerate democrats, socialists and Jews in furnaces.
>
> Today, opposition parties around the world struggle to win elections and form new governments. But this is not a crime. It is a precondition of a democratic regime. Opposition doesn't mean curtsying to the government and politely asking, 'Would your lordship permit me to criticize some of your shortcomings?'

In mid-1945, I wrote a number of pieces defending workers' rights. These only intensified the attacks on *Tan*. Just as it was a crime to criticize the government, the People's Party and the country's economic state, it was also a crime to talk about the workers' plight. In fact, it was the greatest crime of all. In October 1945, I published a series of articles, 'Labourers' Working Conditions', 'Grievances of Workers at the Kartal Cement Factory' and 'Miners' Living Conditions Today'. At that time, workers' organizations were controlled by the state and the bosses, and tram workers were classified as civil servants rather than labourers. In my articles, I argued that workers needed to found their own trade unions and organizations, and pointed out their dire circumstances. These articles also were branded as communist propaganda.

---

[14] TN: Article 50 enabled the government to shut down newspapers and journals for criticizing its policies.

8

The *Görüşler* journal

While these debates continued in the press, I prepared the journal I'd agreed to publish with Celal Bayar and Tevfik Rüştü Aras. We decided to call it *Görüşler*, after my newspaper column. As I mentioned earlier, the journal would be dedicated to a specific political front. The Bayar faction would write for it and so would names like Tevfik Rüştü Aras, Cami Baykut, Niyazi Berkes (the publisher of the journals *Türk ve Dünya* [The Turk and the World] and *Adımlar*), Behice Boran, Pertev Boratav and Sabahaddin Ali. We would solicit articles from everyone who defended democracy against dictatorship and fascism.

Cami Bey proposed that we ask Halide Hanım and Adnan Adıvar to contribute as well. Halide Hanım had returned to Turkey from her self-imposed exile around 1939. These days, she wrote her novels and kept out of politics. Adnan Adıvar, in the meantime, published the *İslam Ansiklopedisi*.[1]

I made an appointment with Halide Hanım and went to her apartment. When I arrived, Adnan Adıvar was sick in bed. I told them about the state of the country and the rising discontent with the oppressive regime among the public and the intellectuals. We talked about the Bayar faction assuming the role of the opposition in the Assembly. I maintained that all opposition forces had to form a united front; if we were divided, we were doomed to be crushed. This, I said, was why we'd decided to publish the journal *Görüşler* and why we wanted Halide Hanım to write for us.

She listened and then spoke in a determined voice. 'I also want to see a democratic regime,' she said. 'This dictatorial system was established by Atatürk. When we opposed it, we were persecuted and forced to leave the country. There is no room for such a system in today's world.

'I don't believe that İnönü will grant us democratic freedoms. He is a wily politician. One day, he leads a totalitarian system. The next day, he appears to support democracy. When the time is right, he uses fascist methods, and then, the day after, he looks like a socialist. He doesn't change because he believes in any of these ideas, but simply because he wants to hold on to power. However, I don't believe a Bayar administration would grant democratic freedoms, either.'

'These men were part of the same system,' I answered. 'They ran it side by side. I have no illusions that they will suddenly convert to democracy and establish a democratic

---

[1] TN: A Turkish-language 'Encyclopedia of Islam', commissioned by the Turkish Ministry of Education.

regime in this country. But the stated goal of the Bayar faction is to abolish the one-party system and to change anti-democratic laws. I don't know how long they'll remain on the democratic bandwagon, but we should travel with them as long as they're on it. We need to unite those who demand a real democracy. *Görüşler* will be a forum for them all, even if their personal beliefs and ideologies diverge from each other.'

Adnan Bey rose up in his bed and rested his head against the pillows. 'Who will write for this journal?' he asked.

'The writers of *Tan*, Cami Baykut, Tevfik Rüştü Aras, Köprülüzade Fuat, Adnan Menderes, Niyazi Berkes – an assistant professor at Ankara University's Faculty of Language, History and Geography – Behice Boran, Pertev Boratav and other leftists. As I said, this journal will be a forum for progressive thinkers.'

Halide Hanım interrupted me.

'Cami Bey is the most honourable man I've ever known. He is sincere in his beliefs. He too was lambasted for opposing Atatürk's dictatorship. He is a true champion of democracy. As for Tevfik Rüştü Aras, I'll concede he truly believes in friendship with the Soviets. But he's only working with the Bayar faction to regain his former position. And Behice Boran – I encountered her at a meeting once. She is as haughty as she is diminutive. She spoke to me so insolently that I had to reprimand her in spite of all my good will. Nevertheless, I will write for *Görüşler*. Just leave me out of the first issue. I'll write for the second one.'

Adnan Bey jumped up.

'Halide, Halide, what are you doing? How dare we oppose İsmet Paşa? Have you forgotten his efforts to bring us back into the country?'

Once again, Halide Hanım spoke decisively: 'No, but I also haven't forgotten that İsmet Paşa supported Atatürk when he forced us to flee the country. He may have granted me a favour once, but I'm willing to forget that to defend a cause I believe in. This is not about you and me. This is about the establishment of a democratic regime in the country.'

Adnan Bey didn't answer. Like him, I didn't see anything left to talk about. A piece by Halide Hanım would be a boost for us, even if it only appeared in the second issue.

A conversation with Köprülüzade Fuat

Köprülüzade Mehmet Fuat was in Istanbul at that time. I visited him in Akbıyık, at his large mansion by the sea. His son opened the door and took me to the library, where Köprülü was working at a desk. He greeted me with compliments. I told him the reason for my visit.

'We all want this journal to appear,' he said. 'The daily newspapers are hampered by a thousand restrictions. They are in constant fear of being shut down. We want a journal in which we can freely express our ideas. Our goal is to establish a democratic regime that will grant equal rights to all individuals. The People's Party started out as a revolutionary party. It did important work. But today, it has lost its revolutionary character. In fact, it damaged the country's credibility by cooperating with fascists. It trampled on everything that stands for freedom and democracy. Our people yearn for freedom. We are founding this party to ensure freedoms and rights of equality.'

'I understand that you support freedom of speech, opinion and belief,' I said. 'But what do you mean by equality?'

Köprülü stood up and started walking up and down the room.

'It isn't enough for citizens to simply be equal before the law,' he said. 'The biggest inequality is that most of the population languishes in hunger and poverty while certain groups amass great fortunes by exploiting the masses. We will work to prevent this.'

'Will you allow workers to organize, start independent unions and defend their rights?'

'Of course. I'm preparing the party programme right now. All these demands will be in it. Personally, I'd like to see the country move toward socialism. But my companions don't support me on this issue.'

This was the first time I heard that Köprülü had socialist tendencies. I smiled. Köprülü was an old Turanist, cooperating with Adnan Menderes, a big landowner, and Celal Bayar, a champion of liberal economy. To claim that he was a socialist was nothing short of laughable.

'We don't see *Görüşler* as a socialist journal,' I said. 'The conditions for a socialist regime are not ripe in this country. We fight for the expansion and completion of the bourgeois democratic revolution. We want freedom of speech, opinion and association to be granted and safeguarded. We want workers to be able to found independent trade unions, peasants to be freed from the yoke of the landlords, and all citizens to be given the right to form associations. If your party introduces these rights, it will have brought the country one step closer to real democracy. We would like you to write for us on these issues.'

'Rest assured that I will,' Köprülü replied. 'As I said, I'm preparing the party programme right now. As soon as I'm done, I'll write an article for you.'

He saw me to the door, affirming that he would keep his promise.

The reversal in state policy and in the press

On 1 November 1945, İsmet İnönü gave his speech reconvening the Assembly. He said the country was moving toward freedom and democracy, that immediate action would be taken on these fronts, and that commissions would be established to explore possible legal changes. He added, 'One can always find parts to be changed in the Law of Associations, the Penal Code and certain other laws. In revising the relevant articles, one must also change the provisions that prevent the founding of new parties and obstruct the rights of assembly and safety.'

This statement showed the People's Party was ready to take action. It indicated that opposition would be permitted. Government circles believed the speech ushered in a whole new era in Turkish political history.

From now on, it was said, all affairs of the state would be approached in a more democratic manner. The Assembly would launch many new initiatives for the good of the country, and opposition representatives would be able to voice serious criticism. In effect, the Declaration of Four submitted to the Assembly by the Bayar faction seemed to have been accepted.

The press started shifting as well. Necmeddin Sadak wrote an article signed 'Democrat' for *Akşam*, maintaining that 'the government mustn't shut down any more newspapers, and this can only be ensured if the laws are changed.'

They'd branded us traitors for demanding the same thing. I called attention to this in the 9 November edition of my column, 'Görüşler', where I wrote a piece called 'What a Traitor!'

> When I made the same argument three months ago, the editor-in-chief of *Akşam* railed against me, as did other newspapers. They maintained there were no unconstitutional laws and accused me of treason. But now, Necmeddin Sadak writes, 'We aren't in favour of special courts for newspaper trials. Such courts will always be unduly harsh. It might be a good idea to convene juries for press-related trials.'
>
> In his articles from three months ago, Sadak didn't even recognize the category of press crimes, maintained that such crimes shouldn't be handled either by special courts or by juries, and claimed that civil courts and the current laws were adequate to deal with them. Now, under the pen name 'Democrat,' he says that 'some laws, for instance the Law of Associations, need to be changed.'

On 17 November 1945, the papers published the following news:

> Unconstitutional laws are being revised. A committee of representatives has been assigned to the project. Article 50 of the Press Law will change, The Law of Public Assembly will be abolished, and some adjustments will be made to the Law of Police Responsibility and Authority.

Without a doubt, revising these articles would help safeguard the freedoms of press and assembly. We'd been demanding changes to these laws for years. And we'd been treated as criminals for it.

In light of these developments, we raised the matter of an amnesty for political prisoners who'd been convicted under the current laws.

On 20 November, Hüseyin Cahit Yalçın published an article entitled 'Confused Ideas on Freedom of Opinion'. His ideas on the matter were as follows:

> Over the last few days, Zekeriya and Sabiha Sertel of *Tan* have persistently highlighted a very important matter. The issue stirred up by our companions is an amnesty for political prisoners. I am not sure that anyone in the country has been convicted because of a dissenting opinion. Mrs Sabiha herself translated the works of Kautsky into Turkish. She was neither imprisoned nor exiled. She wrote in defence of freedom of opinion and was not prosecuted in any way. In fact, I have not heard of anyone being convicted for thinking differently than the government.

Who, then, was convicted? Those who engaged in communist propaganda, some returning to the country after fleeing from Russia. Their actions fall within the scope of Articles 141 and 142 of the Turkish Penal Code. These are the people the Sertels want released from prison through a political amnesty.

It was true; I hadn't been imprisoned for translating the works of Kautsky and August Bebel, which were of a wholly scholarly nature. But police had confiscated the books. Didn't Hüseyin Cahit know about journalists who were dragged into court and imprisoned for failing to parrot the government's line? Hadn't he himself been sent before an Independence Tribunal for his writings? Didn't he know that I'd been taken to court repeatedly for fighting against a dictatorship, that I'd been banned from writing three times, that newspapers kept getting shut down in the country? Of course he knew. But people like Hüseyin Cahit just couldn't accept democratic rights being granted, and so, the call for a political amnesty drove them into a frenzy.

Nazım Hikmet had been sentenced to twenty-eight years under these laws. He hadn't attempted to overthrow the government or secretly spread propaganda. He'd simply given his books, which were freely sold at bookstores, to some young people to read. And for that, he'd been in prison for thirteen years now. Neither history nor humanity will ever forgive the unjust incarceration of this universally acclaimed poet. Our demand for the release of political prisoners frightened those responsible for this disgrace.

Following this exchange of articles, the Prime Minister's Office and the General Press Directorate ordered news vendors to stop selling *Tan* and *Vatan*. This was confirmed by letters we received from the vendors, who assured us they would keep selling *Tan*, come what may.

The *Görüşler* journal and the newspaper *Yeni Dünya*

We completed the first issue of *Görüşler* just as Cami Baykut, Sabahaddin Ali and Esat Adil Müstecaboğlu, a co-founder of the Socialist Party, were preparing to publish a daily newspaper called *Yeni Dünya* [New World]. We hadn't received any articles from Adnan Menderes or Fuat Köprülü. I wrote a letter to Tevfik Rüştü Aras, asking for the pieces and whether we could announce on the cover that Celal Bayar, Menderes, Köprülü and Aras himself were on our editorial board. He answered in the affirmative and told me I'd receive the articles soon. But it was already too late to include them in the first issue.

After handing the journal to the printers, I decided to go to Ankara and secure the articles in person. I called Aras on the phone and told him my travel plans. He said he'd pick me up at the station. I boarded the morning train to Ankara on 28 November.

We arrived in Ankara three hours late. When I got off the train, Aras wasn't there. Instead, I was greeted by a young man, who told me that Aras had come to the station but left again when he heard the train would be late. The man took me to Adnan Menderes' home. A long table had been set in the dining room, but everybody else had already eaten because of my delay.

After finishing my meal, I joined Celal Bayar, Menderes, Köprülü and Aras in the guest hall. They were working at a round table covered in documents. I believe they were discussing the party programme. I told them about the preparations for the journal's first issue and complained that they hadn't submitted their articles.

'As you can see, we're very busy,' Menderes said. 'But we'll definitely submit articles for the second issue. *Tan*'s fight for freedom and democracy is of great interest to us. The country has been waiting a hundred years for democracy. We have to establish it at last; we can't continue with our old ways in this day and age. Even İnönü understands this is necessary. We'll continue our opposition from outside the People's Party. Once we've founded our own party, we'll contest the elections. And even if we aren't successful in the first election, we'll definitely gain a majority in the second one.'

While we were talking, the door opened, and Refik Koraltan, the fourth member of the Bayar opposition group, came in. Koraltan was still a representative for the People's Party, but earlier that day, he'd been questioned at the party caucus meeting about an article he'd written in *Vakit* on 2 November. Bayar and Menderes were anxious to hear the outcome.

Koraltan was very excited. He reported that the party caucus had been chaired by Kütahya deputy Recep Peker. Koraltan's article was found to be in violation of the party charter. Then, the party had expelled him by 280 votes. 'I'm finally free,' he said. He was thrilled by his expulsion.

I'd said all I needed, so I took my leave. Aras showed me to the door.

'Keep up the struggle,' he said. 'And don't neglect to print articles promoting friendship with the Soviets.'

From there, I went to the Akba Publishing House to discuss some matters related to the journal. The store windows were full of ads for *Görüşler* and *Yeni Dünya*. When I entered, I saw Sabahaddin Ali furiously pacing up and down with his head between his hands, shouting loudly.

'What's the matter, Sabahaddin?' I asked. 'Who's gotten you so riled up?'

'Look at what's happened to me!' he said. He pointed to the *Yeni Dünya* poster.

'See the globe on that poster, with the flags of all the nations around it? I made them put the Turkish flag on top, followed by the flags of our allies and other friendly nations. But they changed the order while I wasn't here and put the Soviet flag on top! This is sabotage! This is treason, infamy!'

Sabahaddin's face was bright red. His hands and feet were shaking, and he was cursing incessantly.

'Who could have done that, Sabahaddin? Wasn't Esat Adil overseeing everything?'

'Esat Adil wouldn't have done this. There must be a provocateur among us. But what can I do now? What can I do?' He was beside himself.

There was no doubt our enemies had orchestrated this incident to strike at *Yeni Dünya*.

The same day, we met up at Behice Boran's house to discuss new articles for the journal. When I arrived, many friends were already there, including Sabahaddin Ali, Niyazi Berkes, Pertev Boratav, Muvaffak Şeref and Adnan Cemgil.

Sabahaddin couldn't sit still. He kept jumping up from his chair and telling everyone about the flag incident. Behice was constantly admonishing him:

'Quiet, Sabahaddin, don't shout, the neighbours will hear you ...'

'What do I care about the neighbours? The whole world should hear about this! This is a plot. We're facing a formidable foe!'

As it turned out, that formidable foe had taken many more precautions against us before the journal and newspaper even appeared. But at that point, we had no inkling of this.

When I returned to the station that evening, I found the *Tan* correspondent Emin Karakuş as well as Emin Türk waiting there. My train was about to leave, so I spoke to them from the window. Then, I saw Adnan Menderes and Köprülüzade Fuat appear in the distance. They'd come to see me off. I asked them both once again to send me their articles for the second issue.

'Please don't worry,' they said. 'We will definitely, definitely send them.'

I was back in Istanbul on 29 November. At the printing house, the typesetters, writers and workers from the machine room surrounded me before I even stepped through the door.

'Good news!' they said. 'This morning, we distributed *Görüşler*. It sold out by 11 o'clock. We're swamped with telegraphs from vendors in Anatolia. They want to triple the number they ordered. We started printing the second run without you. It'll be ready in a couple of hours.'

The second print run of *Görüşler* sold out as well. People were still requesting more. The journal was enthusiastically received everywhere.

In the evening, Zekeriya and I went to a restaurant called Degüstasyon in Beyoğlu. Sadreddin Celal had a personal table, where he'd always sit and work. When he saw us, he called us over.

'Have you heard the news?' he said. 'They've likened the letter "G" in "Görüşler" to a sickle. They're spreading rumours that *Görüşler* has appeared with a hammer and sickle on the cover.'

This was another version of the sabotage at *Yeni Dünya*. The calligraphy on the cover was by İhap Hulusi, a painter from a wealthy family, who'd spent most of his life in Europe and had nothing whatsoever to do with socialism or communism. By chance, he came to the restaurant as well, the journal in his hand. We told him about the rumour. He laughed.

'They're making a mountain out of a molehill,' he said.

Görüşler struck in Ankara like a bomb. The People's Party called an extraordinary meeting, renewing instructions to attack the opposition newspapers. The party issued verbal and written orders to prevent news vendors from selling *Tan*, *Yeni Dünya* and *Görüşler*, and to ban state officials and students from reading these publications. Deputies who wrote articles for *Vatan* were purged from the party.

We were determined to continue our fight no matter what. I called Tevfik Rüştü Aras in Ankara to ask for the promised articles, which still hadn't arrived.

'Yes, yes,' he said in a panicked voice. 'We're all together right now. We were just discussing this matter. My companions are hesitant about the articles. I'm trying to convince them, but Adnan is opposed to the idea.'

Figure 8.1 The debut issue of *Görüşler* (Views), 1 December 1945, the Sertels' new political magazine, three days before the destruction of their publishing house. Edited by Sabiha, the magazine was intended to serve as the voice for the new opposition party.

'Is this how you keep your promises?' I asked. 'Didn't you allow me to put your photos on the cover of the first issue? Didn't you have me announce you would all write for us? How can you pull out now?'

Aras apologized. He was contrite but said there was nothing he could do.

Soon, we received a telegram from our correspondent in Ankara:

Recent reports that former Prime Minister Celal Bayar is founding a new party have stirred up a hornet's nest here. The hottest topic is whether he'll write for a certain journal. I approached Bayar himself about the issue. Here's his response:

> I'd like to assure you of my complete and sincere loyalty to Kemalism and its goal of popular sovereignty. As you know, what we call Kemalism is nothing but the fully expressed idea of democracy. I have no connection with any ideology except Kemalism. I've been a part of our revolution from the first day. Time and again, I've shouldered the responsibility for its advancement. It's impossible for me to depart from the principles of our revolution. We'll soon lay bare the ideas that will guide me in my future political life. But I never claimed to be a writer and have no intention of becoming one now. Joining the editorial board of this journal or any other is out of the question.

As I said earlier, Bayar hadn't promised us an article, only an interview. But what was I to make of his statement that he had no connection with *Görüşler*? Hadn't Celal Bayar and Tevfik Rüştü themselves asked for the journal to be published? Hadn't they even offered to provide the capital? There was no way to chalk up this new statement to a lapse of memory. Only yesterday, at Adnan Menderes' house and at the train station, they'd stated that they'd 'definitely, definitely send the articles.' There were witnesses, namely Emin Karakuş, the *Tan* correspondent, and Emin Türk. How could they deny all this?

Perhaps, flip-flopping and breaking one's word was normal for bourgeois politicians, who saw politics as nothing but a game of cunning and contortion. But for supposed champions of freedom, people who never grew tired of repeating how they risked their lives for the cause, it was most unbecoming.

The uniting of all opposition forces and the founding of a new party had frightened the People's Party administration. Visitors from Ankara reported that a cloud of terror and intimidation had settled over the capital.

9

The *Tan* incidents

On 3 December 1945, I wrote an article entitled, 'The Clamour of the Status Quo'. After the *Tan* printing house was destroyed, this article was used as a pretext to take me to court. For this reason, I am reproducing it in its entirety:

> The People's Party is not a majority party but rather a party of alliances. Five to ten of the erstwhile allies have now formed an opposition. But these opposing voices only started to reach the public once the press was granted permission to cover Assembly debates. The opposition newspapers face the same situation. Until now, the 'legally free' press was actually muzzled by laws. And if restrictions under the Press Law weren't sufficient, an ordinance or a phone call by the Press General Directorate tightened the leash. But recently, one or two Turkish newspapers became opposition voices, demanding the establishment of true freedom and democracy, the people's right to determine their own fate, an end to exploitation and profiteering, and control of the entire state machinery by the Turkish people.
>
> This opposition is rooted in the will of the people. But while its numbers in the Assembly and the press are limited, guardians of the status quo are expending an unlimited effort to crush it. As soon as the opposition speaks up in the Assembly, these guardians drown it out with radio interference, trampling feet, banging desk tops and whistles – just as in the war years, when radio stations intentionally broadcast interference to drown out the truth. The opposition is branded as a power-hungry gang trying to take over the state.
>
> Opposition newspapers show great civil courage in speaking the truth. And since this is supposed to be a free country, where all can say what they want, their voices need to be drowned out by 'radio interference'. Papers are accused of saying things they didn't. Their articles are misrepresented, distorted and denounced. They are subjected to a barrage of high-pitched, cacophonous noise.
>
> These are the tactics of the status quo today, employed to confuse the common people, who have let their tongues and minds rust from years of profiteering, exploitation and tyranny. This is the clamour of the status quo, raised to drown out the people's opposition.

The same day, Hüseyin Cahit Yalçın published a full-page, enlarged article in *Tanin*. It was called 'Rise Up, O Patriots!' The subheading, again in large type, announced: 'A National Front is Needed'. The article called on the youth to rise up, stating:

The great patriot Namık Kemal's words must be today's motto. Rise up, o patriots! The struggle begins, and we must engage in it. We cannot allow the most rabid and ruthless propaganda to pour the caustic, chilling and appalling poison of disinformation down the throats of Turkish citizens. Every Turk who wants a fatherland where he can live in freedom and independence is bound by duty to stand up to this propaganda.

When I opened *Görüşler* and read Mrs Sertel's article 'Freedom in Chains',[1] set on a page adorned with crimson bars, I grasped at once what kind of freedom she has in store for us. Mrs Sertel says, 'In a society of free people, the highest maxim must be to sacrifice individual interests, if needed, for the good of the masses.' Those who haven't delved into communist literature might easily miss the hidden meaning of these lines. The place where freedoms are sacrificed for the good of the masses is Russia!

It isn't the government's duty to shut such people up. That duty belongs to able journalists and free citizens!

Hüseyin Cahit Yalçın was openly trampling on the country's law and order. With the command, 'Rise Up, O Patriots!' he was urging the youth and the citizens of the country to riot and silence us. Namık Kemal coined the motto, 'Rise Up, O Patriots!' to call the people to action against the sultanate and dictatorship of Abdülhamid II. But Yalçın was using it to incite citizens to lynch those who fought for freedom and democracy.

This call was not without context. The People's Party and the Saraçoğlu administration had already organized some youth groups from the university to attack the *Tan* printing house the next day, on 4 December. In the pitched battle that had been raging for months, they'd realized that their sabre-rattling couldn't shut us up, that their reactionary ideas weren't embraced by the people, and that, to the contrary, the masses supported champions of freedom and democracy. They were scared. They were scared of freedom. They were scared by the common people's contempt for them. They called for brute force to cover up their defeat in the arena of debate.

After reading Hüseyin Cahit's article, I wrote a piece called 'Don't Fear the Newspapers. Fear Public Opinion,' for the 4 December issue of *Tan*. I can summarize it as follows:

> Recently, the Istanbul chairman of the People's Party called a meeting of pro-government journalists. At this meeting, he advised journalists to continue their struggle against the opposition newspapers. This move shows that the party in government is scared of the opposition. In a democratic country, debate is a natural thing. A party that is sure of its popularity doesn't try to prevent debate.
>
> Publications only have an impact if they reflect the will of the people. If they oppose the ideas and interests of the people, they simply fade away. All the noise made by pro-government journalists to drown out opposition papers won't be enough to fool or confuse the people. Don't fear newspapers. Fear the people.

---

[1] TN: I cannot reproduce this article, since I don't have a copy of the text.

Figure 9.1 On 4 December 1945, the police watched on as thousands of government-orchestrated rioters, swinging pickaxes and sledge hammers, destroyed the Sertels' publishing house, chanting, 'Damn the communists! Damn *Tan* and *Görüşler*!'

This was the last article I wrote in my thirty-two years as a journalist in Turkey. Time has shown my words to be true. Government circles had the *Tan* printing house destroyed, silencing our voices. But in the 1950 elections, the masses' hatred for the People's Party erupted. The party was defeated, and the Democrat Party took power. Ten years later, the same hatred by common people led to the 27 May movement[2] and the demise of the Democrat Party. I will say it once again: Don't fear newspapers. Fear the people.

On 4 December, the day after I wrote this article, the *Tan* printing house was destroyed under orders from the People's Party and Prime Minister Saraçoğlu. The party used secret police to organize youth groups at Istanbul University, some of them fascist and racist, some of them simply naive. These groups were then sent to attack the printing houses of *Tan* and the progressive papers *La Turquie* and *Yeni Dünya*.

In 'Battles in the Press', an article series that appeared in the paper *Yeni İstanbul* [New Istanbul], Tekin Erer describes the destruction of the printing house as follows:

> On the evening of Monday, 3 December, the Istanbul branch of the Republican People's Party issued instructions to the student dormitories, ordering a demonstration against *Tan* the next morning. I was news editor of *Tasviri Efkar* at the time. Our editor-in-chief, the late Nejdet Baytok, arrived at the paper early the next day. He said he'd heard of a large demonstration being planned against the papers that published communist content. But he warned me against telling anyone since the news might be a hoax.

---

[2] TN: The first Turkish coup d'état, which toppled the Menderes administration on 27 May 1960.

It was the morning of 4 December 1945. I went to the university courtyard. Students with flags in their hands were slowly beginning to gather. Many of them held framed photographs of Atatürk and İnönü. Soon, the crowd swelled to 10,000 people. At 9:30, the mob started flowing like a tide from Beyazıt Square toward Çarşıkapı. The A.B.C. Bookstore was on the way to *Tan*. It stood at the top of Cağaloğlu Slope and sold books about communism. It was destroyed within minutes. From there, the crowd moved on to *Tan*.

They were yelling, 'Down with communism! Down with the Sertels! Long live the Turkish Republic!' Wave after wave of youths demolished *Tan*'s windows and doors with stones and iron bars. On the first floor of *Tan* stood one of the largest rotary printing presses in Turkey at the time. They started attacking that press with the pieces of iron they found in the room and completely destroyed it, even smashing the parts they'd broken off.

On the second floor were linotype machines, metal types and other materials and machinery used by the printing house. These were much more easily dismantled and destroyed. Doors, windows and chairs were smashed to bits. Articles, documents and books were taken from drawers and torn to shreds. Some of the rioters found the paper storage room next to the rotary press and rolled reels of paper down the street toward Sirkeci. Others wanted to set the building on fire, stopping only because there were so many people inside.

Some employees had left the buildings as soon as they heard of the rally in Beyazıt. Halil Lütfi Dördüncü, one of the owners of *Tan*, watched on with a heavy heart from the window of the Hofer advertising firm, just across the road, as the newspaper and

Figure 9.2 Rioters ransacking the printing press.

Figure 9.3 Police make no arrests.

building were destroyed. Murat Sertoğlu, editor-in-chief of *Tanin*, was also there, reporting the events via telephone to his paper's head writer, Hüseyin Cahit Yalçın. At some point, Halil Lütfi lost his composure and spoke to Sertoğlu in a harsh voice. 'Remind Hüseyin Cahit of what happened to him during the uprisings of 31 March 1909,'[3] he said. 'Tell him the same thing is happening to me now.' Sertoğlu conveyed the message, word for word.

By 10:30, the destruction of *Tan* was complete. Once the crowd was sure that no more papers could be printed, it crossed the bridge and headed for *Yeni Dünya*. That paper's printing house was in Beyoğlu, on the street at the corner of the Soviet embassy facing Tünel. *La Turquie*, a French-language newspaper, was also printed there. These two papers, just like *Tan*, published pro-communist articles.

At first, it seemed like the planned attack on *Yeni Dünya* would fail. Fearing an incident at the Soviet embassy, the police had blocked the streets with fire engines. But the youths, whipped into a frenzy by the mob, assaulted the firefighters, seizing their hoses and turning them on the police officers. Then, they broke through to *Yeni Dünya*. The printing house was destroyed within minutes. Machinery, furniture, books, newspapers and archives were thrown out into the street and torn to pieces. The Berrak Bookstore in Tünel, which sold leftist publications, was destroyed next, and closed its doors for good.

Some groceries and other stores had the word *Tan* in their names. As soon as they heard of the Babıali incident, they took down their signs or scratched them out. Petro, owner of the *Tan meze* restaurant in Karaköy, didn't have time to remove his sign, so he painted over the letter 'T' with a 'C', and the *Tan* restaurant became the *Can* restaurant.

The *Akşam* newspaper, distributed at 10 a.m., stated, 'This morning's demonstrations had regrettable results.' When the rioters heard this, they left Beyoğlu and headed for

---

[3] TN: The reference is explained further below.

Akşam to destroy that newspaper as well. The editorial board managed to appease the youths, though, calling the statement an unfortunate mistake and promising to correct it in the next print run. The mob kept yelling, 'Down with communism! Long live İnönü!' and scrawling these slogans on walls wherever it passed.

Next, the crowd arrived in front of *Tasviri Efkar* and started chanting for Cihat Baban, Ziyat Ebüzziya, Orhan Seyfi and Peyami Safa to appear. But the only people at the paper were Mithat Perin and myself. We stepped out onto the balcony. Briefly thanking the youths for their praise and affection, Mithat told them that the writers

Figure 9.4 *Cumhuriyet* front page, 5 December 1945. The destruction of *Tan* made headlines in Turkey and wordwide. It effectively silenced the leading progressive voices of the era.

Figure 9.5 On 5 December 1945, the day after the *Tan* riot, *Cumhuriyet* published this caricature of Sertel, depicting pro-government journalists assaulting her. The sign in the background held by Hüseyin Cahit Yalçın says: 'Rise Up, O Patriots,' the title of Yalçın's editorial that rallied protestors.

they wanted to see weren't there. Then, the crowd headed over to *Tanin*. They wanted to salute Hüseyin Cahit, but he wasn't at the newspaper, either.

Originally, the mob had also planned to attack *Vatan*. But security forces had taken very heavy precautions, preventing rioters from even entering the street where *Vatan*'s printing house was located. Around three in the afternoon, the mob finally dispersed.

When the papers appeared the next morning, *Tan*, *Yeni Dünya* and *La Turquie* had vanished. The destruction of *Tan* also marked the end of Zekeriya and Sabiha Sertel's careers in the Turkish press.

This article by Tekin Erer, an eyewitness to the events, confirms that the riot was staged by the government and the party. Quite a while later, Cami Baykut bought a book from a secondhand store in Beyazıt and found a letter inside. The letter was written by a certain Yaşar Çimen and reported the *Tan* incidents to Prime Minister Saraçoğlu. Çimen told Saraçoğlu that he'd carried out the latter's orders and was looking forward to his reward. When I departed Istanbul, I had to leave this document behind.

On 12 April 1967, the newspaper *Yeni Gazete* [New Gazette] published an article called 'I Disclose', written by Kazım Alöç, who was martial law prosecutor[4] at the time of the *Tan* incidents. The article contained two important pieces of information.

---

[4] TN: The north-western provinces of Turkey, including Istanbul, were under martial law from 1940 to 1947.

'The university students who raided *Tan* were led by Ali İhsan Göğüş, who is currently a CHP[5] deputy and also served as minister.' The article also stated: 'Following the incident, the demonstrators who raided *Tan* were cordially welcomed at the police headquarters, where CHP inspector Alaaddin Tiritoğlu offered them cigarettes.'

The CHP members who destroyed *Tan* promote themselves as leftists today. Ali İhsan Göğüş, for instance, is part of the CHP's 'left of the middle' movement.

On Wednesday, 5 December, all newspapers printed a statement issued by the Martial Law Governorship:

> Yesterday, on Tuesday, 4.12.1945, a group of university students attacked two printing houses and some bookstores, committing the crimes they planned in spite of attempts by government and police forces to intervene. Investigations and prosecution have already commenced. This highly regrettable incident will not be tolerated. I hereby declare and advise the population that such conduct will be met with force and that mass gatherings such as this are against the law.
> Lieutenant General Asım Tınaztepe, Martial Law Governor.

Young readers unaware of the events might take this statement to mean that the Martial Law Governor apprehended and punished the culprits. But exposing the culprits would have meant admitting that the People's Party and the Saraçoğlu administration had staged the entire incident. And so, the culprits were neither exposed nor punished. In fact, soon thereafter, we ourselves were arrested.

The Republican People's Party used axes and sledgehammers to respond to criticism by progressive papers. This was an act of barbarism on par with the methods of fascist Germany. Destroying the printing houses of those whom they couldn't defeat in debate was a quintessentially fascist tactic.

Halil Lütfi Dördüncü was correct in comparing this riot to the reactionary movement of 31 March 1909. Back then, Abdülhamid II rallied the bigots around dervish Vahdeti and the *softas*[6] to crush the 1908 revolution.[7] Now, another reactionary movement had rallied university students to destroy not just *Tan* itself, but also the freedom of opinion and democracy that *Tan* represented.

As Tekin Erer's article makes clear, the night before the riot, the Istanbul branch of the CHP issued instructions to the university dormitories and alerted the police. The police were instructed not to protect the printing houses of *Tan* and *La Turquie*, but, to the contrary, to direct and oversee the riot.

It was no coincidence that the publishers of the destroyed papers were branded as communists. The Saraçoğlu administration hoped to kill two birds with one stone. Their first goal was to prevent the Bayar faction from entering an alliance with

---

[5] TN: Abbreviation for *Cumhuriyet Halk Partisi* or the Republican People's Party.
[6] TN: Students at a religious academy (*medrese*).
[7] TN: The so-called Young Turk Revolution, in which military forces led by the Committee of Union and Progress forced Sultan Abdülhamid II to grant a constitution and allow political elections in the Ottoman Empire, turning the empire into a constitutional monarchy.

progressive forces. Their second was to secure US aid by showing Turkey's willingness to fight against communists.

During the war, Turkey had supported fascist Germany. This had estranged Turkey's ally, Britain, as well as the Soviet Union. The country was isolated. İnönü's new plan was to latch on to the USA for support and financial aid. This violent, anti-progressive act was a concession to American imperialism.

The destruction of the printing house and its aftermath

On the morning of 4 December, Zekeriya said to me, 'Don't go to the printing house today. I'm not going myself. I heard they're planning a demonstration against us. But don't stay at home, either.' He'd been informed the night before.

Zekeriya left the house. I followed suit, visiting a woman I knew in Moda. Her husband called and told her about the demonstration over the phone. He said he'd be home once the roads were clear, and that the demonstrators might head for the Sertels' house. I realized that remaining there would put these people in danger, so I left and went to my mother's house on Mektep Street in Moda. Soon, Zekeriya arrived as well.

My mother was an old woman of seventy-eight. She was surprised to see us in the middle of the day.

'What's the matter?' she asked. 'Aren't you working today?'

'No, we wrote our articles yesterday. We're taking a break today.' I didn't want her to know about the demonstration.

We hadn't told İclal, our housemaid, where we were going. We stayed at my mother's until evening, only returning home once it was completely dark. Soon, Vala Nureddin and his wife, Müzehher, dropped by. Vala, who worked for *Akşam* at the time, told us about the demonstration, saying that even Necmeddin Sadak was saddened by it. I couldn't help but laugh.

'After the demonstration,' he said, 'the youths boarded the Kadıköy ferry to come to your house. But when Governor Lütfü Kırdar heard this, he called the captain and ordered him to take the ferry to the Princes' Islands instead.'

Zekeriya jumped up at once and called Governor Kırdar.

'I'd heard there would be an attack on *Tan*, and I reported this to you,' he said to the governor. 'You told me not to worry, that nothing would happen. But the printing house was destroyed. Now I learn they're headed to my home. At least prevent this!'

Zekeriya said that the governor responded by saying, 'That danger has passed. But where are you calling me from?'

'Home.'

'You should get out of there at once.'

So we still weren't safe. Vala offered to take us to their house in Kalamış. We packed a set of clothes and left, urging İclal not to tell anyone where we'd gone. We stayed there for three days and nights. During daytime, I sat around in boredom. At night, I went out for walks on the Fener road, marvelling at how normally democracy was developing in the country.

After three days, we returned home. The ground floor of our house faced the road and the sea. The living room had large windows on all sides. One room was connected to the garden through a veranda which people could easily access. So we remained upstairs.

The next morning, my nephew Osman Binzet came to visit. We were talking when we heard a commotion nearby. We sent İclal to see what was happening. She didn't return.

'We should leave,' Osman said. 'Maybe they're stopping the girl from coming back.'

I threw a coat over my morning gown, and we left by the back door. Zekeriya and I went to the apartment of a family we knew in Moda. Some people said the noise came from students of the French School, who played soccer on Moda Field. But others believed the students were sent there to frighten us. I don't know which story was true. We stayed at that apartment for three days as well.

At one point, Zekeriya called up *Tan*'s lawyer on some business. The lawyer told him we mustn't be seen on the street. The demonstrators, he said, had brought big containers of red ink to the printing house on the day of the riot. If they found Sabiha Sertel, they wanted to douse her in red ink, pin a tag to her chest that read, 'This is what a communist should look like,' and parade her in the streets.

It was then that I understood just how staggering this plot was. They couldn't win the debate, so they were destroying newspapers and even trying to kill their owners. Where was the democracy they'd promised? This was nothing but fascist terror.

I hadn't seen my mother for days. She'd finally heard of the incidents and was worried sick. I went to visit her after dark. When I saw her, she looked so sad that I tried to hide my own desolation. She approached me and put her hand on my shoulder.

'Don't be bitter,' she said, 'that's just how people are.' And she quoted a line of poetry: 'They only throw stones at the tree that bears fruit.'

My mother was a well-read person. In her day, girls weren't allowed to attend school, so she gathered the schoolboys in the neighborhood and took lessons from them. Back then, she was the only literate woman in Salonika. She knew the poems of Ziya Paşa and Namık Kemal by heart.

The days passed in emptiness. Our house was surrounded by uniformed and secret police. They didn't let anyone in. At night, they didn't even allow people to walk down the street. Ostensibly, the governor had taken this precaution to protect us.

We had a neighbourhood doctor, called Doctor Meyh, who treated poor people for free. One night, he passed by our house on the way to one of his patients. When the police wouldn't let him through, he told them his patient was in danger and he needed to get there at once. They assaulted the poor man. When I heard about it the next day, I was heartbroken.

Foreign journalists kept calling. They said they wanted to see us, but the police barred them as well. One day, after midnight, the doorbell rang. We asked who it was – a precaution we now took with every visitor. It turned out to be a well-known British journalist. Knowing of the police restrictions, he'd arrived late, presuming the officers would leave after midnight. He'd risked assault just to see us.

He told us about articles appearing in the foreign press:

Because of this demonstration, Britain and France are very disillusioned with the democracy Turkey vowed to establish. Both the public and statesmen were already appalled with Turkey for aiding fascist Germany during the war. And now, this stance toward a progressive newspaper has created the impression that democracy in Turkey is still many years away.

'Will you continue publishing?' he asked.
That was a hard question to answer.
'Not now. One day, perhaps.'
But that day never came.

A meeting with Sabahaddin Ali

Sabahaddin Ali was in Ankara when the printing houses were destroyed. One evening, after dark, he showed up at our doorstep. He'd just gotten off the train and come straight to our home.

'Sabahaddin, how did you get here?' I asked. 'Weren't you afraid?'
'There was no one around when I arrived,' he said. 'If they'd stopped me, I would've gone back.'

He sat down and we talked. It was the first time I'd seen Sabahaddin act so serious.

'The People's Party may have destroyed our presses and papers, but it didn't destroy us,' he said. 'If anything, it destroyed its own prestige. I wish you could hear the people on the streets! "*Tan* was the only paper voicing our concerns," they say. "By crushing *Tan*, they crushed our hopes of liberation." Even members of the People's Party are grumbling. "İnönü keeps promising more democracy in the caucus meetings and the Assembly," they say. "This operation happened without our knowledge. It shook our confidence in İnönü. It was a bad thing." I heard it from their own mouths.'

Sabahaddin was very excited. He couldn't sit still and constantly fiddled with his glasses. He continued in a spirited voice. At some point, he took a bunch of papers from his pocket. 'I'll read you a story,' he said. 'I just wrote it. It's called 'Sırça Köşk' [The Glass Palace].'

He sat down and started reading. The glass palace stood for the bourgeoisie. It was the palace of those who grew rich by robbing the people. The famished masses came to its gates every day and begged for food. Receiving no answer, they finally started throwing heads of lambs and sheep at the palace windows, breaking them. They threw so many heads at the palace that one day, the whole building came crashing down. Sabahaddin ended the story by saying, 'If you want to destroy the glass palace, you just have to throw some heads at it.'

He looked up to see our reaction.

'Sabahaddin,' I said, 'maybe those heads will destroy the glass palace one day. But in the meantime, I fear they'll throw your own head at it.'

He smiled.

'He who lives by the sword, dies by the sword,' he replied.

Poor Sabahaddin. He did end up 'dying by the sword', lured into a cowardly trap and shot from behind while asleep. But I will talk of his murder later.

*

The house was under constant surveillance. I wasn't allowed to leave. Late one evening, I finally went out for some fresh air. The street by our house was curved like a horseshoe, ending on another street after just one block. I walked back and forth between one end of the horseshoe and the other, trailed by three men. I kept walking up and down, trying to rid my lungs of the stale air I'd been breathing for days.

The men behind me started talking. 'Brother, I'm getting tired,' one said.

I turned around.

'Well, I'm not tired yet,' I said. 'Why doesn't one of you wait at this end of the street and one at the other end? Don't worry, I won't run away.'

'We're not following you.'

'Then why do you walk up and down the street right behind me?'

They didn't answer.

We lived like this for a week. Finally, the uniformed officers left. But not the secret police. Unbeknownst to us, they'd established a base at the Moda Hotel across the street. I saw a hotel window, looking onto our back door, covered with newspapers. When I ran into Monsieur Jacques, the owner, I asked him, 'How could you paper over that window? Is it so hard to replace the glass?'

'We didn't put the newspapers there.' He leaned over and whispered in my ear. 'The police did. They're watching your house through a hole in the paper.'

After a while, the storm subsided. People started visiting us again. One day, our typesetters and machine operators came by. After commiserating with us, they told us about the day of the incident. Cemil, the chief typesetter, reported the following:

> Early that morning, we heard that there'd be a demonstration at the paper. We all assembled outside the building. At some point, two people arrived with enormous bottles of red ink and left them at the store next to the printing house. We became curious, so we went inside and asked. 'The police brought them,' the storeowner said quietly. 'I was told to keep them for now.'
>
> The mob arrived and started breaking the doors and windows with axes. They destroyed whatever they found. They looked for you in every room. We were very worried – if you arrived, they were sure to attack you. We overheard them say they'd brought the ink to paint you red and parade you in the streets. All the workers gathered outside the printing house door. We wanted to prevent an attack on you if you came.

One after the other, they told their stories:

> They found an American journal on Zekeriya Bey's desk, with the picture of an American general on the cover. 'That's Stalin's photograph,' they said. They put the

journal in their bag like evidence. They scattered the types we'd set for the second issue of *Görüşler*. We were also printing the final sheet of the Tevfik Fikret book – they tore it up, and all the drafts as well. Thankfully, you didn't come. That would have been a disaster.

The visits didn't let up. A group of university students came by. They told us how instructions were issued in the dormitories the night before the demonstration. They'd refused to join and asked the dean's permission for a counter-demonstration, but he hadn't allowed it.

Philips Price, a Labour MP from Britain, visited us. He asked me about the underpinnings of political strife in Turkey and the goals of the People's Party and the opposition. I told him about the economic, social and political causes of the strife. He listened patiently.

The disputes you talk about occurred in Britain a hundred years ago,

he finally said.

There were many parties in Britain even back then. The socialists were never imprisoned or deprived of the chance to work in the open. Even the Communist Party was only penalized by having its paper shut down from time to time. The disputes remained in the realm of ideas.

This was the reaction in Turkey and abroad to the attack on *Tan*, *La Turquie* and *Yeni Dünya*.

10

The founding of the Democrat Party and the arrests

On 7 February 1946,[1] the Celal Bayar faction officially announced the foundation of the Democrat Party. Since its founders were already deputies, the party immediately assumed the role of opposition in the Assembly. The party programme, published shortly thereafter, was full of pledges to establish a democracy. But it also made clear the party would protect the interests of private enterprise and promote a liberal economy.

In his conversations with me, Bayar had said he'd recognize workers' rights, safeguard the right to organize and form associations, and even respect workers' right to strike. But these rights weren't enshrined in his party programme, which used ambiguous wording to avoid committing to them. And in the ten years that he was in power, Bayar established a dictatorship that was the exact opposite of these pledges.

The founding of the Socialist Party

In 1946, the Law of Associations was changed, allowing the establishment of class-based political parties. On 14 May of the same year, Esat Adil Müstecaboğlu and his companions founded the Socialist Party of Turkey. Esat Adil was a well-established jurist. He'd served as head assistant at the Kocaeli Prosecutor's Office and as warden of the İmralı Island Prison. He was friends with Nazım Hikmet.

I told Esat Adil I had no intention of joining a party, but many intellectuals and workers gathered around the Socialist Party.

In the twelfth issue of the journal *Gün* [Day], the party's position was outlined as follows:

> There are those who accuse our party programme of deceitful tactics. They should know that ours is not a tactic, but a strategy. Our programme is clear. We regard private property as sacrosanct as long as it doesn't constitute a means for the exploitation of others. This formula, we believe, is the only way to steer our country clear of crises.

---

[1] TN: The correct date is 7 January.

It is obvious that our class of big landowners ruthlessly exploits the mass of peasants, reducing them to the direst living conditions. Ownership of land must be given to those who work on it. In the cities, the situation is similar. The big manufacturing companies are owned by a class that exploits workers, seizes their products and leaves them so destitute they can barely survive. Once the big companies are nationalized and become part of the people's common property, the working class will start raising its standards for welfare and culture.

There are those who call themselves socialists but condone the imperialists' colonial policy and work with all their might to ensure its continuation. To us, they are not socialists but counter-revolutionaries. We wholeheartedly embrace movements of national liberation around the world. Those who cast us in a different light are barking up the wrong tree.

These words were aimed at critics from the left who accused the Socialist Party of betrayal because it engaged in party politics instead of working underground. But as the statement makes clear, this wasn't a collaborationist party indebted to the imperialists. Esat Adil and the other founders simply believed that underground activism was useless given the current conditions in Turkey. Police confiscated flyers before they could reach any workers and arrested many activists. The new law offered an opportunity to work out in the open, and the Socialist Party wanted to take advantage of this opportunity.

The Socialist Labourers' and Peasants' Party of Turkey

On 19 June 1946, another party was founded thanks to the new law permitting class-based parties. This was the Socialist Labourers' and Peasants' Party of Turkey, chaired by Doctor Şefik Hüsnü. During its brief existence, the party founded many trade unions in Istanbul, Izmir and other cities, as well as establishing a youth organization in Istanbul. It published numerous journals, such as *Sendika* [Trade Union], *Ses* [The Voice] and *Yığın* [The Mass].

But the party didn't last long. On 13 December, the police raided its headquarters and Şefik Hüsnü's home. He and the other founders were arrested by the martial law governorship. The Socialist Party of Turkey was banned as well, and Esat Adil Müstecapoğlu and the other founders arrested. The government justified these closures by saying the parties promoted the dominance of one class over another. This, they maintained, was against the Penal Code, which outlawed class struggle.

The revised Law of Associations granted the right to found class-based parties. It was obvious that the socialist parties taking advantage of this law would be based on class. But İnönü wasn't sincere in allowing the creation of these parties. Like a good bourgeois politician, he wanted to lure the socialists out of the underground and catch them all in one fell swoop. The law was just a trap.

Our home is searched

Ostensibly, this was an era of democratization in Turkey, a time when even class-based parties could be founded. In reality, the People's Party was destroying printing houses, banning socialist parties and silencing all its opponents. But it didn't end there.

One night in early February, our doorbell rang at four in the morning. We were asleep and didn't hear the sound. We'd told İclal to check from the balcony before opening the door to strangers, so she went out on the upper balcony and asked the man outside what he wanted. He said he was a courier who'd brought an urgent telegraph. The girl went downstairs and opened the door. Immediately, five or six people stormed inside – the others had been hiding behind the wall.

The girl's scream woke us up. Zekeriya ran to the stairwell and tried to stop them from coming upstairs. He talked about the privacy of the home and asked to see their official papers. An argument broke out.

When I realized they were going to search the house, I set about destroying my private papers. I didn't get dressed; if they tried to come inside, I hoped to stop them by saying I was naked. While they were arguing outside, I unlocked the cupboard, tore up the papers and flushed them down the toilet. Just as I finished, three or four people entered the room. They were led by a short, stout, round-faced man. He introduced himself.

'I am Parmaksız [Fingerless] Hamdi,' he said. 'We're here to search your house. I've shown Zekeriya Bey the official documents.'

'Go ahead and search.'

I'd heard this name before. Parmaksız Hamdi was the chief of the First Branch, which dealt with political offenses. He was notorious among leftists as 'the hangman'. He was the one who interrogated communists and had them tortured.

They started searching the room. They threw the sheets and mattresses on the floor. They looked under the bedsprings. They went through the cupboards, looking in the pockets of all clothes.

While one group of policemen was with me, the other was searching the rooms downstairs with Zekeriya. Parmaksız Hamdi turned to his men. 'One of you stay here,' he said. 'I'll check the other rooms.'

I was left alone with the policeman. I gave him the key to the locked cupboard.

'Open it,' I said.

The policeman looked at me. 'It's alright, sister,' he said. 'I know who you are. I admire your work. I came here under orders, not because I wanted to.'

I was surprised to find such a man among the police and regretted tearing up my papers. The officer briefly skimmed the bathroom and storeroom. Then we went downstairs together. Parmaksız Hamdi was just coming out of the living room.

'Where is the library?' he said. 'Let's go there.'

I took them to the library. This was where Zekeriya and I did our work. Two walls were covered with built-in bookshelves from floor to ceiling. We worked at a wall-to-wall desk in front of the window facing the street. Parmaksız Hamdi went in and took a look at the books.

'We'll need a ladder to get up there,' he said.

'We can bring one,' I replied.

Because he was short and overweight, he was scared to climb a ladder. He got on a chair instead. He took and replaced one book after the other, but couldn't find what he was looking for.

'Are all these books in Frankish?' he asked.

'Yes, they're all in English or French.'

'Don't you have any Turkish books?'

'Almost none.'

He got off the chair.

'We came here unprepared,' he said. 'We should've brought a translator.' He turned to me.

'Are there no Russian books here?'

'No.'

'Do you know Russian?'

'I don't.'

'Have you been to the Soviet Union?'

'I haven't.'

He realized he wouldn't find anything on the bookshelves. But there was a locked cupboard which contained archived files. He told me to open it. Inside was the research I'd done for my *Tan* articles on colonies and imperialism. He gave the folders to the officer standing next to him.

'Put these in the bag,' he said.

I took the folders and looked at their titles. 'The Island of Haiti'. 'The Congo'. I gave them back.

'You should certainly take these,' I said. 'There are very important secrets inside. You'll definitely find what you're looking for.'

He kept randomly pulling out books. *The Popular Front in France*. *The Spanish Civil War*. And many more pamphlets like these. Then he opened my desk drawers and stuffed all my private letters and papers in the bag. He took the three notebooks from the year I'd lost my freedom to write. As I've explained, they contained my commentary on daily events.

The sun was starting to rise. They'd worked from four in the morning until nine. They were tired, and so was I. I hadn't even washed my face or had a cup of tea. I tried to leave the room to put on the kettle. Hamdi grabbed me by the arm.

'Where are you going?' he asked. 'You can't leave.'

'Why not?'

'Because you're in custody.'

'Let me make some tea. We'll drink it together.'

'An officer will go with you,' he said. Tea must have sounded good to him.

I went to the kitchen with the officer and made tea. The man carried the tray. We drank with the other policemen.

After they were finished with the library, we went to the living room. The group with Zekeriya was done as well. Parmaksız Hamdi put everything they'd gathered on the table. They wrote out a list of the books, notebooks and papers they were taking. Then they made us sign it.

'When will you return these to us?' I asked.

'God knows,' he said.

And since God was put in charge, we never saw those books and papers again.

We are arrested

It was the evening of 7 February. The doorbell rang around nine o'clock. İclal opened the door and told us they'd come from the Police Directorate. They wanted to see Zekeriya. He went to the door and, after a short while, came back with the officers. One of them showed us an arrest warrant.

'We're leaving at once,' he said.

A boil had recently formed on Zekeriya's neck. He had to go to the doctor every day for treatment. 'Let us stay at home tonight,' I said to the officer. 'We'll show Zekeriya's boil to the doctor tomorrow and go from there.'

'No,' he said, 'you have to go now.'

They didn't even give us time to pack. We took the automobile ferry from Üsküdar to Istanbul. From there, we went to the Police Directorate. They took us to see a police chief on the third floor. The chief started questioning us without even letting us sit down.

'This is what happens if you disobey the government,' he said in a harsh voice.

We didn't answer. This was democracy under the Saraçoğlu administration, and we expected nothing less.

'You will stay here tonight,' he said.

'Then please allow us to bring linens and beds. The owner of the nearby Karasi Hotel is a relative of ours. We can have beds brought over from there.'

'Out of the question,' he said.

They took us upstairs and into an office steeped in cigarette smoke. Clearly, the policemen who worked there had smoked all day without opening a window.

'You'll spend the night here,' said the officer who took us inside.

'Where will we sleep?'

'You can sleep on these.' He pointed at the dirty desks. 'Sleep on the floor if you want.'

We immediately opened the windows. It was cold outside, but sleeping in that foul air was impossible. After airing out the room, we laid down on the desks. I didn't mind too much, but for Zekeriya, with the wound on his neck, it was torture. We couldn't sleep, not because we'd been arrested, but because we weren't used to sleeping on wooden desks.

Early the next morning, I went to use the bathroom. Cami Baykut was in the hallway. He'd turned up the collar of his coat and was pacing up and down. I tried to approach him but was stopped by a policeman. Halil Lütfi was also there, standing outside an office door, lost in thought as if pondering what he'd done to deserve this.

I went back inside. Soon, the officers working in the room started arriving. While we watched from our chairs, they sat down at their desks and went about their business. We waited like that until noon. Finally, a policeman came in.

'Come on,' he said, 'we're going.'

'Where?'

'To Sultan Ahmet Prison.'

They put us in cars, driving us to the prison as if we were out for a picnic in Göksu.[2] The iron-barred gates opened, and a gendarme escorted us to the warden's office. As soon as we went in, a tall old man with black, curly hair embraced Cami Baykut. This person was Sırrı Bellioğlu. He'd been the minister of transportation in the first Turkish cabinet established at the outset of the War of Independence. Baykut had been a member of the same cabinet. Now, these two ministers of the War of Independence were reunited in prison. It was a sombre sight to behold.

After falling out with Atatürk, Bellioğlu had been removed from his ministry and never given another post. During the Second World War, with fascist movements sweeping the land and Turkey appearing poised to join the German camp, he'd begun sending critical, anonymous letters to Turkish statesmen. He'd finally been caught depositing some of his letters in a mailbox.

Releasing Baykut from his embrace, Bellioğlu came over to me, took my hand and kissed it. He turned to the prison warden, who was sitting at his desk.

'This woman is the greatest hero of them all,' he said.

The warden was a very polite man. 'We'll do whatever we can to ensure your well-being,' he said.

Prior to our arrival, progressive doctors working at the prison had advised against placing me in the same ward as the other female prisoners. They'd arranged a bed for me in the room of Aliye Hanım, a female prison guard. Zekeriya, Cami Baykut and Halil Lütfi were put up in Sırrı Bellioğlu's quarters.

A guard came to fetch me. We left the warden's room, walked back through the entrance hall and onto the quad where the prisoners took their walks. The women's prison was to the right of the quad. We entered through a small, narrow door. Aliye Hanım had an office there, as small as a chicken coop. She came out as soon as she saw us.

'Welcome,' she said.

She took me to her living quarters. We crossed the women's quad, which was no larger than a small room. Some female prisoners were cooking at their barbecues. I felt all eyes on me. We stepped into a moldy-smelling entrance hall. There, Aliye Hanım showed me the infirmary's quarantine room. It was built on a dirt surface. Inside, there were a bunk bed and some large holes in the ground. Newly arrived prisoners slept in those holes for five to ten days.

'There are rats as big as cats in there,' Aliye Hanım said. 'But we won't put you in quarantine.'

Ascending a flight of wooden stairs, we arrived at Aliye Hanım's room. It looked out on Sultan Ahmet Square to one side and the sea to the other. The furniture consisted of two beds, a little desk and two chairs.

I sat down on my bed and began considering how I should pass my time in here.

---

[2] TN: A favourite recreation area for Istanbul dwellers at the time.

Life in prison

The women's prison was an ideal place for conducting social research. I spoke to the inmates every day, listening to why they'd committed their crimes and ended up in prison. There were three rooms on my landing. One was an enormous hall full of bunk beds. It held around thirty beds, with sixty women sleeping in them. When there were too many inmates, two people slept in the same bed. The other ward was smaller. Because the rooms were cold, the women took their braziers to the entrance hall and cooked there. The heavy smell of charcoal filled every room.

There were only two or three murderesses in the prison. The majority of the inmates were thieves and prostitutes. Heroin addicts were a case study in and of themselves. I was a novelty to all of them. They found it extraordinary that a female journalist had been thrown into prison.

The first night I was there, two women came to my room. 'We prepared a show for you tonight,' they said. 'Would you come?'

I went along. All women had gathered at the top of the stairs, some of them sitting on the stairs, some on the floor. A few held self-made instruments to accompany the singer, Nuriye, who'd been a famous bar performer. She sang the song 'Kır Belini Alidayı'.[3] The others kept time and sang along. Even now, whenever I hear this song, I remember my prison days.

Nuriye was in prison for murdering an officer she'd loved. Slowly, I got to know all the prominent inmates. I wrote their petitions to the prosecutor and read out the letters they received. They came to me for advice on everything.

The noisiest day in prison was *hamam* [Turkish bath] day. To go to the *hamam*, we'd take our bags and pass through the men's courtyard. On the way back, the male prisoners would line up on both sides of our path and hand the women letters and heroin. Back in their own quarters, the women would fight over the heroin and love letters. They'd scream and shout, jump on each other, tear out each other's hair, and rough each other up. Occasionally, the fighting grew so bad that Aliye Hanım had to blow her whistle and call in the gendarmes. It was amusing to see fighting women separated by gendarmes. Sometimes, the women returned to their wards covered in blood.

One night, they invited me over to the big ward. They told me it was trial night; once a month, they held a session to interrogate new arrivals. I saw them put a large desk in the middle of the ward. Three women sat down at it, a chief judge and two other members of the court. Another woman sat across from them, pretending to take minutes. Two inmates were brought before the court. One of them was in prison for stealing, the other for prostitution. The judge first spoke to the thief, asking her why she had stolen.

'I have three children,' the woman answered. 'I'm a widow and can't find work. I stole to feed my children.' She never tried to deny her crime.

The second inmate said the following:

---

[3] TN: Roughly, 'Shake your hips, Uncle Ali'.

> I used to work at a factory and as a charwoman. When I lost my jobs, a woman in the neighbourhood convinced me to start selling myself. The job brought in more money than all the others. The police arrested me for unlicensed prostitution. There are hundreds of women who work in licensed brothels, and the police don't touch them. But they jailed me for not having a licence.

The women playing the judges knew the proper procedure from their many sessions in court. After listening to the culprits, they started whispering among themselves. Then, the chief judge stood up. She sentenced the prostitute to five years and the thief to three. When the culprits heard the verdict, all hell broke loose. The woman sentenced to five years demanded to know why prostitution was a greater crime than theft.

'I'm the one selling myself!' she yelled. 'What's it to the police or the government? I'm okay with it, and the men I see are okay with it too! So what's it to them? I'm not stealing anyone's property. Theft is the real crime!'

Now the thief started yelling.

'I'm stealing because I have to,' she said. 'What's your excuse for disobeying the government?'

The argument grew. The other thieves and prostitutes in the ward each stood up for their companion. Finally, they all fell upon each other, hitting one another and ripping out each other's hair. Aliye Hanım blew her whistle, and the gendarmes stormed inside. The women attacked the gendarmes as well. I escaped to my room.

Sociologists and psychologists write volumes on the issue of crime and punishment. But these women, with their highly realistic approach, solved the issue in a matter of minutes. In a capitalist society, it wasn't a crime for a woman to sell her flesh. But the government issued licences and confined the profession to brothels. If selling one's flesh wasn't illegal, why was it a crime to do it without a licence? The thief's reasoning was equally sound: if a woman with three children couldn't find a job, what could she do but steal?

Once a week, the inmates were allowed family visits. On such occasions, they and their families lined up on opposite sides of the iron bars. We were exempt from this rule and could receive visitors every day. Zekeriya, Cami Baykut, Halil Lütfi and some imprisoned merchants met their guests in a room next to the warden's office. I joined them there in the afternoons to talk to the visitors. One day, A. M., an imprisoned merchant, told me about a female inmate. Her name was Madame Atina, and she'd been the owner of Beyoğlu's most luxurious brothel.

'Talk to her,' he said. 'She can tell you many political secrets.'

I made friends with Madame Atina. She was a rather beautiful middle-aged woman. The police had been extorting her at the brothel. When she hadn't paid the amount they demanded, they'd found a pretext to lock her up.

I made my own tea in the mornings, so I invited her over one day. After some trivial questions, I asked if any statesmen and prominent people visited her establishment.

'Just a few,' she said. 'Usually, they told us to set up a big table for them. They ate, drank and talked, spreading their documents out on the table and calculating things. More often than not, they brought along some German military officers. The Germans put bundles and bundles of dollars on the table. They didn't let us inside, so I observed them through a crack in the door.'

'Who came, for instance?'

'S. K. H., the Secretary General of the People's Party; General Ş. N.; and S. S. from the Foreign Ministry.'

Each time we spoke, Madame Atina gave me more names. It was clear that important people found her establishment safe for conducting such transactions. But soon, she started avoiding me. One day, we met in the courtyard.

'I can't come to your room anymore,' she said. 'I was called to the Police Directorate. They forbade me to talk to you.'

I laughed. It seemed the police had grown suspicious of our conversations.

Around that time, I received a letter from my younger daughter, Yıldız, who was studying in London. She'd read the British papers' reports on the destruction of *Tan*. She told me about the coverage and included some newspaper clippings. During a speech in the House of Commons about Turkish–British relations, Labour MP Philips Price had said to the Prime Minister, 'You claim Turkey is our ally. But we haven't forgotten this ally's wartime conduct. Even today, the Turkish government destroys the printing presses of those who oppose fascism, bans socialist parties and imprisons their founders. It locks up intellectuals like Sabiha Sertel with murderers and thieves.'

I had to laugh when I read this. I wondered what Philips Price would have said if he'd heard that Madame Atina, a brothel owner, had been banned from talking to me because I compromised her virtue.

Yıldız also wrote disapprovingly about Ahmet Emin Yalman. When she'd heard he was in London, she'd met him at the embassy to get some news about us. After telling her what happened, Yalman had said to her, 'I also fought for democracy, but your parents went too far. They championed leftist ideas. They deserve their punishment.'

A few days later, Yalman came to visit us. We were all surprised to see him walk through the door. He held out his hand to Zekeriya, but Zekeriya didn't take it. Then he held it out to me. I said, 'How can you shake hands with people who deserve to be punished?' He was mortified and walked off with his tail between his legs. If Yalman wasn't punished like us, he owed it to the Americans who had pulled strings and to the bourgeois friends who had shielded him.

The trial begins

The prosecutor's office informed the prison that our trial would begin on 5 March 1946. According to the warden, the gendarmerie would allow us to take a car to the courthouse. I would've preferred to walk. I felt like a mill horse from circling around and around inside the prison. I was dizzy; I needed to walk and get some fresh air. But this was deemed unnecessary.

Early in the morning, the gendarmes drove Zekeriya, Cami Baykut, Halil Lütfi and me to the courthouse. Cami Bey and I were in the same car. When we arrived, Zekeriya was paying the driver.

'Who're the old man and the woman?' the driver asked.

'Cami Baykut and Sabiha Sertel,' Zekeriya answered.

The driver dropped Zekeriya's money on the ground.

'Do you think I'd charge Sabiha Sertel for a ride?' he said. 'She's in this mess for defending our cause!'

Zekeriya insisted, but to no avail. The incident was very heartening for me.

After climbing endless stairs, we arrived at the hall of the Second High Criminal Court. The Police Directorate had taken precautions to prevent crowds from gathering at the courthouse. As a result, there were only a few people inside. We entered the defendants' box, which was enclosed with bars like a cage. At our front and back were policemen, gendarmes and soldiers with bayonets. The panel of judges consisted of Chief Judge Salim Başol and Judges Aza Nüsret and Nevres Tiryakioğlu. In the prosecutor's seat was Hicabi Dinç, Deputy Prosecutor and Chief of the Second Investigative Bureau.

They began by reading the First Investigative Court's verdict from February 18, 1946. It stated that Sabiha Sertel would be tried for the article 'The Clamour of the Status Quo', which was published in her *Tan* column, 'Görüşler', on 3 September 1945. Cami Baykut was on trial for the article 'The Historical Role of the Intellectual Class', published in the same newspaper on 5 September 1945. Finally, Zekeriya Sertel would be tried for the article 'Can We Expect Anything from the Government and the Assembly?' in the 27 September 1945, issue of the same paper. These articles were found to publicly insult and deride the Grand National Assembly and the government's moral character. Therefore, Zekeriya Sertel, Sabiha Sertel and Cami Baykut would face charges under Articles 159-1, 173-3, 59 and 69 of the Penal Code, while Halil Lütfi would face charges under all of the above except Article 59. In accordance with Articles 196 and 200 of the Law of Criminal Procedure, the defendants would remain in custody for the duration of the trial.

Chief Judge Başol asked whether we preferred an open or closed trial. We saw no need for a closed trial; we had nothing to hide from the public. And so, the court decided on an open trial.

Next, the court heard from Zekeriya Sertel. 'My article contains no element of insult to the moral character of the Assembly and the government,' he said. 'For this to be ascertained, the prosecution must provide a definition of insult. Since we live in a democratic country, it is within my rights to voice criticism.'

I was heard after Zekeriya. 'My article "The Clamour of the Status Quo" concerns the struggle between the status quo and its opposition in the Assembly and the press,' I said. 'It contains no insult to the moral character of the Assembly and the government. In essence, the article describes the pressure exerted by the People's Party on the opposition party in the Assembly and on opposition writers in the press. In his indictment, the prosecutor finds no need to analyse the article's substance. Instead, he simply defends the People's Party. But this case was not opened by the People's Party. Does the prosecutor represent the People's Party or the public? Whether the article contains an insult depends on the prosecutor's interpretation. There is no proof of an actual insult.'

Finally, the court heard from Cami Baykut. 'My article "The Historical Role of the Intellectual Class" concerns intellectuals regardless of nationality,' he said. 'There is

Figure 10.1 Istanbul, March 1946. The only people arrested after the *Tan* riot were the Sertels and *Tan* colleagues. Sabiha defended herself in the headline-making trial.

nothing here that insults the moral character of the Assembly and the government. If such an insult is present, the prosecution needs to identify the precise words and expressions that constitute it. And there was definitely no intent to insult.'

As soon as the defendants had spoken, Hicabi Dinç, the prosecutor, rose in anger.

'Sabiha Sertel accuses me of acting as an advocate for the People's Party. My office has no connection with politics. We are charged with protecting the public interest. We exercise our duty no differently in press crimes than in any other crimes. This country is under the rule of justice. We cannot allow the highest institutions of our society and state, such as the Grand National Assembly, to be defamed.

'The defendant Zekeriya Sertel demands to know how the state prosecution defines criticism and freedom in the democratic country of Turkey. That kind of academic discussion is impossible here. Before the law, the best freedom is that which benefits the country, reflects the moral quality of the people, and protects the rights and interests of the state.'

In effect, the prosecutor confessed that his definition of freedom protected not the people's rights, but the rights and interests of the state.

The court rejected our lawyers' request to form a panel of experts. The case was adjourned to 10 March, when the prosecutor would present his statement with regard to the accusations.

We returned to the prison, where we found the visiting room crowded with friends. Before even asking us about the trial, they showed us the newspapers. The People's Party had removed the expression 'Permanent Chairman' from its charter, replacing it with 'Chairman'. Phrases like 'Eternal Chief' and 'Permanent Chairman', reserved for dictators, were becoming history. Whatever the outcome of the trial, this was a battle that we'd won.

The second session

The second court session began with prosecutor Hicabi Dinç reading out the indictment before the same panel of judges. The document was several pages long, so it took a while. The prosecutor claimed to have studied the three newspaper articles at length. He'd arrived at the conclusion that they insulted the moral character of the government and the Assembly. He declared that the press was only free within the limits of the law and that the Constitution was clear on this matter. Accordingly, he stated, Zekeriya Sertel, myself and Halil Lütfi Dördüncü were guilty of insulting the Grand National Assembly and the government of the Republic. The other defendant, Cami Baykut, was only guilty of insulting the moral character of the Grand National Assembly.

The prosecutor requested that the court implement the Penal Code as outlined in the first session. Article 159 called for a prison sentence of one to six years. Article 173, Paragraph 3 required continued police supervision after completion of the sentence. Finally, Article 69 called for the fullest punishment available by law in the case of repeat offenders, which Hicabi Dinç claimed we were.

The prosecutor concluded his speech. Chief Judge Başol asked if we, along with our lawyers, would present our defence now. We asked for time to prepare. The trial was adjourned to 26 March.

We had six days to ready our defence. Our case was so clear and our cause so just that describing and defending them would be much easier than waging our battles in the press. I prepared my defence in two nights. The day after I finished, Aliye Hanım told me a female lawyer had come to see me. I went to the visiting room and greeted the woman, whom I'd met before.

'A. I., the secretary of the party's Istanbul branch, sends his regards,' she said. 'He asks you to present a tempered defence. If you accept, they will release you.'

I answered without hesitation.

'A conviction will cost me nothing,' I said. 'It's not in my nature to be submissive. Send my greetings to the secretary. Those who defend a just cause have no fear of being convicted.'

She'd barely left when I was joined by my older brother Celal Deriş, a lawyer. He wanted to read my defence. I gave it to him.

'This is too harsh,' he said. 'Let's soften it a bit.'

'I'm not just defending myself before the court,' I replied, 'but before the public as well. The people's verdict concerns me more than the verdict of the court.'

He tried to change my mind, but I stood my ground.

On the night of 14 March, I took to bed with a fever of 39 degrees Celsius. The doctor said it was pneumonia and wrote a letter to the prosecutor's office excusing me from the trial. The next day, I put the letter in my bag and went to the courthouse, fever be damned. The lawyers delivered their defence speeches. Then, Salim Başol gave the word to Zekeriya Sertel. I will only recount a few lines of his lengthy defence:

> I stand trial for an article that contains no criminal element. In fact, it's a highly objective and truthful piece of criticism. The prosecutor ascribes words to me that I never uttered. We live in an age when our statesmen keep stressing the need for more democracy, and yet we imprison and prosecute a citizen for writing a critical article. This proves there is no freedom in the country. This trial is a disgrace for our nation!

I was called on next. As I write these lines, I don't have a copy of my defence speech at hand, so I'll only highlight its main points. In summary, here is what I said:

> My article concerns the People's Party and the newly established opposition party. Despite all claims of democracy, the People's Party has resorted to terror, intimidation and censorship to crush the opposition in the Assembly and the press. Parties are independent organizations. They do not represent the Assembly or the authority of the state. Consequently, criticism of a party does not equal criticism of the state's authority or the government. There is no law against criticizing parties. This is the basis of my critique of this country's 'One Party, One Chief' system.[4]

After the defence speeches, Hicabi Dinç spoke again and accused the defendants of demagoguery. The Chief Judge declared the trial concluded and asked our lawyers if they had anything to add. The lawyers rested their case. The defendants were granted the final word, which led to another dispute between the prosecutor and us.

'The prosecution accuses us of demagoguery,' I said. 'This accusation is baseless. Our defence is not political, but politics inevitably plays a role in any trial about political publications. The prosecution also accuses us of harbouring ulterior motives. This, too, is an unfounded accusation. We are confident the High Court will let justice and right prevail. I'd like to close by saying that it isn't Sabiha Sertel who sits in this defendant's chair, but democracy itself. Democracy will be convicted or acquitted today.'

Cami Baykut declared he was in full agreement with our statements and asked that they be recorded in the minutes.

The trial was over, and we awaited the verdict. But Hicabi Dinç stood up one last time.

---

[4] Because the papers didn't print our defence arguments, we published them in a pamphlet called *Davamız ve Müdafaamız* [Our Trial and Our Defence]. Sadly, I have no copy at my disposal. [TN: The word 'davamız' in the original Turkish title can be translated as 'our trial' or 'our cause', a double meaning that surely was not lost on the Sertels.]

'It is not customary for the prosecution to speak after the defence,' he said. 'And in the previous court session, I replied to Sabiha and Zekeriya Sertel's slanderous allegations – allegations that exceeded the limits of justifiable defence. Nonetheless, in this session, they used my accusation of demagoguery to attack me once again and repeated the libellous remarks in their written defence. Therefore, I am forced to respond.

'I cannot accept the baseless attacks and false accusations levelled against me by the defendants Sabiha and Zekeriya Sertel. They have abused the immunity granted by their right to present a defence. They have obfuscated this trial by interjecting all manner of irrelevant, weighty ideas. Well, I turn their accusations right back on them. These defendants have tried to paint themselves as scholars, professors of democracy, even as heroes. But as I pointed out earlier, this effort only served to expose their aggressive and destructive character. Demagoguery is too light a word to describe the defendants' conduct. I repeat my statement from the prior session: A nation in which the champions of truth have less courage than its enemies has no chance of surviving or arriving at the truth.'

These words were an object lesson in the prosecutor's own demagoguery. His efforts to have us convicted were basically an application for an Assembly seat on the People's Party ticket.

The Chief Judge ended the session, and the court announced its verdict:

> The defendants' actions constitute a crime under Article 159 of the Turkish Penal Code. This court unanimously finds Zekeriya Sertel, Sabiha Sertel and Cami Baykut guilty of insulting and deriding the Grand National Assembly. Under Article 159, Paragraph 1 of the Turkish Penal Code, they are each hereby sentenced to one year in prison. Since Cami Baykut is over 65 years old, his sentence is reduced by one-sixth under Article 59 of the same code. He will serve ten months in prison. Halil Lütfi Dördüncü is also sentenced to one year of prison under Article 159, but his sentence is reduced by one-sixth under Article 20 of the Press Law. The defendants are acquitted of insulting the government's moral character. The verdict may be appealed.

Long story short, each of us was sentenced to one year in prison.

Through the prison window

We appealed the verdict. We were watching the world and current events through a prison window now.

The press reported important news. On 5 April, *Ulus* proclaimed, 'The *Missouri*, one of the largest US battleships, has arrived in Turkey. The American sailors are coming ashore. Parades are being staged everywhere, and all of Istanbul is in a festive mood.'

Falih Rıfkı Atay described the festivities as follows:

> The *Missouri*'s arrival in the Bosporus has been interpreted in various ways. This battleship is a genuine titan of the sea. The flag it carries represents the largest

military force in the world today. But the Turks, like all other Mediterranean nations, salute this flag as a harbinger of freedom and peace.

We know what America wants: a world based on the mutual safety of free, equal and sovereign nations. A world without war and aggression. A world ruled only by the bonds and treaties of virtue and law. Those who desire such a world see the American flag as their guiding star. The *Missouri*'s voyage is not about pomp and circumstance. But it should reassure us of America's resolve to prevent military aggression and deliver freedom, peace and security to all nations. The *Missouri* is an invincible manifestation of this very resolve. The admirals, officers and soldiers who came to Istanbul on the *Missouri* and other battleships are guests of the Turkish people. They bring happiness and joy to every home.

As I write these lines today, I wonder if Falih Rıfkı Atay feels any shame at all when he thinks of US machinations to deprive people of their freedom and independence, crushing movements of national liberation in Latin America, Asia and Africa. I wonder if he thinks of Vietnam, where the USA bombed innocent people with napalm, turning the entire country into a river of blood. Falih was thrilled to see his country hit the jackpot with American colonialism.

This was how people greeted the same country that we fight today to regain our independence.

After prison

On 30 June, Şükrü Saraçoğlu made the following statement to the *Daily Telegraph*: 'Turkey's foreign policy decisions are binding, and we are fully committed to them. The country is not divided, nor has it turned quisling.[5] There may be domestic disputes between the parties, but we stand united on foreign policy. In this area, there is not the slightest discrepancy.'

Both parties were in agreement on opening the country to foreign capital and handing over the reins of our economy to the USA. We had to watch these momentous decisions from prison. Progressive papers and journals had been closed down. Socialist parties were banned. Nobody could raise their voice as the country was sold off to America.

The People's Party and the Democrat Party both were preparing for the elections. In order to boost its chances, the Democrat Party wanted to recruit Marshal Fevzi Çakmak as a candidate.[6] Çakmak had been retired from duty for opposing the People's Party. He was still a party member and had a seat in the Assembly, but it was rumoured he would resign.

---

[5] TN: This expression, which Sertel employs with a capital 'Q', originated under the administration of Vidkun Quisling (1887–1945), who was head of the government of Norway during the country's occupation by Nazi Germany. Due to his enthusiastic support for Nazi policies, Quisling was executed at the end of the Second World War, and his name became synonymous with 'collaborator' or 'traitor'.

[6] TN: Fevzi Çakmak (1876–1950) was one of the most prominent military commanders of the Turkish War of Independence.

Around this time, the First Chamber of the Supreme Court of Appeals reached its decision in our case:

> After a review of the newspaper articles leading to the investigation and conviction, the following verdict has been reached: The Istanbul Court regarded the abovementioned articles as sufficient grounds for punishment. However, it failed to present the necessary rationale for this decision. It also failed to probe the defendants' motives. According to the First Penal Chamber of the Supreme Court of Appeals, the articles contain no insult. They do not overstep the limits of legitimate criticism. The sentences of the four convicts are hereby overturned. They are to be released from prison at once.

The warden's office was notified of the verdict. I was in my room, exhausted from pacing up and down the quad. Aliye Hanım ran up to me.

'You're leaving,' she said. 'You've been acquitted!'

I couldn't believe it. She took me to the warden. Zekeriya, Cami Baykut, Halil Lütfi and Sırrı Bellioğlu were already there. We were all overjoyed. Since it was evening, the warden told us to stay that night so the necessary procedures could be completed. One more night in prison hardly made a difference to us.

When I returned to the women's prison, the inmates approached me. They'd already heard about my release.

'We'll give you a send-off tonight,' they said. 'It's our tradition here. We hold a farewell celebration for anyone who leaves.'

There was an empty space under the stairs leading up to the second floor. The inmates considered it to be a shrine. They lit candles for me there. After dinner, everyone gathered in the big ward. Nuriye and some others took turns singing songs like 'Hapishane Çeşmesi Yandan Akar' and 'Köyümde Akan Irmaklar'.[7] These weren't songs of celebration; they expressed the inmates' longing for freedom, home and loved ones.

The next morning, I said goodbye to my boarding house of four months.

---

[7] TN: Roughly, 'The Prison's Fountain Runs to the Side' and 'The Brooks that Flow in My Village'.

11

The Human Rights Association

We were back home, but had no opportunity to work. Cami Baykut came to visit us twice a week, full of energy despite his advanced age.

As a young military officer, during the age of Abdülhamid II, Baykut was exiled to the deserts of Tripolitania, spending years away from his homeland. After many adventures and hardships, he became an aide to Recep Paşa, the Ottoman military commander of the province.

He joined the Committee of Union and Progress, playing a major role in toppling Abdülhamid during the 1908 Revolution. With the Unionists in power, he won a seat in the first Ottoman Assembly as deputy for Fezzan. But when the Committee of Union and Progress established a dictatorship, Cami Bey aligned with the opposition. His efforts in opposition failed, however, and he retired from political life.

Following the occupation of Istanbul and Izmir after the First World War, Cami Bey went to Ankara and joined the War of Independence, serving as interior minister in Atatürk's first cabinet. But soon, he started criticizing Atatürk's regime as well and was forced to retire.

He re-emerged during the Second World War, especially the Saraçoğlu years, when he fought against those who pushed for Turkey to throw in its lot with Germany. Undergoing a major ideological change, he started to view socialism as Turkey's path to liberation. But he lacked a clear vision of how socialism could be achieved in the country.

To him, the biggest threats were Catholics and the Pope. He suspected their involvement in all kinds of political events. But he believed in harnessing the power of religion on the path to socialism. Villagers made up 80 per cent of Turkey's population, he maintained, and all of them were religious. He claimed that many Qur'anic verses and principles were compatible with socialist ideology. One ought to use these, he said, to spread the ideology among the masses.

According to Cami Bey, Islam accepted the concept of private property but opposed large fortunes being amassed in the hands of the few. That was why Islam introduced the obligation of *zekat*.[1] Islam also emphasized the importance of public property. Thus, the *Mecelle*[2] decreed that underground resources and large estates should be managed by the state. Finally, Cami Bey stressed Islam's opposition to making profit by charging interest.

---

[1] TN: One of the five pillars of Islam, *zekat* is an obligatory redistributive religious tax.
[2] TN: The Ottoman Civil Code that took effect in 1877.

Cami Bey conceded that socialism today couldn't be based on these principles, and that industrialization and class struggle hadn't existed in Muhammad's time. But he insisted one should make tactical use of religion to promote socialism.

Even after prison, Cami Bey kept urging us to oppose those who fought ideas with hatchets. Roosevelt's Four Freedoms and the Treaty of San Francisco[3] had undeniably triggered a trend toward democratization in the country. This trend, he said, should be harnessed to establish a human rights association. He enlisted the help of Tevfik Rüştü Aras and Zekeriya Sertel to found such an organization. As its chair, he envisioned Marshal Fevzi Çakmak.

Baykut and Marshal Çakmak had been comrades-in-arms and fellow cabinet members during the War of Independence. They had great fondness and respect for each other. Çakmak also knew Tevfik Rüştü Aras from the latter's days as foreign minister. The marshal had been an early supporter of the Democrat Party (DP), declaring he'd contest the elections as an independent candidate on the party's ticket. He was highly critical of the Republican People's Party and İnönü in particular.

The Democrat Party's election campaign was gathering momentum. Large parts of the population were so fed up with the CHP that they rallied around the DP without even knowing its programme. The election was seen as a fight for freedom, a war against dictatorship. The Democrat Party posters depicted a raised hand with its palm facing outward and the word 'enough' underneath. They became a symbol capturing everyone's feelings. People regarded the DP as a saviour.

The DP's initial plan was to leverage Marshal Çakmak's prestige. Having him on their ticket, even as an independent candidate, was sure to help them win the people's hearts. For this reason, they welcomed the idea of a Human Rights Association founded by the marshal, Aras and Baykut. At the same time, though, they were wary of the marshal's popularity and clout with the public, fearing he might seize the reins of the party one day.

The Interior Ministry announced that the election would be held on 21 July 1946. The Human Rights Association prepared its launch, holding meetings at our house. Cami Baykut was in close contact with the marshal, who assured him that he was prepared to give his life for the liberation of the country. These proclamations of self-sacrifice were frequently used by Tevfik Rüştü Aras and other DP founders. During an election rally in Izmir, the marshal repeated these words before the crowd. The pro-government newspapers attacked him at once.

Marshal Çakmak's Izmir rally was a great success. People flocked from towns and villages to see him. They hoisted his car on their shoulders, yelling, 'You are the father of the people; save us!' The government was embroiled in an economic crisis. People were hungry and destitute, and they yearned for deliverance. Unaware of how to achieve this on their own, they pinned their hopes on the marshal and the Democrat Party.

The marshal returned to Istanbul triumphantly. He invited Baykut, Zekeriya and Aras to his mansion. Prior to the visit, Cami Bey came to our house. He was accompanied

---

[3] TN: Again, Sertel is likely referring to the United Nations Conference on International Organization held in San Francisco in 1945.

by Evliyazade Özdemir, a student of his and Adnan Menderes' nephew. Özdemir deeply respected Cami Bey and was always by his side. Aras dropped by as well. They'd planned to visit the marshal together, but Aras kept making excuses, refusing to go. We all tried to convince him until finally, Özdemir became angry.

'You're all the same,' he said. 'My uncle Adnan Menderes, you, Celal Bayar – you only care about your own interests. Freedom, democracy, the people – these are just political passports you use to climb the ranks. You want the DP to give you an Assembly seat, so you'll do whatever Bayar says. And Bayar has grown scared of the marshal because of his reception in Izmir and the attacks on him by right-wing papers. He's turning his back on the marshal. But Fevzi Çakmak is an asset for you. The People's Party is trying to rob you of that asset, and you're falling for it!'

Aras went beet red. 'I cannot act on my own in this matter,' he finally said. 'Let me talk to my associates.'

I was surprised by Özdemir's courage. I was even more surprised when I read much later, in exile, that during the Yassıada trials,[4] he'd admitted to being a police informer. He seemed like such a pure, honourable man. When Cami Bey died, he wept bitterly at the funeral. It was hard to believe he'd been working for the police all along. What a perfect actor he turned out to be.

Cami Bey, Zekeriya and Özdemir went to see the marshal, leaving me alone with Aras. I asked him why he'd refused to go.

'It's an honour for me to work with the marshal,' he said. 'But everyone is worried by his sudden rise and the Izmir rally, not just the People's Party but my friends in the DP as well. They fear he may become another Atatürk.'

'But the Human Rights Association isn't a political party,' I replied. 'How would it harm the DP if you joined it and worked with the marshal?'

'The People's Party would use it against us. As a matter of fact, they already do.'

'You keep saying you'd put your life on the line for the cause. How can you retreat at the first sign of trouble?'

'I'm not saying I won't join the Human Rights Association. I just need to talk to my associates first.'

Soon afterward, Cami Bey and the others returned. They said the marshal was very happy and had instructed them to prepare the Association's programme.

'The marshal is equally upset with the People's Party and the founders of the DP,' Cami Bey said. 'As he puts it, "Both parties criticize Tevfik Rüştü Aras for advocating friendship with the Soviets. But Aras is right. We need the USSR to be our friend. They say the Soviets demand Kars and Ardahan[5] from us. But they also demanded many provinces after the First World War, all the way to Van. We sat down and talked with them. Not only did they abandon their claims, but they also gave us Kars and Ardahan, which were theirs at the time. Just like then, we need to sit down with the Soviets and have a conversation. Antagonizing them won't solve anything," he says.'

---

4 TN: The trials against the Democrat Party following the 1960 coup d'état.
5 TN: North-eastern provinces of Turkey, bordering the former Soviet Union.

Cami Bey was thrilled by the marshal's interest in the Human Rights Association. But newspapers continued their attacks on the marshal and the Soviet Union. This was just the beginning of a campaign to beat him into submission.

Fearing a DP landslide, the People's Party moved up the election date. They won the July elections by a slim margin.[6] İnönü remained president, Kazım Karabekir became chairman of the Assembly and Recep Peker was appointed prime minister.

Following a trip to Ankara, the marshal stepped up his involvement in the Human Rights Association. By this time, political circles in the capital had grown alarmed by his collaboration with Aras, Baykut and Zekeriya. Falih Rıfkı Atay, writing for the pro-government paper *Ulus*, started targeting Aras in his articles, focusing on Aras's support for Turkish–Soviet friendship:

> Tevfik Rüştü Aras, Secretary General of the Human Rights Association, wants us to resolve our issues with Russia through direct negotiation. These views were made public a year ago, in the newspaper *Tan*. Time and again, Aras's articles appeared in that paper along with those of Zekeriya Sertel and Cami Baykut. But now, when I point this out, Aras denies he holds these views. And not just that – he wants us to believe nobody else holds them, either, that I invented the whole thing!
>
> Aras is a former foreign minister, a politician who allegedly cares about protecting his name against false rumours in foreign countries. And yet, he wrote for *Tan*, a paper that opposes and stands far outside mainstream domestic and foreign policy, and he established close friendships with its writers. Wasn't he afraid this would raise suspicions about his own views?
>
> Around the time he wrote for *Tan*, Aras spoke with a *New York Times* correspondent about the Polish borders. Here's what he said, word for word: 'We must consider this: the Soviets rightfully feel they've shouldered the whole weight of the war for the past two years, spilling their blood like a river. Now, they're taking precautions so the Russian people won't ever endure such a slaughter again. No one can blame them for this. Clearly, one way for them to prevent future wars is to establish friendly governments in countries near their borders.'

Atay regarded Aras's desire for friendship with the Soviets as a crime, even treason. In the same article, he also touched on the Human Rights Association:

> We read in the papers that Marshal Fevzi Çakmak and Tevfik Rüştü Aras travelled on the same train from Ankara to Istanbul one day. The next thing we know, a Human Rights Association was founded, and Zekeriya Sertel, Tevfik Rüştü Aras and Cami Baykut were on its board of directors. Many people were surprised to see Marshal Çakmak among the founders. The Democrat Party quickly distanced itself from this association. We heard the marshal was urged to leave as well.

---

[6] TN: Historians widely consider this election to have been rigged by the People's Party.

> The latest news is that Marshal Fevzi Çakmak attended a Human Rights Association meeting before leaving Istanbul for his Izmir rally. At this meeting, he was elected chairman of the Association and Tevfik Rüştü Aras became Secretary General. Cami Baykut also was elected to the board.
>
> We don't know how this movement will evolve. But we understand that it labels some citizens as fascists and shuts them out. Until now, Radio Moscow was the only source discussing fascists in Turkey.

On 20 October 1946, the Human Rights Association was officially launched. Apart from the marshal, Aras, Zekeriya and Baykut, its founders included Kenan Öner, the Democrat Party's Istanbul chairman; Sadık Aldoğan, a retired general; Hasan Rıza Soyak, a former deputy; Hamdi Artak, former ambassador to Berlin; and Raşit Karel, a finance minister of the Ottoman Constitutional Era. The day before, the Association held its first official meeting at Kenan Öner's office in Karaköy Palas, electing Fevzi Çakmak as its Chairman.

An alliance among Marshal Çakmak, the DP and the leftists posed a grave danger to İnönü's reign. The People's Party took steps to sabotage the Association, and Atay's smear campaign against the movement was embraced by all newspapers. The Democrat Party, intimidated by how the Association was being used to attack Aras and the marshal, cut its ties with both of them. On 22 October, Atay published the following article in *Ulus*:

> For some politicians [referring to Aras and the marshal], the only goal is toppling the CHP government. To achieve this goal, they threw all their weight behind the Democrat Party. But the Democrats didn't accept them, showing enough prudence to keep them at bay although they were friends. The Human Rights Association, chaired by the marshal, caused much alarm in Istanbul, and rightly so. The leftists in this organization are so red that it's difficult to ignore.
>
> Here is what we'd like to know: Is the marshal's name like a magic spell, cast to rally anti-CHP movements, no matter how dubious their membership? The marshal is an Assembly member. He should speak from the podium or write for newspapers. It is unimaginable that the marshal has never read *Tan* or doesn't have the capacity to understand the questionable nature of its contents.

The attacks on the Human Rights Association reached a fevered pitch. When the marshal found himself accused of being a communist, he abandoned the left at once, telling the papers he'd severed his ties with the Association. Celal Bayar was next to announce that he had no connection with the movement. Kenan Öner then cut his ties as well.

On 22 October, *Ulus* reported on the developments:

> The Human Rights Association chaired by Marshal Çakmak has reached an impasse. Just the other day, Marshal Fevzi Çakmak, Cami Baykut, Zekeriya Sertel and the other founders delivered a statement to the newspapers, officially announcing the association's launch. But things started changing once the marshal's

statement was published, and now he has issued another statement. This time, the chairman of the association proclaims: 'People afflicted with extreme leftism may be described as red fascists due to their beliefs. Any leftism based on the "One Chief" system should be considered inhuman and illegal.' He further maintains that he can't agree to work with extreme leftists or those whose opinions diverge from the national mainstream.

Only yesterday, the marshal stated, 'Our movement is not about nationality or political ideology; we simply demand human rights. It's this demand for human rights that unites ideologically opposite poles.' There are three signatures on the founding document of the Human Rights Association submitted to the governor: those of Marshal Fevzi Çakmak, Tevfik Rüştü Aras and Kenan Öner.

The pro-government press had a field day with the marshal's hasty U-turn. After his astonishing second statement appeared in newspapers, Cami Baykut went to visit him. From there, he came straight to our home. He was very upset. We all wanted to hear what the marshal had told him. I asked why Çakmak had gone back on his word in less than 24 hours.

'Wasn't the marshal going to give his life to defend human rights and the rights of the people?' I asked.

Cami Bey made a gesture as if swatting away a fly.

'There's a lesson in all this,' he said. 'The people cannot entrust their rights to these political parties or to elder statesmen with outdated philosophies. They can only trust organizations established by themselves. If workers, peasants and the whole population want to protect these rights, they'll have to start fighting for their own cause.'

As usual, Özdemir had come along with Cami Bey. 'The marshal didn't do this because he was afraid,' he said. 'He was stopped by the reactionaries around him from working with you.'

But there was no excuse for the marshal breaking his word just because he'd been called a communist. He could have easily refuted any ties between communism and himself. The truth was that the marshal didn't have any political ideals. He'd simply joined the opposition on account of personal grudges. And so, he abandoned the left the minute he felt the Human Rights Association was hurting his image.

İnönü had systematically eliminated his greatest rival. Celal Bayar was pleased as well. They'd done away with a force that could have challenged them both. The biggest loser in the whole affair was Tevfik Rüştü Aras, who had fallen between two stools. The press continued its campaign against him. On 12 November, he wrote an article in *Akşam*, defending himself against Falih Rıfkı Atay's relentless attacks:

There are those whose only desire is to follow the path forged by Atatürk,

he wrote.

And then, there are those who have found, claim to have found or fancy themselves to have found another path. Ultimately, they all must seek to serve the country. I'm one of those who believe that progress is tied to Kemalism, which has already carried our country to much success. I share this belief with the marshal, and I'm honoured and delighted to work by his side. Through our many years of collaboration, this feeling has never changed.

The Human Rights Association's chair and members were on the defensive. The political victory belonged to İnönü. A collaboration between leftists and parts of the bourgeoisie would have threatened his plans to hand the country's reins to the USA. He wanted to secure US financial aid, and to do that, he needed to show the Americans that there were no fascist or communist movements in the country, and that the government would crush any that emerged.

The printing houses of *Tan* and *La Turquie* were destroyed. The paper *Yeni Dünya* was shut down. The Socialist Party and the Socialist Labourers' and Peasants' Party were banned. And now, the Human Rights Association was dismantled. These actions were all taken to appease the USA.

The leftist professors

The assault on progressive papers, journals and ideas wasn't over yet. In June 1946, Recep Peker replaced Saraçoğlu as Prime Minister. Hasan Ali Yücel, Minister of Education under Saraçoğlu, had protected university professors with leftist leanings. Now, he was replaced with Reşat Şemseddin Sürer, who immediately dismantled many of his predecessor's achievements.

A campaign was launched to dismiss Pertev Boratav, Niyazi Berkes and Behice Boran from the Faculty of Language, History and Geography, where Boratav worked as Professor of Folklore and the others as associate professors. Some twenty to thirty students were instructed to sign a letter calling for the dismissal of these progressive professors. The letter was then published in *Ulus*. At the same time, the student body was incited against them, especially at the Faculty of Law. These steps were coordinated by the Demirtepe Centre of the People's Party in Yenişehir, Ankara. A series of conferences were held there, aimed at provoking the students against leftist and progressive movements. They were chiefly organized by Kemal Çağlar.

On 5–6 March 1947, a student rally was staged to protest a conference organized by Pertev Boratav. And on 27 December, another rally was held against the university president for granting professorships to these scholars. The president was nearly lynched; he barely made it out alive.

Next, the professors were taken to the Ankara Trial Court on charges of abusing their positions. The case began in early 1948 and concluded in February 1950, with the acquittal of Pertev Boratav and the conviction of Behice Boran and Niyazi Berkes. The Court of Appeals overturned the decision, acquitting Behice and Niyazi as well.

One would have expected the story to end there. But the reactionaries were so determined to crush progressive movements that they paid no mind to democracy, justice and law. Tahsin Banguoğlu, who took over as minister of education from Reşat Şemseddin, started a campaign in the National Assembly against the progressive professors. The movement was led by the notorious fascists Fahri Kurtuluş, Behçet Kemal Çağlar and Emin Soysal. These demagogues created such a furor that the Faculty of Language, History and Geography decided to rescind the professorships. That meant discontinuing all sociology and folklore classes. Along with the three professors, they fired twenty-one lecturers as well. Only two Assembly members protested these dismissals: Adnan Adıvar and the *paşa* Sadık Aldoğan.

And so, these exceptionally valuable national assets were neutralized and banished from intellectual life. Some of them were even forced to leave the country. This was Turkey's loss and other countries' gain, as they found positions at foreign universities. Today, Pertev Boratav is a highly acclaimed professor of folklore at the Sorbonne. Muzaffer Şerif is a famous professor of psychology, whose works are used as textbooks at US universities. Niyazi Berkes is a professor of sociology in Canada and the author of many important works on Turkey. Behice Boran, who remained in Turkey, plays a leading role in the caucus of the Workers' Party.[7]

This episode was yet another sad example of the bourgeoisie's reactionary policy against progressives and intellectuals in Turkey.

---

[7] TN: Eventually, following the 1980 Turkish coup d'état and long after Sabiha Sertel's death, Boran was also forced into exile.

12

The provocations continue

Ever since our release from prison, we'd been receiving a steady stream of visitors. Some of these were our friends, but others were complete strangers. Ostensibly, they'd come to wish us well, but it wasn't hard to see they were provocateurs sent by the police.

One day, we were visited by a bearded young man called Arslan Kumbaracı. He told us a sob story about how he was under police surveillance and wanted to flee to Israel to publish a book about Turkey. He asked Zekeriya and me to contribute chapters to his book. I told him that he could write a book about Turkey without leaving the country, and that I'd decided to take a break from writing. But he kept on visiting, goading us daily. Much later, we learned that this young man was an international spy who worked for the British and Americans.

We encountered many such attempts to provoke us. We couldn't publish newspapers anymore. It was impossible to continue our struggle under these conditions.

Sedat Simavi, an old friend and the publisher of *Hürriyet* [Liberty], came by to visit. I offered to write anonymous pieces for his paper.

'I have a lot of respect for you,' he answered morosely. 'But I'm too scared to print any of your articles, anonymous or not.'

'I could translate detective stories,' I offered.

'I'm scared of being associated with you in any way,' he said.

Clearly, we wouldn't find any work in the press. The police pressure was so intense we could hardly breathe.

I kept thinking of Gogol's story 'Ivan Fyodorovitch Shponka and His Aunt'. Ivan Fyodorovitch is a retired army officer. His aunt invites him to stay with her and manage her estate. She also proposes a match for him. But Ivan is fiercely averse to women and marriage. One night, he dreams that someone is sleeping in a bed next to his own. 'Who are you?' he asks. 'I'm your wife,' she answers. Turning to his left, Ivan finds another woman lying there. 'Who are you?' he asks again. 'I'm your wife,' she answers. Ivan jumps out of bed and hurries into the garden. He takes off his hat. There's a woman on it, as well. He puts his hand in his pocket. Out comes yet another woman.

Just like Ivan Fyodorovitch, I felt that if I put my hand in my pocket, I'd find a policeman in there.

After the professors' dismissal from the Faculty of Language, History and Geography, the ministry of education started hunting down all progressives working at universities, art institutes and theatres. They were either temporarily suspended, exiled to schools in remote parts of Anatolia or summarily dismissed. Sabahaddin Ali lost his post at the conservatory and returned from Ankara to Istanbul.

One day, he came to see us. He told us that he and Aziz Nesin were going to publish a satirical journal called *Marko Paşa*. Once again, he couldn't sit still. He kept taking off his glasses and squinting at us with his tiny eyes.

'This journal,' he said, 'will make people devour politics, ideology and social issues like candy!'

The alliance of two prodigious forces such as Sabahaddin and Aziz Nesin yielded a groundbreaking type of satirical journal. Aziz Nesin put his comical talent on full display for the first time. *Marko Paşa* became the most successful journal of its day. With a print run of 60,000, it was read in villages, towns and cities alike. Throughout Anatolia, common people embraced it like a new Nasreddin Hoca.[1]

Of course, the powers that be grew scared of the journal's success. The government and the police did all they could to stop its publication. But Sabahaddin and Aziz Nesin didn't give up. When *Marko Paşa* was shut down, they published *Merhum Paşa* [The Deceased Pasha] instead. And when that journal was shut down as well, they continued with *Malum Paşa* [The Same Pasha].

As far as I remember, the journal lasted around a year. In the end, police pressure and provocations forced it to close for good. The prosecutor's office launched various court cases against Sabahaddin for his articles. He was arrested and put in Üsküdar prison, where we visited him frequently.

Some friends told us that Sabahaddin's wife, Aliye, and daughter, Filiz, who lived in Ankara, wanted to visit him in Istanbul but lacked money and accommodations. They asked if Aliye and Filiz could stay with us. We were happy to help.

Once Aliye and Filiz arrived, we went to see Sabahaddin together. He was waiting for us in a small room next to the warden's office. When he saw us, he embraced Filiz and started weeping like a baby. Seeing her father like this, Filiz also began crying. Aliye took the girl outside.

'Sabahaddin, what's going on?' I asked once we were alone. 'Does crying suit a man like you?'

He leaned over and whispered in my ear.

'They'll leave me to rot in prison, just like Nazım Hikmet,' he said. 'They've filed five lawsuits against me. I've decided to escape. I met a man called H. in here. He's part of an organization that can get me out of the country in 24 hours. I'll run away.'

'How can you entrust your life to someone you barely know?'

'It's not like that. Some of my trusted friends know him as well.'

Sabahaddin was as naïve as a child. He believed whatever he was told.

'If that's your decision, why did you tell me? No one must know!'

'You're the only one I've told,' he said.

But later, I heard he'd told his secret to others as well. This lack of discretion was partly to blame for all that befell him.

---

[1] TN: A traditional folkloric figure whose exploits relate didactic and socially relevant messages in the form of jokes.

Eventually, Sabahaddin was released from prison and moved in as a guest of a family he knew. He came to visit us again.

'I've decided to go into commerce,' he said. 'They won't let me work anywhere. There's this rich lady, an acquaintance of the family I'm staying with. She takes struggling artists and writers under her wing. They told her about my plans and asked her to buy me a truck. She accepted. The truck is ready. Now we're looking for a driver. As soon as I have one, I'm heading for Anatolia.'

After his Anatolian trip, Sabahaddin dropped by again.

'Looks like you can't make a merchant out of a novelist!' he said. 'We loaded the truck with goods, but on the way back, we got stuck in snow. So we unloaded the goods, put them on a train and returned, leaving the truck behind!' He was howling with laughter.

Sometime afterward, Sabahaddin paid us another visit.

'I'm finally escaping,' he said. 'The man I met in prison, H., arranged everything. A. Hanım, with whom I'm staying, has already packed my suitcase. She even wrote my initials on the clothes. Aliye and Filiz don't know. I'll write to them once I'm in Bulgaria.'

And so, Sabahaddin disappeared. For months, we heard nothing. We were all sure he'd made it out.

The Progressives keep up their struggle

We watched from a distance as events unfolded. The fight between the People's Party and the Democrat Party intensified. The Democrats, in opposition, kept attacking the People's Party in hopes of winning the next election.

Halet Çambel, an associate professor of Archeology, paid us a visit. She was a highly energetic woman, who'd studied in France and spoke German, French and English like her mother tongue. I complained to her about the university professors' stance.

'We fought for freedom and democracy,' I said. 'But instead of supporting the cause, the university sent its students to attack us. When the printing houses were destroyed, not a single professor or faculty member spoke out on our behalf.'

'That's not true,' Halet replied. 'Some professors support the cause. After the destruction of the printing presses, Mehmet Ali Aybar[2] spoke very courageously to his students in class. He criticized the government.'

This was the only voice that had been raised at the university.

'If you want, I can introduce you to him,' Halet said.

We gladly accepted. We knew Mehmet Ali Aybar from his forceful, pro-democratic articles in *Vatan*, but we'd never met him in person.

Mehmet Ali turned out to be a young progressive, who'd studied law in France. He was very knowledgeable about Marxism and had truly interesting ideas about advancing the country and developing social movements.

Whenever we met up with him, we all complained about our lack of action. But Mehmet Ali kept busy. With a friend, he published *Nuhun Gemisi* [Noah's Ark], a

---

[2] Current Chairman of the Workers' Party.

Figure 12.1 At the Sertels' villa, 1948, Sabiha reads to their visiting grandchildren Sevim and Denis O'Brien, a respite in the aftermath of *Tan*'s destruction. The Sertels were under round-the-clock police surveillance and unable to work.

journal that analyzed current affairs, criticized concessions to the US and stood up for the country's independence. *Nuhun Gemisi* was closed down after a few issues. Next, Aybar launched a journal called *Zincirli Hürriyet* [Freedom in Chains]. The Martial Law Governorship of Istanbul didn't allow him to publish it, so he went to Izmir, where the journal appeared in 1947 to popular acclaim. These two journals were the first sparks of a backlash against the American yoke. But soon, reactionaries and racists incited by the police attacked *Zincirli Hürriyet*'s printing house and burned all copies.

Upon returning to Istanbul, Mehmet Ali was sued by the prosecutor's office. He was thrown into Üsküdar Prison, where he remained for the duration of his trial. While under arrest, he was stripped of his professorship by government order and a resolution of the university senate. Üsküdar's proximity to Moda allowed us to visit him frequently. Mehmet Ali stood as firm as a rock, undaunted by the attacks on him, like a true idealist determined to defend his cause to the end.

The few progressive journals that still appeared were quickly shut down and their owners imprisoned. Our Moda home became a hub for jobless intellectuals. We'd often gather there and commiserate with each other. The country's most valuable minds had been neutralized.

Sabahaddin is murdered

It was 1948. We opened the papers one day and saw the following news: 'The corpse of Sabahaddin Ali was found in a forest on the Turkish–Bulgarian border.'

The story ran roughly like this:

Some smugglers were apprehended by an anti-smuggling unit of the police. One of them was discovered wearing Sabahaddin Ali's clothes. The investigation was extended. It emerged that the smuggler had bought the clothes from Ali Ertekin, a Yugoslavian immigrant. Upon his arrest, Ertekin stated that Sabahaddin Ali had offered him money to drive him to the Bulgarian border in a truck, and he'd previously driven Ali to Anatolia in the same truck. Ertekin asked why Ali was fleeing to Bulgaria. Ali supposedly replied, 'I'm a communist and am going there to work with other communists.' This offended Ertekin's national pride, and he killed Ali.

This story made no sense at all. I was acquainted with M. Hanım, who'd bought the truck for Sabahaddin, so I arranged a meeting with her to learn more. I found her on pins and needles, worried her name would crop up in the papers. She told me about the purchase of the truck. Her story matched Sabahaddin's. The truck had been bought with the help of A. Hanım, Sabahaddin's host, and her husband.

I asked who'd found the driver for her.

'K. A. Bey, a police superintendent,' she said. 'I rang him up this morning. He told me not to worry, that my name wouldn't be in the papers.'

These words explained a great deal. Clearly, the police were involved in Sabahaddin's murder. We were heartbroken. They'd set this trap for Sabahaddin all the way back in Üsküdar Prison. And Sabahaddin had flung himself into this dangerous adventure, trusting people he barely knew.

By now, Mehmet Ali was out of prison. That night, we went to visit him at his house in Kuzguncuk. Some other friends were there as well. Everyone was speculating about Sabahaddin's death. Since we knew he'd been planning his escape for a long time, none of us could believe the newspaper stories. According to one report, Ali Ertekin had killed Sabahaddin for his money. But when the police found Sabahaddin, he still had some money on him. Supposedly, his bag was full of books by Marx and Lenin. But a man fleeing to Bulgaria had absolutely no need of such books. Clearly, a source was feeding the papers stories while concealing the facts. Today, Sabahaddin's murder still hasn't been fully explained.

The persecution and torture of leftists were daily occurrences in Turkey. But now, these acts had taken the form of undisguised terror. From time to time, deaths occurred among those who were beaten in police custody. But the killing of a writer, one of the country's best-known novelists, was something that had never happened before. On the day that *Tan* was destroyed, they'd come after me with bottles of red ink. Had I been at the printing house, I might have been killed as well.

While we were talking with Mehmet Ali, the doorbell rang. It was 11 o'clock at night. We opened the door, and in came Arslan Kumbaracı, looking inconsolable.

'They're bringing Sabahaddin's remains to Istanbul tomorrow,' he said. 'We must all go to his funeral.'

We knew at once this was another attempt to provoke us. They wanted to lure us out so they could claim we were staging a communist demonstration at Sabahaddin's funeral. Perhaps they would even arrest all of us. Attending the funeral would have been a tactical mistake.

When we left Mehmet Ali's home around midnight, we saw two buggies waiting a little down the road. It was impossible to find a cab in Kuzguncuk at that hour. Clearly, Arslan Kumbaracı had told his cab to wait and brought another one in tow. The police were watching our every step.

And in this horrifying manner, we lost our friend Sabahaddin.

Nazım Hikmet is released

In spite of the oppression, progressives maintained their struggle. We fought for the release of Nazım Hikmet, who'd been in prison for fourteen years. Even the bourgeois papers adopted this cause. Ahmet Emin Yalman started an amnesty campaign for Nazım in his paper, *Vatan*, where the lawyer Mehmet Ali Sebük wrote about legal issues involved with a pardon.

It's a mystery why Yalman took up this cause at a time when communists, leftists and progressives were persecuted so fiercely. One theory is that he was encouraged by reactionary groups. Even from prison, Nazım remained a great influence on the youth and workers. His poems were passed around secretly from person to person. The reactionaries wanted to assassinate him. But this was hard to achieve in prison; one attempt already had failed.

Nazım personally described this incident to me in 1942, when I visited him in Bursa Prison. A fascist army officer entered the prison posing as an inmate. Once there, he paid off a few murderers to kill Nazım. But most inmates revered Nazım like a father and took shifts watching over him. Hearing of the assassination plot, these friends seized the murderers on the night of the planned attempt. The warden, who was very fond of Nazım, transferred the fascist officer elsewhere, and Nazım was saved.

There were those who saw Yalman's amnesty campaign as the prelude to another assassination attempt. They claimed that the reactionaries were using Yalman as a pawn. Another rumour pointed to Yalman's cooperation with the Democrat Party at that time. By supporting a pardon, it was said, the DP hoped to win over progressives.

I don't know which rumour was true. But once again, it was the progressives who truly championed Nazım's release. Some youths published a journal entitled *Nazım Hikmet*, printing his poems and calling for an amnesty. Celile Hanım, Nazım's blind, elderly mother, wandered the bridges and highways with a sign around her neck that read, 'I want my son back alive.' She petitioned the state. Some papers published articles about the cruelty Nazım had endured.

Finally, Nazım's supporters gathered at the Çelik Palas convention hall to give speeches on his behalf. Nazım's mother herself gave a heartrending speech. But the meeting was raided by fascist youths, with the blessing of the police. They attacked whoever they encountered, roughing them up. The police simply watched. In the end, the meeting's participants were led away through a secret door and directly to the police station. They were held in custody overnight, while the fascists walked off scot-free, continuing to attack any Nazım supporters they saw on the street, spitting in their faces.

This fascist initiative prompted campaigns of support in the Soviet Union as well as in France and other European nations. The disgrace visited upon Nazım Hikmet, one of the world's greatest poets, weighed heavily on the conscience of mankind. Beset by domestic and international pressure, the government decided to move Nazım from Bursa Prison to a jail in Istanbul, supposedly because he was ill. But it flat out rejected the idea of releasing him. Nazım was transferred to Üsküdar Prison. To protest this decision and force his release, he began a hunger strike.

This occurred around the same time that Mehmet Ali Aybar was convicted in the *Zincirli Hürriyet* case. Aybar landed in Üsküdar Prison as well. I paid him a visit.

'Can't they at least give him vitamins?' I asked.

'Impossible,' he said. 'He won't even drink water.'

Nazım's condition kept deteriorating. We gathered at our house every day, trying to find ways to save him. When prison doctors announced he only had one or two days to live, we panicked. He had to be saved, no matter what. Many of us felt he needed to end his hunger strike. We sent the painter Abidin Dino and Zekeriya Sertel to see him and convey our plea. Nazım didn't refuse us. He ended his hunger strike. In return, the government decided to release him.

Nazım left prison and moved into Vala Nureddin's house. Soon after, I visited him there. He'd recovered a little by then, and we talked at length about our past work together, the destruction of *Tan* and the current situation. Here is exactly what he said:

> Fourteen years, they imprisoned me, for nothing. I didn't do anything. All I did was give my books to some youths, who could've bought them in stores anyway. Even the Inquisition may not have considered that a crime! Fourteen years, that's easy to say, but to carry the pain of one's innocence in one's heart for fourteen years is the greatest torture of all. That's what truly broke my heart. If I'd actually committed a crime, I wouldn't have minded so much!

Nazım rose in anger. He started pacing up and down the room.

'My innocence will be proven one day,' he said. 'But how will I regain the fourteen years that I lost? My heart, my heart tells me that my remaining days are numbered.'

He sat down again, placing his head in his hands.

'They won't let us work in this country anymore,' he said. He was very worried. The thing that distressed him most was the daunting prospect of making a living under these conditions.

We were wary of meeting with Nazım too often. One night, after ten o'clock, Zekeriya and I went to see him at his mother's house in Cevizlik. We'd heard that the police officers observing the house left at that hour. We were greeted by his mother, Celile Hanım. She was overjoyed and ushered us into her decrepit wooden home. When we climbed the creaky stairs, we found Nazım waiting for us at the top. He'd heard us arrive and stepped out of his room. His wife, Münevver, also was there. They were very happy to see us. We entered his room, where a young man was sitting. Nazım introduced him.

'Balaban, a painter,' he said, 'my friend from prison.'

The walls of the room were covered with Balaban's paintings. They dazzled my eyes as if caught in a torrent of colour. Nazım told us about the paintings and how he'd trained Balaban as a painter in prison. We were amazed by the aptitude of this simple village boy.

Nazım turned to his desk and gathered up some pages he'd written on his typewriter.

'I write children's poems now,' he said. 'I have to make a living. Who would've thought that children's poetry was so difficult to write?'

We send soldiers to Korea

After the Second World War, several socialist states were founded in Central Europe. Many parts of Asia and Africa waged wars of liberation. But the USA, aiming to establish a global hegemony, was determined to crush these socialist revolutions and national liberation movements. Turkey was politically and economically vital to America's monopolies.[3] It could serve as a springboard in any war the USA might plan against the Soviet Union and socialist nations. At the same time, the underdeveloped country could be used as a market for US capital. For these reasons, the USA resolved to bring Turkey under its yoke.

The People's Party had lost the public's trust because of its oppressive policies during and after the war. It had estranged Britain, its wartime ally, as well as the Soviet Union. Finding itself isolated, it turned to America for help in the form of the Marshall Plan and related agreements. The Turkish bourgeoisie also hoped to benefit from collaborating with US monopolies.

Immediately exploiting the situation, the Americans instructed Turkey to draft soldiers for the US war against North Korea. These Turkish soldiers would be sent to Korea under the UN banner.

America was holding the whole world ransom with its nuclear weapons and the threat of a third world war. The UN was merely a puppet carrying out US orders. America's war on communism was not aimed just at the Soviet Union, but at all independence movements in underdeveloped nations. Anti-communist rhetoric was merely a passport used by the US to penetrate these nations and exploit them.

China's shift to communism cost the US a market totalling 600 million people. Other parts of Asia followed suit, establishing governments with socialist leanings. Korea expelled its Japanese invaders with the Soviet Union's help and went on to found an independent state. In North Korea, a movement to build a socialist regime started gaining ground.

American monopolies already had seized Korea's mines and natural resources. Just as they armed the government of Formosa under Chiang Kai-shek against China, they supplied weapons to reactionary forces in Korea. Under UN cover, they incited these

---

[3] TN: Sertel seems to be referring to the economic, ideological and political power of monopolies that she perceives the USA is trying to establish on a global scale through its private sector and the state.

forces to attack the new democratic government, dragging the country into a civil war. And now, the American imperialists were ordering Turkey to join this war.

The Turkish Government agreed to deploy forces. The news struck the public like a bomb. Why was Turkey doing this? Korea hadn't attacked us. We weren't historical enemies. There was no conflict between us. The common people's reaction can be summed up with the following anecdote:

> I was on the Kalamış seashore, hoping to take a rowboat over to Moda. The sea was rough, with white-capped blue waves crashing against the waterfront. Osman Ağa, a well-known Kalamış boatman, stood in the water cleaning his rowboat, his trousers pulled up to his knees. I called out to him.
>
> 'Osman Ağa,' I said, 'can we make it over to Moda?'
>
> 'Of course!' he answered. 'Why wouldn't we?'
>
> We set out to sea. The waves kept tossing the boat from side to side, but Osman Ağa hardly seemed to notice. At some point, he slowed down the rowboat.
>
> 'Sister,' he said, 'tell me, where is Korea?'
>
> It was hard to explain Korea to someone like Osman Ağa.
>
> 'It's far away,' I said, 'very far away. Beyond mighty seas.'
>
> 'Why are we sending soldiers there? Did they attack us? Did they do us any harm?'
>
> 'They didn't attack us. And no, they didn't do us any harm. America attacked them. And our government wants to help America.'
>
> Osman Ağa furrowed his brow.
>
> 'What do I care about those infidels?' he said. 'What's Korea got to do with us? I got a letter from my son in the village. They're calling him to the army. I'll tell him not to go, to hide in the mountains instead.'

'What's Korea got to do with us?' The question was on everyone's minds. But we did send our soldiers to Korea, beyond the mighty seas. On the snowy mountains of Kunu-ri and many other fronts, we sacrificed our sons for the sake of US monopolies. America sent Turkish soldiers into the line of fire, frittering them away like small chips at the casino. Falih Rıfkı Atay was wrong: the US battleships hadn't conquered the Turkish people's hearts, but their independence. We paid for America's dollars with the blood we shed in Korea, with graves that rose in mounds.

The Friends of Peace Society

After the Second World War, progressive forces around the globe launched a struggle to counter the threat of a third world war. The World Peace Council was founded with the Soviet Union's help. Peace organizations sprang up everywhere and started collecting signatures. The movement was well received among peace-loving Turkish people, and shortly before the Korean War, the Friends of Peace Society was established under the chairmanship of Behice Boran.

I attended some of the society's meetings but took no active role, fearing that after *Tan*'s destruction, my involvement might harm the movement. Still, I wrote anonymous pieces for *Barış Dergisi* [Peace Journal], the society's publication. This was around the time of the announcement that soldiers would be deployed to Korea. The news didn't just cause a backlash among common people but also prompted many progressives to join the peace movement. The cause united progressives, opponents of war and the vast majority of the population: they all rejected America's criminal acts and refused to sacrifice Turkish sons for the sake of the USA. The Friends of Peace Society published a declaration protesting the government's decision.

The day that the declaration was published, Zekeriya and I went to visit the painter Abidin Dino. His house was in Caddebostan, an elegant seaside mansion surrounded by an expansive garden. Abidin's wife, Güzin, greeted us at the door. Nazım Hikmet, Melih Cevdet, Oktay Rifat and some other friends were there, bathing in the sea or sitting in the garden and discussing the Korean War. Nazım was astounded by the decision to deploy troops.

'The big patriots have sold out the country.' He buried his head in his hands. 'Brothers, we've been bought and paid for.'

The Korean War was all we could talk about that day. After a while, Nazım took us to a room on the ground floor. There, laid out on the floor, were Dino's paintings illustrating Nazım's *Milli Kurtuluş Destanı*.[4] They were truly wonderful works of art. Nazım showed me the paintings.

'You'll see,' he said, 'one day, Dino will be a world-renowned painter.'

We went back into the garden, where we were joined by some friends who'd prepared and handed out the declarations. They told us how well the public had responded. Adnan Cemgil paced up and down the garden, recounting how all copies had been snatched up.

The struggle for peace became the first priority for progressive intellectuals. But the government needed to hide the criminal nature of its actions from the public. It confiscated the declarations and imprisoned those who distributed them. Soon, the Friends of Peace Society was banned. Behice Boran and her companions were taken to court and each sentenced to one year of prison. By the time they were sentenced, we'd already left the country.

Even advocating peace was considered a crime. We lived in an era in which the government pompously announced the transition to an 'advanced democracy'. But the same government saw treason in all attempts to criticize it for acts that harmed the nation and the people. Every progressive movement was branded as communist and silenced.

Government circles were gearing up for the next election. The Democrat Party, which had promised to bring democracy, freedom and peace to the country, was vying with the People's Party for control of Assembly seats. But both these parties were united in their foreign policy, which consisted of handing over the country to the Americans. They were selling out the country while calling themselves nationalists and patriots. And we, who defended the people's interests and the nation's independence, were labelled as criminals.

---

[4] TN: *Epic of National Liberation*, an alternate title for the poet's *Epic of the War of Liberation* mentioned above.

To conceal their crimes, they kept attacking progressives. Sabahaddin Ali, one of Turkey's greatest novelists, was murdered. Journals like *Marko Paşa, Zincirli Hürriyet* and *Nuhun Gemisi* were shut down and their owners imprisoned. The Friends of Peace Society was banned and its founders taken to court. Progressives lived under constant police surveillance. True patriots were deprived of all means to defend the nation.

One evening, we were entertaining some friends on the seaside balcony of our Moda home. They'd all lost their jobs. Not only were they unable to serve the nation; they couldn't even make a living anymore.

'I found a new job,' Adnan Cemgil proudly announced. 'A friend of mine owns a water truck. I'll be delivering water canisters to people's homes.'

How bitter a moment it was, witnessing an intellectual like Adnan Cemgil thrilled by the prospect of delivering water!

Behice Boran and her husband, Nevzat, had opened an agency that translated merchants' letters into English and other languages. Niyazi Berkes had founded a small printing house with his brother's help, but the police barred it from operating. Pertev Boratav kept travelling back and forth between Ankara and Istanbul, tormented by unemployment. Abidin Dino was taken to court for a figure he'd drawn on a ceramic pot. They'd spotted a hammer and sickle in his drawing, just as they'd found a sickle in the 'G' of *Görüşler*. The country's rulers were wearing out these crucial individuals over trifles, rendering them unable to work.

I looked at all the intellectuals who'd been cast aside like pebbles. My heart sank – the news of Adnan's job had really depressed me. I decided we could all use a good laugh at our own pitiful state.

'Guys,' I said, 'these are not jobs for us. Tomorrow, they'll take away Adnan's water canisters as well. They'll close down the translation agency. Come, let's open a restaurant instead. Behice Boran, Nazife Cemgil, Mediha Berkes and I will cook, and the men will be waiters and stewards.'

Adnan Cemgil jumped up at once.

'What are you saying?' he demanded. 'They'll claim the restaurant is a front for the communists' secret activities, that we're using the basement to hold clandestine meetings and print pamphlets! They'll lock us all up!'

He was joking, of course, but there was some truth to his words. We couldn't even open a restaurant in this country anymore. In fact, we could hardly breathe. The country's most progressive forces were deprived of the freedom to speak, think, move, and even work. O glorious democracy, rising on Turkey like a sun!

After all our years of struggle, we'd run out of ways to defend the nation's and people's cause. We'd run out of ways to speak out for peace and fight for our ideals. We were exiled in our own homeland. Our days were barren and empty; our lives were without purpose.

It was March 1950 when Zekeriya Sertel suggested a journey abroad to escape the country's stifling atmosphere. I was happy to accept. We requested passports from the police for a trip to Paris. We waited six months. Finally, Zekeriya wrote a telegraph to Adnan Menderes. The Democrat Party had won the elections, and Menderes was prime minister.

'When we worked together,' Zekeriya wrote, 'you promised to bring freedom and democracy to the country. How can we believe democracy will come when I can't even obtain a passport to travel abroad, when my freedom to travel is curtailed? I insist you order the police to issue my passport.'

And so, after six months and a thousand adversities, we obtained our passports to travel to Paris. On 9 September 1950, Zekeriya, my youngest daughter, Yıldız, and I drove to Yeşilköy Airport. Each of us took only one small bag. We were consumed by fear that they'd seize our passports. We didn't pack anything written, not one of the books and journals we'd published. This was how we were leaving our motherland, whose people we'd spent years defending. It hurt.

With a heavy heart, I slowly climbed the stairs to the plane. I knew this wasn't an ordinary trip. Who knew when I would return to my beloved country, my people, my friends, my brothers?

As the plane takes off, I watch Istanbul through the round window. Yeşilköy, the minarets, the houses – one by one, they fall away. I see the green treetops. Then I enter the clouds. I no longer can see anything.

I leaned my head against the seat and closed my eyes. I was leaving behind a life of struggle. The people for whom I'd sacrificed so much faced their most difficult hour, and I lacked the freedom to defend them. My heart ached. I felt the warmth of tears on my lips.

13

To my countrypeople

Many years have passed since that September in 1950, when I left behind my country. So much water has flowed under the bridge. The İnönü dictatorship ended, only to be followed by the Menderes dictatorship. But that dictatorship met its end as well. Under the heavy hand of the bourgeoisie and its governments, my country failed to complete its democratic revolution and achieve the freedom it craved for 200 years.

Still, the movement of 27 May 1960[1] produced a new constitution that granted many rights to the masses. Today, freedom of speech, opinion and association are enshrined in the Constitution. Workers won the right to form unions and strike. They attained consciousness and started defending their own cause, founding their own parties.

Young people are at the forefront of the battle for democracy. Intellectuals and progressives fight against compradors[2] who collaborate with the American bourgeoisie. They fight against the Turkish bourgeois government and against the American yoke. Socialist movements are gaining ground. It comforts me to witness these developments, even from afar.[3]

Under the harshest of conditions, we fought for democracy and against dictatorship. We fought for our country's independence against imperialism and its yoke on underdeveloped nations. We fought against exploiters who prey on peasants, workers and the poor. We fought against fascism and its quest for hegemony over smaller nations – a quest it pursues through religious, nationalist and racist propaganda as well as through brute force. The reactionary bourgeoisie attacked our ideas with axes and sledgehammers. It tried to crush our struggle for freedom, social justice and democracy. It destroyed not only printing presses that championed liberty, but all progressive movements that emerged in the country.

The struggle we left unfinished continues today. New progressive forces have emerged, fighting for this cause with all their might. But the compradors paid by America and the CIA lie in wait to crush these movements as well. I wish the

---

[1] TN: Sertel is referring to the first Turkish military coup in 1960.
[2] TN: A local who acts as an agent for foreign interests.
[3] TN: Since Sabiha Sertel wrote these lines, the country has experienced two military coups (in 1971 and 1980) and many smaller military interventions, negating many of the trends Sertel outlines. Following the 1980 coup, the country became fully integrated in the global economic system. In 2017, it passed constitutional changes, all but enshrining autocratic one-man rule. Sertel's ideals of political and economic independence as well as social justice seem more distant than ever.

progressives and all my countrypeople success in this arduous fight for freedom and independence.

My memoirs depict our era, our struggle and the hardships that forced us to leave behind our country, people and friends. We sacrificed everything for our cause. Today, we live in exile, anguished at having to watch from afar as the struggle we began is carried on by capable hands.

In a sense, we aren't in exile after all. Here in the Soviet Union and Azerbaijan, we are among brothers and friends. I am eternally grateful for their hospitality. But nothing can ease the yearning for one's own country.

As I write these lines and recall my thirty-two years of work in the nation's service, I take solace in having done my duty. Let me end these memoirs, so much like a novel, by repeating my parting wish for all my brothers and sisters in the cause: May success be yours.

Figure 13.1 Yalta, 24 April 1966. While exiled in the Soviet Union, two years before her death, Sertel sent this photo to her elder daughter and grandchildren in the USA to show she was well.

Glossary

Bourgeoisie, national In the Turkish case, this term refers to a Muslim and ethnically Turkish bourgeoisie. It consciously excludes people who may be bourgeois and citizens of the Turkish state, but are non-Turkish and/or non-Muslim.

Bourgeoisie, petty In Marxist thought, this term denotes a class above the proletariat, but below and beholden to the capitalist high bourgeoisie. Often, the petty bourgeoisie is a clerical and managerial class employed by the high bourgeoisie.

Bourgeoisie, trade A bourgeois class that comes into being as a result of commerce rather than capitalist production. Sertel uses the term interchangeably with 'trade capitalists'.

Democratic bourgeois revolution In Marxist thought, this term denotes a revolution aimed at abolishing a feudal system and/or wresting national independence from colonial rule while establishing the bourgeoisie as the country's dominant class and capitalism as its economic system. Once these goals are attained, the country may become ready for a proletarian revolution, in which the working class attempts to overthrow the bourgeoisie itself. Throughout her memoirs, Sertel remains convinced that Turkey has not been able to successfully complete its bourgeois revolution.

Dialectical materialism A philosophical position maintaining that the world consists solely of matter in motion. This world, or reality, is taken to be in a constant process of change through struggle.

Kemalism A term used to describe the political thought and programme of Mustafa Kemal Atatürk and his followers. Most commonly associated with the 'six principles' or 'six arrows' of republicanism, nationalism, statism, populism, laicism, and revolutionism. Nationalism and republicanism note that the Ottoman Empire has been replaced by the Turkish nation-state, and that the former's monarchy has given way to a constitutional republic. Populism maintains that sovereignty belongs to the public rather than to an autocratic ruler. Statism advocates state regulation of all major economic activity in the country. Laicism (or secularism), in the Turkish case, stands for a non-religious state controlling all organized religious activity in the country through a special directorate. Finally, revolutionism (or reformism) maintains that the Kemalist reforms are to be regarded as an ongoing process rather than as completed historical events.

Ottomanism An ideology advocating the reorganization of the Ottoman Empire as a modern nation-state under the continued leadership of the Ottoman sultan. Sertel uses the term interchangeably with New Ottomanism.

Turkism An ideology advocating the political union of Turkic-speaking populations spread across Central and Western Asian countries. Sertel uses the term interchangeably with Pan-Turkism and Turanism.

Index

Abdülhamid II, xvii, 83, 88, 95, 102, 192, 198, 221
Adıvar, Adnan, 36, 51, 181–2, 187, 228, see Doctor Adnan
Adıvar, Halide Edip, 4, see Halide Edip
Adsız, Nihal, 123, 137, 160–3
Ağaoğlu Ahmet Bey, 12, 37, 40, 105, 122
Ali, Sabahaddin, xxii
   arrest and escape, 230–1
   literary debates, 94
   Marko Paşa, 230
   murder of, 232–4, 239
   Nazım Hikmet and, 75
   Resimli Ay, 50, 73
   Tan, 144, 165
   trial and attacks on, 137–8, 162–3
   Yeni Dünya, 185–7
   Yurt ve Dünya, 146
Aras, Tevfik Rüştü, 142, 144–6, 165, 170, 181–2, 185, 187, 189, 222–6
Atatürk, *see* Mustafa Kemal
   army, establishing of, 25
   death of, 119–21
   Kemalism, 243
   Liberal Republican Party, 105, 108, 170
   Nutuk, 151
   principles of, opposition, 136
   reforms, opposition to, 58–9
   Republic, founding of, 35–7
      Constitution, 1924 of, 41
      powers of, schism, 36, 38–9
   Soviet Union, 128–9, 140
   see also Grand National Assembly
Atay, Falih Rıfkı, 144, 155, 166–7, 169, 218–19, 224–6, 237
Aybar, Mehmet Ali, 231–2, 235

Balkan Pact, 118–19, 124
Bayar, Celal
   appoints İnönü president, 121
   Atatürk's funeral, 119

'Declaration of Four', 168–9, 184
   dictatorship of, 205
   founds Democrat Party, 146, 205
   Görüşler, 181, 183, 185–6, 189, 198
   Human Rights Association, 223, 225–6
   İş Bankası, 109
   opposition in Assembly, 176, 179
   opposition in People's Party, 164–5
   opposition to İnönü, 144–5
   seeks *Tan*'s support for new journal, 170–1
   sidelined by İnönü, 124
Baykut, Cami, 165, 181–2, 185, 197, 209–10, 212–14, 216–18, 220–2, 224–6
Bekirağa Prison, 2, 12–13
Berkes, Niyazi, 146, 181–2, 186, 227, 228, 239
Boran, Behice, 137, 146, 165, 181–2, 186–7, 227–8, 237–9
Boratav, Pertev, 137–8, 146, 181–2, 186, 227–8, 239
Büyük Mecmua, xviii, 5–6, 8, 10–14, 16–18

Çakmak, Fevzi, Marshall, 222–3
Cemal Pasha, 1
Cemgil, Adnan, 146, 165, 186, 238–9
Cevat Şakir, 59, 61, 63, 111, *see* Halikarnas Balıkçısı
CHP, xxi, xxiv, 198, 222, 225, *see* Republican People's Party
Cici Anne, xix, 47
Çıtra Royla Babası, 111
Çocuk Ansiklopedisi, 59, 61–2, 69, 71
Columbia University, xvi, 19–21, 111, *see also* New York School of Social Work; New York Teachers College
Committee of Union and Progress, xv, 1, 53, 221, *see* CUP

Constitution, 1924 of, 38, 39, 41, 121
Cumhuriyet, 51–2, 59, 71, 100, 123, 131–2, 154, 196–7
CUP, xvii, 2, 3, 12, 18, 38, 61, see Committee of Union and Progress

Damat Ferit, 3, 11, 15, 17, 110
Declaration of Family Rights, 55
Deriş, Celal, xvii, 10, 63, 65, 216
Deriş, Neşet, 10, 140
Derviş, Suat, 50, 73, 102, 112, 116, 135–6
Detroit Solidarity Association, 28
Dino, Abidin, 136, 235, 238–9
Directorate General of the Press, 36, 134
Doctor Adnan, 51, see Adıvar, Adnan
Doctor Fuat Bey, 32–4, 42–4
Doctor Şefik Hüsnü, 60–1, 206
Dönme, xvi, xvii, xx, 5, 172
Dördüncü, Halil Lütfü, 105, 109, 194–5, 198, 209–10, 212–14, 216, 218, 220

Enver Pasha, 1, 3, 12, 38
Eren, Hidayet, 9
Eren, Mecdi, 9, 65
Ertem, Sadri, 50, 60, 73, 75–6, 79–80, 89–90, 102, 144

Fikret, Tevfik, 52, 95, 128, 130–1, 136, 172, 203
First World War, 1, 19, 84, 99, 111, 120, 122–3, 128, 134, 154, 221, 223, see Great War
Friends of Peace Society, 237–9

Gökalp, Ziya, 6, 12, 19, 42–4, 152
Görüşler (journal), 181–9, 192–3, 203, 239
Grand National Assembly, 36, 38, 51, 124, 152, see National Assembly
Great War, 10, 118, see First World War
Gülcemal, 32

Halide Edip, xviii, 3, 11, 13–15, 17, 35–6, 51, 84, 181–2, see Adıvar, Halide Edip
Halikarnas Balıkçısı, 111, see Cevat Şakir
Hamdullah Suphi, 79, 81, 2
Hamid, Abdülhak, 76, 78–9, 81–3, 102

Hayat Ansiklopedisi, 108–9
Human Rights Association, 221–7
Hüseyin Cahit, 51, 62, 175–6, 178, 185, 192, 195, 197, see Yalçın, Hüseyin Cahit

Independence Tribunal, 57, 59–63, 69, 185
İnönü, İsmet, xix, 51, 121, 132–3, 145, 183

Karabekir, Kazım, 35, 38, 51, 58, 224
Kaya, Şükrü, 116–18, 139–41, 144–5
Köprülü, Fuat, 164, 168–9, 182–3, 185–6, see Köprülüzade Mehmet Fuat
Köprülüzade Mehmet Fuat, 5, 11, 13, 182, 187, see Köprülü, Fuat
Koraltan, Refik, 164, 186
Korea, xxiii, 144, 167, 236–8

La Turquie, 165, 170, 175, 193, 195, 197–8, 203, 227
Labour Law, 60, 70, 85
Latife Hanım, xvii, 42–4
Lexington Community Center, 22
Liberal Party, 105, 108–9, see Liberal Republican Party
Liberal Republican Party, 105, 170, see Liberal Party

Mehmet Akif, 102, 128–9
Mehmet Emin, 5, 79, 80–1, 102
Menderes, Adnan, 164, 168–9, 179, 182–3, 185–7, 189, 223, 239, 241
Mustafa Kemal, 8, 13, 15–17, 32, 40–2, 69, 105, 243, see Atatürk
Müstecaboğlu, Esat Adil, 165, 185–6, 205–6

National Assembly, 38, 55, 58, 70, 109, 124, 133, 145, 147, 227, see Grand National Assembly
National Bloc, 4, 17
National War of Independence, 69, see War of Independence
Nazım Hikmet, see Ran, Nazım Hikmet
Ali, Sabahaddin, 75
imprisonment of, 121, 164, 185, 234–5

poems, impact of, 76
Resimli Ay, 50, 72–3, 78, 80–1, 89–90, 92, 95, 101–4
Second World War, reaction to, 141
see also Resimli Ay
Nesin, Aziz, 165, 230
New York School of Social Work, 21–2, 42, see also Columbia University
New York Teachers College, 28, 72, see also Columbia University
Nur, Rıza, 160
Nureddin, Vala, 50, 69, 73, 79, 87, 94, 199, 235

Okyar, Fethi, 43, 53, 105
'One Party, One Chief', 39, 121, 134, 164, 168, 170, 217
Orhan Seyfi, 5, 13, 79, 137, 196
Ottoman (National) Assembly, 13, 15, 17, 221

Pan-Turkism, 120, 131, 151, 243, see also Pan-Turkists; Turkism
Pan-Turkists, 6, 103, 4, 122, 137, 154, see also Pan-Turkism; Turkism
Papen, Franz von, 132–4, 142, 145, 150, 154, 160
Peker, Recep, 119, 186, 224, 227
People's Party, see Republican People's Party; CHP
Pocket Books, 110
Projektör, 117
Public Debt Administration, xxi, 10

Ran, Nazım Hikmet, xxi, see Nazım Hikmet
Red Crescent Association, 28–30, 32, see Red Crescent
Red Crescent, 31–2, see Red Crescent Association
Republican People's Party (People's Party), see CHP
  alleged German ties, 212–13
  creation of, xxi, 39, 50
  Democrat Party, 231, 238
  elections of, 1946, 219, 224–5
  İnönü, 121
  internal opposition, 137, 146, 164, 168–70, 176, 179, 182

  opposition to, 51, 108–9, 179, 186, 189, 191, 193, 203, 207, 227
  patronage of, 70
  post Second World War, 236
  press, criticism of, 187
  program, 153
  reorganization of, 216
  single party rule, 58, 105, 171, 183
  Tan, destruction of, 191–3, 196, 198, 201, 214–15, 217
Reşat Nuri, 5, 50, 69
Resimli Ay
  Breaking the Idols campaign in, 75, 79, 102
  closure of, 102–5
  column writing, new style of, 51
  controversail articles in, 54–8
  editorial staff, 50
  launching of, 47–9
  literary debates at, 94–8
  missionaries, campaign against, 83–5
  Nazım Hikmet at, 72–5, 77–8, 94
  second period of, 69–70
  trial of, 87–94
  workers' rights in, 85–6
Resimli Perşembe, 58–9, 61–7, 94
Resimli Yıl, 59

Safa, Peyami, 69, 73–4, 79, 89–90, 94–5, 97–8, 131–2, 177, 196
Salonica, xvi, xvii, 8, 9, 80, see Thessaloniki
Saraçoğlu, Rüştü, 137, 138, 227
  Atatürk's funeral, at, 119
  foreign policy of, 141, 156–7, 159, 164, 219
  measures against opposition and press, of, 171, 178
  opposition to, 145, 176
  Press Law, 179
  servitude to Germany of, 154, 156
  Soviet-German Pact, on, 127
  statement at end of war, 166
  Tan incidents, role in, 192–3, 197–8
  Turkish nationalism, on, 152, 164
Second World War, 74, 111, 118, 125, 144, 147, 154–5, 164, 167–8, 236, 237

Sertel O'Brien, Sevim, 4, 12, 19, 34, 36, 64, 72, 77, 111, 145
Sertel, Zekeriya, 4, 17, 51, 229, 238
   arrests, 12–13, 16, 61–5, 69, 109, 207–10, 212
   Büyük Mecmua, 5–6, 11
   Columbia University, 19–20, 23–4, 28
   exile, 239–40
   Directorate of Press, 36, 41, 45
   Human Rights Association, 222–5
   Nazım Hikmet, 72–3, 235
   Resimli Ay, 47, 50, 57, 67, 69, 103
   Son Posta, 105, 109
   Tan, 109–10, 139, 170, 175
      destruction of, 197, 199–200, 202
      trial, 213–18, 220
   see also *Büyük Mecmua*; *Resimli Ay*; *Tan*
Sevimli Ay, 66–9
Sèvres, Treaty of, xvii, xviii, 1
Seyfeddin, Ömer, 5, 11, 13, 18
Social Survey Project, 41–3
Socialist Labourers' and Peasants' Party of Turkey, 206, 227
Socialist Party of Turkey, 165, 185, 205–6, 227
Society for the Protection of Children, 33, 41, 43
Soviet-German Pact, 127
Spanish Civil War, 34, 112, 208
Sultan Ahmet (Square), 14, 53, 210
Sultan Ahmet Prison, 132, 210
Suudi Bey, 47, 64–6

Tabouis, Geneviève, 113–14
Talat Pasha, 1, 12, 38
Tan
   Ali, Sabahaddin, 144, 165
   anti-fascist stand, 143–4, 157
   Atatürk, death of, 119–20
   censorship of, 134–5, 178–9, 185, 187
      banned, writing for 139–41, 151–2, 154–5
   destruction of, 191–5, 199, 202
      aftermath of, 200–3, 207–9, 233
      arrest and trial of, 209–19
      Democrat Party, support of 168–71
      press coverage of, 195–8, 200–1
   early years, 109–10
   Görüşler (column), 132, 141, 155, 171, 184, 214

   press attacks, 174–6, 178–9, 184
   pro-democracy, campaign for, 128, 165
   Romanian Foreign Minister, interview of 118–19
Tasvir-i Efkar, 35, 60, 67, 123, 131, 133, 154, 177, 193, 196
Tevetoğlu, Fethi, 161–2
Thessaloniki, xvi, 9, see Salonica
Togan, Zeki Velidi, 160–1, 163
Turanism, 129, 154, 161–3, 243, see also Turanist
Turanist, 6, 12, 123–4, 131, 137, 152, 159–62, 164, 177, 183, see also Turanism
Türk Teavün Cemiyeti, 27, see Turkish Solidarity Association
Turkish Hearth, 19, 37, 40, 43, 81, 104
Turkish Solidarity Association, 27, 30, 32, see Türk Teavün Cemiyeti
Turkish-German Pact, 133–4
Turkism, 6, 10–11, 129, 131, 152, 161, 243, see also Pan-Turkism; Pan-Turkists
Türkkan, Reha Oğuz, 137, 160, 162–3

United Nations, xxiii, 159, 168

Vahdeddin, 3
Voix Européenne, 114, 116–17

War of Independence, the, 1, 16, 18, 37, 39, 50, 56–8, 110, 120, see National War of Independence
   aftermath of, 35, 48, 57, 69, 98
   alliances in, 37–8, 120
   Baykut, Cami in, 165, 210, 221–2
   ideological significance of, 35
   Nazım Hikmet's epic poem on, 98
   Soviet support for, 140, 145
   support for, 25
Wealth Tax, xx, 147–51
Wilson Society, 3, 4

Yakup Kadri, 50, 79, 80, 82, 95
Yalçın, Hüseyin Cahit, 127, 175–6, 178, 184, 191–2, 195, 197, see Hüseyin Cahit
Yalman, Ahmet Emin, 3, 51, 60, 62, 84, 109, 139, 178, 213, 234
Yücel, Hasan Ali, 11, 137, 227
Yunus Nadi Bey, 37, 51–2, 109, 132

www.ingramcontent.com/pod-product-compliance
Lightning Source LLC
Chambersburg PA
CBHW052217300426
44115CB00011B/1721